the **complete** book of
sailing

D1540986

the **complete** book of
sailing

EQUIPMENT
BOATS
COMPETITION
TECHNIQUES

Bob **Bond**

David **Pelly**

Brian **Grant**

Jonathan **Clark**

Adrian **Morgan**

hamlyn

First published in Great Britain in 1987 by Hamlyn an
imprint of the Octopus Publishing Group,
2–4 Heron Quays
London E14 4JP

Reprinted 1989, 1990, 1993, 1995
Revised and updated 1997
Reprinted 1999

Copyright © Bookbourne Limited 1997
The Old Farmhouse
Newton
Sleaford
Lincs NG34 OD1

Distributed in the United States by
Sterling Publishing Co., Inc.
387 Park Avenue South
New York
NY 10016-8810

ISBN 0 600 59946 9

All rights reserved. No part of this publication may be
reproduced, stored in a retrieval system, or transmitted in
any form or by means, electronic, mechanical,
photocopying, recording or otherwise, without the prior
permission of the copyright holders.

Produced by Toppan

Printed in China

FOREWORD

No single publication can hope to cover every aspect or specific interest of a sport as complex as sailing, so what we have done as writers, photographers, designers and editors is to put together a book that highlights the principal aspects of the sport as it exists today.

One of the great attractions of sailing is that the sailboat is a 'vehicle' to be used as the owner sees fit. One day it can be a racing machine, the next a platform for a family picnic, the next a way to whisk the occupants to a distant shore. It is this freedom and diversity of use that attracts so many people to boating in general and sailboating in particular.

The traditional pattern of first 'learning the ropes' in a small dinghy, and then graduating to a larger dayboat or cruiser racer, has been eroded in recent years by an influx into the sport of sailors in their twenties and thirties who want to learn from the outset in the type of their choice.

In Europe, a large number of sailing schools has grown up to meet this demand, whereas in the United States very few sailing schools cater for adults, largely because so many young people learn to sail through the many camps, college and sailing club summer programmes, and return to sailing in later years.

Throughout the complicated latticework of sailing skills you will encounter various views, theories and dogma. However, there is no specific 'one way' of doing anything connected with sailing, and what we have presented here are tried and tested methods, devised by experienced practitioners who appreciate that each sailor is unique and will develop his or her own peculiar methods of sailing and sailboat management.

Whatever your experience and skill level, I hope that you will find something in the book that will help you enjoy your sailing to the full.

BOB BOND

CONTENTS

EQUIPMENT

When you first start sailing you accept that the boat, its gear and its fittings are standardized. In fact, you are usually so busy learning to sail that you don't have much time to think about how the boat is laid out and whether there are alternatives to the multitude of ropes and fittings that you have to learn to use.

Later on, when you have more experience, or if you happen to visit a chandler's shop or look at a catalogue of sailboat equipment, you will begin to realize that many inventive minds have been applied to devising many alternatives for each piece of equipment. This section sets out the basics of each of the principal equipment groupings and gives just a few of the many alternatives.

Just a quick flip through the pages of any sailing publication will show that there are hundreds of different boat designs and thousands of marine businesses, each with its own specialist products, servicing the sailboat market.

Sailing clothing, for example, has been developed to the point where materials and designs are so good that manufacturers have moved into the 'designer' market to encourage colour-coordinated crews and the use of pastel shades for dinghy and inshore use. Offshore clothing now incorporates dayglow colours and reflective strips so that the wearer can be seen easily both day and night.

Unless you come into sailing by first building your own boat, you will not normally need to worry too much about the choice or construction of equipment until you have sufficient sailing experience and the mechanical and design skills to change the way your boat is rigged, or until you have to replace broken or worn equipment. It is at this point that you will appreciate the complexity of the sport and notice the paucity of impartial hard advice available.

Masts and booms are usually made of an aluminium alloy and come in a range of shapes. Recent developments include in-mast or in-boom mainsail furling systems to make sail handling simpler and safer without a dramatic loss of sailing performance. Sails for most applications are made of woven synthetics. It is only the racing sector which has moved into the exotic sheet and film products which give short-lived advantages.

Ropes have improved as synthetic fibres have been developed for specific applications. Characteristics such as stretch, wear, grip and feel are listed in manufacturers' catalogues to enable the rope purchaser to make a satisfactory choice when replacing or buying new. This readily-available information is especially important to the owners of racing dinghies, because many classes have opened up their class rules to permit a multiplicity of sail and rig controls.

On dinghies, the development of 'muscle boxes', which are essentially miniaturized versions of the multi-purchase tackles, have been matched on larger boats by the introduction of the self-tailing winch. The standard winch requires two people, the wincher and the tailer, to operate it, but the self-tailing winch is operated by one person and virtually eliminates the dreaded 'riding turn' which immobilizes the standard winch. In anchoring, the most significant developments have been the introduction of the one-piece Bruce anchor and the return to the vertical windlass, usually electric, to replace the mechanical anchor-chain handling systems.

Protecting a wooden boat requires the frequent application of a bewildering array of paints and varnishes, but plastic hulls may need to be repainted only every fifteen or twenty years, and only the antifouling and the wooden trim need to be attended to on an annual basis. Environmental concerns have led to the widespread banning of harmful tributyl tin derivatives as antifouling agents, and forced a return to the traditional copper-based products, but most boatowners have been pleased with the results.

It is a well-known fact that diesel engines thrive on hard work, but until the revolution in shipboard electronics most sailboat diesels died of neglect and lack of use. The increased requirements for electrical power to drive the extensive electrical and electronic systems of boats have made frequent engine use essential, to keep the batteries charged, and brought about the development of more efficient alternators and batteries. In addition, the engines themselves are smaller and lighter because of the developments that have taken place in the automotive industry.

The electronic instruments can do almost everything the human navigator can, and more in some cases, but the important thing to remember is that they are all merely aids to navigation and when it comes down to the wire it is the ability of skipper and crew that counts most.

Nowhere is the importance of this ability more evident than in the area of safety where, despite the increasing array of sophisticated equipment designed to rescue or save, it is still better not to abandon your boat until you can step *up* into the liferaft.

PARTS OF A BOAT

The language of the sea and seafarers is so intermingled with the English language that you will have no difficulty recognizing many of the terms used in sailing, but many others may be new to you.

In plan view, most boats have a pointed front end and a squared-off back end. A few have two pointed ends and others have two squared-off ends, but no matter what shape it is the front of any boat is called the *bow* and the back is the *stern*.

The sides of the boat are identified by facing the bow: The *port* side is to the left and the *starboard* side is to the right. When sailing, all objects appearing on the left side of the boat are described as being *to port*, those on the right *to starboard*.

Ahead, abeam and *astern* mean in front, to the side and behind the boat, and *fore* and *aft* mean at or toward the front and the rear respectively. The *beam* of a boat is its width, measured at its widest point, and its *length overall* is the length from the most forward part of the bow to the most rearward part of the stern.

The *hull* is the main body of a boat, and the dividing line between the part below the water and the part above it is the *waterline*. The hull above the line is the *topsides* and the vertical measurement from the waterline to the *gunwale* (or *gunnel*) where the sides join the deck is referred to as the *freeboard*; that below the line is the *underbody*. The bow and stern usually extend ahead of and behind the waterline, and this gives *bow and stern overhangs*.

Everything mounted on the deck to handle the sails or anchors is the *deck hardware*, and it includes the mast and boom that support the sails. On most boats the mast is held in place by wires called *standing rigging*. The ropes or wires used to hoist, lower and control the sails are called the *running rigging*.

At the stern of the boat the *rudder*, which helps to steer it, is controlled by a *tiller* or, on many cruisers, a *wheel*. Beneath the hull, there is a *centreboard*, a *daggerboard* or a *keel* to prevent the boat from drifting sideways when under sail.

The *forefoot* is the underwater angle of the bow as it curves back to the keel (or, on some boats, the keels). The back corner of the keel is the *heel* and the front is often referred to as the *foot* or *forefoot*. The front face is the *leading edge* and the back the *trailing edge*.

RIGGING

The ropes and wires used to raise, lower and control the sails are called the running rigging. This includes the halyards, which raise and lower the sails, and the sheets, which adjust and

DINGHIES

The typical dinghy is a relatively small, open sailboat with a single mast. The smaller dinghies, such as the Laser and the Optimist, have unstayed (self-supporting) masts, but the larger boats have stayed masts held in place by wires (the shrouds and the forestay). A dinghy has no fixed keel, but uses an adjustable board — a pivoting centreboard or a sliding daggerboard — that functions as a keel to give lateral stability. There are some large, dinghy-like boats, such as the Flying Fifteen, that have keels instead of boards; these are called keelboats.

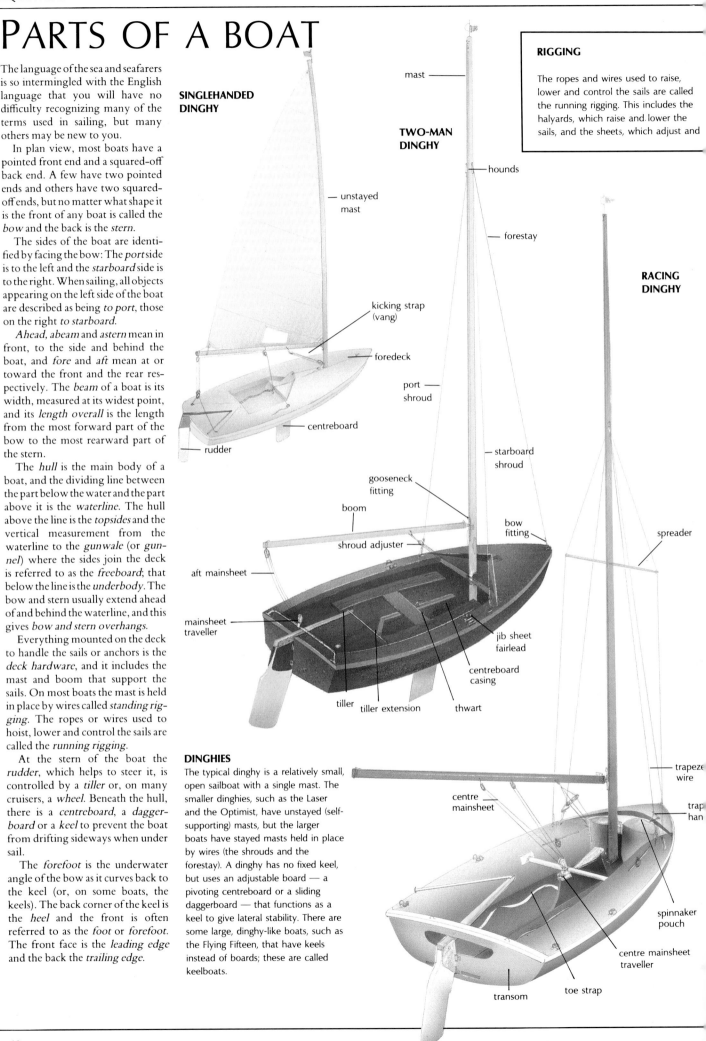

SINGLEHANDED DINGHY

unstayed mast

kicking strap (vang)

foredeck

centreboard

rudder

TWO-MAN DINGHY

mast

hounds

forestay

port shroud

starboard shroud

gooseneck fitting

boom

shroud adjuster

bow fitting

aft mainsheet

mainsheet traveller

jib sheet fairlead

centreboard casing

tiller

tiller extension

thwart

RACING DINGHY

spreader

trapeze wire

trap han

centre mainsheet

spinnaker pouch

centre mainsheet traveller

toe strap

transom

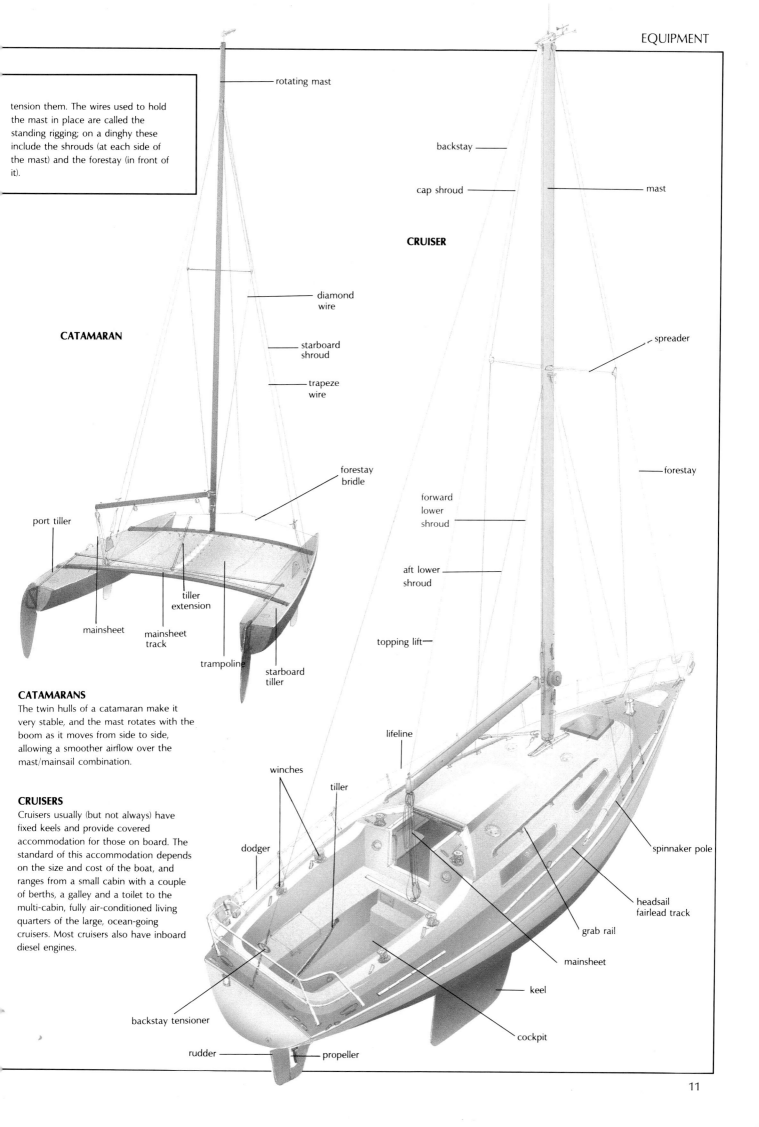

tension them. The wires used to hold the mast in place are called the standing rigging; on a dinghy these include the shrouds (at each side of the mast) and the forestay (in front of it).

rotating mast

CRUISER

backstay

cap shroud

mast

diamond wire

CATAMARAN

spreader

starboard shroud

trapeze wire

forestay

forestay bridle

forward lower shroud

port tiller

aft lower shroud

tiller extension

topping lift

mainsheet

mainsheet track

trampoline

starboard tiller

lifeline

CATAMARANS

The twin hulls of a catamaran make it very stable, and the mast rotates with the boom as it moves from side to side, allowing a smoother airflow over the mast/mainsail combination.

CRUISERS

Cruisers usually (but not always) have fixed keels and provide covered accommodation for those on board. The standard of this accommodation depends on the size and cost of the boat, and ranges from a small cabin with a couple of berths, a galley and a toilet to the multi-cabin, fully air-conditioned living quarters of the large, ocean-going cruisers. Most cruisers also have inboard diesel engines.

winches

tiller

dodger

spinnaker pole

headsail fairlead track

grab rail

mainsheet

keel

backstay tensioner

cockpit

rudder

propeller

SAILS

Sail design and manufacture are nowadays the province of the engineer. The engineer's tools are the computer and laser, but there is still a good deal of instinctive skill involved and the end results can often seem more like works of art than sophisticated pieces of technical equipment.

The introduction of new strong, lightweight materials has been crucial to the development of sails, which continues at a rapid pace. Major racing events, in particular the America's Cup, force the development of new materials and techniques, which then filter down to the rest of the sailing world.

In the past, sails had to be made from whatever natural materials were available, such as hide, flax, cotton, bamboo, coconut fibre and jute. All of these suffered from shrinkage or stretch depending on whether they were wet or dry, decayed over time, and lost a proportion of the wind's energy as the air blew through them.

As yacht racing became more popular during the 19th century, sails made from thick and heavy flax canvas gave way to the much smoother and finer fibres of cotton.

The search for better performance led sailmakers to look for better sail shapes, which in turn demanded improved construction. When most yachts had gaff mainsails, these were made with vertical panels whose seams gave the sail much of its strength. But when yachts changed over to Bermudan mainsails and larger headsails, this layout was no longer satisfactory. Woven cloth of any kind is strongest along the axis of the 'warp' threads, or exactly at right-angles, on the axis of the 'weft' or 'fill' threads. But it is weak and stretchy on the 'bias', when the

load falls diagonally and all the little squares formed by the weave turn into little diamonds when force is applied.

To get over this, the clothmaker must try to make the sailcloth as stable as possible, by tightening the weave and by using fillers to lock the threads in position. The sail-maker, meanwhile has to devise panel layouts in which the cloth is made to take the greatest strain along its strongest axis.

The first big revolution in sailmaking occurred in the 1950s, when synthetic cloth became available, under the trademarks Terylene in Britain and Dacron in the USA. At first it was stretchy, but it gradually became more stable as makers learned how to coat it with polyurethane filler. This had the unfortunate effect of giving a hard and crackly finish to sails, which as a result were difficult to handle and did not stay in good condition for long. In the 1970s, a much stronger and stiffer fibre, Kevlar, made its appearance, and at the same time sailmakers began to use computers to produce better sail shapes and layouts. This resulted in some very complex-looking sails which had masses of seams radiating from the stress points.

In the 1980s, experiments began with composite sails in which the basic shapes are created using panels of a nonwoven plastic, such as Mylar, to which reinforcing threads of glassfibre or Kevlar are bonded. Next, the reinforcing threads were applied in a complex pattern that reflects the stresses that the sail experiences in use.

In all sails up to this point, the basic aerofoil shape was produced by rounding the luff (leading edge) of the sail and by tapering the seams between panels. Nowadays

KT 6161 is using sails with radial-cut panels. The mainsail is a mix of Kevlar and Dacron. G 3417 is using contour-cut sails designed to eliminate the hard spots of the radial cut.

the precise outline of each panel is calculated by computer and cut out by a laser knife in order to produce exactly the shape that the designer intends. However, a completely new method of sailmaking was introduced for the 1995 America's Cup series.

In this method, the whole sail is constructed in one piece over a mould, rather as glassfibre is laid up in a mould to produce the hull of a boat. These '3DL' sails are made by laying threads of synthetic yarn over a mould and then locking them in place by bonding on a layer of nonwoven plastic. There are no seams, no cloth, and the shape is totally 'built-in'.

For the time being, such sails are very expensive and only of interest to the top echelon of yacht racers, but at the same time the new materials such as Spectra and Vectran

have resulted in cruising sails that are strong, light, soft- handling and last for many years. This is especially important when many cruising yachts have sails that roller-furl and are never removed from the boat. As a rule, cruising yachts have only one mainsail, which has to serve in every type of weather.

Spinnakers are made from lightweight nylon woven into a 'rip-stop' cloth that is traditionally sold in a variety of bright colours. The lightest 'gossamer' cloths weigh as little as half an ounce per square yard while a typical all-purpose spinnaker for a 30-footer might use a 1.5 ounce cloth. Different shapes and constructions depend on what the sail is intended for running, reaching, or all-purpose use.

Many of the newer racing classes use 'assymetrics', which are hybrid sails that combine the features of a genoa and a spinnaker and are particularly effective for high-speed reaching. In place of the usual spinnaker pole that has to be changed over every time the boat gybes, assymetrics normally have their forward corner (the tack) attached to a bowsprit with sheets to either side of the boat, like a foresail.

While this method works very well on lightweight dinghies, which mostly sail downwind on a series of reaches, larger boats are often compelled by tactics to sail a square run and in this case a conventional spinnaker and pole is found to be superior.

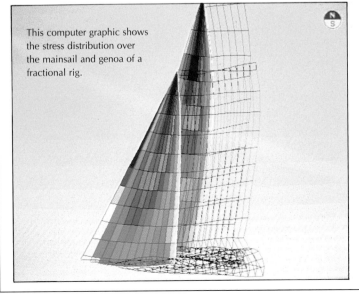

This computer graphic shows the stress distribution over the mainsail and genoa of a fractional rig.

This 3-panel, horizontal-cut Optimist sail sets perfectly on the hard-to-trim-spritsail rig.

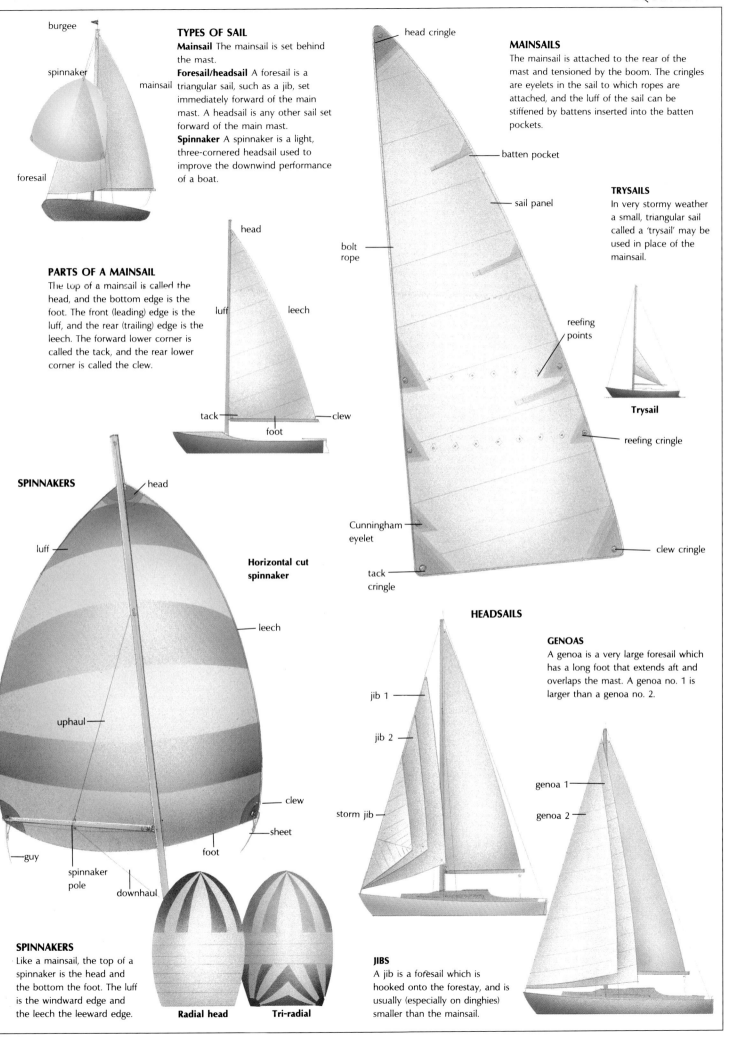

TYPES OF SAIL

Mainsail The mainsail is set behind the mast.

Foresail/headsail A foresail is a triangular sail, such as a jib, set immediately forward of the main mast. A headsail is any other sail set forward of the main mast.

Spinnaker A spinnaker is a light, three-cornered headsail used to improve the downwind performance of a boat.

burgee

spinnaker

mainsail

foresail

PARTS OF A MAINSAIL

The top of a mainsail is called the head, and the bottom edge is the foot. The front (leading) edge is the luff, and the rear (trailing) edge is the leech. The forward lower corner is called the tack, and the rear lower corner is called the clew.

head

luff

leech

tack

clew

foot

SPINNAKERS

head

luff

Horizontal cut spinnaker

leech

uphaul

clew

sheet

foot

guy

spinnaker pole

downhaul

SPINNAKERS

Like a mainsail, the top of a spinnaker is the head and the bottom the foot. The luff is the windward edge and the leech the leeway edge.

Radial head   **Tri-radial**

head cringle

MAINSAILS

The mainsail is attached to the rear of the mast and tensioned by the boom. The cringles are eyelets in the sail to which ropes are attached, and the luff of the sail can be stiffened by battens inserted into the batten pockets.

batten pocket

sail panel

bolt rope

TRYSAILS

In very stormy weather a small, triangular sail called a 'trysail' may be used in place of the mainsail.

reefing points

Trysail

reefing cringle

Cunningham eyelet

tack cringle

clew cringle

HEADSAILS

GENOAS

A genoa is a very large foresail which has a long foot that extends aft and overlaps the mast. A genoa no. 1 is larger than a genoa no. 2.

jib 1

jib 2

storm jib

genoa 1

genoa 2

JIBS

A jib is a foresail which is hooked onto the forestay, and is usually (especially on dinghies) smaller than the mainsail.

MASTS & BOOMS

A keel-stepped mast with deck seal and gaiter. Crash bars give protection to the crew, and the spinnaker pole is stowed on the mast.

The mast and boom form the supporting structure for most sails. Generally speaking, only the most exotic racing machines can exploit the state-of-the-art developments which have taken place. The majority of owners have to be content with the standard oversize (for safety) sections which can be produced in quantity. Wood, aluminium and carbonfibre are the most frequently used materials, aluminium being the normal choice, and the standard mast cross-section is elliptical, with an integral luff groove at its trailing edge.

The hollow spars (a collective term for masts, booms and other sail-supporting structures) are initially formed by extruding aluminium under immense pressure through a shaped die. Mast makers buy in a range of extruded sections, and then fabricate each mast to a set of precise design specifications. Where large spar sections cannot be extruded, they are fabricated from rolled panels which are glued, welded or riveted into the appropriate shape.

One of the first considerations of the mast designer is the bend characteristics of the finished spar. The bend of a mast is measured in the fore-and-aft plane, and can be quite considerable: up to three feet in some fractionally-rigged racing craft.

Pre-bend is the amount of bend placed in a mast when the main shrouds are tightened. This is achieved by angling the spreaders back and fixing them rigidly in position. Once the sails are rigged, the amount of draft (aerofoil shape) in the sail can be increased by straightening the mast to make the sails fuller, or decreased by bending the mast to make the sails flatter.

The rake of the mast forward or behind the vertical helps determine the amount of weather helm (tendency to turn into the wind) the boat carries. Foward rake, used when downwind sailing, decreases it, backward rake, used in upwind sailing, increases it. The backstay tensioner controls mast rake, and the mainsheet, boom vang and backstay all influence mast bend.

Athwartships (transverse) bend or sag of the mast is eliminated by the wires supporting it. In a typical cruiser there is a single spreader, about midway between the deck and the jib sheave (pulley), which carries the main shroud. The inboard end of the spreader is called the root, and any intermediate or lower shrouds are attached just below the spreader roots. Two shrouds on each side, led about two feet forward and aft of the mast, help support the bottom half of it. An inner forestay prevents the mast popping backward if the mast flexes 'out of column' in a seaway.

The multi-spreader rigs used on offshore racing boats use very thin mast sections which rely totally on an intricate web of supporting wires for their strength and stability.

When fabricating a spar, the mast maker carries out a series of standard operations and a limited number of custom options. Most dinghy spars have tapered top ends achieved by cutting a V-shaped section from the leading edge, and compressing the spar to be welded and then profiled with a grinder. Offshore racing boats and some cruiser/racers also have tapered spars.

Current practice is to attach all shrouds and stays internally, using specially-developed captive T-bars and in-mast terminals in an effort to cut down the considerable windage created by external tangs and toggles. The spinnaker pole track is mounted on the leading edge of the mast, and the gooseneck that holds the boom is on the trailing edge.

Halyards, control lines and electric and electronic instrument cables must all be carried inside the masts of larger boats. Conduits are provided within the mast to ensure that the halyards and electrics are kept apart. Special moulded alloy or fabricated stainless steel sheave boxes are incorporated into the masthead and halyard exit points. The masthead is also the mounting base for wind instruments, the tricolour navigation light and the VHF aerial, and can become very cluttered, while the foot of the mast often resembles a mushroom farm because of the large number of pulley blocks used to disperse the halyards and controls to their destinations via turning blocks and rope stoppers.

Deck-stepped masts are usually mounted on an inverted T-shaped angle. Keel-stepped masts must be chocked tightly at deck level using wedges, and a neoprene gaiter covering the point where the mast passes through the deck prevents water finding its way below.

Booms perform a similar function to masts. They support the foot of the sail and, by use of the boom vang and mainsheet, can be used to control the draft of the sail and the degree of mast bend.

Booms usually have deep cross-sections to combat the excessive bending forces produced by the boom vang and mainsheet. As with masts, exotic racing machines sport booms with lightening holes, cutaway end sections and fabric covering to decrease weight without jeopardizing stiffness. The ordinary cruiser will have a standard oversize boom.

Slab reefing systems require specially fabricated end fittings. Inboard, the reefing lines run through quick-release stoppers, and outboard the reefing lines lead up from their appropriate places on the boom through the reef cringles to pulleys housed in the boom end.

Spinnaker poles are usually circular in section and equipped with specialized end fittings which vary from those of the permanently mast-mounted dipping pole, which has a different fitting at each end, to those of the end-for-end pole which

has identical fittings at each end.

The rapid development of in-mast and in-boom reefing systems has given mast makers the opportunity to produce specially-shaped sections which will accommodate the furled sail within the enlarged luff groove. The sails used with these systems must have hollow-cut leeches because battens cannot be fitted.

Racing multihulls often fit wing masts, which form an integral part of the overall aerofoil shape of the mast/sail combination. Laminated wood, aluminium and carbonfibre are the principal building materials used for these.

The masts and booms of small dinghies, such as the Laser, are generally very simple wooden or alloy structures. Singlehanded, single-sailed boats usually have unstayed masts, with no supporting shrouds or stays, but boats for two or more people, or those that carry more than one sail, have their masts supported by standing rigging comprising a shroud at each side and a forestay attached to the bow.

Above *This keel-stepped 505 rig features a boom with lightening holes, foredeck-mounted mast strut and boom-mounted pole stowage.*
Top right *By contrast the deck-mounted mast of a cruiser racer incorporates a slab-reefing winch, boom vang and halyard winches.*
Right *Another deck-mounted mast, with all halyards led aft via turning blocks at the base of the mast. The boom vang incorporates a spring-loaded strut.*

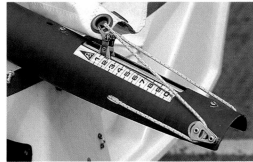

Above *The outboard end of this dinghy boom is cut away to save weight and incorporates a simple clew outhaul purchase.*
Left *A general view of a spar shop manufacturing a wide range of spars in a variety of sections and lengths.*

ROPES, CLEATS & SHACKLES

The choice of ropes, cleats and shackles facing the yachtsman or dinghy sailor is now wider than ever, but the most important factor to consider when you are buying one of these items is that it should be of the correct style and strength for its intended application. Safe working load figures for these products are available from your chandler or from their manufacturers, so if you know the working loads they will have to cope with, it is easy to choose the correct size when making a purchase. If in doubt, look at what size of rope or shackle is used for the same job on a boat of similar size to your own.

The commonest ropemaking materials are nylon, polyester and polypropylene, and the two principal forms of lay-up (rope structure) are 3-strand and 9-plait. Some ropes have an inner core made of a low-stretch polymer, such as Kevlar, Spectra or Dyneema, and such ropes are commonly used for spinnaker sheets and runner tails.

A basic 3-strand polypropylene rope will float and has good abrasion resistance, and so it is an ideal mooring rope. It is also highly resistant to degradation by sunlight, which enhances its longevity. 3-strand nylon can also be used for mooring ropes and again will float, and it usually has a hairy finish which helps it to knot well. Lightweight 3-strand nylon rope is sometimes used for halyard tails, but it will not withstand high loads.

The range of plaited ropes starts with plaited polypropylene, which is a soft and flexible floating rope that can be used for sheets in small yachts. Multiplait nylon is strong but it stretches, making it unsuitable for sheets. However, since it can readily absorb shock loads, this rope makes an ideal anchor warp.

For most yacht applications a multiplait polyester is the workhorse. There are two main types, one a pre-stretched rope and the other a hard-finish, close-knit braid ('hard finish' means that each strand has a lot of twist).

The pre-stretched type is a good choice for ropes under constant tension, particularly control lines and sheets, and its matt finish makes for ease of handling. The hard-finish braid is a good rope for sheets and halyards, where very low stretch and high strength are needed.

Finally, there are the 'exotics' of which the Kevlar-cored polyester was the first; these ropes have very low stretch but they are expensive. They are most commonly found on racing yachts, where expense is not necessarily a primary consideration,

and their applications include running rigging and control lines. The latest exotic, Dyneema, is specifically designed for high load applications where a rope of very low stretch must turn tight corners.

The function of a cleat is to hold a rope from slipping, and there are three principal designs: the two-armed deck cleat, the cam cleat and the clam cleat. Of these, the deck cleat is the most simple, having no moving parts and merely requiring a rope to be wrapped around it or clove hitched across it to function. This type of cleat is commonly used for securing genoa sheets, halyards and mooring ropes, and is usually made of acetal resin or high magnesium-content aluminium alloy.

The cam cleat has moving jaws that are controlled by a spring and which grip the rope to prevent it slipping. A wide variety of sizes and types of cam cleat are available, and they often have fairleads to aid handling. It is essential that a cam cleat be able to accept the size of rope chosen and that it should be capable of being released under pressure.

This type of cleat is typically used for those control lines which need frequent adjustment. A mainsheet system, for instance, will usually include a cam cleat incorporated into a suitable multiblock system. Cam cleats are also used to secure jib sheets on many yachts of 28 feet or below, as they can provide a quick-acting system.

Clam cleats have no moving parts, the ropes being held in a ribbed slot. These cleats are made of plastic or aluminium, and a variety of sizes is available to suit the rope diameters commonly in use. This type of cleat is ideally suited to securing halyards and control lines such as the kicking strap.

As well as cleats, rope clutches and sheet jammers may be used to secure ropes. Racing yachts commonly have a row of rope clutches on their coachroofs, and sheet jammers are used on genoa sheet turning blocks to allow sheets to be secured when changing sheets.

Shackles come in two main forms, the strip shackle and the polished steel forged shackle. Some shackles are available with captive pins, and these can be useful on main halyards. All shackles are designed to specific breaking loads, and other design points to consider when choosing a shackle are the pin diameter, the width of the shackle and the length. In general terms, strip shackles will be of less practical application on a yacht than will forged shackles, which will be more able to withstand high working loads.

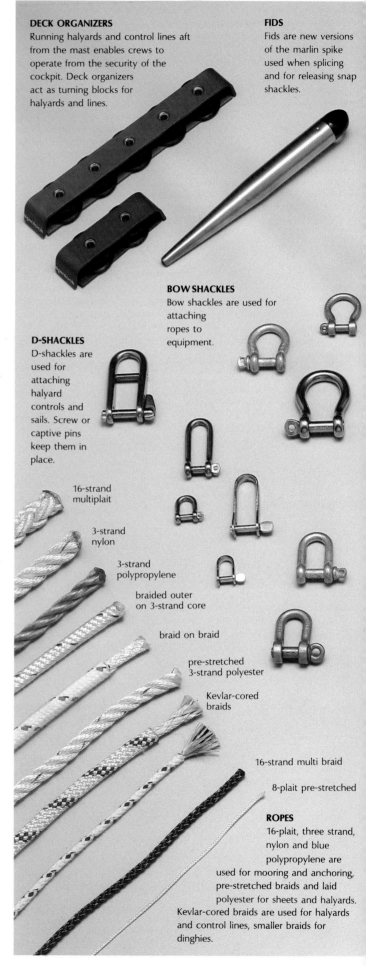

DECK ORGANIZERS
Running halyards and control lines aft from the mast enables crews to operate from the security of the cockpit. Deck organizers act as turning blocks for halyards and lines.

FIDS
Fids are new versions of the marlin spike used when splicing and for releasing snap shackles.

BOW SHACKLES
Bow shackles are used for attaching ropes to equipment.

D-SHACKLES
D-shackles are used for attaching halyard controls and sails. Screw or captive pins keep them in place.

16-strand multiplait

3-strand nylon

3-strand polypropylene

braided outer on 3-strand core

braid on braid

pre-stretched 3-strand polyester

Kevlar-cored braids

16-strand multi braid

8-plait pre-stretched

ROPES
16-plait, three strand, nylon and blue polypropylene are used for mooring and anchoring, pre-stretched braids and laid polyester for sheets and halyards. Kevlar-cored braids are used for halyards and control lines, smaller braids for dinghies.

CAM JAMMERS
When control lines and halyards are led back from the mast to the winches at the aft end of the coachroof, they are held in position by cam jammers. When the levers are lifted the ropes run freely; when they are lowered, the ropes are held in place.

TWISTED SHACKLE
Used where the fitting to be attached needs to be aligned with the shackle pin. Normally used with non-swivelling blocks.

FID-OPERATED SNAP SHACKLE
This shackle can endure the enormous loads imposed by spinnakers.

SNAPHOOK
Used on equipment that needs to be removed quickly, such as vangs.

LEVER-OPERATED CAM
The rope is held by a lever-operated cam.

CARBINE HOOKS
These heavy-duty self-locking hooks are used for non-permanent attachment of a rope or wire.

SAFETY SNAP SHACKLE
The only type of snap shackle to use with safety harness.

CLEATS
The horned cleat is the traditional fitting for securing a rope, which is wound in a figure-of-eight or clove hitches.

PISTON-RELEASE SNAP SHACKLES
These bronze or stainless steel shackles are for spinnaker work. The steel version shown here has a ring attached to the piston to make releasing under tension easier.

RING-PIN RELEASE
A short length of tape attached to the ring enables the crew to 'trip' a spinnaker prior to lowering it.

CORD-RELEASE SPINNAKER SHACKLE
The cord is attached to the internal cam release system, and kept short to avoid accidental tripping.

CAM CLEAT
The cam cleat or crab's claw is used where a sheet or control line is always led off in the same direction. The rope can be pulled in easily but can't return because the jaws close tightly under tension.

CAM CLEAT
This simple cleat has no moving parts. Its inward-slanting grooves ensure that a rope under tension forces itself into the cleat, making the grip even tighter.

WINCHES & BLOCKS

Marine winches, powered or manual, control the various ropes, wires and chains used in many of the activities involved in yacht sailing. Sails are hoisted, reefed and trimmed, crewmen are hoisted for rigging checks, parts of the rigging are tensioned, mooring lines are hauled, booms' angles are controlled, and anchors, dinghies, lifting keels and gangways are lowered or raised by winch or windlass.

The smallest and simplest design is the 'snubbing winch'. Like most bigger winches, it is designed to rotate in one direction and ratchet-lock in the other. A few turns of a loaded rope around the drum will sustain a high load through friction on the drum surface, provided that a light tension is maintained by hand on the loose 'tail' of the rope.

Pulling on the rope tail rotates the winch and gains rope from the loaded end, while easing the tension allows the turns to slip on the drum, so that the loaded rope is paid out under control but can be stopped again immediately (snubbed) by restoring the tail tension. Greater forces can be controlled by fitting a handle at the centre of the winch to provide leverage longer than the radius of the drum.

Further mechanical advantage is obtained by employing two or three levels of gearing between the handle and the drum. This is achieved extremely neatly on the majority of winches while still leaving the handle and the drum on the same rotational axis.

Most commonly, headsails are trimmed through ropes (sheets) running to two-speed winches. Turning the handle one way gives direct drive, and reversing it when the load increases gives a lower gearing, though the drum always rotates in the same direction. Once the sail is set, the tail of the rope is cleated fast. Alternatively, the loaded side is passed through a levered 'stopper' so that the rope can be released from the winch, leaving it available for other use. With an array of stoppers, one winch can serve many different ropes.

A 'self-tailing' winch has additional height to accommodate a circular groove into which the rope tail jams to provide the necessary tension, but can feed out as the drum rotates. This enables heavier loads to be managed singlehanded, though the action may be slightly slower than with two crewmen attending to the separate tasks of 'winding' and 'tailing'.

On larger yachts, three-speed winches are used. The third speed is selected by a button, which is

TWIN TURNING BLOCK
Turning blocks ensure a constant lead angle into winches for sheets and control lines, and can be mounted flat or on edge. Twin blocks usually have a lifting back section for easy loading.

FOOT BLOCK
The foot block serves the same purpose as a turning block. It is usually used on the deck where lines may need to be turned, or as part of a sail or track control system.

BLOCKS
Blocks are pulley wheels that enable mechanical advantages to be gained by linking numbers of them together. The three below are a single with a fixed eye; a double with a swivel eye; and a triple with a swivel eye and a becket (loop), over the central sheave (wheel), to which the rope is attached.

FIDDLE BLOCK WITH SNAP HOOK
This specialist block would be used to position the spinnaker guy and sheet on the toe rail.

SWIVEL FIDDLE WITH BECKET
Used on most mainsheets, this block produces a 4:1 purchase when used with a double block.

RING BLOCK
This unusual block has a rotating ball race to spread the sheet loads. The becket is a plastic saddle which enables the end of the rope to be attached through the centre of the block.

SNATCH BLOCKS
Snatch blocks are used where it is necessary to move ropes to different sheeting positions. The largest block shown here has a snap shackle to enable it to be repositioned on the toe rail, and is opened by pressing the 'snap' locking mechanism.

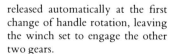

released automatically at the first change of handle rotation, leaving the winch set to engage the other two gears.

The crews of the largest racing yachts need to inject a large amount of manual energy into a single winch quickly and with maximum ergonomic efficiency. For this, one or more vertical pedestals with large double handles are linked to big winches a short distance away. This enables several crew to wind simultaneously, concentrating on putting all their musclepower into one winch while one man is entirely responsible for the tailing. Such an arrangement is known as a 'coffee grinder'.

Both in this case and in small boats with simple two-speed winches, the task of sheeting is the same. As a sail is tacked, the sheet is hauled rapidly and manually under light load, as with a snubbing winch. As the sail fills, the load increases with progressive winching and it becomes

WINCHES

The winch is a device for handling sheets, halyards and control lines. The winch on the right is a conventional two-speed winch with a 14:1 retrieve power ratio and a 42:1 tensioning power ratio. The winch on the left is self-tailing and so it can be used by one person. The self-tailing mechanism grips the rope and strips it off a bale arm similar to those on fishing reels.

TRACK EYE

The sliding track eye carries a sheet block. It fits onto a T-section deck track and is positioned by lifting its spring-loaded piston and sliding it along the track.

WINCH HANDLES

The length of a handle's arm determines its mechanical advantage. The two-handled version shown here is designed for serious racing and is fabricated from chromed bronze. Black anodized alloy is used for handles which are not severely stressed.

However, for the expensive superyachts a whole new range of powered 'captive' winches is emerging. These are placed below the decks where the sheets are led to large drum reels or first to a capstan drum and then onto separate drum stowage. This can result in very clear decks with all trimming under push-button control from the helmsman's station.

For yachts over 10 metres length overall, anchor handling is usually relieved by a powered windlass, which must either be reversible for raising or lowering anchors, or else have a lever-operated clutch to allow the cable to run out. It must also be capable of handling either chain or rope. The rope will pass over a smooth drum but the chain has to be gripped in a special wheel called a 'gypsy'.

The majority of traditional windlasses have two drums, one either side of the motor and gears and on a horizontal axis athwartships, and one side is used for rope and the other for chain.

There is a recent fashion on smaller craft for a vertical drum in the form of the ancient capstan. This is neat and unobstructive because the motor can be placed below deck, protected from seawater, leaving only the small profile of a winch that looks similar to a sheet winch. Its main difference is that the gypsy occupies the lower section below the rope drum. The power and direction of rotation is controlled by footpads set flush in the deck.

More recently, like many other devices, even yacht winches are seeing the influence of electronic control. Information can be provided on the instantaneous load in each line, so that within preset limits a drum can be stopped if a line goes slack, or eased if overloaded.

Blocks, casings containing one or more pulley wheels, are used extensively on all sailboats. Some, such as turning blocks and foot blocks, are used to change the directions of sheets and halyards, while others are arranged in combinations that provide *mechanical advantage*. The mechanical advantage of a pulley system is the ratio of its output force to the amount of force applied to it. For instance, if a mainsheet system has a mechanical advantage of 8:1, then pulling on the mainsheet with a force of 1 kg would result in a force of 8 kg being applied to the boom.

However, the price you pay for the mechanical advantage is that you have to pull the mainsheet farther than the distance the boom will be pulled by the system.

necessary to work down through the gears.

In winch design, the racing sailor has different requirements and criteria from the cruising sailor. For racing, the emphasis is on light weight, involving expensive materials like titanium and carbon-fibre, and since only manual operation is allowed, optimum gearing is essential to make the best of the crew manpower. For cruising, durability and low maintenance are more important, and in larger yachts electrical or hydraulic power reduces the dependence on multiple gears.

Reel winches are, as the name implies, those which (like a fishing reel) hold all the line that they wind in. On a simple drum, this technique is only suitable for thin line and was formerly used mainly for wire halyards which could not be tailed by hand. Since the advent of aramid fibres such as Kevlar for making ropes as strong as steel, wire halyards are decreasingly used.

ANCHORS

In spite of their apparent simplicity, anchors are probably the least understood of sailing paraphernalia. While everyone knows what they are intended to do, there is remarkably little scientific knowledge of how well they perform in all practical circumstances. This is because of the difficulty of watching them, especially when they are buried in the seabed, and because their behaviour depends primarily on the texture and strength of the seabed itself, factors which can vary greatly.

It is not the anchor that actually 'holds', but the shear strength of the ground that it tries to penetrate. Trials in artificial test tanks can be misleading, and only recently have anchors begun to be instrumented for study of their behaviour in detail. For these reasons it is impossible to say that this or that anchor is best overall.

There will often be a preference for a certain type of anchor in a particular locality, as a result of experience. Fashions come and go as experience tempers the claims of successive marketing promotions, and boats on extensive cruises often carry a variety of designs for use in different types of ground.

It is interesting that Classification Societies recommend weights of anchor in relation to size of boat, but avoid the controversy of specifying types. Indeed, plenty of weight and plenty of chain is an effective solution whatever the anchor, because the heavy chain itself absorbs much of the energy of a tossing boat before any disturbing force can reach the anchor. However, the desire is to save weight carried aboard, and many boats now carry nylon warp in preference to chain.

Although the nylon can absorb energy by its elasticity, it has little weight in water so averaged loads go direct to the anchor, putting more reliance on its ultimate holding performance. It is still essential

Anchors have developed from the basic four-pronged grapnel (**right**). The plough anchor (**top**) performs well in a wide variety of seabed conditions, while the Danforth (**far right**) works well in sand and mud but jams on small rocks. The Bruce anchor (**above**) has no moving parts and is designed to dig deep into the seabed.

The majority of cruising yachts stow their anchors lashed securely in bow rollers ready for immediate use (**left**).

PARTS OF AN ANCHOR

Anchors come in many different shapes but share the same components

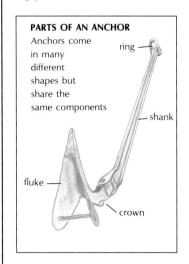

ring

shank

fluke

crown

to have a few metres of chain (the leader) between the warp and the anchor to absorb the worst peaks of snatch loading.

Anchoring in light weather is no problem, and for this a kedge is used. A kedge is any anchor that is conveniently lighter than the bower (main) anchor. For serious anchoring in heavier wind and wave conditions, there is no substitute for as heavy an anchor as can be handled and carried. This is especially so for emergency anchoring where the all-important choice of holding ground and shelter is not available.

The most long-standing and universally-recognized type of anchor is the 'fisherman', still popular for many applications. Whichever way up it lands on the seabed, one of its flukes (points) will be in a downward position ready to penetrate the ground. A stock (crossbar) at the opposite end of the shank lies horizontally on the bed, keeping the flukes vertical.

Partly because most of the weight is felt at the tip of the fluke, this form is good on rock, weed and firm soils but is limited in soft ground by the small amount of fluke area available

to resist dragging. Moreover, the stock resists going deep to find firmer ground. The fisherman's attributes are its consistent performance in a wide variety of seabeds and its ability to reset quickly if dragged out.

In the same family is the grapnel, which has four flukes on cruciform arms and does not need a stock. Grapnel anchors are popular among fisherfolk in areas of hard sand and rock, but they are not easily stowed on yachts.

Most other forms are classed as 'high holding power' or 'stockless'.

They have relatively large fluke areas and are intended to bury themselves deeply. When they do, much higher performance is achieved but certain seabeds make them inconsistent in their holding power, which is the ratio of the force they can sustain compared to their weight.

Tumbling fluke anchors, typified by the Danforth or Meon, have a hinge which allows the flukes to 'tumble' either side of the shank, ready to point downward whichever side they land on on the bed. A significant attribute is that this form

stows easily because it can lie flat on the deck ready for use. Although usable on rock, it is not ideal on hard ground but good in soft ground where its large flukes are effective.

Big ship anchors are similar in principle, and popular because they are stowed easily by drawing them directly into a hawse pipe. At the limit of their holding power these designs tend to roll out of the ground and may not reset if they have collected a stone between the shank and the fluke.

Plough anchors also have a large fluke area and are popular in spite of

being cumbersome. The best known is the CQR, which has a strongly-forged hinge between the plough-shares and the shank. This assists the digging-in phase by causing the plough to 'screw' its way into the ground in an attitude which puts much weight on the fluke. These are good all-round performers, excelling in softer soils where they can penetrate deeply.

Recent design work, resulting from studying the point of break-out, promises a significant improvement in the optimum performance of plough anchors.

A radically different form is the Bruce, famous for its two curved horns which rotate the main fluke into the ground. It is good on softer ground but sometimes does not compete with other designs on harder ground if it cannot penetrate far. It has the advantage, on intermediate ground, that even if tending to roll out it usually retains some holding and has a fair chance of digging in again.

Some anchors, such as the mushroom and the rond, are not self-burying and are carefully placed in the ground for long-term use.

PAINTS & VARNISHES

Tree resins, natural tar, animal fats and vegetable oils were all used by the early boatbuilders to preserve the structure and ensure the watertight integrity of wooden hulls, and the addition of pigments to these materials gave the colours which encouraged owners to decorate their vessels.

Today, there are three basic types of protective coatings: oil-based paints which dry by the evaporation of some of the oil; polyurethanes, which include varnishes and cure when in contact with the air; and two-part epoxies which cure by chemical reactions between the two parts.

Varnishes are produced without pigments and are used to bring out the natural colour of all wooden surfaces, including the on-deck varnished woodwork or 'brightwork'. On traditionally-decorated wooden boats the darker varnished mahogany of cabin sides, hatches and cockpit contrasts with the paler scrubbed teak decks and cockpit gratings.

Other teak structures, such as grabrails, are treated with teak oil which penetrates the wood and preserves its natural oiliness and gives it a slightly darker appearance.

The interiors of wooden boats were often finished with contrasting white planking and varnished beams and furniture. Matt finishes often gave a better contrast than the bright finishes which also showed up areas of wear.

The bilge area, often susceptible to rot, was usually treated with coal tar derivatives, or specially-mixed bilge paints containing fungicides, to prevent the onset of dry rot. The bilge is a particularly difficult area to keep clean, and is a repository for stagnant water and engine oil spillages.

The topsides of the boat were the obvious areas for the development of finishes which could be applied evenly and would dry to a perfect, hard gloss finish.

White has always been a favourite with owners but is one of the most difficult to apply because it shows up every blemish. This is particularly so now that older GRP hulls require painting to prevent the ingress of water into the laminate through a deteriorating gel coat.

The boot topping is the junction between sea and air on the hull and extends about three inches above the waterline. Boot top paints are a mixture of the harder topside paints and the softer, leaching antifoulings (paints that keep the hull clear of fouling, such as weed growth, by slowly releasing or 'leaching' their active ingredients). Most owners use a contrasting colour for boot tops.

The real battle between the hull and the elements takes place below the waterline, where the growth of weed and barnacles causes fouling resulting in a considerable loss of performance. In tropical waters, harmful marine borers penetrate wooden hulls and, once inside, chew away happily along the grain until the boat finally collapses.

Copper sheathing and copper and arsenic-impregnated antifouling paints were highly successful in combating growth and borers, but hulls still needed periodic scrubbing off during the sailing season.

The introduction of tributyl tin (TBT) in the 1970s revolutionized the protective coatings industry. TBT paints were excellent antifouling agents, but their harmful effects on shellfish populations and other marine life resulted in a complete ban on their use in the late 1980s and a return to the copper- and arsenic-based paints of previous decades.

Two grades of antifouling are produced. The hard racing finishes can be sanded smooth and leach slowly, while the softer cruising versions form a thicker protective coating which leaches quickly to prevent weed and barnacles from gaining a foothold.

The application of paint is one of the most skilled boat maintenance tasks and requires considerable time, patience and perfect working conditions. Successful finishes rely upon fastidious preparation of the surface to be protected or decorated, and unpainted wood and GRP surfaces must be filled and sanded so that all blemishes are removed.

The resulting surface will then have to be cleaned several times with degreasers and thinners, to ensure that the first phase of the paint system can key into the porous structure so that the whole finish does not flake off. Many layers of paint are applied, and throughout the application process each successive coat must be sanded down with wet-

and-dry paper and cleaned with a 'tack rag' to remove all traces of dust.

Most systems start with a primer, which acts as a keying agent and filler. Sometimes the primer is combined with an undercoat, but if not, a specified number of undercoats is applied after the primer. After the priming and undercoating, a number of top coats are applied to give the sort of immaculate finish displayed on the side of the paint can. Brushes, rollers and mohair pads are all used to assist in producing the desired result.

Paint manufacturers have to balance the quick-drying properties their products need to prevent runs, with the need to preserve a 'wet edge' that allows successive strips of painted boat to merge into one smooth skin free of brushmarks.

The treatment of GRP hulls is often best left to the professional spray shop. The aim is to use two-part epoxies to replace the original gel coat finish with an impervious coating, and so extend the life of the boat.

The treatment of the undersides of the hull to remove blistering caused by osmosis involves the removal of the entire gel coat by gritblasting or sanding. Osmosis is the slow seepage of water into the laminate, and it causes leaching of the resins which shows up as blisters.

The exposed laminate must be dried before a new epoxy barrier is built up and sanded to a perfect finish. Again, this is such an important process that it is best left to the professionals.

Steel and aluminium hulls also require treatment with appropriate paint systems. The first coat of primer is an inhibitor to prevent the formation of rust or corrosion. Thereafter, the paint systems are designed to build up an elastic protective layer to prevent moisture getting near the metal.

As with all sophisticated products, the wide variety of finishes available to the boat owner must be researched thoroughly before purchase. If you want a traditional but renewable finish, traditional paints and varnishes are the answer. Polyurethanes tend to give quicker results but varnishes especially can peel off if moisture gets into the wood. Clear epoxy finishes may need a final protective coat of ultra-violet light stabilizer to prevent them going cloudy after prolonged exposure to sunlight.

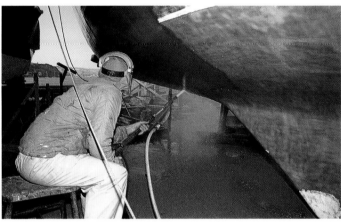

Good preparation is essential; steel hulls are sandblasted to bare metal.

Wooden hulls need many layers of paint and varnish for a proper finish.

Left *When using spray paint protective clothing is a must, as here preparing the Courtaulds yacht.* Inset: *The finished product.*

Above *The contrast between a rich varnish and a light-coloured paint can be extremely effective.*

NAVIGATION INSTRUMENTS

Modern electronic navigation instruments are so easy to use, so accurate and so reliable that it is extremely easy to become over-dependent on them. It must be borne in mind that at all times the most important instrument on board is a skilled human navigator, and that person must always be ready for the moment when all the instruments on board go blank.

This is not simply a hypothetical situation; virtually all modern instruments depend on electricity, and its traditional enemy remains seawater. Even with the most elaborate backup arrangements and the most careful sealing, there is always a risk of water getting into the works. The old-fashioned chart, magnetic compass, pencil and ruler are the instruments that almost never go wrong and therefore must always be carried.

One instrument, the sextant, used to be considered essential on any yacht sailing long passages but has now been relegated to the status of standby. It is sad that these this wonderful piece of precision equipment, which took many centuries to develop, finds decreasing use, but the truth is that the GPS (Global Positioning System) receiver is both more accurate and a great deal easier to use. However, if you sail long passages, a sextant is a valuable backup instrument to have in case your electronics fail.

Every boat that goes to sea, however small, must be able to mount a magnetic steering compass and fortunately there are some very neat compasses designed for racing that are also perfectly adequate for coastal cruising. If the boat has an engine, then the compass must be installed as far away from it as possible and adjusted for magnetic deviation—the error caused by a big lump of metal (such as the engine) distorting the magnetic field.

Many small yachts carry a bulkhead compass with a card that can be read either from above or along the edge. Although these are fairly easy to use, the great difficulty lies in mounting them so they will not be obscured by other members of the crew. A better solution, found on the majority of larger boats, is to mount a traditional dome-type compass on the top of a console that also supports the steering wheel and the other sailing instruments. This brings the compass to an ideal position on the yacht's centreline and close to the helmsman's face.

The next requirement is for some sort of chart table, and even an open boat can have a plywood square with a piece of clear plastic over it. Any boat with a cabin should have a proper desk, either fixed or folding, measuring at least 60 x 75 cm (24 x 30 in) in order to take a standard Admiralty chart folded in half. To draw on the chart, you need soft pencils, an eraser, and one of the many types

TRADITIONAL INSTRUMENTS

The traditional plotting instruments are brass dividers, centre right, and the parallel rule, top centre. These have been joined by plastic plotters such as the Douglas square protractor, top centre, and the Breton plotter, bottom centre. The rotating card handbearing compass, bottom right, has a new electronic fluxgate rival complete with memory, bottom left. The sextant, top left, is still one of the most valuable of all navigational instruments.

of parallel rule or plotter, plus a pair of dividers to measure distances on the chart.

The basic skill requirement is to be able to rule off a course and then measure the bearing that it makes, and to rule in bearings of land or seamarks to fix your position. The traditional type of parallel rule, consisting of two sections joined by swinging arms, is the easiest to use on a nice steady table ashore but almost impossible on a small yacht jumping along in a seaway with everything sliding around. A better solution afloat is a clear plastic plotter such as the Hurst, which has a moveable arm, or the Breton plotter, which has a rotating compass rose. Simplest of all is the square Douglas plotter, which has no moving parts at all and has the bearing marks engraved along its edges.

The other essentials are a handbearing compass—and here it is well worth having the 'point and shoot' type that memorizes three bearings—plus a pair of binoculars. The price range of binoculars is quite extraordinary as you can pay anything from about £50 to £1,000. For marine use, a 7 x 50

(7-times magnification, 50 mm object glass) is usually the best as it is very hard to get a steady view with more magnification than this. A wide field of view is very important and this requirement disqualifies the usual types of 'pocket' binoculars. The very best instruments are water-resistant, rubber-armoured and have a built-in bearing compass, but these tend to be very expensive.

The basic elements of dead-reckoning are course and distance; the compass tells you the course steered, and you also need a 'log' to measure distance sailed. The commonest type of log these days is an electronic instrument that shows both speed and distance run, very much like the speedo and milometer on a car. Driven by a tiny impeller (a propeller or paddle-wheel projecting through the hull), it is very reliable unless weed jams the moving part, when it becomes necessary to withdraw the impeller and clean it.

The final essential instrument is a depth sounder, which modern electronics has made a very reliable piece of equipment indeed. In addition to a basic indication of

WIND INDICATORS
Because the wind plays such a vital role in sailing a boat well, very precise measuring instruments have been devised. Masthead sensors, **top**, detect the wind direction and speed, and information from them is shown on instruments such as a wind direction indicator, **above**.

MULTI SYSTEM The chart desk of a racing yacht shows some of the equipment available to the modern navigator. It includes satellite navigation receivers, communications equipment and instruments to monitor the yacht's performance. There is even an old-fashioned paper chart; good navigation makes use of all.

depth in either feet or metres, it is common to find alarms that can be preset to a particular depth, and graphic sounders that display a profile of the bottom as the boat moves along. In addition to the obvious safety benefit, a sounder can be a very useful navigation tool, allowing you to make a run (series) of soundings and compare them with the charted depths.

Although they are not strictly navigation instruments, many sailing yachts carry wind speed and direction instruments as these make it so much easier to sail the yacht to the best advantage, especially when racing. It is important to realize that the wind speed and direction felt by sensors at the masthead can only be 'apparent wind', a combination of the true wind and the yacht's own movement. The more complex instruments, which integrate information from the log as well as from the wind instruments, can also give an indication of the true wind speed and direction.

The increasing trend in instrumentation is to have one multifunction 'instrument panel', which is capable of giving a wide variety of different information on

HAND HELD GPS This neat little hand-held GPS receiver by Garmin gives an accurate latitude and longitude position anywhere in the world and can give the bearing and distance of a series of 'waypoints' programmed in by the user.

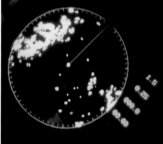

RADAR Thanks to major improvements in design, radar is a practical proposition on even small yachts. However, the range achieved is still dependent on the height of the antenna above sea level.

demand. This can include speed, distance run, depth, wind speed and direction, and compass heading using information from a fluxgate compass that has no moving parts and therefore does not swing like the traditional type.

Even the smallest sea-going yacht must have a minimum library that includes one of the combined handbooks, such as *The Macmillan Almanac*, which contain a mass of information on subjects such as the tides, port and coastal details, weather forecasts and many other matters of interest to the navigator.

COMPASSES This Plastimo hand bearing compass, **above right**, is one of the coastal navigator's most basic and useful tools as it allows him or her to fix the ship's position very accurately simply by taking bearings of three or more fixed objects. The 'porthole' spherical compass, **right**, features a card that can be edge- or top-read.

MULTI DISPLAY
The display of the Brookes and Gatehouse Hydra 2 appears simple but the instrument is capable of giving a mass of different information about the yacht's performance, wind speed and direction, and navigational information.

ELECTRONIC SYSTEMS

The microelectronics revolution has affected nearly every part of daily life, including life aboard ship, where there is now an incredible variety of equipment available to make life easier for the mariner. The three main areas to benefit from this are navigation, communication and safety.

Until about 1990, there was a number of electronic navigation systems competing in the marketplace, the main players being Loran, Decca, satnav (satellite navigation) and RDF (radio direction finding), but since that date the American Global Positioning System (GPS) has rapidly moved into a dominant position. Originally developed as a military system, GPS consists of a constellation of satellites that between them provide worldwide coverage 24 hours per day.

The receiving set integrates the signals from three or more satellites to provide a position accurate to around 200 metres. The system itself is actually considerably more precise, but the service available (free) to civil users is deliberately downgraded. However, the inaccuracy can be removed by a clever additional service (which you have to pay for) called Differential GPS, which gives a position accurate to around 10 metres.

With such accurate positioning available from hand-held sets costing less than £500, all the other systems are relegated to the status of standby in case GPS should suffer a breakdown or the US Government should decide to switch it off. The Decca system is expected to be withdrawn after a few more years, leaving Loran as the main standby. The more sophisticated instrument sets can receive both GPS and Loran.

The electronic revolution has also changed the style of navigation, as even the most basic GPS sets are able to store a number of 'waypoints'—electronic landmarks that you can position anywhere you wish, for instance 250 metres outside the harbour you intend to visit. As soon as you select this waypoint, the set will tell you its distance from you, its bearing, and the time needed to reach it at present speed. A coastal passage therefore becomes a string of waypoints that are selected in turn.

To make this even easier, the almanac publishers now give the latitude and longitude of hundreds of seamarks and coastal features so that you can quickly load them as waypoints without needing to plot them on a chart.

The next stage is to do away with paper charts entirely by replacing them with CD-ROM discs and displaying the chart on a screen. Such a chart can also be overlaid onto a radar display while a cursor can be moved around the screen to pick off and display the waypoints.

Communication with other vessels, or with coastal radio stations, is universally carried by VHF radiotelephone and this is another piece of equipment that has become dramatically cheaper in recent years. Even open boats with no power supply can carry a hand-portable set with all the marine channels and about 10 miles range. This is an enormously valuable safety aid, especially now that coastguard lookouts are few and far between. Coastal radio stations provide the means of linking into the normal telephone system, but a lot of this work has now been taken over by mobile phones, which often give a range of 20 miles or more over water.

For radio communication over a longer range there are two alternatives: HF (high-frequency) radio, also called SSB (single sideband), and satellite. HF radio can give worldwide range but the sets are quite expensive and a certain amount of training is needed to obtain an operator's licence.

Satellite communication (or satcom) using the Inmarsat system is rapidly growing in popularity and the antenna domes needed for telephone calls are frequently seen on large motor yachts, but both the equipment and the calls are exceedingly expensive. The lower-cost alternative for sailing yachts is Inmarsat Standard-C, which transmits text but not speech and requires only a small antenna.

A very special quality of satcom is that the set can be 'polled' from a shore station and will respond by giving its position, obtained from GPS. So the organizer of something such as the Whitbread Round the World Race can find the position of all the yachts in the race within a few minutes without any action on the part of the crews. In an emergency, the crew of a yacht can press a 'panic button' causing the satcom to transmit an automatic distress call accompanied by the boat's position.

Another very useful aid is the Navtex receiver, which receives weather and safety information and prints it out. The great benefit is that you no longer run the risk of missing an important message such as a gale warning. You can also select the types of information you want to receive.

Radar, which was once the province of big ships, can now be found on many small yachts though there is no escaping the basic fact that range depends on the height of the antenna above the sea. But both the size and the price of sets have come down enormously, as has the power requirement, while the quality of picture is far better than it was.

Most of the devices already mentioned have important safety benefits, but there are others that are exclusively concerned with safety. The most important are EPIRBs (Emergency Position Indicating Radio Beacons), very robust automatic distress beacons whose signals are picked up by satellites, aircraft and shore stations.

Ships and fishing vessels have to carry the type that automatically floats clear and begins sending if the vessel sinks, but yachtsmen are more likely to carry the miniature version that can be sewn into a foul-weather jacket or carried in a pocket. In addition to sending a distress signal, the EPIRB transmits a code identifying the user while the COSPAS-SARSAT satellites are able to pin down its position to within about a square mile.

Tiny beacons, designed to be worn on foul-weather clothing, sound the alarm if the wearer falls overboard and are made by both Sea Marshall and Jonbuoy. Their signal acts as a homing beacon to help find the person in the water and cause the boat's GPS set to mark the position as a waypoint that can be returned to.

Above A powerful, high-frequency transceiver and a single sideband radio provide long-range radio communication.

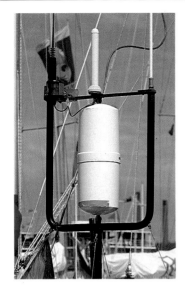

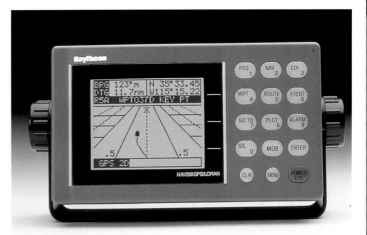

Above An antenna array housing a radar reflector (*centre*), satellite navigation antenna (*left*), Decca navigation antenna (*centre top*) and VHF antenna (*right*).

Above For any kind of small boat, a light, compact, hand-held VHF radio, such as this water-resistant Navico Axis 200, is an invaluable safety aid.

Above Cross-track error is shown on this Raytheon 398, which is a combined GPS and LORAN navigator. Although GPS has rapidly become the first-choice navigation system for yachtsmen because of its accuracy and reliability, it is always wise to have a standby system—which is provided by this Raytheon unit. It is able to make use of the land-based LORAN system in addition to the satellite-based GPS.

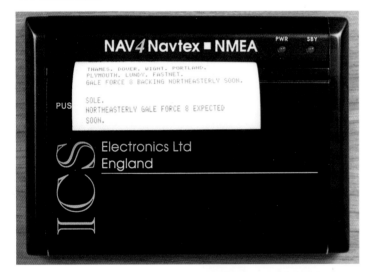

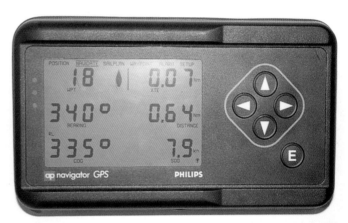

Above A Philips GPS navigator system, shown here set up to display a 'sail plan'—a list or series of waypoints that are linked to form the yacht's intended route—relies on signals from satellites.

Above This Navtex unit can receive and print out navigation and weather infomation as it is required by the operator.

Right Paper charts are gradually being replaced by electronic versions that can be stored in the form of CD-ROM discs and displayed on instruments such as this Lowrance Global Map display. Navigational tasks can be carried out entirely on screen.

Left Even when going around the world, like Tracey Edwards in *Maiden Great Britain*, and surrounded by high tech equipment, one essential is a VHF radio. So vital is this equipment that it is obligatory on yachts in most countries around the world.

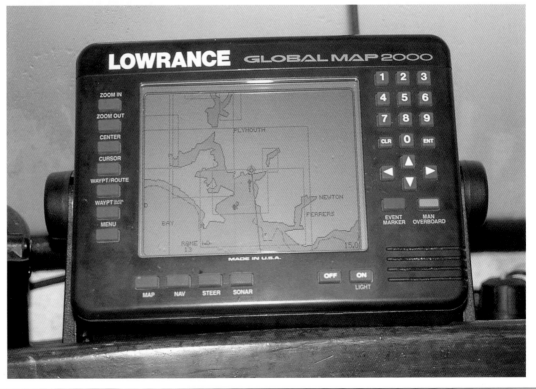

AUTOPILOTS & SELF-STEERING GEAR

Provided it is used responsibly, automatic steering is one of the greatest aids to modern cruising because it frees the person on watch from the need to be constantly at the helm, something that is particularly valuable when short-handed. On a small yacht, it becomes reasonable to have only one person on watch as, with the chore of steering taken care of, this person can trim the sails, navigate, make a cup of tea or simply sit and read a book while keeping a regular lookout for other traffic.

Model yachts with windvane self-steering were the inspiration for a whole series of ingenious systems for steering yachts automatically. These systems have now been replaced almost entirely by electrically-powered autopilots, except for standby use or on small yachts with poor battery capacity.

Windvane steering systems can steer a sailing yacht to windward extremely well, but are much less able to steer a straight course downwind when the pressure of the apparent wind on the vane is much less. This is especially true on lightweight modern yachts that surf down the waves so readily that at times they feel almost no apparent wind. For these boats a powered, compass-controlled autopilot is a far superior option.

Before powered systems took over, some extremely ingenious designs of self-steering gear were produced, the aim being to amplify the weak force felt on a vane when the yacht went off course into a stronger one capable of operating the steering. The most effective type uses a windvane to turn a deep, narrow servo rudder. This rudder harnesses the boat's own speed through the water to produce a strong force that is transferred to the main rudder via lines and pulleys.

As well as being bad at steering downwind, the weakness of virtually all windvane systems is that they consist of relatively delicate mechanisms projecting over the stern of the yacht, where they are vulnerable to damage from severe weather. Also, because they steer with reference to wind direction rather than compass course, if the wind changes, you may end up sailing in a circle. On the other hand, if sailing to windward, you do want the yacht to respond to wind shifts and therefore it is better to have windvane sensing, even if it is applied to an electric autopilot.

Compact tillerpilot systems have probably done more to popularize automatic steering than any other type because they are so easy to install and to use. The tiller-pilot is a self-contained unit consisting of a push-pull ram, one end of which is attached to a hinged bracket on the side of the cockpit and the other to a fitting on the tiller. The motor, controls and compass are all built into the unit and it is only necessary to 'plug in' to the ship's electrical supply and switch on.

Autohelm manufactures a wide range of tillerpilots costing from as little as £300 upwards. An extremely important feature of these tillerpilots is the ability to remove the complete unit in just a few seconds so that it can be locked in the cabin or taken home—unfortunately, theft from boats is increasingly common these days, especially at marinas.

Wheel steering calls for a different type of autopilot, usually a motor connected to the wheel hub via a toothed rubber belt. These systems can be simple and removable, but on wheel-steered cruising yachts of over 10 metres (33 feet) it is more normal to find a system that is built into the wheel pedestal with the motor fully protected from the effects of spray and the weather.

With more powerful, built-in autopilots come much more sophisticated controls. The important thing is to be able to 'tune' the pilot to suit the boat so that it steers a good course with the minimum of effort. If the autopilot is constantly making small movements of the helm, like a nervous driver, battery drain will be excessive and the whole system will suffer from premature wear.

The first adjustment, therefore, is sensitivity, which in effect means the amount the boat is permitted to wander off course before the autopilot responds. When sailing in waves, the boat is bound to weave from side to side and the aim is to achieve the correct average course without steering too much. The sensitivity needs to be progressively reduced as the sea-state increases, to prevent the autopilot from working too hard.

The next most important control is amplitude, or response, which means the amount of helm the autopilot applies to achieve the required correction of course. The more old-fashioned types of boat with rudders attached to the keel tend to need quite a firm application of rudder before they respond, whereas modern, lightweight designs with spade rudders react much more precisely.

A problem facing the designers of autopilots is that the big wave that knocks the boat off-course also makes the compass spin. Part of the answer is to use a fluxgate compass with no moving parts, but

Wheel steering systems can be driven by an autopilot linked to the rudder quadrant or, as in this example, the much more convenient demountable drive system. The sensing compass, at the front of the cockpit, activates the motor to turn the wheel via a toothed belt driving a hub-mounted drum.

Vane steering systems are designed to keep the boat on course relative to the wind, not the compass. The vertical axis drive, **far left**, is linked via gears to an auxiliary rudder. The pendulum type, **left**, activates a small servo rudder that turns the tiller to keep the boat on course.

Below The main elements of a 'built-in' autopilot, the Brookes and Gatehouse Hydra Pilot. On the right are the cockpit controller and display unit, on the left the power unit, and in the centre is the ram, which is connected below deck to the rudder via a universal joint.

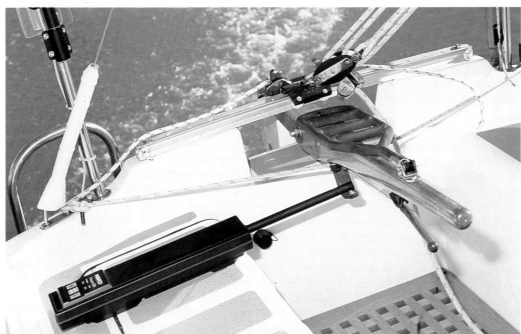

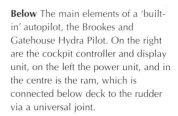

The Navico **tiller-mounted autopilot, left,** can be programmed to cope with a wide variety of conditions. Its remote control unit, **above,** can be used to programme it with instructions for course changing, tack and waypoint programming.

Modern autopilots, like this Cetrek 780, can be linked to other navigation systems in various ways so that, for instance, the yacht automatically steers to a waypoint.

the more sophisticated systems also incorporate a gyro that can tell the difference between slowly drifting off-course and being violently spun by a wave.

When they are sailing to windward, most boats exhibit what is known as 'weather helm', which means that a small but constant pressure in one direction is needed on the helm to keep them on course. This calls for a bias adjustment in the autopilot and for a tacking switch so that the correct bias can be applied in the opposite direction after tacking. The autopilot also needs to be told the angle through which the boat will tack.

The autopilot can be linked to other navigation instruments. Most GPS sets, for instance can work out 'cross-track error' and then give the autopilot the correct course adjustment to bring the yacht back onto the correct track.

A really useful adjunct to the autopilot is a remote-control keypad. This allows the watchkeeper to try, for instance, small adjustments of course while standing at the mast studying the set of the sails, or in an emergency to take over manual control quickly with a 'dodge' button and then let the autopilot resume control when the danger has been passed.

ELECTRICAL SYSTEMS

The modern yacht is highly dependent on its electrical power supply, which provides power for both its luxury and its navigational equipment. While the electrical system of a small yacht needs to supply at least navigation and cabin lights, essential instruments and engine-starting capacity, the large yacht will have many additional luxury items including refrigeration, air conditioning and electrically-operated pumps and winches.

The basic source of power is the 12-volt lead-acid battery as used on motor vehicles. A yacht will carry at least two batteries which can be used together in parallel or separately. Although 12-volt supplies tend to predominate, some craft, especially in the United States, are equipped with 24-volt systems. The very large yachts, in addition to a bank of batteries, have independent motor-generators and provide power at several voltages including 230 and 110 volts ac for running standard appliances.

The principal source of battery charging is the standard alternator (and associated regulator) driven by the vessel's propulsion engine. The duty cycle of boat batteries is more demanding than that of automotive batteries. A car uses its battery for starting, then immediately takes its electrical power directly from the alternator, which also recharges the battery so that it remains fully charged and ready for the next start; overall, the battery spends little time supplying current on its own.

By contrast, the use of the navigation and other electrical equipment of a boat, particularly of a sailing yacht, may run down much of the battery's charge. Then, when it is needed to start an engine, its charge may be at its lowest. This 'deep cycling' is very hard on conventional batteries and limits their life, although the modern low-maintenance battery, which uses calcium in the lead instead of antimony, is much more tolerant. Nevertheless, most boats have some provision for battery charging from sources other than the engine-driven alternator.

In simple installations, it is common practice to reserve one battery for engine starting and use the other for services. Then, if the service (auxiliary) battery is depleted there is no worry about engine starting to recharge. The alternative school of thought is to keep both batteries balanced by using them together, but to monitor their state carefully, even using automatic alarms to avoid over-depletion. A useful standby is a 'torque battery' which

can hold its charge for many months and then, for engine start, can deliver typically 100 amps for about a minute.

In marinas, where running engines to charge batteries is unpopular or forbidden, shore power supplies are available for use with mains chargers. The shore power input should be controlled by earth-leakage circuit breakers ('earth-current trips'), which will break the circuit instantly should any dangerous stray currents arise.

If battery charging is to be unsupervised (for instance if the charger is left on between weekends of sailing), use only the more expensive chargers which take account of the charge state and reduce the supply accordingly. Cheap chargers can overcharge unless watched, and this causes gassing and will diminish battery life. Charge state can be indicated by a range of instruments, from complex indicators of percentage charge to simple voltmeters with an expanded scale covering the critical voltage range. Monitoring of current in and out is done by inserting a very low value resistor in the main cable and measuring the voltage drop across it with a remote meter.

Battery isolation and selector switches enable selection of one, two, none or both batteries, but a running alternator can be destroyed if disconnected from all batteries, even for an instant, so switches must be of high quality with built-in safeguards to prevent the alternator running open-circuited.

When batteries are connected

directly in parallel, a strong one will be bled by a weak one and the discharge can continue almost indefinitely. To counter this, large diodes should be connected between the batteries to prevent current flowing from one into the other.

Large yachts have built-in diesel motor-generator sets, which have watercooling and exhaust systems and are encased in acoustic silencing material. These can work when the main engines are off, and they use much less fuel.

Smaller yachts, on long ocean passages, cannot carry sufficient fuel to allow them to run the propulsion engine long enough to keep the batteries properly charged, so resort to several other charging methods. The most reliable reserve source of significant energy is a small, portable, aircooled petrol generator, which may be no bigger than a large briefcase and can be used on deck in fair weather.

Another option for sailing yachts on long passages is to use shaft generation. A large pulley on the propellor shaft (which is allowed to rotate in neutral gear while the boat is travelling under sail) drives a special alternator that can generate useful power at low revolutions. This can provide one amp per knot of sailing speed.

Wind generators are a good source of 'topping up' charging power on long-distance cruises, though they seldom provide for all the needs of a modern boat. One version, made by Ampair, allows the generator component to be driven either by windmill blades or

by a spinner towed in the water.

Solar panels, another source of topping-up power, are becoming more efficient and economic. In daylight they yield around 100 watts per square metre, and they typically cost about £1000 per square metre. A small panel with a 15-watt output will top-up between weekends, and several large panels on the wide deckspace of a multihull will provide most of the energy needed.

While much marine equipment is designed for 12- or 24-volt dc operation, it is also useful to have a modest level of ac supply at domestic voltages to allow on-board use of, for example, an electric drill or a video recorder. A solid-state inverter can provide this but will not stand heavy current loads.

For equipment which is used temporarily on deck, waterproof plugs and sockets are available. These are generally sealed with O-rings and successfully resist dangerous water ingress when in use, but the sockets must be capped with sealing covers when the plugs are removed.

Quite elaborate switch panels are now often provided to control the ever-increasing electrical circuits of yachts. These panels often have mimic lights indicating which circuits are energized, and there is a trend toward the use of small individual circuit-breakers in place of switches and fuses.

Water and electricity are a dangerous combination, so any electrical installation work on board a boat must be carried out to the highest standards to minimize the risk of shocks or fire.

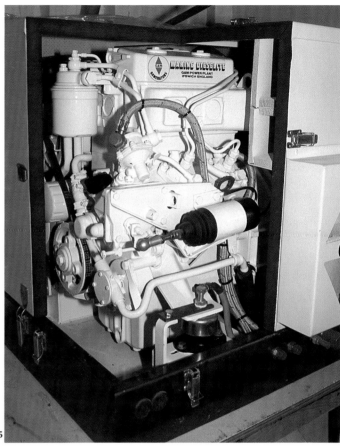

POWER SOURCES

In addition to the standard engine-mounted generator there is an increasing number of alternative power sources. The wind generators (**2** and **3**) and the solar panels (**4**) harness the freely-available natural power sources. Generally, they provide a trickle charge to keep batteries topped up, rather than powering equipment directly. Solar panels are robust and require a reasonably flat mounting surface, preferably away from areas of intense crew activity. As with all electrical generating systems, blocking or switching diodes are fitted to ensure that no discharge is possible when conditions are not suitable for generating electrical power. The self-contained gasoline or diesel generator (**5**) is a purpose-built generating station, usually mounted in an insulated housing to cut out noise and vibration. The Powerpack (**6**) is a rechargeable portable power source which can be taken on board to power a range of tools or appliances with a modest current requirement.

The well-designed marine switch panel (picture **1**) has separate controls for each electrical circuit on the boat, and meters to indicate battery state and charge. This example also incorporates fuel gauges, a clock and a heating and ventilation control. The marine alternator (**7**) is fitted with diodes which enables two batteries to be charged automatically, and the four-position isolation switch (**8**) allows manual switching between two batteries.

The gas detector (**9**) sounds an alarm if its bilge-mounted probe detects a buildup of explosive gas.

CRUISER FIXTURES & FITTINGS

The modern cruiser provides comfortable accommodation and is often as well-equipped as most homes, with hot and cold running water, full cooking facilities, central heating and air conditioning.

The most widely used method of central heating in boats of all sizes is ducted air warmed by a diesel oil burner. The oil is conveniently supplied from the engine fuel tank, with the draw pipe set higher in the tank than the engine supply pipe, for obvious reasons. The heater is started and controlled electrically and the airflow, which is fresh rather than recirculated, is forced through the ducting by a fan.

Older methods of heating include wood stoves (still to be found in classic boats, albeit often now made of stainless steel) and charcoal stoves. The latter are still quite common due to their safety, compactness and simplicity; a combusting layer works its way slowly up through a cylinder of charcoal, and the heat it produces is radiated and convected from the metal casing. Paraffin, petroleum spirit (SBP) and bottled gas are also used.

Where the combustion heats the cabin air directly, it has the disadvantage of producing water vapour equal to the weight of fuel, and so will only reduce humidity if there is good ventilation. For safety, gas and spirit heaters are preferably of catalytic form; the fuel is passed over a platinum gauze which glows hot, and there is no naked flame.

Air conditioning units, similar to those used in road vehicles, are used in motor vessels and the larger yachts. They generally consume electricity at a level only available by continuous engine running or the use of shore power. On smaller yachts, a sailcloth wind scoop can be effective for directing breeze down the forehatch. At sea, sailing yachts usually rely on natural ventilation through the familiar Tannoy vents or deck cowlings with Dorade boxes, boxes designed to pass air while intercepting water.

Cooking facilities vary from the simplest paraffin camping stoves to split-level cookers of the domestic type. Bottled gas appliances are the most commonly used because of their convenience and low fuel costs. They need careful handling because the gas is heavier than air, and leaking gas will accumulate in the bilge and form an explosive mixture. The danger of this is not as high as it once was, thanks to the introduction of 'flame-out' protection on stoves and gas bottle lockers that ventilate overboard. However, a reliable gas alarm should always

Top An attractive wooden interior with non-absorbent upholstery fabric. The fold-down table incorporates the mast support.
Above This well thought-out galley incorporates deep sinks, accessible storage and secure lockers.
Right Gimbals, a fiddle rail and a substantial crash bar ensure safe cooker operation in rough weather.

be fitted to warn you of any leaks.

The main alternative to gas cookers, for galleys that are going to be used at sea, is a paraffin pressure stove. These are very effective but a burner needs heating with methylated spirit for a minute each time it is started. Stoves using only methylated spirit are convenient and safe but the fuel is generally costly.

Large yachts whose generators produce kilowatts of power, or those spending most nights in a marina with accessible shore power, enjoy all the conveniences of domestic-style electric cooking. A

modern alternative to an electric cooker is the microwave oven, which is suitable for most types of vessel because its total power consumption is small. Even a small yacht can conveniently run its engine and alternator for the few minutes a microwave takes to complete each cooking operation.

Good marine cookers differ from those in the domestic or camping market in several important ways. The materials should not easily corrode, and the whole unit should be gimballed in the roll axis (only) of the vessel. With the movement of a

boat at sea, the utensils will slide or even jump off the stove unless constrained by special frames called 'fiddles'. These should be at least half the height of the utensils.

In good cooker designs, attention is also given to retention of grillpans and oven trays, whose contents can cause serious burns or scalds if spilled by the motion of the boat. The pressure cooker is a favourite utensil at sea because, being sealed shut during use, it does not spill its contents. It is also efficient in its use of fuel, and can keep several items of food piping hot so they don't need to be eaten

Above On large boats engine heat or electric power is used to convert seawater to fresh.
Left This 'heads' installation is unusual in that the bowl is mounted fore-and-aft, which might create problems for users when the boat is heeled.
Below A well-equipped 'heads' with hot and cold running water and a shower.

immediately after cooking.

Refrigerators for yachts include designs similar to camping and domestic units, and are operated by gas, thermoelectric or compression systems. The compression types have low electrical consumption, and one uniquely suited to any motorized boat has 'eutectic plates', inside the coolbox, through which Freon (or an ozone-friendly alternative) is pumped directly from a special compressor on the main engine. If the engine is run for at least 30 minutes each day, the thermal capacity of the plates will maintain normal refrigeration (including a small freezer compartment) for 24 hours.

Of the thermoelectric types, a compact and easily-fitted, solid state unit consisting of aircooled Peltier plates can maintain low (but not freezing) temperatures in a coolbox. The elements within the Peltier plates consist of layers of semiconductor material sandwiched between two sets of metallic strips. When an electric current is passed through the elements, heat is absorbed from the inner set of metallic strips (and thus from the coolbox) and emitted to the outside of the unit by the other set.

The heat is carried away from the unit by the aircooling of the plates. If the plates are watercooled, even lower temperatures can be maintained. However, Peltier plate refrigerators are not as popular as gas or compression types because they cannot produce really low temperatures.

Water storage tanks are made of metal, GRP or flexible fabric. There are generally few contamination problems with these if the original water supply is good and if light does not penetrate the tanks. An annual scouring with proprietary treatments based on chlorine is then sufficient precaution to ensure safe drinking water. The ideal source of the purest water is by desalination of seawater taken from well offshore. This desalination can be by evaporation, using the cooling water heat of large engines, or more commonly by a process called reverse osmosis.

INBOARD & OUTBOARD MOTORS

Sailing has become the weekend leisure activity of thousands of ordinary people whose commitments require them to be back at work on Monday mornings. This is one of the factors that has increased the demand for sailing boats fitted with engines, which can get their owners home in time.

Engines for boats are of two types: inboard and outboard. Both have been improved out of all recognition in recent years, becoming smaller and lighter for a given power output and infinitely more reliable. Originally, nearly all inboard marine engines were fuelled by petrol or paraffin (kerosene), but during the past 25 years there has been a steady, inexorable move to diesel. In the USA, where gasoline is relatively cheap, fast powerboats with powerful 'gas' engines are still fairly common, but in Europe they are practically unknown except for racing.

Although the cost of the fuel is itself a strong reason for favouring diesel (marine diesel being taxed less heavily than road fuel), the main arguments for diesel have to do with safety and reliability. Being heavier than air, petrol vapour sinks downward. With cars this is not a problem as spilled petrol can normally evaporate safely but in boats the vapour collects in the lowest part of the hull where it presents a

deadly danger of explosion. For a petrol-engined boat to be safe, the fuel system must be designed with special care to avoid any possibility of leakage and the engine compartment has to be ventilated by special fans with spark-proof motors. And even then there is always a worry about spilling petrol while refuelling.

The other big objection to petrol engines has always been the unreliability of spark-plug ignition systems in the marine environment. Modern electronic ignition is far superior in this respect to the magnetos and distributors of old, but there is still the worry of dampness and corrosion caused by sea air. Boats that spend their entire life on fresh water are a slightly different story, of course.

The objection to diesel engines in the past was that most of them were big, heavy, noisy converted truck engines. But this has changed, because now that so many cars and vans have diesel engines, there are compact, lightweight diesel blocks available for conversion into marine engines. Safe, economical and reliable, they make the auxiliary motors.

Many specialist engineering companies such as Sabre, Westerbeke and Volvo-Penta completely transform a stock diesel engine to turn it into a marine

auxiliary. First, a completely different cooling system is required. Formerly, cooling water used to be run through the engine straight from the sea but this is now rare as it carries the risk of corrosion and of salt gradually accumulating in the cooling galleries. Instead, fresh water containing corrosion inhibitors circulates through the engine, and is cooled in turn by a seawater heat exchanger. This method also makes it possible to run the primary cooling circuit through another heat exchanger, producing hot water for use within the boat.

Instead of a vehicle-type gearbox with different ratios, the marine engine requires only ahead, astern and neutral. The gearbox often incorporates a down-angle at the output end so that the engine can be installed reasonably level.

Almost as important as pushing the boat along is the need to generate electricity, with the result that marine engines have oversized alternators. Nearly all boats have two sets of batteries, one for general use and the other exclusively for engine starting, and these are charged through a splitting diode so that the power cannot trickle from one battery to the other. Both alternator and starter need to be installed high up on the engine, out of the way of bilge water.

A good marine engine will have all the main maintenance points, such as oil dipstick, sump pump, filters and belts, mounted on the front of the engine where they are accessible without taking the entire boat to pieces.

Volvo-Penta make the Saildrive, which combines some of the advantages of both inboard and outboard installations. A special right-angle gearbox incorporates an outboard-type 'leg', which projects through the bottom of the boat via a waterproof membrane and terminates with a neat folding propeller. The whole outfit is easy to install and causes very little drag when sailing.

While inboard engines have become steadily smaller, outboards have swelled ever larger. It is now possible to buy stock outboards of 150 bhp from all the major manufacturers and even more powerful ones for competition. In effect they have replaced petrol inboards for high-speed craft up to the point where turbocharged diesels take over. These multicylinder two-stroke engines have a formidable power/weight ratio but they are thirsty beasts that demand high-priced petrol. Manual starting being impractical for motors over about 25 bhp, these big outboards have alternators and they usually incorporate electric trim and lift

Outboards have improved greatly in recent years. They are used to power tenders and as auxiliaries on smaller yachts and multihulls. A tender's outboard can be stowed on a pushpit-mounted bracket (**above**). Note the safety lanyard. The engine on the right is a four-stroke outboard; four-stroke outboards are steadily becoming more popular than two-strokes.

VOLVO
PENTA MD31/MS4

The Volvo-Penta MD 31 is a mid-range diesel for use in yachts in excess of 35 feet. Note the flexible mounting blocks and the down-angle of the final drive coupling. Modern marine diesels for yachts incorporate heat exchangers to cool the engine indirectly with seawater and also to provide a supply of hot water for use within the boat.

A clever combination of the advantages of inboard and outboard motors, the Volvo-Penta Saildrive is installed through the bottom of the boat and eliminates all the difficulty of fitting a conventional shaft and propeller. For sailing yachts, a special folding propeller is fitted to minimize drag when the engine is not in use.

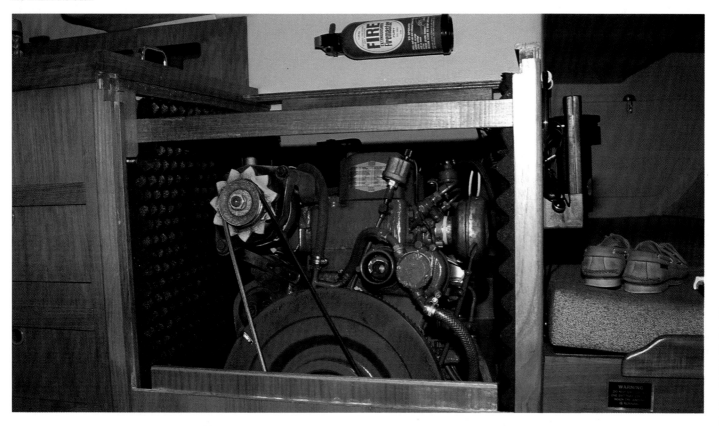

Because the space below the cockpit sole is quite small it is the traditional home of the auxiliary engine. By careful design, marine engineers have placed most of the service points at the front of the engine. The surrounding furniture is removable for easy access.

controls and electric starting. Diesel outboards exist but have never become popular, whereas 4-stroke outboards are useful where economy is especially important.

Although outboards up to about 70 bhp are commonly found on the rigid inflatable boats (RIBs) used by many yachtsmen as tenders, small ones of 10 bhp or less are of much more interest to yachtsmen, either as auxiliaries for small yachts or as power units for tenders. Tiny outboards of 1.5 bhp that you can easily pick up with one hand are ideal motors for inflatable dinghies. To keep the weight down, these usually have no gearbox so you turn the motor right around to reverse. A tiny petrol tank holding just a litre or so is built into the motor, so avoiding the expense and nuisance of a separate tank and fuel line.

An outboard of 6–10 bhp, fitted with a fine-pitch prop, will push a surprisingly big yacht along. The drawbacks are the need to mount the motor on a stern bracket, where it tends to jump out of the water in waves, and the need to stow it away when not in use.

An ingenious solution can be seen on the Hunter 7-0-7 sports-boat, where the outboard is stowed in a well under the cockpit floor. When the motor is needed, a plug is removed from the hull skin and the motor can be mounted in its place in just a few seconds. This method is both easier and safer than a stern mounting.

CRUISER SAFETY EQUIPMENT

Because a yacht is both a working platform and a living space, it has, of necessity, to incorporate safety systems for a wide variety of emergencies. Safety equipment can be complex and expensive and seldom used in anger but when it is, it must perform properly.

On deck, the main risk is of falling overboard and the precautions are in two stages: firstly to prevent people going overboard and secondly to ensure their survival if they do. Lifelines right around the yacht, supported on strong stanchions, are the first line of defence. The drawback to lifelines is that they can easily act as 'trip-lines' if someone stumbles against them, and so personal safety harnesses are at least as important and should be worn on deck at all times except in calm conditions.

Harnesses are no use unless proper strongpoints are built into the yacht. These should include U-bolts around the cockpit, including one that can be reached from the hatch before emerging. A continuous wire or webbing line along either side-deck makes it possible to walk forward in safety.

The skipper of any boat is responsible for telling crew when they must wear harness and lifejackets. The latter must naturally be of an approved type and properly stowed in an easily accessible position. The type that depends exclusively on foam for buoyancy tends to be bulky and annoying for long-term wear. Gas-inflated types are much neater, but are expensive and need to be checked regularly.

If the worst happens and a member of the crew goes overboard, the first line of defence is a horseshoe lifebuoy, which must be attached to a length of line terminating in a dan buoy and drogue. The drogue stops the lifebuoy from being blown out of reach of the person in the water, while the dan buoy carries a flag and light to help the yacht return to the right place.

Modern yachts tend to have decks a considerable distance above the water (high freeboard). This can make it exceptionally difficult to get someone back on board, especially when their clothing has become sodden. The best solution is a yacht with a bathing platform in the stern, or failing that a fold-down boarding ladder. If neither of these is available, it is essential to carry one of the devices for winching a person up using a halyard.

The next emergency to consider is the yacht sinking. Any vessel larger than a sailing dinghy must carry appropriate bilge pumps, the

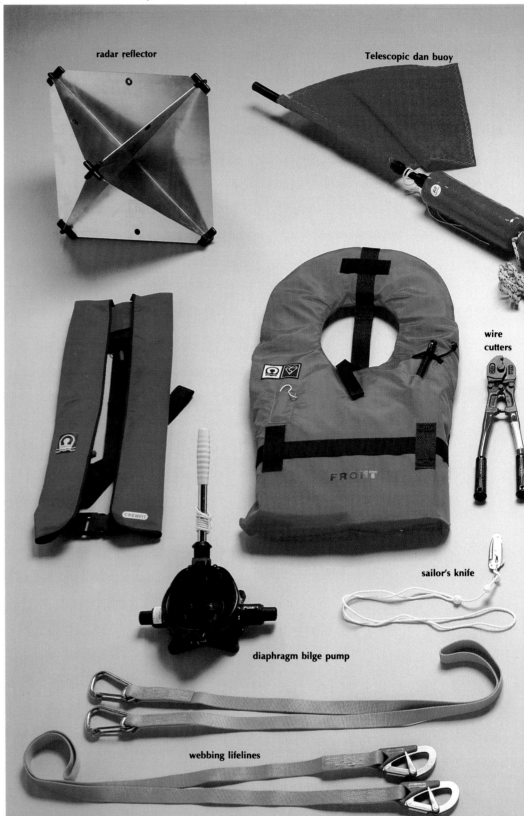

radar reflector

Telescopic dan buoy

wire cutters

FRONT

sailor's knife

diaphragm bilge pump

webbing lifelines

Radar reflectors are designed to reflect the incoming radar beam back to the sender. The example shown folds flat for stowage. **Lifejackets** should be chosen to suit their intended working environment, and the best option for offshore use is the CO_2-inflated jacket incorporating a safety harness. The foam-filled jacket is ideal for day sailing or for going ashore in the tender. **Webbing lifelines** clip to either a safety harness or to a specially-adapted lifejacket. When moving about the deck at night, or in rough weather, the wearer clips the snap clip to a jackstay running along the side deck or to strongpoints. The **diaphragm bilge pump** is a simple pump which enables large quantities of water to be pumped overboard. It is operated by rocking the handle to and fro. The **sailor's knife** usually incorporates a marlin spike for splicing ropes and a shackle key for tightening and loosening shackle pins.

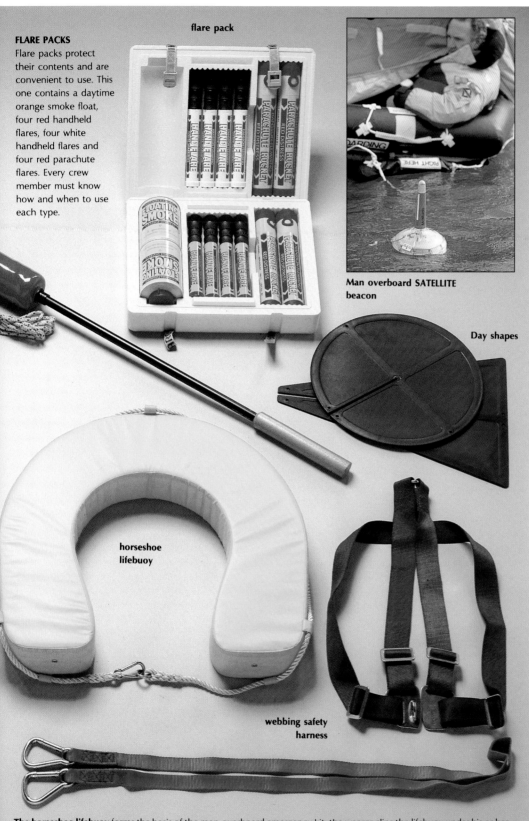

FLARE PACKS

Flare packs protect their contents and are convenient to use. This one contains a daytime orange smoke float, four red handheld flares, four white handheld flares and four red parachute flares. Every crew member must know how and when to use each type.

flare pack

Man overboard SATELLITE beacon

Day shapes

horseshoe lifebuoy

webbing safety harness

The horseshoe lifebuoy forms the basis of the man-overboard emergency kit; the wearer clips the lifebuoy under his or her arms for additional support. The **telescopic dan buoy** incorporates a flashing light which can be seen by the returning vessel. It is attached to the horseshoe lifebuoy and should have a drogue fitted to prevent undue drift in strong winds. The man-overboard/shipwreck **satellite beacon** is representative of electronic devices which when released pinpoint the position of the victim or vessel. Mechanical systems are designed to give the victim support and to enable the crew to winch him or her back to the boat. **Webbing safety harnesses** are designed to be worn over all protective clothing, but they are often difficult to get into unless properly adjusted beforehand. The front buckle is normally locked by inserting the snaphook of the lifeline. **Day shapes** are signals shown at the fore part of a vessel. A black ball denotes that the boat is anchored, while a black cone, apex down, shows that the boat is under power.

most useful being the diaphragm type that can operate in spite of a certain amount of debris in the water. It is also worth carrying a hole-stopping device of the type that opens like an umbrella.

The next essential for sea-going yachts is a liferaft appropriate for the number of people carried. The liferaft's painter must be strongly attached to the yacht and a knife must be available nearby to cut it. Certain inflatable dinghies are acceptable as dual-purpose tenders and liferafts, the essential extra being gas inflation. However, they generally lack two very important features of a liferaft: water pockets on the underside to reduce drift and reduce the risk of capsize, and a canopy to shelter the occupants.

Attracting attention is the next priority, and there is no doubt that VHF radio is the first choice as it enables you to make direct and immediate contact with the coast-guard service. Because an accident involving the boat being flooded is liable to short out the electrics, it is well worth carrying at least one hand-portable VHF set that can be taken into the liferaft with you.

The difficulty with distress flares is that you do not normally know if they have been seen, and often the most important service they can render is to identify a vessel in trouble when a helicopter or lifeboat is searching for it. Coloured smoke flares are best for attracting the attention of an air-craft, while rockets are more likely to be seen from sea level; hand-held flares cannot be seen from a long distance away. The important thing is to have a set of flares in a proper pack that can be quickly grabbed and put into the liferaft.

Fire at sea is especially danger-ous because of the fuel and cook-ing gas stored on board and the risk of crew getting trapped below. Because of the risk of fumes below deck, use only water and dry pow-der extinguishers in the cabin. Vaporizing liquids such as BCF are recommended only for automatic systems in an engine room. For cooker flare-ups, a fire blanket is best and this should be stowed near but not right next to the cooker.

Water is the best answer for any fire involving wood or fabric, but it should never be used if fuel, oil or high-voltage electricity is involved. Engine fires almost invariably involve leaking fuel or oil, so if the engine is stopped and the fuel cut off at the tank, the fire should die out. Keep the engine covers on to restrict the air supply and squirt the fire extinguisher in through a vent.

CLOTHING & FOOTWEAR

Splash proof thermal jacket

Splash proof thermal long-john

padded waistcoat

polo neck sweater

towel scarf

rugby shirt

thermal socks

boot liners

cotton trousers

thermal underwear

The rapid rise in the popularity of sailing in recent years can be attributed in part to the remarkable improvement in protective clothing that makes it possible to remain warm and dry in most conditions. When the normal wear for dinghy sailing was shorts and some kind of light waterproof jacket, the sport was restricted to the summer months and a capsize called for a rapid return to shore. Nowadays, sailing continues throughout the year and ending up in the water is a minor incident.

The improvement in offshore clothing has been, if possible, even more dramatic, thanks largely to the development of the new 'breathable' fabrics that allow perspiration to evaporate and escape without letting seawater in.

If you are dinghy sailing where the weather and water are warm, or cruising on a warm, dry day, your choice of clothing basically depends upon your personal preferences and perhaps on the current fashions. Most large chandlers sell a good range of casual clothing—such as shirts, sweaters and caps—designed specifically for the leisure cruising market, but they also stock the more practical clothing that you will need for serious sailing in cold weather and rough seas.

Sailing clothing has two main roles to perform: to keep you dry and to keep you at the right temperature, neither too hot nor too cold. Sailing footwear also has a dual purpose, in that it should enable you to remain securely on your feet as you walk about the boat, and be capable of providing some form of weatherproof protection for your feet.

For dinghy sailing, the choice of clothing is between drysuits and wetsuits. Neoprene foam drysuits are relatively cheap and are available in a choice of thicknesses and styles depending on the degree of protection needed. For summer sailing, a lightweight 'shortie' wetsuit that leaves the arms and lower legs uncovered can be the best bet, while colder water calls for a full suit covered by a light one-piece overall. For winter use, a 'steamer' with seals at the neck, ankle and wrist would be appropriate.

The next step up is to a fully waterproof drysuit with seals at the ankles, wrists and neck. These suits

The thin, non-absorbent **thermal undergarments** wick the moisture away from the skin and prevent moving air from cooling the body. The intermediate-layer clothing has a thin, lightweight outer shell that is water-repellent but still permits body water vapour to pass through. The inner lining of non-absorbent material creates a thick layer of trapped air that insulates the wearer from the elements. Available in high-waist or **long-john trousers**, with waistcoat and long-sleeved jacket, this style of clothing is very popular with cruising and racing crews. **Thermal socks** and **boot liners** ensure that the feet and legs remain warm, while a **towelling scarf** will prevent water dribbling uncomfortably down one's neck. For casual wear, **rugby shirts** loose **cotton trousers** and **deck shoes** combine warmth and protection with style.

were originally developed for diving and were very stiff, heavy and awkward. Getting in or out of one was an act worthy of Houdini, especially as the waterproof zip ran across the back.

Dramatic improvements in materials have transformed the drysuit into something easy and quick to put on and offering total protection. Formerly, one could not wear a drysuit for an extended period because undergarments gradually became soaked with perspiration, but with the development of breathable fabrics, that objection no longer applies.

The challenge of major events such as the Whitbread Round the World Race led to a rapid improvement in offshore clothing.

Out went oiled wool sweaters and sweaty PVC waterproofs, and in came a series of 'multilayer' systems based on modern synthetic fabrics. A key feature of these systems is that each layer can be used on its own or as part of an outfit suitable for the most hostile conditions of cold and bad weather.

Underwear made of lightweight fibre-pile is designed to keep the skin dry by 'wicking' moisture outwards. The next layer, usually consisting of a long-john suit made of fibre-pile covered with a light waterproof covering, provides most of the warmth and can be worn without additional covering in fine conditions or below deck.

The outer layer, made of fully waterproof material, is the most important. All the main clothing manufacturers, such as Musto, Henri-Lloyd, Splashdown, Helly-Hansen and Gill make outerwear in a series of grades depending on whether they are for small-boat racing, coastal cruising and racing or serious offshore work.

In every case, waterproof trousers should be cut high so there is never a gap at waist level. The legs must have ankle tighteners. Except on the cheapest suits, there should be reinforcement on the seat and knees and a lining to prevent condensation forming on the inside. A jacket for coastal use can be a fairly straightforward waterproof whereas an offshore jacket needs waterproof cuffs, a high collar and hood that between them protect most of the head, spaces for a built-in harness and buoyancy, and lots of pockets for equipment. Reflective patches that make the wearer more visible at night are recommended.

Until the introduction of new materials, the problem with such jackets was that they became heavier and heavier as more features were added, eventually resembling suits of armour. The appearance of lightweight, vapour-permeable materials such as Gore-Tex was therefore especially welcome. Being much lighter and more flexible than the older type of proofed nylon, they are far more pleasant to wear. But they are not cheap, and a full offshore outfit calls for a serious cash outlay.

The ever-popular leather deckshoes are the footwear of choice in temperate conditions, except on racing dinghies where special zip-up boots are used over drysuit feet. When buying leather shoes, be sure they really are designed for use afloat rather than as fashion items. The 'real thing' has specially-tanned leather that will survive repeated wetting and drying and is sewn with rotproof thread.

Offshore, good boots with thick, well-insulated soles are essential. Beware of the foam rubber insole that having once become wet takes about a week to dry. Boots should always be knee-high as short ones tend to pop out from oilskin trousers when you are sitting down, with the result that they immediately fill with water.

Gloves are essential for most types of sailing. Gloves for small-boat sailing are intended to provide protection when handling rope, and the leather gloves made for this purpose usually have the ends of the fingers cut off so that one can still grasp small objects such as shackle pins. Gloves for more serious sailing cover the whole hand and have either a leather or rubber palm for grip, but do not claim to be waterproof. For events such as the Whitbread, where both cold and wet are the problem, two layers of gloves are called for—a warm pair covered by tough rubber gauntlets with long wrists that tuck under the jacket cuff. Ski gloves are no good because they rely for their insulation on foam, which quickly becomes sodden.

Finally, never forget that a high proportion of body heat loss is from the head, so a warm hat of some kind is essential for most types of sailing. In summer, when the sun glares brightly, a peaked cap and sunglasses are recommended. When the wind blows, wear a close-fitting woollen cap that covers the ears. The type that is a cap when folded and then pulls down to become a balaclava is ideal.

A harsh sailing environment often necessitates the wearing of a totally waterproof outer layer of clothing that stands up to heavy abrasion. The majority of materials used for this type of clothing are designed to prevent water passing through and are often lined with a permeable layer so that body vapour condenses on the inside of the outer shell material and runs off it.

High-lift pants are kept up with elastic suspenders, and a Velcro adjuster permits the bottoms to be fitted snugly to deck boots. Hooded jackets totally protect the upper body and are the key to an efficient waterproofing system.

Deck boots are designed to protect and to give a good grip, while thick socks or thermal liners keep the feet warm. Gloves and a wool hat complete the protection of the offshore sailor. Deck shoes and a yachting cap can be worn on sunny days or when going ashore.

TIDES & WEATHER

Together, the individual and combined natural forces of the tides and the weather still preoccupy the thinking of all those who sail on the sea. For all but a small band of dedicated racing and long-distance cruising crews, the decision to set sail is primarily dependent upon the forecast wind and wave conditions.

Once under way, the destination of a sailboat is often determined by any improvement or deterioration in the existing conditions. All the time, the skipper is weighing up the seaworthiness of the boat, the welfare of the crew (usually the family), and his or her ability to second-guess the mass of readily available broadcast weather information.

Sailing, especially out of sight of land, presents one of the few frontier challenges left to modern man, but there is a marked contrast between today's sailors, with their banks of electronic equipment, weather printouts and instant radio contact, and their seafaring ancestors whose survival depended on their ability to interpret sea, sky and seabed. Yet each generation shares the common elements of seamanship and decision-making, and experience in dealing with the unexpected is still an important attribute.

There *are* sailing areas, such as Southern California and the Mediterranean, where 'ideal' sailing conditions can be found for much of the year. However, most of the world's sailors, living in the northern latitudes of Europe and North America, have to learn to live with the changeable weather dished out by the prevailing westerly airstream and with the changes in the height of the surface of the sea caused by the twice-daily tides.

Unlike the difficult business of predicting the weather, it is possible to predict the times and heights of each day's tides a long time in advance and with a great deal of accuracy. These predictions are published as tide tables and are available on a national and local basis in most popular sailing areas.

The force that generates the tides is the strong gravitational pull of the moon, which is relatively close to the earth, combined with the weaker gravitational pull of the more distant sun.

The predictability of tides is due to the regular movement of the moon around the earth once every 24 hours and 50 minutes. This regular movement, combined with the relative position of the sun, gives us our two-week cycles of spring and neap tides.

We talk about weather systems because there is a semblance of order about weather patterns, and in predicting the weather the barometer has long maintained its importance as an essential indicator of approaching weather systems. Its function is to display the pressure of the atmosphere at the earth's surface, this pressure being measured in inches (of mercury) or in millibars.

The original standard measuring instrument, invented in the 17th century by Italian physicist Evangelista Torricelli, was a column of mercury contained in a 32-inch test tube upended in a dish of mercury. Pressure fluctuations are only about 20 percent of the column, seldom exceeding a low of 25.5 inches (863.5 millibars) or a high of 31.5 inches (1066.7 millibars).

The invention of the less accurate (but more convenient) aneroid barometer, by Lucius Vidi in 1843, was a welcome advance. Pressure is shown on a clock-like display by a pointer, activated by a mechanical linkage attached to a thin-walled, partially-evacuated metal container that expands and contracts as pressure decreases and increases.

A second pointer can be moved by hand to record existing pressure, thereafter becoming a reference point that shows clearly whether the air pressure is rising or falling.

A refinement of the aneroid barometer is the barograph, which makes a continuous record of pressure changes by marking them on a paper chart wrapped around a slowly-revolving drum. This delicate instrument can be taken to sea if suitably damped (insulated from shocks) and gives a comprehensive record of pressure patterns.

Sailors need to know the trends of pressure changes because these are closely related to well-documented weather patterns associated with large masses of high- and low-pressure air.

Most barometers are marked up to show the general conditions to expect when pressure is rising or falling, but these markings (such as 'fair' and 'rain') are only an approximate guide and should not be relied upon.

Excesses of pressure differences, especially in areas of extremely low-pressure air originating in the tropics or at the interface of polar and tropical air, combine to produce intense and sometimes extensive storms. These storms — typhoons, hurricanes and localized tornados — cause considerable damage and loss of life and are bad news for the unwary sailor.

The combination of wind-induced waves, rapid changes in pressure and the movement of surface water can produce awesome sea conditions. Hurricane-force winds produce short, unstable waves that can exceed 40 feet from trough to crest and will easily overwhelm small craft.

Given that seafarers need a lot of help to ensure their safety, it is not surprising that weather forecasts are of special importance. These are available from a wide variety of agencies including TV, radio, coastguard stations and newspapers.

Specialist marine or 'shipping' forecasts give stylized predictions for designated sea areas, as well as giving reports from weather stations enabling experienced sailors to draw their own weather charts. In addition, many craft carry weatherfax equipment that prints out weather charts at regular intervals to give a visual update of prevailing conditions.

TIDES

As the moon orbits the earth, its gravitational pull causes two tidal 'waves', on opposite sides of the world, to follow its progress. These waves do not rush around the oceans causing havoc, but rather they are bulges causing up to fifty feet of change in sea level between high and low water.

A tidal bulge becomes most noticeable when it approaches the shallows of the continents and is translated into the lateral movement of water—the incoming flood tides, and the outgoing ebb tides.

When the sun and the moon are both in line with the earth — at new moon and full moon — their gravitational pulls combine to produce the highest high tides (the spring high tides) and the greatest movement of water.

At the neap tides, the sun and moon are at 90° to each other relative to the earth — the first and last quarters of the moon — and so their gravitational pulls work against each other, producing the lowest high tides and the least amount of movement of water.

Fortunately, the predictability of the relative positions of the sun and moon enables hydrographers to produce tide tables years in advance of the event. These are published as nautical almanacs covering numerous ports or tidal stations, or as localized tide tables, and are available from chandlers or fishing tackle shops.

Since the moon orbits the earth once every 24 hours and 50 minutes, the two tidal waves representing high water occur approximately every 12 hours and 25 minutes.

Low water occurs between 5 and 6½ hours after high water, depending on the location of the tidal station.

As with most simple concepts there is a plethora of names to describe the various phenomena related to tides. For instance, the *chart datum* is the level from which measurements are made to determine the heights of tides. It is normally the level of low water at the time of the *lowest astronomical tide* (LAT). Everything above this line is shown on charts (maps of the coast and seabed) as *drying heights*. Everything below this line is shown as *charted depths* in metres.

Tide tables give the times of high and low water together with the height of high water (above chart datum) and the height of low water (above chart datum). Subtracting low water from high water heights gives the *range* of the tide which is the depth of the moon's tidal wave.

Sooner or later, most sailors have to sail over areas of the seabed which dry out at low water. The first essential for this is to know how much water there is at a given point at a given time to enable your boat to sail over it without striking the seabed or an obstruction.

A very rough guide, but one which is better than a blind guess, is the *rule of twelfths*. This is based on observations that show that in the six hours between low and high water, the hourly depth changes related to the range (difference in tidal heights) are:

- first hour — 1/12 range
- second hour — 2/12 range
- third hour — 3/12 range
- fourth hour — 3/12 range
- fifth hour — 2/12 range
- sixth hour — 1/12 range

These twelfths of the tidal range can be memorized easily, as they are simply 1, 2, 3 and then 3, 2, 1, over the six-hour period.

On a falling (ebb) tide you cannot afford to make a mistake, for once aground you will stay there until the moon drags the next tidal wave to your rescue. A more accurate method is to use the published tidal curves to calculate the depth.

The rhythmic cycle of the tide creates accompanying periodic river-like movements of water, especially where the oceans shallow along coastlines. The effect is greatest around headlands and in restricted shallow waters.

These horizontal movements of water are known in the United States as currents, and in Britain as tidal streams. To the English, currents are the non-periodic horizontal movements of water caused by the major wind systems of the world. These non-periodic movements include the Gulf Stream, originating in the Caribbean and flowing to the Newfoundland Banks, and the North Atlantic Drift, sustained by the prevailing westerly winds and carrying water from the North American coast to well within the Arctic Circle.

Because of their predictability, sailors can learn to use tidal streams to their advantage by sailing with them whenever possible and by gauging the depths of water so that they can traverse shallows at high tide.

On the downside, when the wind and a tidal stream are in opposition they can create life-threatening rips and tidal races in narrows and off prominent headlands.

You should also remember that, when you are sailing against the tide, if the stream is running faster than your boat can sail you will find yourself going backward, even though your sails are full and you

Above *Slipways make it easy to launch dinghies at low tide.*
Right *When anchoring, allow for the rise and fall of the tide.*

seem to be making good speed over the water. If you are approaching the shore under these conditions, the stream will carry you farther out to sea; if you are heading out to sea, it can wash you back to the shore, and possibly aground or onto rocks.

Most of the tidal stream atlases that are published contain 13 charts showing tidal streams at hourly intervals from 6 hours before high water to 6 hours after it at a designated Standard Port.

Before delving into tidal stream atlases, though, it's important to appreciate that tidal flow can be observed and that this is always the best guide to its direction, especially in estuaries.

A pole, buoy, moored boat or a rock will all show a wake streaming out in the direction that the water is moving. It's almost as if they are moving through stationary water and, if the stream is strong, they will have a bow wave on the upstream side. Moored boats will point into the tide if the wind is light.

If you are afloat and uncertain of the direction of the stream, let the boat drift and observe the relative positions of a shoreline feature and a feature somewhere behind it. Imagine that the front mark is stationary. Any apparent movement of the back marker will be in the same direction as that of the tidal stream.

In estuaries, the strongest stream is in the deepest channel and, should you find yourself battling against an adverse stream, back eddies and weaker streams are to be found at the edge — but watch the depth of water beneath you!

ESTIMATING DIRECTION OF TIDAL FLOW

A pole, buoy, moored boat or a rock will show a wake streaming in the direction that the water is moving

flow

USING A TRANSIT TO GAUGE TIDAL FLOW

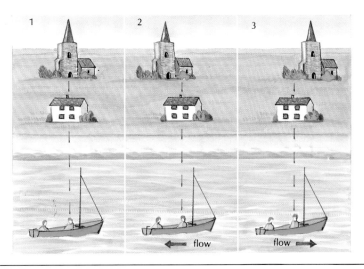

1   2   3

flow   flow

1 To find the direction of a tidal stream or current, let your boat drift and observe the positions of shoreline features. When two are in line with each other, as seen from the boat, the imaginary line joining them is a 'line of transit'.
2 and 3 Any apparent movement of the back marker (here a church tower) relative to the front marker (the house) will be in the same direction as the tidal stream or current is flowing.

ESTIMATING TIDE RISE

You can use your tide tables and the 'rule of twelfths' to estimate the depth of the water at a particular time and place. The rule of twelfths is based on the amount the tide rises and falls during each successive hour from low to high tide and vice versa.

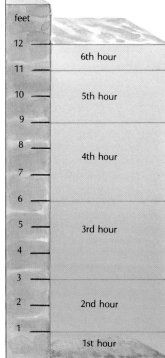

feet	
12	6th hour
11	
10	5th hour
9	
8	4th hour
7	
6	
5	3rd hour
4	
3	
2	2nd hour
1	
	1st hour

The approximate hourly rise of a twelve-foot tide from low to high water. The actual time from low to high water is only 6 hours approximately.

AIR MASSES & CLOUDS

Left *Clouds are a useful indicator of what is happening with the weather.*

The weather is the result of the nature, motion and interaction of low-pressure and high-pressure air masses. To find out where these large areas of low and high pressure air originate we have to look at what drives the weather — the heat from the sun.

When the sun shines on the earth's surface it heats it, and as a result the air above it heats up, expands and rises. This rising warmed air creates a partial vacuum — an area of low pressure — and as it rises, surrounding higher-pressure air flows in to replace it.

When the sun doesn't shine — at night, or during polar winters — the earth's surface cools and so the air above it cools, contracts and sinks. This denser, heavier high-pressure air flows outward, displacing the surrounding lighter low-pressure air.

Because the sun's effects are greater in the tropics than at the poles, there are semipermanent bands of high- and low-pressure air masses around the earth at different latitudes. There is a region of high pressure at each pole, and a band of low pressure around the equator.

Warmed air rising from the equatorial regions spreads to the north and the south, and as it does so it cools and sinks again over the Horse Latitudes, forming bands of high-pressure air masses (the subtropical highs) at about 30°N and 30°S. Between these bands of high pressure and the polar high pressure regions are further bands of low pressure, at about 60°N and 60°S. Each pressure band is sustained by the global and local heating effects of the sun.

Air returning to the equatorial zone from the adjacent high pressure bands is deflected to the west by the Coriolis Effect — a result of the

earth's rotation — to become the Northeast Trades in the Northern Hemisphere and the Southeast Trades in the Southern.

Air flowing to higher latitudes from these high pressure bands becomes the Prevailing Westerlies of the Northern and Southern Hemispheres, while the outward flow from the areas of cold, dense air at the poles is deflected to the west by the rotation of the earth to create the Polar Easterlies.

There are four categories of air mass, each with its own characteristics and classified according to where it originated. These are Continental Polar air (cold and dry, originating over land near the poles), Continental Tropical (warm and dry, originating over land in the tropics), Maritime Polar (cold and wet, formed over seas near the poles) and Maritime Tropical (warm and wet, formed over tropical seas).

An air mass may thus be warm or cold, and wet or dry, but once formed, it tends to retain those characteristics even when in contact with different air masses. Different air masses do not readily mix and it is this characteristic which creates the weather systems, especially at the interface or *front line* of converging masses of air.

In the Northern Hemisphere, air flowing out of the high pressure zones is diverted to the right by the Coriolis effect. This results in slow-moving high-pressure air masses (anticyclones) that rotate slowly in a clockwise direction. In the Southern Hemisphere, the flow of high pressure air is deflected to the left, and so the southern anticyclones rotate in a counterclockwise direction. Anticyclones usually bring clear, settled weather.

Sea-based low pressure areas are established in northern and southern latitudes over water which is warmer than the adjacent polar ice-caps. Air flowing into these low pressure areas is deflected by the

Coriolis effect, producing a vortex spiral (counterclockwise in the Northern Hemisphere, clockwise in the Southern) which is seen at its most extreme in hurricanes and typhoons. Low pressure is characterized by mostly unsettled, moist and windy conditions.

The opposite rotation of pockets of warm and cold air enables them to intermesh like a giant system of cogs in a global gearbox. It is only at the junctions between high- and low-pressure air masses that conflict occurs, and the battle intensifies as the air masses intermingle and either gradually lose their identity or combine to produce destructive forces.

For most of the time, warm, moist, low-pressure air rises, cools, deposits its excess moisture and descends without a great deal of fuss, but it can sometimes act as a catalyst to produce violent weather conditions.

A depression forms when the convex leading edge of an approaching cold, high-pressure air mass slides under the concave edge of the lighter, warm air of a low-pressure air mass, forcing it to rise. The line of interface between the two, with its attendant high, white cloud, slopes away from the observer. This is the often-volatile *cold front*, with its attendant thunderstorms and strong, veering winds.

Warm moist air overtaking cool denser air climbs up and over the convex slope, creating clouds as it rises and cools. The line of interface and its cloud formations slope toward the observer, and the first indication of this approaching *warm front* is the high cloud of the already-mixing air. This is followed

POLAR AND TROPICAL AIR MASSES

This map shows the average movement of the world's major Maritime Polar (MP), Maritime Tropical (MT), Continental Polar (CP) and Continental Tropical CT) air masses.

→ MP
→ MT
→ CP
→ CT
----- Equator

Average movement of Polar and Tropical air masses

CLOUD CLASSIFICATION

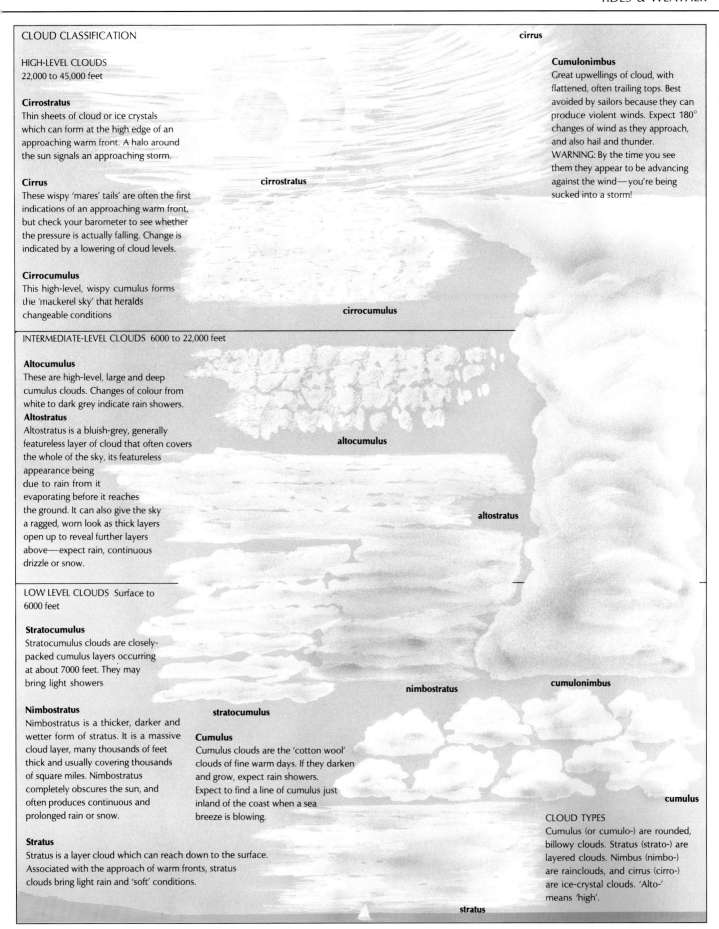

HIGH-LEVEL CLOUDS
22,000 to 45,000 feet

Cirrostratus
Thin sheets of cloud or ice crystals which can form at the high edge of an approaching warm front. A halo around the sun signals an approaching storm.

Cirrus
These wispy 'mares' tails' are often the first indications of an approaching warm front, but check your barometer to see whether the pressure is actually falling. Change is indicated by a lowering of cloud levels.

Cirrocumulus
This high-level, wispy cumulus forms the 'mackerel sky' that heralds changeable conditions

cirrus

cirrostratus

cirrocumulus

Cumulonimbus
Great upwellings of cloud, with flattened, often trailing tops. Best avoided by sailors because they can produce violent winds. Expect 180° changes of wind as they approach, and also hail and thunder.
WARNING: By the time you see them they appear to be advancing against the wind—you're being sucked into a storm!

INTERMEDIATE-LEVEL CLOUDS 6000 to 22,000 feet

Altocumulus
These are high-level, large and deep cumulus clouds. Changes of colour from white to dark grey indicate rain showers.

Altostratus
Altostratus is a bluish-grey, generally featureless layer of cloud that often covers the whole of the sky, its featureless appearance being due to rain from it evaporating before it reaches the ground. It can also give the sky a ragged, worn look as thick layers open up to reveal further layers above—expect rain, continuous drizzle or snow.

altocumulus

altostratus

LOW LEVEL CLOUDS Surface to 6000 feet

Stratocumulus
Stratocumulus clouds are closely-packed cumulus layers occurring at about 7000 feet. They may bring light showers

Nimbostratus
Nimbostratus is a thicker, darker and wetter form of stratus. It is a massive cloud layer, many thousands of feet thick and usually covering thousands of square miles. Nimbostratus completely obscures the sun, and often produces continuous and prolonged rain or snow.

Stratus
Stratus is a layer cloud which can reach down to the surface. Associated with the approach of warm fronts, stratus clouds bring light rain and 'soft' conditions.

nimbostratus

stratocumulus

cumulonimbus

Cumulus
Cumulus clouds are the 'cotton wool' clouds of fine warm days. If they darken and grow, expect rain showers. Expect to find a line of cumulus just inland of the coast when a sea breeze is blowing.

cumulus

CLOUD TYPES
Cumulus (or cumulo-) are rounded, billowy clouds. Stratus (strato-) are layered clouds. Nimbus (nimbo-) are rainclouds, and cirrus (cirro-) are ice-crystal clouds. 'Alto-' means 'high'.

stratus

by a period of rain and poor visibility until the arrival of the next air mass.

An *occluded front* occurs when one wedge of cold air catches up with a preceding one, and the warm air that was separating them is squeezed upwards en masse. This gives rise to strong winds and rain if the cold and warm air masses differ considerably in temperature and humidity.

Clouds, which are classified according to their shape, colour and height, are useful indicators of approaching weather systems. Because each family of clouds is created by specific circumstances of temperature, humidity and height, clouds tell the experienced observer what is happening with the weather and what is to come, hence their importance to navigators world-wide.

WINDS & STORMS

Sailboats are designed to derive most of their power from the effect of the wind on the sails, yet many recreational sailors choose to sail in only a very small range of the winds available to them.

20 knots of wind is a fresh breeze, and will have many family cruisers scurrying for shelter. 30 kts is a yachtsman's gale. Beyond 30 kts those who choose to leave harbour must have the experience and the type of craft to cope with extreme conditions. 40 knots of wind means the air is moving at 46 mph — try keeping your arm extended out of the window of a car moving at that speed and you will begin to appreciate the power of strong winds.

The main reason for the general dislike of fresh to strong winds is not the wind itself, but the choppy seas it generates in a relatively short time, especially when the wind is blowing against the tide.

Inexperienced family crews or friends out for the day quickly succumb to the large angles of heel, the cold spray and seasickness. The wise, experienced skipper will pay careful attention to the forecasts and choose the days which best suit his or her chosen style and crew.

Winds are caused by air moving from an area of high atmospheric pressure to one of lower pressure. These areas of differing pressure may be air masses such as anticyclones and depressions, or they may be of more local origin. For instance, air cooling and sinking over a cold expanse of water will cause a localized increase in pressure, while air being heated and rising over adjacent warm land will cause a localized drop in pressure.

Whatever their origin, the closer the centres of high and low pressure are to each other, and the

greater the pressure difference between them, the stronger the wind will be.

Some of the most violent and destructive winds are associated with some of the smallest weather systems. The principal culprits are cumulonimbus clouds; because of their vertical development and unstable air, these create vortexes and whirlpools of air that, at their worst, result in tornados or waterspouts.

The rapidly-rising air associated with cumulonimbus clouds sucks in surrounding air with a rotary motion. The centre of rotation can develop into an intense area of low pressure which reaches down to the earth's surface and, like a huge vacuum cleaner, sucks up solid objects and explodes buildings.

At sea, waterspouts are created in thundery conditions associated with an extremely cold front breaking up hot, humid weather.

Tornados and waterspouts experienced in Britain are usually weak compared with those of the central states of the USA. However, infrequent but violent line squalls are a feature of UK weather, especially along the south coast of England. Again, they are associated with the approach of a cold front following a period of settled weather, or the rapid development of massive cumulus clouds on a hot day.

If, when you are sailing, the wind suddenly changes direction by 180°, look at the sky in the downwind direction — the direction in which the new wind is travelling. If the sky there is dark grey, or black, or greenish purple, and the sun becomes progressively obscured, prepare yourself, your crew and your boat for a violent squall, or seek immediate (within 15 minutes) shelter. On open water you will see an

intense white line at the junction of sea and sky. This bright line is the rain hitting the sea; don't ask any more questions — act!

The squall, usually another 180° change of wind, will be preceded by violent rain falling out of the front of massively-developed thunder heads. In such conditions, winds of up to 70 knots have been recorded on what were previously hot summer days.

The term 'depression' — formerly used to denote interactions between cold and warm air masses— is now also used to describe larger, well-developed areas

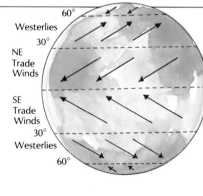

Above *Even experienced racing crews can have problems in very strong winds.*

of strong to hurricane-force winds.

The classic ingredients of a depression are fairly large masses of well-developed cold polar air and warm moist tropical air thrown together over a warm land mass or, better still, over a warm sea.

The stirring motion that mixes the depression is supplied by the natural cogwheel-like interaction between the different air masses, and it is the rotation of the low-pressure warm air that drags in, and down from the upper atmosphere, the

---

AIR MOVEMENT
Winds are caused by air flowing out of an area of high pressure into adjacent areas of low pressure

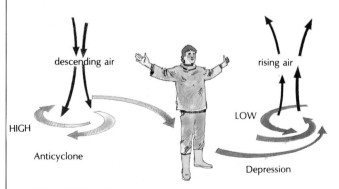

descending air

rising air

HIGH

LOW

Anticyclone

Depression

BUYS BALLOT'S LAW In the Northern Hemisphere, if you stand with your back to the wind you will have low pressure to your left (in the Southern Hemisphere it will be to your right)

THE PREVAILING WINDS
This is the basic pattern of prevailing winds around the world.
In practice, this pattern is distorted by the land masses and the passage of weather systems.

60°
Westerlies
30°
NE Trade Winds
SE Trade Winds
30°
Westerlies
60°

LAND AND SEA BREEZES
These breezes are the result of differences in temperature between the air over the land and that over the sea.

Sea breeze

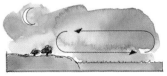

Land breeze

THE BEAUFORT WIND SCALE

SCALE	DESCRIPTION	WIND SPEED km/hour	knots	VISIBLE SIGNS	SAILING CRITERIA
0	Calm	<1	<1	Flat, calm sea. On land, smoke rises vertically, leaves are still.	Dinghies should be heeled to reduce wetted area and allow the sails to form aerofoil shape. Cruisers need to use engines to make steerage way.
1	Light air	1–5	1–3	Slight rippling of the sea. Smoke drifts, wind vanes unaffected.	Dinghies can make gentle forward motion with flattened sails, and balanced to be slightly bow-down and heeled to leeward. Cruisers need engine power.
2	Light breeze	6–11	4–6	Small wavelets develop. Leaves rustle, flags and weather vanes stir. The wind can be felt on the face.	Dinghies can sail upright at a reasonable speed and with full sails. With 6 knots of wind, a good cruiser racer may make 3 to 4 kts; other cruisers need engine power.
3	Gentle breeze	12–19	7–10	Wave crests begin to break. Leaves move continuously, light flags are extended.	Ideal conditions for dinghies because there is sufficient wind and the waves are still quite small. Cruisers can make steady progress under sail.
4	Moderate breeze	20–28	11–16	Wave lengths increase, with frequent white horses. Most flags extended, light branches move and dust may be raised.	Good for experienced dinghy sailors but learners should go ashore. Most cruisers can reach hull speed; some need reefed mainsails and part-furled headsails.
5	Fresh breeze	29–38	17–21	Many breaking wave crests. Small, leafy trees begin to sway, tops of all trees move.	Excellent for experienced dinghy crews; the less experienced may be capsized. Ideal for cruisers, but light boats need to use smaller sails to reduce heeling.
6	Strong breeze	39–49	22–27	Large waves develop, with foamy crests and spray. Large tree branches move, wind whistles in telephone and electricity lines.	Most dinghy crews at their limit; many will be overpowered. Most cruisers will head for shelter, with mainsails double-reefed and crews wearing harness.
7	Near gale	50–61	28–33	Waves heap and foam is blown downwind. Whole trees sway, and walking against the wind becomes tiresome.	Dinghies should stay on shore. Most cruiser crews will find it hard to cope and should seek shelter or, if gales are forecast, heave to and ride out the storm.
8	Gale	62–74	34–40	Waves become large with deep troughs and much blown foam. Twigs break off trees, and walking is difficult.	Dinghies should be securely tied down. Cruisers should have deeply reefed main and small headsails; all except essential crew should be safely below deck.
9	Strong gale	75–88	41–47	High foam-streaked waves with breaking crests. On land, roofs, chimneys and fences may be damaged.	Cruisers in danger of knockdown. Even the most experienced of crews will have problems, and most will need to lower the sails and lash the tiller.
10	Storm	89–102	48–55	Waves very high with breaking crests and large, frothy patches of foam. Trees are uprooted; much structural damage.	Wave heights of 20 to 35 feet can capsize large cruiser racers lying a-hull. Breaking crests can pitchpole a large yacht running with or across them.
11	Violent storm	103–117	56–63	Waves become extremely high, and sea surface obscured by driving foam. Severe structural damage on land.	Extreme danger, especially when close to a shelving coast. Capsize and 90° knockdowns possible. Keep well away from coastline if at all possible.
12	Hurricane	>117	>63	Huge waves. The sea becomes completely white and visibility is seriously affected by driving foam.	The worst possible danger. Survival is the most you can hope for, and your only priority.

The Beaufort Scale of wind speeds was devised by the English admiral Sir Francis Beaufort in the 19th century. The scale is not linear; the range of wind speeds for each number of the scale increases progressively up the scale.

cold air that disperses the original pocket of warm air.

An interesting feature of a depression is that the cold air drawn into it is induced to change its flow from clockwise to counter-clockwise rotation (in the Northern Hemisphere; it's from counter-clockwise to clockwise in the Sou-thern) and that the direction of tra-vel of the depression is governed by the winds in the warm air. Particu-larly destructive depressions shoot down the corridors formed by older, more static depressions, using them to change direction and increase their speed.

Superimposed on the global pat-tern of heating and cooling, and the air masses and winds that it pro-duces, is the daily cycle produced by the sun. In many coastal and inland areas, local winds override the gradient winds (those created by anticyclones and depressions) to give more predictable patterns to sail by. These local winds include sea breezes and land breezes.

Sea breezes are onshore winds caused by the replacement of rising, heated inland air by cooler air from off the coast. Land breezes are off-shore winds which occur mostly at night, when the cooling land-based air sinks and flows out to the now-warmer sea.

FOG & MIST

Over the last decade or so, the miniaturization (and the easy availability) of electronic navigation equipment has changed the attitude of long-time sailors and is taken for granted by newcomers to the sport.

The great differences between the newcomers and the small-boat sailors who sailed before the electronic revolution is that the latter can quickly revert to using their old, well-practised skills when necessary, for instance in fog, but those who rely implicitly on their little black boxes will risk being well and truly lost unless they learn the traditional back-up navigational skills.

To the car driver, fog can be a daunting experience, and many drivers pull off the road to avoid having to drive in it. The sailor does not usually have any option but to sail on when he encounters fog, and unless he is sailing close inshore or in an estuary, anchoring will not be a viable alternative.

In fog, not being able to see more than a few few feet, and not being able to focus properly on a fixed point of reference, can cause spatial disorientation. So the use of sensible boat-handling strategies is essential if the safe navigation of the craft and the safety of its crew are to be ensured.

The various types of fog are essentially clouds which form at the earth's surface, and are products of temperature differences and moisture in the air.

The amount of moisture a given amount of air can contain, in the form of invisible water vapour, depends on its temperature: warm air can hold more water vapour than cold air can. The ratio of the *actual* amount of water vapour in the air, at a particular temperature, to the maximum amount of water vapour that it *could* hold at that temperature, is called the *relative humidity*.

The relative humidity is expressed as a percentage; air containing the maximum amount of water possible at a given temperature has a relative humidity of 100 percent, and is said to be *saturated*.

As warm, moisture-laden air cools, its relative humidity increases, and if it is cooled sufficiently it will reach saturation. The temperature at which this happens is called the *dewpoint temperature*, because at that point the moisture will begin to condense out of the air and form water droplets, creating dew, clouds or fog.

Radiation fog may form when the sun sets and the earth begins to radiate its heat. If the sky is cloudy, it acts in the same way as roof insulation and traps a warm layer of air between the clouds and the earth's surface.

If there is no cloud, though, the heat radiates out into the atmosphere and the surface air cools rapidly as the earth's surface cools. Strong winds will remove this layer of cooled air, but a gentle breeze will simply stir it up into a deeper layer that continues to cool.

Under these conditions, if the ground is damp or the humidity already high, continued cooling to and beyond the dewpoint causes condensation in the form of dew and mist. Further cooling produces dense fog in layers extending to hundreds of feet above the ground. In valleys, mist and fog roll down the hillsides forming cold 'lakes' of air containing mist and fog and capped by warmer air. In winter, hoar frost forms when the dewpoint is below 0°C (32°F).

Seasonal differences are marked. In summer, the rising sun soon burns the fog off or causes it to rise as dispersing stratus cloud. In spring and autumn, there is additional moisture in the air and the weaker, later-rising sun takes time to disperse the fog.

In winter — especially in settled conditions of high pressure — radiation fog, fuelled by vehicle exhaust gases and industrial pollution, may persist for days.

Sailors moored or anchored in sheltered estuaries may experience this type of reduced visibility, but offshore the only noticeable effect of these conditions will be that they inhibit the formation of sea breezes in settled spring and autumn weather.

Advection fog is the product of moving air. Humid air blowing over a cold surface capable of

cooling it below its dewpoint will produce fog. This occurs especially in spring, when the sea is cold and the returning sun is warming the often-saturated winter land to produce saturated air. When this air is blown over the cold sea, advection fog may form. Maritime tropical air, with its high moisture content, is also liable to produce thick banks of advection fog as it reaches the cooler waters of higher latitudes.

Sailors can expect advection sea fog to be accompanied by winds of up to 12 knots and exceptionally of 20 knots if the incoming air is already at or near dewpoint.

Onshore winds meeting cliffs or mountains often lift the fog a little for up to a mile offshore, creating a corridor of visibility along the shore. Use your VHF radio to contact any yachts or fishermen who may already be in the clear zone.

Warm sector mists may form in the area of warm moist air trapped between two colder fronts in a depression. The compressed warm air becomes increasingly saturated as occlusion takes place, so that only a small drop in temperature by contact with a cold sea, or air in the

EQUIPMENT USEFUL IN FOG

Echo sounder

An efficient, frequently-used echo sounder will give you a known dimension: the depth of water under your boat. If it has shallow and deep alarms you can set them to enable you to traverse a seabed contour that will lead you safely to the shore.

Radar

Radar is the 'eye' which penetrates the surrounding gloom and which in experienced hands, can be used in conjunction with the echo sounder to guide you to your destination and to avoid collision with other vessels.

Radar reflection

Being visible to radar is essential. Make sure your reflector has been proven to work and is not filled with junk. Hoist it high to increase the distance from which it can be detected.

VHF radio

If caught out in the shipping lanes, especially in heavy traffic, go with the traffic flow and cross behind passing ships as the opportunity arises.

Speak to surrounding craft, even using a Securite message if you think you have not been detected on their radar. You must know your vessel's approximate position before sending a Securite warning.

Position indicator

Decca, LORAN and satnavs, when properly used and calibrated, are excellent navigation aids; but note that fog banks can distort the incoming signals. Known waypoints which have been achieved time and again should be used when closing a familiar coast.

cold sector, is needed to produce fog.

One further type of fog, sometimes seen in the United States in very hard winters but not often met in the UK, is arctic sea smoke. Supercooled continental polar air, blowing over yet-to-be-frozen sea water, produces lanes of fog. These seldom rise above 10 to 15 feet.

Most sailors rely on professional forecasters to warn them of impending foggy conditions, but you can predict them yourself with some degree of success if you have a humidity meter on your craft. If it reaches 90 to 95 percent, and the sea water temperature is 5°C to 10°C, there's a good chance of fog.

A more accurate way to determine the likelihood of fog is to use a hygrometer to find the dewpoint temperature of the air.

A typical hygrometer, called a psychrometer, consists of two thermometers — one wet bulb, one dry bulb — that are used to determine the relative humidity of the air. When you know the air's relative humidity, you can find its dewpoint temperature by referring to tables. If the dewpoint temperature is just a few °C below the actual air temperature, expect fog as night approaches. If your boat doesn't have a hygrometer, you should listen carefully to broadcast weather forecasts, especially during settled

As soon as you see mist or fog developing, establish your position as precisely as you can.

conditions of high pressure and in spring and autumn.

At the onset of mist or fog, establish your position as exactly as you can; knowing where you are, or cannot possibly be, is the key to safe conduct in reduced visibility. Thereafter, update your estimated position (EP) at half-hourly intervals or when major changes of direction are made, and pay particular attention to tidal streams as these will still be operating as they would on a sunny day. Double-check all EPs and fixes, and verify them by using the echo sounder.

When approaching land or a chosen harbour, *always* estimate your time of arrival, consult the tidal stream atlas, and initially aim for a point some miles upstream of your actual destination.

This permits you to close the shoreline, choose a seabed contour to follow, correct for the height of the tide, and then change direction toward your chosen destination with some degree of confidence.

Whenever possible, during fog everyone should be on deck, or ready to come up at a moment's notice. Considerable danger of collision exists in busy shipping lanes, at the entrance to busy harbours and on fishing grounds, so lookouts should be given two white flares and posted bow and amidships to look and listen for approaching ships. The fog signal should be sounded as appropriate for sailing or motoring to warn other vessels of your presence.

WEATHER FORECASTS

Forecasting the weather is always going to be an inexact science in areas of complex pressure and temperature changes. Most of the time, professional forecasting agencies and government departments get it right, and that saves each of us a lot of time watching the sky, barometer and bits of seaweed for signs of a change in the weather.

What is needed of today's sailors is the ability to look at a chart representing the weather at a given point in the past, or near future, recognize the important features and trends, and compare the forecast to what is actually happening to the barometric pressure, visibility, sea and sky in their locality.

Weather maps are drawn, in the form of 'contour maps' from thousands of simultaneous observations taken at land and seaborne weather stations around the world. Observers measure temperature, humidity, barometric pressure, sunshine, precipitation, windspeed, wind direction, cloud type, cloud cover, visibility and, where applicable, sea state.

This information is then telexed or sent via satellite to hundreds of central plotting stations as the raw material for the production of weather charts by computer, or sometimes manually by experienced forecasters.

Large agencies such as the US National Weather Service and the UK Meteorological Office have sophisticated computers — among the most powerful in the world — that construct predictive models based on the information supplied, augmented by the information derived from records of previous similar weather patterns.

In the UK, special forecasts for Port Areas can be obtained by telephoning one of the thirteen Regional Met Office forecasting centres. These will also give reports of present weather, which can be extremely valuable if you are planning to sail in their area. Another useful source of weather information is ITV's Teletext service. This gives forecasts for the next 24 hours for each sea area on page 107 and for inland waters on page 108.

In the United States, special VHF weather radios equipped with severe weather alarms are used to receive a continuous flow of updated weather information. Most local airfields and some coastguard stations contribute to this information service.

The US National Weather Service broadcasts it on 102.40 MHz, 162.475 MHz and 162.55 MHz. All shipborne VHF radios are able to receive one or more of these Wx channels devoted solely to continuous weather broadcasts.

In the UK, sailors have to consult lists of the times of weather bulletins on a wide variety of frequencies, ranging from the shipping forecasts on 198 kHz (1515 m) AM long wave to VHF forecasts broadcast by Coast Radio Stations. However, since 1989, HM Coastguard has advised those wishing to obtain a forecast to telephone for one, and the use of VHF for weather forecasts will be increasingly discouraged by them.

In addition, because of frequent changes to broadcast weather forecast services in the UK, you should consult the 'weather' sections of up-to-date nautical almanacs for all information relating to the frequencies and times of all Coast Radio and BBC forecasts.

Official British Met Office forecasts are broadcast by the BBC on long wave (198 kHz, 1515 m) at 0048 hrs, 0555 hrs, 1355 hrs and 1750 hrs. The standardized format and speed of delivery used in these forecasts is intended to permit the skilled listener to record the details in meteorological 'shorthand' for use in compiling a personal weather chart. Experience shows that a pocket tape recorder is very useful for this.

These forecasts are based on specific sea areas extending from Iceland to northern Spain, and they can be received in all the sea areas that they cover. Books of charts of these sea areas, with spaces to record the forecasts, are available from the Royal Yachting Association and the Met Office.

Each broadcast begins with a list of gale warnings. This is followed by a general synopsis giving the position and movement of pressure fronts and depressions in the next 24 hours. Forecasts for the next 24 hours are given for each sea area, commencing with Viking, Forties and Cromarty and continuing in a generally clockwise direction, finishing with South East Iceland.

Details given include wind direction and Beaufort speed with expected changes and weather and visibility. This is followed by reports from coastal stations giving wind force and direction, weather, visibility, barometric pressure and barometric change.

Constructing your own chart from the broadcast information takes some practice, but with some outside help and reference to professional maps you can soon grasp the basics, especially if you have the forecast chart from your previous day's newspaper to refer to.

The coastal station reports give you the basic data you need, such as pressure and wind speed, and you should enter these on your chart at the appropriate station.

Pressure is shown in millibars, and wind as an arrow blowing away from the observed direction. The wind's force is represented by oblique lines on the tail of the arrow, the force being numerically equal to twice the number of lines.

Check the weather forecast before you set out, to make sure you will not be sailing into potentially difficult or dangerous conditions.

SHIPPING FORECAST LANGUAGE

Each word or phrase of the Shipping Forecast has a precise meaning:

Gales indicates mean winds of Force 8, with gusts to 43 knots.
Severe gale indicates mean winds of Force 9, with gusts to 52 kts.
Storm indicates mean winds of Force 10, with gusts to 61 kts.
Imminent means 'arriving within 6 hours'.
Soon means 'arriving within 6 to 12 hours'.
Later means 'arriving more than 12 hours later'.

For example, a wind force of 4 is represented by two lines, and one of force 7 by three and a half lines.

The general synopsis part of the broadcast will have given you the centres of pressure areas and the positions of fronts. Pencil these in at the correct positions, writing 'H' for high and 'L' for low.

Isobars are the lines on a weather chart joining areas of equal pressure. You now have to draw in isobars at 2-millibar intervals relative to the pressure reading that you've already written against each coastal station on the chart. For example, if a station reported a pressure of 1021 mb, then the 1020 mb and 1022 mb lines go either side of that station.

Wind speeds are a guide to the spacing of the isobars. The *geostrophic scales* printed at the top of the chart show the spacing to use for given wind speeds (this spacing is labelled 'Beaufort force' on the scales).

The forecast information for sea areas concerns the 24-hour period following the time your chart relates to. You can now enter this forecast information to show the pattern of change over the next 24 hours.

Of course, if fiddling about with shipping forecasts late at night or early in the morning does not appeal to you, you can always invest in an electronic aid such as a weatherfax machine. This will happily print out a range of accurate weather charts for you to ponder over, but as with most electronic equipment it is essential that you get proper training in its use if you are to get the best out of it.

BOATS

There surely could not be a greater contrast between the tiny Optimist, a first-time training dinghy for children, and the USS *Eagle*, an 1800-ton square-rigged ship. What they share, of course, is that both are dependent on the wind, that infuriatingly fickle source of motive power that has been making life so difficult for sailors for thousands of years.

It is this variety in boats that makes them so fascinating and in the following pages you will find sporty ones, sturdy ones, ones that you need the agility of an acrobat to stay aboard and ones that are complete floating homes ready to carry you all over the oceans of the world.

Sailing was once the sport of the rich but nowadays virtually everyone who wants to can get afloat in something. There are even boats specially designed for the disabled and a ship they can go aboard in a wheelchair. Smaller and cheaper boats have put the sport of sailing within the reach of most people and, as a result, it is now one of the most popular of all leisure activities.

This popularity is reflected by the huge increase in the ownership of cruising yachts, whose owners demand ever-increasing standards of reliability and comfort, plus easy handling. Reliability means a sturdy hull and rig, well fitted-out with strong but simple gear that is easy to handle and will not let you down in an emergency. In addition, virtually every cruising yacht is now fitted with a diesel engine to reduce dependency on favourable wind conditions, make the boat easier to manoeuvre in marinas or other confined spaces, charge the batteries and in many cases to provide hot water as well.

To be able to live comfortably aboard a boat for more than a few days calls for roomy accommodation, with a degree of privacy if possible, and plenty of stowage space for clothing and personal gear. The galley must be capable of producing full cooked meals, not just snacks, and have room to store sufficient food to last for weeks at a time; most people consider a fridge or freezer virtually essential today. A chart table with room for a small library of books and guides is also essential, as is sufficient room for navigational instruments and radios.

Racing crews tolerate spartan conditions, sleeping (if at all) in their clothes and staggering ashore to the club shower-room to get cleaned up after the race.

The cruising sailor, however, expects to be able to live as normally as possible when on board and this calls for a decent washroom (with a hot shower if possible) and space to keep towels and washing gear. Above all, the modern cruising yacht must have a pleasant, welcoming ambience with room for those aboard to sit down and relax in comfort when not on deck. The idea, after all, is to make sailing a pleasure rather than an ordeal.

When you're choosing a boat, think carefully about what you want from it and take full account of what owning it will involve, in terms of finance, time, convenience and your own (and your potential crew's) ability to handle it.

For instance, small dinghies are cheaper to buy and easier to care for than larger boats and can be launched and recovered by one or two people, whereas most cruisers must be craned or launched by professionals at boatyards or marinas, and you then have to foot the bill for the berthing or mooring of the boat when you're not sailing it.

Once afloat, however, the dinghy is far more responsive and tippy to sail than a cruiser, and will capsize easily given the right conditions, whereas most cruisers, especially the newer ones, are very stable and relatively easy to handle, and sail well.

Basically, though, the decision to buy a particular type of boat – such as a dinghy which is kept ashore, or a trailer sailer which is kept at home and trailed to various sailing venues, or a cruising boat which is kept on a mooring or in a marina – is usually governed by the potential owner's financial status.

All boats, even secondhand ones, tend to be expensive and it is therefore essential that prospective owners who know nothing about sailing should seek the help of a qualified marine surveyor once they have chosen the boat most likely to suit their purposes. When buying a used boat, as when buying any secondhand vehicle, the buyer should beware.

The boats that appear on the following pages have been carefully chosen to show a little bit of every type of sailing and are among the best-known internationally. Yet this survey only scratches the surface of a vast fleet with literally thousands of different designs, and every year there are more, as designers and builders strive to squeeze just a little bit more into their latest models.

CHOOSING A BOAT

If you are already a sailor, you will have some idea of what type of boats you like to sail and the type of boat that would suit your particular circumstances. If you are new to sailing, but are determined to be a boat owner before you know how to sail – don't get a big one!

In most cases, the purchase will be influenced by the availability of finance, and as with the purchase of other expensive items there will be many agencies only too willing to lend you the money and charge you interest on it. Remortgaging your home is a worthwhile option unless interest rates look to be moving against you.

Before setting foot in a broker's office you should have worked out a maximum outlay figure, bearing in mind that the annual upkeep of a boat is about 10 percent of its purchase price and that mooring and marina fees can treble that if you live in a popular sailing area.

Make a realistic appraisal of your

The Cadet is one of the many classes of dinghy intended specifically for young people to sail.

family and their enthusiasm for sailing. Do you regularly go out together? Do you take holidays or go camping together? Do they have any interest in your project? If the answer is no on all counts, buy a singlehander. Alternatively, ask your friends if they are interested and whether they are keen enough to share the purchase price.

Before you set out to buy, decide whether you want a dinghy, a dayboat, a cruiser or a racer. Bear in mind not just your current interest in sailing but how your interest might develop in the future, and that while dinghies and small keelboats can be trailed behind the family car and launched and recovered by the crew, cruisers need specialist handling equipment and cradles and have to be 'shipped'.

The nature of your home port will decide whether your boat is kept afloat or ashore. If you want a cruiser, can you have a fin keeler or must it have bilge or lifting keels because the mudflats dry out? Do you have to row out to it or is there a launch service? Is the boat's berth accessible at all states of the tide?

If you want a cruiser, scan the 'for sale' ads in the many yachting magazines to get a feel of the price of used craft compared with that of new ones, remembering that new boats need to be equipped with all safety gear, clothing, warps, anchors, dinghies, instruments and so on and that you will need to add 20 to 25 percent to the advertised price to ensure that you have everything needed to go to sea.

If you don't know anything about boats you will not recognize an O'Day from a Westerly and therefore you would be wise to visit a broker's display lot and choose a few boats to look over. Don't be afraid to let the appearance of a boat influence your choice. Ugly boats *are* ugly: they don't look right and they don't sail right, so if the shape doesn't appeal to you leave it for someone else.

If you buy a new yacht you will be getting a known product at a reasonably competitive price. There are a lot of add-ons, but the dealer can be persuaded to make a considerable discount for the gear in order to secure the sale of the boat. You should haggle, and if the dealer won't bargain then try the guy down the road with similar products.

When you decide to order a new boat which has yet to be built, beware! You will need to consult your lawyer to ensure that your deposit and stage payments are safeguarded should the company fold. It is usually better to make the agreement with the dealer rather than the builder, because the dealer has to supply you with alternative merchandise if the builder goes under.

There is a commissioning period for any new boat, during which you should thoroughly test all systems and make a list of defects to be corrected. Should you decide to follow

The 505 is a large, fast two-man dinghy, exciting to sail but not a boat for the inexperienced sailor.

the used-boat route, on the basis that you will get more for your money, you would be wise to bear in mind that the 'more' could include trouble.

Alone, or with a friend, visit the brokers' lots and the locally-advertised boats to get a feel of what is available in the category of boat you want. Choose two or three as a final shortlist and go over them with a fine-toothed comb making a list of good and bad points.

Choose your boat from the shortlist and determine, by haggling, what is the lowest price the vendor will accept. Make an offer *subject to survey* but don't part with any money yet. Engage the services of a certified Marine Surveyor, who will carry out a detailed inspection and submit a written inspection report pointing out work and repairs needed, the overall condition of the yacht and its approximate value as it stands. If you still want the boat, pay the offer price subject to all defects being put right by a boatyard to the satisfaction of the surveyor. Otherwise, offer a reduced price to take account of survey defects.

Once the offer is accepted a deal is struck and you will have problems backing out of it, so be sure that you really want to buy before you commit yourself to the purchase. In addition, get your lawyer to ascertain that the vendor does actually own the vessel which, in turn, is free from all debts and writs.

Above left *Catamarans are fast and relatively stable.*
Above right *A small cruiser is simple to rig and handle, and a good choice for the beginner.*
Right *When you buy a cruiser, have it surveyed to make sure it's seaworthy.*

Experienced sailors, who may already own or have owned a boat, can fall into the trap of thinking that they know enough about general defects and the condition of used boats to dispense with the services of a surveyor. However, wood, steel, aluminium and GRP hulls all need inspection by a specialist who is skilled in interpreting certain features as pointers to serious structural defects.

Newcomers would be wise to start with a small boat which is simple to rig, easy to manoeuvre and which will withstand the inevitable knocks experienced in the first season of ownership. Get an expert opinion of the type of rig and how it should be reefed, and steer clear of one-off and experimental rigs. Go for a used production boat that has retained its original specification, and not been heavily modified.

The size of boat you buy will depend on how many people you expect to go sailing in it at any one time, but as a rough guide, if it's a dinghy you want go for a 14- to 16-footer. If it's a cruiser, go for one of 25 to 30 feet, and select the boat which has got the best equipment if all else is reasonably equal.

TYPES OF RIG

When we think of rigs, we tend to think of the development of triangular sails from the square sails that predominated until the early 20th century. This ignores the quite separate development of a wide variety of rigs, such as the junk, lateen and crab's claw, which have been in use for thousands of years.

The junk rig, as used in eastern Asia, is a refined, multipurpose trading rig which, while not being close-winded, is very efficient off the wind. There have been attempts to popularize the rig in the West, and 'Blondie' Hasler, one of the originators of the singlehanded transatlantic races, used such a rig on the now-legendary *Jester*, a wooden folkboat which was a regular entrant in these races.

One of the attractions of the rig is the ease with which it can be set and reefed, operating on the same principle as horizontal-slatted window shades. The original junk sail was made up of closely-spaced split bamboo or vegetable fibres, and therefore lent itself to quick reefing, and the modern sail has full-length battens, usually made of bamboo, which self-stow when lowered.

The control of the twist and set of the sail is achieved by control lines led from the helmsman to a complex single, solid wood block which has lines leading to the end of each batten. Other control lines are used for hoisting and for determining the fore-and-aft position of the sail on the unstayed mast. Large ocean-going junks can have up to four masts, but two or three is the norm.

Most junk masts are raked forward, and a similar forward rake is used by the traders and fishermen of the Arabian seas to support the weight of the lateen rigs of their fast and powerful dhows. The dhow's mast is short but the yard supporting the sail is both long and heavy. The triangular sail is efficient because it has such a long leading edge and can be sheeted close to the wind.

The feluccas of the Nile have a similar rig, carried higher to catch the wind above the river banks. Again it is a trading rig which developed over thousands of years, and was used in every type of boat on the Nile until engine-powered boats arrived. The popular Sunfish dinghy, like the dhow and the felucca, has a lateen rig.

Out on its own is the crab's claw rig, which is similar to a lateen sail in basic shape except that it has a spar on each of the two longer edges. In use, the sail is set point-down with both spars angled upward. Recent research with this rig shows that it may have the potential to produce

Above *A gaff rig, efficient but difficult to hoist and control.*
Left *The sprit-rigged Optimist.*

more power than any other sail type on all but a close-hauled course.

The square sail is a great downwind rig because it can be wider than it is high, thus keeping its centre of effort (the capsizing factor) low, but it is not possible to use it closer than about 60 degress to the wind.

In its original form, the square sail had a spar at its upper edge that was controlled by lines to set it, and the sail, to the desired angle to the wind.

Square sails set in this fashion developed in complexity and size to power vessels such as the 19th-century tea clipper *Cutty Sark* (named after the witch in Robert Burns' poem *Tam O'Shanter*, who wore only a short skirt or 'cutty sark').

The use of square sails on small

TYPES OF RIG

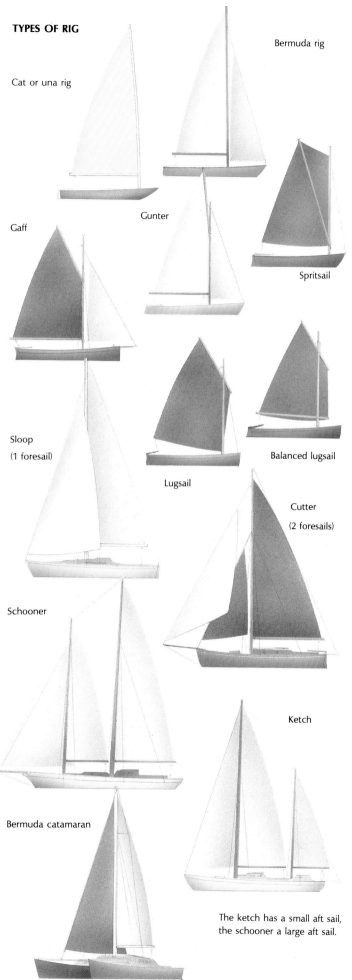

inshore boats led to the development of the sprit and lugsail versions. The lugsail has its tack set at the mast, which results in the yard being cocked up at an angle or, more commonly, led forward to the windward gunwale where it is attached to a tack hook. When changing tacks, the yard was lowered on its mast traveller so that it could be dipped around the mast to be hoisted and set on the leeward side. Meantime, the tack was moved to the windward tack hook.

The sprit rig is still used on the Optimist dinghy and the Thames Sailing Barges. Its configuration lent itself ideally to converting the inefficient square sail into a good upwind rig. It is an extremely rewarding sail to tune to get the best out of it.

The popularity of the gaff rig, with or without a boom, arose because it was a rig which created the power needed by fishermen, pilots and coasting trading vessels. It is a fairly complicated rig and requires considerable effort to hoist and control. Once up and drawing, though, especially from a close reach to a run, it is very efficient at harnessing the wind's power.

Splitting the rig up into smaller sails gave rise to the classic two-masted gaff ketch and schooner rigs. The schooner differs from the ketch in that the main mast is taller than the foremast. This rig was developed to perfection on the fishing schooners of the Grand Banks.

Above *The very popular Bermuda rig requires additional sails for downwind work.*

For the inshore fisherman, the small mizzen and larger main of the ketch gave the correct degree of balance when trawling, especially with the addition of a large and powerful overlapping tow foresail.

The gunter rig developed the four-cornered sail into something resembling the now familiar Bermuda rig. The gaff was designed to be hoisted almost parallel to the mast to give the sail height. In dinghies, it ensured that the spars were short enough to stow in the boat.

The Bermuda rig, with its triangular sails, is reputed to have come from the sails used on the islands' dinghies which, in turn, were developed from ships' boats. The transition from the two spars of the gunter rig to the single Bermuda spar would have been a natural development, and as triangular sails were used for the headsails of most square-riggers, their efficiency was well known. The familiar triangular-sailed rigs of today have been developed for upwind work and require additional special sails for downwind work.

Single-sailed Bermuda-rigged boats, or those designed without headsails, are described as being cat-rigged or una-rigged; multiple-masted versions are cat-rigged ketches or cat-rigged schooners.

JUNIOR SINGLEHANDED TRAINERS

There is no doubt whatever that the best time to learn sailing is when young. Children have an amazing ability to learn quickly by imitation, especially if it involves something they enjoy. In the past, most children learned sailing either from their parents or friends but today it is much more common to go on a training course, either at a commercially run sailing school or on a club's junior programme.

The training that sailing instructors receive enables them to take a newcomer methodically through the basic skills in a short time, without losing sight of the fact that the whole activity is supposed to be fun.

The question of when a child is ready to begin learning to sail is really impossible to answer as it depends on the individual's ability to concentrate on a new task for a reasonable length of time.

The child must also have developed sufficient strength and agility to handle a small boat successfully. In Britain, the fact that a child under the age of 8 years old may only be taught by a registered child-minder tends to make this the minimum age for most sailing schools, but this is a completely arbitrary level.

Although one might think that the best way to learn is from an instructor sitting opposite you in the same boat, this turns out to be incorrect for young children. They learn best by example, and often simply switch off to what adults are telling them. From experience it has been found that children learn best while sailing on their own but as part of a supervised group.

Back in 1947 in Tampa, Florida, boatbuilder Clark Mills was asked to build the simplest possible dinghy for an existing youth club called 'The Optimists' so they could go sailing on the wonderful Tampa Bay. He made a tiny, almost square, soapbox of a boat only 7 feet (2.3 m) in length and gave it a short pole mast and a sprit that held out the top corner of a rectangular sail. A short plywood 'dagger' extending through a waterproof box stopped the boat drifting sideways while a basic rudder was fixed to the transom.

With a little refinement, Mills' 'basic box' turned into the International Optimist dinghy, which is now used throughout the world as a first trainer and racing boat for children. The surprising fact about the Optimist is that it sails really well, and to see a championship fleet of these tiny boats racing in tough conditions on the sea is a revelation.

Unfortunately, the pressure of racing has resulted in the Optimist becoming a sophisticated little machine with a composite construction hull, aluminium spars, scientifically-shaped foils and a top-quality sail. The result is that a new boat to racing specification can cost around £3,000.

The good thing is that 16 years old is the maximum age permitted in the class, with the result that there is always a lively secondhand market for Optimists, with racing boats gradually filtering down to become beginners' boats after a few years in use.

Although the Optimist is by far the most popular one-person junior boat, with a huge international following, there are plenty of other designs that serve a similar purpose. Good examples are the New Zealand P-Class, which introduced many of the top Kiwi yachtsmen to the sport, and the Sabot, which is widely used on the West Coast of the USA. This little pram dinghy does not even have a

THE TOPPER (below)
Its reputation for being nearly indestructible makes the Topper an obvious choice as an instructional boat. Larger and speedier than the Optimist, it can be used as a first boat by teenagers or adults and is also a popular fun-boat.

THE OPTIMIST (right)
The Optimist is used almost universally as a first boat for children. It started life as the simplest possible 'soapbox' boat and has developed over the years into quite a sophisticated little racer. Fortunately, there are always plenty of older models available at reasonable prices for beginners to cut their teeth on.

daggerboard but instead has a hinged leeboard fitted to either side of the boat.

Young people who take up sailing as teenagers are more likely to take their first tacks in a Topper, which is larger and faster than the Optimist. It has a very special appeal to sailing schools, being as near as possible indestructible. This is achieved by making the hull from solid polypropylene rather than glassfibre, and Toppers can shrug off the bumps and bangs that are an inevitable part of learning. As well as being a trainer, the Topper is keenly raced and is very good fun to sail in a fresh breeze.

Although, strictly-speaking, it was not designed as a trainer, the Sunfish often gives people their first experience of sailing due to the fact that it is so often to be found on holiday beaches in the warm parts of the world. An ultra-simple 'sailing surfboard', the Sunfish is possibly the wettest boat ever made and therefore one to be avoided unless the water is warm enough to make getting thoroughly soaked a pleasure.

The same applies to the Hobie 14 catamaran, which was cleverly designed without centreboards so that it can sail straight up the beach without damage. Also universally found on holiday beaches, the smallest of the Hobie range provides greatt fun for a teenager who has already done some basic training and wants to try something a little more exciting. In a strong breeze, the Hobie 14 certainly provides 'thrills and spills' as it has the reputation of being able to capsize in any of four directions; forwards, backwards, sideways or diagonally.

Being able to right a capsized boat is a vital part of safety training for although singlehanded beginners must always be accompanied by a safety boat, the idea is to teach them the techniques of 'self-rescue' as soon as possible. In this connection, it is worth noting that dinghies that are stable the right way up, such as the Optimist, tend to be just as stable upside down, unlike something like a Topper, which rolls over easily and can be righted just as easily.

Properly positioned buoyancy can help a great deal, but the vital points to remember with beginners are first that they must wear personal buoyancy at all times when afloat, and second that if they are dressed in good-quality clothing, preferably a wetsuit or drysuit, capsizing will hold no great terror or danger in any case.

TWO-PERSON TRAINERS

Valuable though boats like the Optimist and Topper are as basic trainers, their very simplicity means that they leave the student in ignorance of anything to do with multisail and multicrew boats. The next step up is therefore into a two-person dinghy.

Back in the 1950s, the editor of *Yachting World* magazine, 'Teddy' Haylock, saw the need for a new, cheap-to-build children's trainer and commissioned boatbuilder Jack Holt to design one. Haylock saw the need for it to be a complete miniature yacht with mainsail, jib and spinnaker, and Holt brought this concept to life as the International Cadet. Over the years, this boat has produced many thousands of racing yachtsmen including a good number of Olympic medallists.

Simply built in plywood, the Cadet was very similar in concept to the Optimist but designed for two youngsters instead of one. It takes training much further than the Optimist and similar boats, as the all-important spinnaker has to be mastered, giving the entrée to larger and more exciting racing boats. The whole boat is so small that it is physically impossible for an adult to sail one and this also makes it imperative for a teenaged skipper to take on and train a very young and lightweight crew.

A little later in Jack Holt's career, he was asked to collaborate with home improvement expert Barry Bucknell, who had devised a new way of assembling a small boat using glassfibre tape to join sheets of plywood. From this slightly unpromising start emerged one of the most successful small boats of all time, the Mirror dinghy. Although not specifically designed as a trainer, the Mirror has proved to be ideal in that role, especially as it is one of the smallest boats in which an adult can comfortably sit while a very small person has a first try at steering.

Like the Cadet, the Mirror sports a mainsail, jib and spinnaker, but the sails are considerably larger and the boat itself is able to carry more weight. Designed from the outset for 'DIY' construction, the Mirror has formed the basis of many a family carpentry project, though opinions might vary as to whether this created more family togetherness or friction.

Light enough to car-top, the Mirror is a true multipurpose dinghy, being as capable of carrying a family and dog on a picnic expedition as it is of turning out for club races at weekends.

The teenage years bring, in equal measure, increasing physical strength and an overpowering desire for independence, which can be usefully channelled into a two-person youth dinghy. The best known of these, which has been used for international youth competition for a number of years, is the 420. In spite of a rather uninspiring design, it is a pure racing boat and introduces the young sailor to some important new skills.

In addition to a spinnaker of reasonable size, the 420 is equipped with a trapeze for the crew, and this brings with it the need for much more agility and better coordination between the two people. Relatively sophisticated rig controls, which are not really possible on a boat such as the Mirror, also make their appearance. A proper understanding of these is vital for anyone intending to go on to 'serious' racing.

It is unfortunate that the 'youth' area of yachting has become a bit complicated and confused recently. In Britain, the Royal Yachting Association saw the need for a new high-performance youth dinghy—probably thinking of something like a modernized Cadet. This resulted in the 405, which is markedly bigger and faster than the Cadet but only a little smaller than the 420, which it clearly overlaps in the marketplace. However, the 405 does at least look forward to the

MIRROR

Although it is somewhat antiquated in design, the Mirror dinghy remains one of the best introductions to sailing as it is a true multipurpose boat that can be cruised or raced by people of almost any size and weight. A Mirror can also be the basis for a fun DIY project.

modern era of high-performance planing dinghies rather than back to the 1970s.

Meanwhile, many international youth events are now held in the Laser 2, which represents another step up in size and performance. The result is that schools, colleges and parents are presented with a confusing choice of youth boats, leading to a reluctance to spend in the region of £4,000 per boat.

The 'youth' years end at 18, when keen young dinghy sailors either move on to one of the high-performance dinghies or to crew on a larger boat of some kind. Before doing so, they may well become involved in university

sailing, which is the stronghold of team racing. After a number of years in which it appeared to be in danger of dying out, team racing is making a strong recovery with college teams forming the backbone of what is now a worldwide sport.

For team racing, the type of boat used is not the most important thing and simple but sturdy two-person dinghies such as the Firefly, Lark or Enterprise tend to be the most popular. The normal type of team race is for teams of three boats, with the major regattas being for a dozen or more teams that are gradually eliminated in a league-type competition until the two top teams face each other for a

three-race final. The races are short but extremely intense, with the boats manoeuvring aggressively to obstruct their opponents in ways that are not usually allowed in normal racing.

Good boat handling, good knowledge of the rules, and above all quick thinking are the qualities called for in team racing. Young sailors who have honed these qualities while at university are always in demand in the wider world of yacht racing.

When adults learn to sail, it is more usual to use the one-on-one teaching method and a stable, durable dinghy such as the Wayfarer. Although these are

405

The 405 youth racing trainer allows teenagers to enjoy a modern light-weight planing hull, spinnaker and trapeze wrapped up in a package that is deliberately designed to be too small for most adults. Though planned for use with an asymmetric spinnaker and bowsprit, these are not normally fitted on the 405.

expensive, they last for many years and form the backbone of many sailing school fleets. Thanks to its size and stability, a Wayfarer dinghy can carry two or even three students plus an instructor, and is seaworthy enough for sailing in coastal locations.

SINGLEHANDERS

It suits many people to sail alone either through difficulty in finding a crew in their locality or because they prefer it. Sailing on one's own is a special pleasure and also a special challenge which many people find uniquely satisfying.

As we have already noted, those who learn as children very often do so in an Optimist or Topper, and the obvious next step is towards a Laser. Designed by the Canadian Bruce Kirby, the Laser has been one of the most successful dinghies of all time and the first to make full use of the possibilities of volume production.

Kirby's vision was of a high-performance dinghy with the simplest possible layout in order to keep it cheap and easy to manage. The mast is made from two lengths of aluminium tube, one of which fits into the other, with no rigging whatever. The sail has a sleeve sewn into its forward edge, which slips over the mast. This in turn is fitted into a hole in the deck. Daggerboard and rudder are solid plastic mouldings and the sheet, vang and Cunningham are virtually the only adjustments.

Just as important as the design itself was the concept of a 'Manufacturer's one-design'; in effect a method of ensuring that all the boats sold are identical without recourse to the elaborate measurement procedures that bedevil other classes. To achieve complete uniformity at major regattas, competitors rent a brand-new boat through their entry fee and have the opportunity to buy it at a special price after the event. These imaginative concepts ensure that racing a Laser really is a fair competition in which only personal ability counts. The concept received its ultimate endorsement when the Laser was adopted for Olympic competition in 1996, all equipment being supplied by the organizers.

However 'fair' you make a sailing race, it is not possible to get away from the fact that a particular type of boat is likely to favour people of a particular physique. Top competitors in the Laser, for instance, tend to be tall, athletic and weigh at least 10 stone (65 kg). A smaller dinghy, such as a Moth or its derivative, the Europe, is more suitable for shorter, lighter individuals while the really big men tend to gravitate towards the Finn, a hefty dinghy in which strength and stamina are all-important.

Several manufacturers have entered the market in recent years with singlehanders slightly smaller and cheaper than the Laser in an effort to capture the 'club' market. The Splash, Byte, Blaze and Pico are examples, but the Laser itself offers a low-cost entry route—you can buy a used boat with one of the reduced-sized rigs such as the Laser Radial. The appeal of this arrangement is that you can easily trade up to a full-sized rig without changing boat.

For some people, simplicity holds no appeal and for them a range of more advanced and complex singlehanders is available. The Contender, planned as a replacement for the Olympic Finn dinghy, proved too advanced a concept for the sports bureaucrats of the day to get their minds around. But with a big single sail and a trapeze it presents a real challenge in a strong breeze, especially downwind.

Sailing singlehanded from the trapeze calls for skill, agility and coordination rather than strength, making the Contender the ideal boat for the dedicated sailor of medium build. The trapeze allows the helmsman to balance the power of the rig exactly while fully extended over the side and steering the boat with the extra-long tiller extension. Fast and relatively easy to sail to windward, these boats are exceptionally demanding on a windy reach when body weight, helm and sheet all have to be kept in synchronization if a disastrous 'death roll' is to be avoided.

The Contender is fairly beamy whereas the modern design tendency is towards dinghies with a narrow hull and outriggers. The RS600 singlehander shows how far this idea can be taken, with the helmsman trapezing from a substantial outrigger.

The epoxy foam sandwich hull and carbonfibre mast are both feather-light and the Mylar sail is enormous, giving the boat an extraordinarily favourable power-to-weight ratio. This exciting type of singlehander is definitely not for the fainthearted.

Strangely enough, one of the most extreme small-boat designs of all is also one of the oldest: the 10 Square Metre Canoe that was developed by Uffa Fox and others in the 1930s. The name refers to the maximum permitted sail area, while the design of the hull and equipment is optional. As these boats developed from canoes rather than small sailing boats, they were always narrow and light. In order to obtain stability, a plank was fixed across the hull to give the helmsman somewhere to sit. The plank was then made movable so you could extend it to either side so that the helmsman was no longer in contact with the hull at all.

The Canoe is a connoisseur's singlehander with a multiplicity of rig and tuning controls, and sailing one calls for a great deal of skill and finesse. In the right hands, the Canoe can be the fastest single-hulled boat on the water and has often been referred to as a 'one-hulled catamaran'.

For many normal weekend sailors, dinghies such as the 10 Square Metre Canoe or the RS600 are in the realms of fantasy, especially as they are unsuitable for most inland waters. But there are many hundreds who own and race less-demanding singlehanders such as the Comet or Solo, which perform well with helmsmen of varied weights and heights and are equally at home on the sea or a small lake. The freedom of being able to go sailing without involving anyone else is a pleasure shared only with sailboards. It is nevertheless one that ensures that singlehanded dinghies will always form an important part of the overall fleet.

THE INTERNATIONAL MOTH (above)
A development class with very open rules, the International Moth tends to produce experimental shapes such as this one with narrow hull and wide sitting-out wings, an idea that many other classes have been quick to borrow. The Moth is extremely quick for its size.

THE SPLASH (right)
Specifically designed as a youth sin-glehander, the Splash is a little smaller and less powerful than a Laser with full-sized rig, and also has a more conventional mast with a luff groove instead of a sleeve. A good compro-mise design suitable for both inland and coastal racing.

THE RS 600 (left)
Typical of the new style of dinghy designs, the RS 600 features a narrow, self-draining skiff hull, trapeze and standing-out frame. Exceedingly fast and tippy, this is not the boat for the faint-hearted.

FAMILY TWO-HANDERS AND DAYBOATS

Many of the people who are keenest on sailing have no wish to race at all—or only occasionally. For them, the pleasures of sailing are the noncompetitive ones, including the satisfaction of being close to nature and of harnessing one of its basic forces, the wind. Rigging, launching and sailing a small boat in a completely seamanlike way is a challenge in itself, while the tug of the sheet and the sound of the water are sensations dear to the hearts of all who love sailing.

Back in the 1950s, that prolific designer of small boats, Jack Holt, saw the need for an all-round 'General Purpose' dinghy and met it with the sturdy GP14, which was planned from the outset for amateur construction. In those austere years after the Second World War, this was the only way in which most people could ever hope to get afloat. Soon, school workshops, domestic front rooms and garages up and down the country were filled with the rasp of saws and the swish of planes.

The GP14 sailed well enough to race and soon became a popular class. but it was also an ideal 'potterer' and could be fitted with the smallest type of Seagull, which was the main type of low-powered outboard motor in those days.

In due course, Jack Holt out-designed himself with the Enterprise, which was lighter, cheaper and sailed faster than the GP14. With its relatively large sail area, the blue-sailed Enterprise came to be seen as the ideal boat for inland waters, while the GP14 continued to reign supreme on coastal waters.

The ultimate expression of this type of boat was designed not by Holt but Ian Proctor, whose 16-foot Wayfarer dinghy has been unsurpassed as a general purpose dinghy during the last 30 years. Sturdy and stable but with a good performance, the Wayfarer had some important new safety features including a generous amount of built-in buoyancy in the form of large watertight lockers at either end of the hull. In addition to keeping the boat afloat in case of capsize, these can be used to store dry clothing, a picnic, camping gear or anything else required.

The raised floorboards of the Wayfarer are just large enough to permit two people to stretch out, and with the addition of a tent cover, this makes it possible to use the boat as a camping cruiser. Over the years, some extraordinarily ambitious cruises have been made in Wayfarers including lengthy sea passages. It has also become the most commonly used dinghy for one-to-one sailing instruction and is used by virtually all the UK-based sailing schools.

Like the GP14 and the Enterprise, the Wayfarer was designed to be built in plywood as can easily be seen from the 'chines'

THE WAYFARER
The 16-foot Wayfarer is something of a split-personality dinghy because on the one hand it is keenly raced, while on the other it is one of the most commonly-found boats at sailing schools courtesy of its stability and exceptionally robust construction. It sails well and is an exciting boat to race, and there is room in the cockpit for four, or even five, crew, not to mention ample storage space.

THE GP 14

Designed originally for amateur construction, the GP 14 dates from the early 1950s and is a simple, sturdy two-man dinghy that lasts for many years. The GP 14 is still raced keenly at a number of sailing clubs, and it has a large and faithful following and provides an excellent introduction to racing.

or angles between the flat panels that make up the hull. All three have long since converted to glass-fibre construction, though it is still possible for enthusiasts to build wooden ones if they prefer.

The three boats mentioned so far are all multipurpose, but others, such as the Drascombe Lugger, have a purely cruising character. Looking for all the world like some jaunty small fishing boat of yester-year, the Drascombe Lugger is immensely strongly built and is one of the most seaworthy boats of its

size in existence. As well as adding to the boat's characterful appear-ance, the yawl rig means that all the sails are quite small and easy to handle. The fact that the sails are 'loose-footed' rather than being set on the usual boom, makes this a particularly suitable boat for very young children, who can sit in the middle without fear of being bashed on the head.

The limitation to a boat such as the Drascombe is that it is too heavy to pull out of the water after every trip. It therefore needs a mooring and in turn a smaller dinghy to get to the mooring. On the other hand, being fitted with a centreboard it is suitable for the type of mooring that dries out at low tide, unlike fixed-keel boats, which fall over on their sides when the tide goes out.

Topper have taken a fresh look at this concept with the Cruz. This is also a yawl, but being much

lighter than the Drascombe Lugger is speedier and easier to launch, though probably not as durable. There are, in fact, dozens of non-racing boats of around 15–18 feet in length, many of them specific to particular parts of the world.

With this type of boat, seaman-ship starts to enter the equation as the kind of mini-cruise that the boats are suitable for is very likely to be unaccompanied and out of sight of club and rescue boat. In fact, self-sufficiency is an important part of the appeal.

Before setting off, tide and weather must be checked and a kit-bag packed with extra clothes and supplies. Getting becalmed for a few hours, or going aground, can be a minor adventure if you have the right things with you, but a bit of a disaster if the weather turns bad and you haven't enough warm clothes and nothing to eat or drink. Always remember to tell

someone where you are going and make sure they understand that, within reason, a delayed return is normally nothing to worry about.

With a boat such as the Cruz or the Drascome Lugger, it is sensible to invest in a small outboard motor—one of 5 bhp is plenty for this size of boat. It enormously increases the pleasure of many expeditions if you know that, for instance, you will be able to return home without any difficulty after the wind has died—as it so often does on a summer evening. It also allows you to explore small rivers and creeks where there is insuffi-cient room to sail.

An overboom cover is a cheap extra that opens up the possibility of the occasional night afloat. Conditions will be pretty basic, of course—similar to life in a small tent—but the rewards can be immense. Your very first steps towards cruising!

CONVENTIONAL RACING DINGHIES

The 1960s and 1970s brought a rush of new racing dinghy designs, many of which are still popular today, although these conventional racing dinghies are facing increasing competition from the 'new-wave' designs featured overleaf. A conventional dinghy of 14 to 16 feet is big enough for two grown men to race but not too large for two teenagers or a couple. It is seaworthy enough for open sea racing but still light enough for easy trailing or cartopping and fits into a standard-sized garage.

revolution, and boats such as the 5-0-5 were able to remain at the leading edge of racing for some 30 years as a result. At the same time, new dinghies such as the Lark, 470, and much later the Laser 2, were designed for glass-fibre from the outset. Most of the boats in this category can carry a spin-

naker for extra downwind speed while some, such as the 5-0-5, Fireball and 470, have a trapeze for the crew.

Although it might seem rather alarming to be hanging outside the boat on the end of a wire, in fact trapezing is less of a strain on the body than sitting out vigorously. It

A curious fact about sailing is that people become fanatically loyal to one particular design and continue to race it long after it has become outdated. A good example is the 12 Square Metre Sharpie, a 1922 Dutch design that was used in the 1956 Olympics. Built from solid mahogany planks before marine plywood became available, and with a gaff rig, these heavy boats are lovingly preserved by a dedicated band of enthusiastic owners.

This happens partly because of people's genuine affection for some of the older designs but also for social reasons. Each class gradually becomes a club in which people meet, make friends and organize a programme of sailing and socializing. Since racing makes very little sense unless there are a reasonable number of similar boats involved, particular designs are always found in pockets within their own area.

Economics as much as anything dictates the type of small boat that people sail, and the huge expansion in sailing from the 1960s onwards was due to the fact that dinghies could be built quickly and cheaply in plywood. The Hornet, the Graduate, the Enterprise, the Scorpion, the Heron, the Wayfarer and the Fireball, among many others, were designed from the outset to use this material and have a 'hard-chine' hull shape as a result.

A smoothly rounded hull can be made from wood by building up two or more layers of thin strips of wood glued together over a mould. This 'cold-moulded' construction tends to be expensive due to the amount of work involved but it is also strong and light. As a result, it was used in the past for some of the more advanced racing dinghies such as the Flying Dutchman and the 5-0-5.

A further refinement is to use thermosetting glue which is set off under heat and pressure in a kind of giant pressure cooker called an autoclave. The Fairey Aviation company formed a marine division to exploit this method and produced a series of popular and very durable small boats including the Firefly, Swordfish and Albacore.

These smooth-hulled dinghies were well placed for the glass-fibre

THE FIREBALL
One of the earliest high-performance dinghies, the Fireball has a scow hull-form, a trapeze for the crew and a good-sized spinnaker. It is another example of a dinghy originally designed for amateur construction in plywood and which gradually changed over to plastics construction, although beautifully made wooden examples still exist.

also has the big advantage of increasing the effectiveness of a lightweight crew, and this is why trapeze dinghies are often the best choice for all-female crews or mixed crews.

It is important to choose a dinghy that suits your sailing area. The powerful and fast dinghies, such as the Fireball and 5-0-5, need plenty of space and clear wind. The 5-0-5 in particular is a dinghy that calls for rather big, strong crews because of its large sail area. A couple of lightweights would find themselves overwhelmed in any kind of breeze in one. If you sail mostly on a river or small lake, then a dinghy without a trapeze and which manoeuvres quickly, such as a Lark or Merlin-Rocket might be a better choice.

For the greatest efficiency, expert dinghy sailors like to have a fixed-position rudder and a daggerboard because these present the correct foil section to the water flow all the time. But if you sail where shallows are a problem or launching can be tricky, then it is wiser to select a boat with a tipping centreboard and lifting rudder. These features are also essential where weed in the water is a problem, as there is nothing more frustrating than constantly having to lean over the stern to remove tangled strands of weed from a fixed rudder blade.

Racing dinghies can be organized in various ways: the 'strict' one-designs such as all the members of the Laser family have a standard hull and equipment that cannot be altered in any way, except to replace old parts with exactly similar new ones. This suits people who just want to buy a boat and race it without anything else to worry about.

Semi one-designs, such as the 5-0-5 and Fireball, have a fixed hull shape and a long list of measurements that must be adhered to, but there is considerable freedom in the layout and equipment that can be used. This suits those people who take a keen interest in the technical side of sailing and enjoy tailoring boats to the layouts that they like to work with.

Development classes, such as the National 12-foot Dinghy and National Merlin-Rocket have lists of minimum and maximum weights, sail areas and dimensions, but no laid-down designs. This suits people with a very strong interest in design who may very well want to build and equip boats for themselves. The intention behind these classes is to keep on trying new ideas. To race in such a class is always interesting but it is also frequently expensive, as today's leading-edge design may be next year's museum piece.

The development classes are important to the whole sailing world because the novel ideas they try out gradually become refined and filter down to production boats. An example might be the International Moth, which tends to have an extremely narrow hull with winglike extensions for the helmsman to sit on. This basic idea has since been copied by many other classes in a less extreme form.

THE ALBACORE (above)
One of a series of Uffa Fox designs originally built by Faireys in hot-moulded wood, the Albacore was clearly based on Fox's series of pre-war International 14 dinghies. Sturdy and relatively heavy, it has no aids to stability other than the helmsman and crew sitting out to windward as far as they can.

THE ENTERPRISE (right)
Designed for home construction in marine plywood, the Enterprise has proved to be one of the most successful and popular all-round dinghies, its generous sail area making it a good performer on inland waters. Like many dinghies of the post-war era, it changed over to glass-fibre construction in due course. Notice the large wooden carrying handles—a trade-mark feature of the designer, Jack Holt.

NEW-WAVE RACING DINGHIES

The big thing to hit sailing in the 1970s and 1980s was windsurfing. There was already a tendency on the part of the youngsters of that era to turn their backs on dinghy sailing because it was something their parents did, and therefore had to be boring. Then along came the new sport of windsurfing, which offered a new excitement and freedom, and dinghy sailing nose-dived in popularity. In due course, the dinghy world responded by launching a new fleet of boats that were even more exciting and dramatic than windsurfers, but the irony was that they took their cue from one of the oldest of dinghy classes, the International 14, which has been around since the 1920s.

The curious thing about the International 14 is that although it has advanced design tremendously at various times, it has done this in a series of stop-go lurches. Shortly after the class was formed, Uffa Fox designed Avenger, the world's first effective planing dinghy, which in the 1928 season won 52 first places in 57 races and totally changed small-boat design for ever. But ten years later, when Peter Scott and John Winter tried out Beecher Moore's idea of the crew hanging over the side on a wire from the mast, this new 'trapeze' was promptly banned.

The International 14-foot Class later banned self-draining hulls and other modern developments and became a thoroughly fossilized organization until, with extinction practically staring it in the face in the early 1980s, the class suddenly reinvented itself.

It freed up the rules to permit much lighter boats, twin trapezes, a bowsprit, asymmetric spinnakers and virtually anything else you could think of in a maximum hull length of 14 feet. The result was a really wild, supercharged skiff—something like a smaller version of the Sydney Harbour 18-foot Skiffs that are allegedly the fastest dinghies in the world.

With the International 14 as an example, the production builders soon followed suit with new high-performance dinghies such as the

THE INTERNATIONAL 14 (above) is a tinkerers paradise. Being a 'restricted development class', the International 14 is able to take advantage of new ideas in the sport. In recent years, it has reduced all-up weight and introduced twin trapezes and a large gennaker which is set on an extending bowsprit—developments subsequently adopted by a number of other classes. The International 14 is a very fast and demanding boat to sail, and it is certainly not suitable for complete beginners.

THE LASER 4000 (below) The Laser 4000 shows how various high-performance features can be incorporated into a production dinghy. The lightweight, self-draining hull is fitted with adjustable racks to compensate for differing crew weights, and there is an asymmetric spinnaker set on a reefing bowsprit. The adjustable standing-out racks enable crews of differing physiques to make the best use of their weight.

Iso. This has, among other features, a self-draining hull, fully-battened mainsail, asymmetric spinnaker and trapeze. And unlike the International 14, which is a development class and hence a tinkerer's paradise, the new boats were sold as complete ready-to-sail packages—just add water and away you go. Derisively referred to by more traditional sailors as 'pop-outs', the new boats undoubtedly succeeded in bringing a new sense of excitement to dinghy sailing.

At about the same time, a group of sailors on the South Coast of England was working on a much more advanced concept that was unashamedly aimed at the Olympics. In addition to all the high-performance features already mentioned, the Laser 5000 has an ingenious weight compensation system consisting of adjustable standing-out racks.

Prior to a regatta, the crew are weighed and the racks set to the appropriate position, and ballast weights added so that light crews are able to get their centres of gravity further outboard than heavier ones. This very fast and fairly big

dinghy was soon matched by their rivals Topper with the Boss, which is if anything even more sophisticated with its carbonfibre spars and carbon/foam hull.

It is very interesting to see the way in which Topper, which is a marketing organization rather than a boatbuilder, has set about making a boat such as the Boss attractive to the buyer. Heavy advertising followed by free demonstrations is the obvious first step, and if the customer does decide to buy, he or she is offered a boat-handling and race-training course.

For such an advanced dinghy this is surely sensible, if only for safety reasons, and can be seen as equivalent to the courses offered to buyers of high-performance cars. Next, there is a 3-year warranty and a company-supported class organization that sets up and runs the regatta programme. This kind of 'after-sales support' is something relatively new to sailing, although a familiar part of life in many other fields. It is a far cry from the days when boat ownership began with buying a set of plans, followed by a visit to the timber merchant.

Although the Laser 5000 and the Boss blazed the trail, in the event neither of them received the nod to become a new Olympic class, as this honour went to the rather smaller and simpler 49-er (see pages 76–77). For the time being, however, these two boats probably represent the pinnacle of dinghy-sailing—in Europe, at least. It is appropriate, therefore, that they are boats that appeal to physically fit people with a fondness for high-adrenaline sports, and with healthy bank balances.

Not all the new-wave dinghies are quite so 'hairy' as the Laser 5000 or Boss, which need a lot of space to rush around in. Since a high proportion of dinghy sailors are based for at least part of the time on inland waters, it would be silly to ignore their needs. LDC Racing Sailboats, therefore, commissioned a high-performance dinghy without racks or trapezes from one of the best English dinghy designers, Phil Morrison.

Drawing on his long experience of the Merlin-Rocket and other development classes, Morrison created the RS400, a fast two-person

THE RS 400

The RS 400 was designed to be a compromise dinghy able to perform as well on inland as on coastal waters. It therefore has a high-performance rig, including an asymmetric spinnaker set on a swinging bowsprit, but it has no trapezes because these are seldom useful on the comparatively sheltered waters of inland lakes and rivers.

dinghy with an asymmetric spinnaker. Noting the weakness of this type of sail when running nearly dead downwind, he gave the new boat a retractable bowsprit that may be swung from side to side so that the spinnaker can set more like a conventional sail.

The RS400 has proved to be an excellent all-rounder and it is creating a new generation of club racing scene to replace the one that withered so severely in the 1980s. Like the other pop-outs, it is sold as a complete package ready to race from the day you buy it, and such convenience is playing an important part of the revival of interest in dinghy racing.

PRO-SPORT DINGHIES

One of the major complaints of sailing enthusiasts is that their sport is not shown much on television. The problem is twofold: sailing is difficult and expensive to film, and on screen often seems to be taking place in slow motion. To make sailing 'televisual' it was necessary to create a new type of race in which fast and exciting boats compete at close quarters on a small course within viewing distance of the shore. The course has to consist of a large number of short legs so that the crew are kept constantly busy; rushing around the boat and setting or recovering sails.

The other thing that television requires is familiar faces, and to strike the chord of familiarity it is necessary to create a 'circuit' involving a small number of skippers whose names may eventually seep into public awareness through endless repetition.

The first people to achieve something along these lines were those who sail the Sydney Harbour 18-foot Skiffs, the 'Aydeens'. Sydney is one of those rare places that are perfect for sailing, with warm water, strong winds and a beautiful harbour that forms a vast natural amphitheatre. For many years there has been this special class of boat that is sailed by professionals and attracts a big following of spectators.

Since the rules of the class allow practically anything within a hull length of 18 feet, these boats used to have up to five crew and set a vast cloud of sail on their groaning spars. But efficiency gradually prevailed and over the years the skiffs of Sydney Harbour have developed into very light, dart-shaped boats with narrow hulls and wide standing-out frames.

They carry a crew of three exceptionally skilled people, and with their exceptional power-to-weight ratio they are spectacular performers and provide some very good TV footage.

Attempts to export the Sydney Harbour Skiffs to other countries, including Britain, have met with mixed success. Less favourable

weather and a different sponsorship background in Europe have made it hard for the skiffs to achieve the same level of impact in Europe as they have in Australia.

Instead, Britain has grown its own spectacular pro-sailing class, the Ultra 30. This originally took its cue from an American group that set up a professional sailing circus based on a boat called the Ultimate 30. But this was a development class, like the Sydney Harbour boats, which meant that a rich sponsor could buy success by going to the next level of design sophistication, and this led to high costs and poor racing. A group of British enthusiasts then decided to try a one-design version of the same idea, which they called the Ultra 30.

The Ultra is a giant open dinghy, 30 feet in length, that carries up to nine crew. It is extremely tricky to handle and frequently capsizes. A group of skippers that includes Lawrie Smith, Russell Peters, Pete Newlands and Glyn Charles owns the boats and finds sponsors for them. The number of boats in use at any one time varies between six and eight, and there

THE ULTRA (above)
Big, powerful and very tricky to sail, the Ultra 30 is the successful British professional sailing class. Six of the crew can stand out on trapezes on the extension racks, when they are not busy setting or recovering the huge gennaker. Mark roundings tend to be spectacular because of the high speeds and frequent capsizes caused by the inertia of the rigs.

THE SKIFF (right)
Lighter and more efficient than the Ultras, the Sydney Harbour 18-foot Skiffs are the fastest of all dinghies. After years of development, the number of crew has been reduced to three, who must be highly skilled to control the boat, especially when the huge gennaker is in use. However, adverse sailing and sponsorship conditions have limited the Skiffs' success.

are no plans to increase this number because the impact per sponsor would be reduced.

A professional agency arranges a programme of just four 'grand prix' regattas each year, which are televised. The races consist of repeated laps of a short course close to the shore. Naturally, each boat carries

its sponsor's name prominently on sails, hull and crew uniforms. Because they are big, fast, and carry a lot of people, the Ultras look interesting on the screen even in less than perfect weather, and are so far the only pro-dinghy racing outfit to have stood the test of time in Britain.

The only other professional small-boat sailing of note in Europe is the Open Class on Lake Garda, in Northern Italy. These boats are created specially for an annual 100-mile race around the lake, and includes some extremely large and spectacular dinghies that carry as many as twenty people, all of them hanging outboard on trapezes. Unfortunately, the Open Class boats are so specialized that they would not be able to compete successfully in any other type of racing and therefore remain 'fabulous monsters'.

Professional small-boat racing faces some of the same pressures as grand prix motor racing, in which the Formula 1 cars become more and more efficient until they resemble a minimal bullet in which the driver's head can just be seen. As these are no more interesting to watch on TV than toy cars, the viewer tends to turn to fringe events such as truck racing or stock cars. The Ultra 30s are a bit like truck racing in that everyone knows they could be made more efficient and everyone knows that at some stage the crews are going to end up in the water. At least when an Ultra 30 'crashes and burns' no-one gets hurt.

DAY-SAILING MULTIHULLS

The two things that govern the performance of a sailing boat are power-to-weight ratio and stability. You can give a dinghy an enormous sail plan, but it will be useless if the first puff of wind knocks the boat flat on its side. To make effective use of its sails, a sailing boat needs stability to hold the rig up and turn the wind's energy into power. The best way to achieve more stability is to make the boat wider, but this eventually becomes impractical so it becomes worthwhile to split the boat in two.

The Pacific islanders have known this for centuries, of course, but their outrigger canoes and twin-hulled boats astonished the first Europeans to visit the region, and it was not until after the Second World War that yachtsmen began to experiment with multihulls, with groups in Australia, the United States and Britain all working more or less in parallel.

A key advantage of a multihull is that because it achieves its stability from its width, the individual hulls do not need any stability at all and hence can be made very slim with a semicircular section, a bit like a rowing eight. These slim hulls are very easily driven and are able to reach a high speed without planing. As soon as the first decently put-together catamarans such as the 16-foot Shearwater made their appearance, it was clear that they had an enormous speed advantage over the typical monohull dinghies of the period.

From the earliest days, multihull sailors were regarded as cranks and their boats as a bit of a nuisance as they took up so much room in the dinghy park and were difficult to fit into normal events because they were so much faster. As a result, it was many years before multihulls became really popular and were accepted into the sailing scene. That this did eventually happen was due in large measure to boats such as the Hobiecat and Dart, which are easy-to-use standard products but nevertheless are still fantastic fun to sail.

Though very different in shape, these two boats share a common feature: neither has a centreboard. Wanting a cat that could be run up the beach without damage, Californian Hobie Alter gave his design a deeply rockered 'banana' shape with the crew sitting on an aluminium frame above the hulls. Rodney March, who had already designed the Tornado (currently used in the Olympics), took a different approach, giving the Dart a streamlined skeg that is part of the hull moulding but is very effective in stopping the boat from sliding off sideways.

For really high performance, however, there is no substitute for an aerofoil-section daggerboard, as fitted to the Tornado and other dedicated racing catamarans. The drawback is the expense and difficulty of making them strong enough to resist the phenomenal sideforce that a catamaran develops at full speed.

Because catamarans are so much faster than normal dinghies, it was soon found that the usual kind of soft cloth sail set on a round mast did not unlock the boat's potential. More aerodynamically-efficient solutions were sought, such as streamlined masts that rotate so they can be aligned accurately with the airflow, and fully battened sails made from stiff cloth that come as close as possible to emulating an aerofoil shape.

For major international events, such as the International Catamaran Challenge Trophy, solid wing sails like a glider's wing standing on end have been used. But these are impractical for normal use both because of expense and because they need to be derigged every time the boat comes ashore to prevent it taking off on its own.

Racing a catamaran is very different from racing a normal dinghy. Because of their width, tacking is a relatively slow business that needs to be kept to a minimum, whereas small differences in tuning can mean big differences in speed. Cats therefore sail to windward in a series of big, fast tacks instead of

THE HOBIE 14

Although it has been around for some years, the Hobie 16 is still one of the most popular two-person racing catamarans. Like the smaller Hobie 14, it has deeply-rockered hulls to compensate for the lack of centreboard and a raised crew platform on a tubular aluminium frame. The fully-battened rig is powerful and there is one trapeze for the crew.

THE DART 18 (above)

The Dart 18 can be seen as the British answer to the Hobie 16, because it is another catamaran that combines simplicity and moderate cost with high performance. Like the Hobie it has no centreboards, but in this case lateral resistance is provided by a stream-lined skeg. Another clever feature is that the usual boom is replaced by a stiff batten in the mainsail

THE HOBIE TIGER (left)

The second-generation Hobie Tiger shows off its high-performance features, which include round-bottomed hulls with fully-profiled daggerboards, twin trapezes and a bowsprit for set-ting a gennaker—the cross between a genoa and a spinnaker that makes the Tiger a potent performer downwind.

engaging in dogfights like small racing dinghies. Downwind, the apparent wind becomes all important. Because of their speed, cats pull the apparent wind ahead and increase it, and the trick is to keep this effect going by reaching downwind in a series of gybes. Sailing straight downwind turns out to be much slower.

Most cats sail best with one hull fully immersed in the water and the other just kissing it, so as to reduced 'wetted surface', the area of boat actually touching the water. This can involve the crew deliberately sitting on the 'wrong' side of the boat to make it heel, something that sounds bizarre for a boat whose main advantage is its stability.

Nowadays, catamarans form a substantial proportion of the small-boat population, although they still tend to be concentrated on a relatively small number of clubs that have sufficient space both ashore and afloat. The number of classes, which at one time threatened to become ridiculous as more and more manufacturers fought for a share of a limited market, has also settled down.

For singlehanders the choice lies between the Dart 15 and the Hobie 14, while the 'club-level' two-handers include the Dart 18, Hobie 16 or 17, the Prindle 18 and the NACRA. The Tornado stands on its own, being a bit too expensive unless you are seriously interested in the Olympics, but the boat that was built as a 'trainer' for it, the twin-trapeze Hurricane 5.9, is more reasonably priced and has a considerable following, as does its rival the Hobie 18. If you really want speed, you could try the Formula 18, a rule that encompasses various designs such as the very advanced Dart Hawk with twin trapezes and gennaker, or the somewhat similar Hobie 21.

OFFSHORE MULTIHULLS

Offshore multihulls can be divided pretty neatly into two groups—cruising and racing—although there are naturally some compromise designs. The reason for this division has a lot to do with safety.

For more than 25 years, it has been beyond dispute that unballasted multihulls have a far greater speed potential than ballasted monohulls, but at the same time there has been a very large question mark over the safety of offshore multihulls. For this reason, development has tended to proceed along two broad streams, one leading to safe and comfortable cruising yachts and the other to high-performance racers.

The trouble with multihulls of all types—as anyone who has sailed a small cat off the beach can testify— is that although they are very stable when the right way up, they are equally stable upside down. Unlike a ballasted keelboat, which will eventually bob up from any angle, once a multihull reaches the point of no return and capsizes, that's it. A point in favour of multihulls, however, is that they normally remain buoyant when capsized, giving the crew a better-than-average chance of rescue.

In addition to being potentially faster than keelboats, cruising catamarans can offer a great deal of space, thanks to their generally square shape. A cruising catamaran of 10–12 metres (35–40 feet) overall can easily offer four private double cabins in the hulls in addition to a large and pleasant saloon on the bridge deck. Furthermore, it heels very little, making life aboard more pleasant than on a comparable keelboat.

One drawback is that because of their slender hulls, catamarans are generally poor weight-carriers and the temptation to fill all that wonderful space with heavy cruising gear must be firmly resisted. Another is that they are generally more expensive to keep in a marina where charges are often 50 percent more than the rate for monohulls. Conversely, as the multihulls do not have deep fixed keels, they can sometimes be found moorings in water that is too shallow for keelboats.

This lack of deep draught is also a very nice cruising feature, because most cruising multihulls can take the ground without any problems and are therefore ideal for visiting shallow bays and beaches. The evocative advertising for the well-known Catalac cruising yachts always used to show one of these boats high and dry on a beach, with children playing in the sand.

Prouts of Canvey Island have for many years been one of the most successful builders of cruising multihulls, with a range of comfortable, well-built catamarans up to 45 feet in length. French builders such as

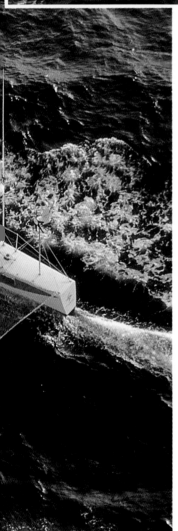

THE FREEBIRD (above)

This Freebird cruising catamaran clearly shows the advantages of the type: lots of space, both inside and on deck, good performance, doesn't keel over, can be sailed in shallow water. Conversely, it is not a very good weight-carrier and could capsize in ultimate conditions.

THE ENZA (left)

Round-the-World record-holder ENZA showing how most of the deck has been eliminated to save weight and resistance. The crew live in the hulls with the central 'pod' being used for control and navigation. This is a high performance multihull.

Multiplast and Edel concentrate on larger cats that are suitable for charter use, and many of these can be seen in the Caribbean where their comfortable accommodation is appreciated by charter clients with limited sailing experience.

In between the racing and cruising extremes are compromise designs such as the old Iroquois cat and the modern Dragonfly 920 trimaran, which is quite fast and has a comfortable cruising interior and a diesel auxiliary. All the Dragonflies address the problem of marina costs by having folding outriggers, which makes it possible to reduce overall beam to about the same amount as a typical cruising yacht of the same overall length. Their drawback is that they have considerably less internal space than the equivalent catamaran. Trimarans, in fact, always tend to be like long, thin keelboats inside, even if the hull is swelled out above the waterline.

At the other end of the spectrum are sporty, high-performance catamarans and trimarans that are mainly used for racing. The smallest and most popular are the 'micro-multihulls' which operate as a restricted class and are about 25 feet in length. The smallest of the Dragonfly trimarans, built in Denmark, fit into this category as do the British-built Firebird catamaran, the Farrier trimarans from the USA and several other designs.

These are boats that you can sleep on, if you must, but they are fantastically fast little racing boats that go skittering along balanced on one hull even in relatively light winds. They need to be sailed just like high-performance dinghies and capsizes are not infrequent.

For real offshore racing, trimarans are generally more popular than cats as they are easier to rig and tend to be faster to windward when the weather hull is kept permanently airborne. At one time, there was an 'open' class that resulted in boats of around 80 feet in length, but these became so expensive that there was a general agreement to bring the maximum size down to 60 feet.

These are the type of multihulls that are used in some of the major ocean races such as the singlehanded transatlantic races, the Route du Rhum and others. They are, without question, the fastest seagoing sailing boats in the world and hold many of the trans-ocean records. It is ironic that they are so often used for singlehanded racing in what is clearly a very dangerous type of competition, one in which the boats sail very fast in bad weather and in the dark. As the American Steve Fossett has shown, a 60-foot racing trimaran is capable of a staggering performance when sailed by four really good people who can keep it going at maximum speed all the time.

A number of top sailors have lost their lives in these singlehanded 'ocean spectaculars', which really are in the same sort of sporting category as Formula 1 motor racing. The boats certainly represent the leading edge of maritime design, being constructed of sophisticated lightweight materials such as carbonfibre and Kevlar. Masts are normally rotating aerofoils like those on day-racing cats but enormously larger, while fully-battened mainsails in the latest material are also *de rigeur*. It is appropriate to use a French term here as the great majority of these ocean fliers are French, even though one of the leading designers, Nigel Irens, is English.

OLYMPIC CLASSES

There are now eight different types of boat used in the yachting events of the Olympic Games. These are a sailboard (the IMCO one-design), three types of singlehanded dinghy (the Europe, Finn and Laser), one double-handed dinghy (the 470), a high-performance dinghy (the 49-er), a multihull (the Tornado), and a keelboat (the Soling).

The question of which boats are sailed in the Olympic competitions tends to be highly political, because there are always a large number of people and groups with an axe to grind when it comes to the five-ringed circus.

For a start, the International Olympic Committee (IOC) insists on classifying all the events as 'disciplines' rather than as classes, because its collective mind-set is towards athletics, where it is the activity that counts rather than the equipment. Furthermore, as far as the IOC is concerned, all events are either for men, for women or are 'open'. So, for instance, what sailors think of as the Soling Class competition is, to the IOC, 'Keelboat, three-person, open, fleet and match-racing'.

Sailors, on the other hand have always tried to choose boats that are popular and give good competition in many parts of the world. The idea has traditionally been to cover the broad spectrum of yachting competition, though in recent years there has been more emphasis on the smaller boats, especially the singlehanders. The Olympic movement is massively conservative and there is always fierce resistance to any proposal to change the boats in use, because they represent an investment in both equipment and training.

The representatives of the well-established classes also tend to have a lot of power within the governing body of sailing, the International Sailing Federation, enabling them to sabotage progressive ideas. It therefore called for a major effort on behalf of the federation to introduce the new 49-er dinghy in time for the 2000 Olympics, especially as it involved displacing the Star two-person keelboat, which had been in the Olympics since 1932.

The disciplines and the boats used for the 2000 Olympics are as follows. Women's sailboard and men's sailboard: IMCO one-design; Singlehanded, women: Europe; Singlehanded, men: Finn; Open singlehanded dinghy: Laser; Open high-performance dinghy: 49-er; Double-handed, women and double-handed, men: 470; Open multihull: Tornado; Fleet/match racing keelboat: Soling.

It will be seen from this list that three classes are reserved for men, three are reserved for women and three are theoretically 'open', although the chances of a woman sailing competitively in the Laser, Tornado or Soling are remote. It will also be seen that five of the ten classes are singlehanded. The sailboards, the Finns and the Lasers are provided by the organizers as a means of increasing participation and fairness, and there is a suggestion that this may also be the case with the 49-er.

Sailing in the Olympics represents the pinnacle of achievement for a small-boat sailor and in most cases is the result of a nonstop four-year training programme. The days in which gifted amateurs could sail in a few trial races and end up representing their country are, unfortunately, over. In addition to the highest levels of skill and fitness, the Olympic sailors needs a flawless knowledge of the racing rules and an exceptionally good feel for weather conditions.

The influence of the Olympic regatta extends throughout sailing

THE SOLING

The Soling three-man keelboat plays a unique part in the Olympics because it is used first in normal fleet races to select a top group that competes in a match-racing tournament to decide the medals. Thus the participants need to excel in two quite different types of racing to succeed in Olympic competition.

because of the tendency of regatta organizers to use 'Olympic courses' and score using 'Olympic points'. For many years, the course was based on a triangle that presented the competing yachts with a series of beating, reaching and running legs, with the race always starting and finishing to windward. However, from 1996 onward, the emphasis has been on a larger number of shorter races over a trapezoidal course, with more emphasis on beating and running and a reaching finish.

Due to the perceived need to make the Olympic regatta easy to follow for TV viewers, the IOC was keen to have a competition in which the gold medal would be decided by the final race, and this was achieved by inventing a hybrid fleet and match-racing regatta which is used for the Soling Class. First, they sail a series of normal races, after which the top twelve

THE TORNADO (right)
The only multihull to be sailed in the Olympics, the Tornado is a 1970s design that is beginning to show its age but is still a very fast and demanding boat to race.

THE 49-ER (below)
The exciting Australian-designed '49-er' was chosen for use at the 2000 Olympics in Sydney—an appropriate choice since it is a typical Australian-style skiff with narrow, lightweight hull, standing-out frames, twin trapezes and lots of sail. A boat to bring sailing into the realm of athletic competition.

teams go into a match-racing tournament. However, it is more likely that the new 49-er races will prove to be the most exciting for the TV audience.

The 49-er, an exciting new two-person skiff, is an Australian design very much in the tradition of the Sydney Harbour 18-foot skiffs, and provides some spectacular racing when the breeze is up. The people who sail them need to be very athletic in contrast to those who sail heavy dinghies such as the Finn, which are exhausting but basically sedentary.

In fact it is extraordinary that the Finn is still in use, because it overlaps with the much livelier and more interesting Laser. At the Atlanta Olympics, the Laser

provided by far the closest and most exciting competition, and it showed itself to be an ideal Olympic boat because every boat in the fleet was identical and the only difference in performance was that resulting from the skill of the sailors.

It is interesting to note that the first ever Olympic medal of any kind to be won by Hong Kong was in the women's sailboard class at Atlanta. The rapid spread and relatively low cost of this new branch of sailing has been totally successful in bringing in new competitors who are not from one of the traditional yachting nations.

The exact opposite applies to the Tornado catamaran, which is expensive to acquire and run and

calls for a lot of background technical knowledge. For instance, it would be useless for anyone to embark on a Tornado Olympic campaign unless he or she had access to a top-class sailmaker with long experience of the class, and unless there were other good Tornados in his or her country to train against.

Many people feel that the Olympics have an excessive influence on sailing as a whole, especially as the top sailing nations tend to devote a high proportion of their training effort toward winning medals. Yet if the Olympics did not exist it would probably be necessary to invent them, as any sport tends to be 'rudderless' without a competitive pinnacle.

DAY-RACING KEELBOATS

Yacht racing had its origins in competitions for relatively large yachts that took place during daylight hours. Both dinghy racing and long-distance racing came later. For many years, day keelboat racing was in decline, but now it has recovered and is again one of the most popular types of competition.

The whole pattern of yacht clubs grew up to satisfy the needs of keelboat racing. Since these are not boats that you can sleep aboard, accommodation is needed ashore and also a base from which to organize the racing. Events such as Cowes Week originally consisted entirely of day keelboat racing, and this type of racing still provides the backbone of that event and many others like it.

The racing yachts of the nineteenth century were huge and were sailed by a professional skipper and crew: the owner was usually more or less a spectator aboard his own vessel. Over the years, as the sport became more amateur, yachts became smaller and owner-skippers the norm. In the 1920s and 1930s, keelboats of 45 to 60 feet in length were thought of as relatively small racing yachts, whereas now they are considered expensive monsters.

The interwar years saw the emergence of much more modest keelboats, such as the three-person Dragon and the two-person X-O-D, both of which are still popular today. The diminishing size of keelboats reached its ultimate with the 2.4-metre, a scale-model 12-metre that is just large enough for one person to sit in. This has become an international class for the disabled, in which they can compete against able-bodied sailors without disadvantage.

A traditional drawback of the keelboat is that it requires a mooring afloat and this is an expense not incurred in dinghy racing. Nowadays, however, thanks to plastic hulls and modern cranes, it is practical to 'dry-sail' keelboats as large as a Dragon or an Etchells. When not in use, they are kept on cradles or road trailers and remain clean and light, unlike boats afloat which inevitably take up weight and become weedy unless they are regularly scrubbed. Plastics have also cut down the other major bugbear of keelboat ownership—maintenance. The annual ritual of scraping, sanding and painting has in most cases been reduced to a quick wash-down with the power spray followed by overhaul of the fittings with an oilcan.

Keelboat racing is a somewhat more leisurely affair than dinghy

THE ETCHELLS 22
The Etchells 22 can be seen as a more modern version of the Dragon theme. Lighter, faster and more efficient than the older boat, it is popular in the USA, Great Britain and Australia.

THE INTERNATIONAL DRAGON

Although dating back to the 1930s, the International Dragon is still one of the top day-racing keelboats and is found in most of the leading yachting countries. It has more tuning adjustments than almost any other small boat.

racing and normally goes on for longer. Because athleticism is not too important, people of almost any age can compete on a reasonably equal basis. Teamwork is of the essence, especially on the boats with three or more crew, and the successful teams are those in which each member of the crew plays a full part.

For instance, in a three-man keelboat such as a Dragon or an Etchells, the helmsman concentrates on steering, the middleman is in charge of sail trim and advises the helmsman on tactics, while the front man does a lot of the physical work involved in tacking or gybing.

Years ago, almost every major club had its own keelboat class. Although the best of these still survive, there is more concentration on international classes these days. One of the best-known is the International Star, a 22-foot, two-person keelboat that was designed back in 1908 and was used in the Olympics from 1932 to 1996 with one short gap.

With its tall, thin mast and big mainsail, the Star is particularly difficult to sail well, with a strong emphasis on tuning the rig to suit the exact wind and sea conditions. It is very popular in North America and various parts of Europe, especially where racing takes place on fairly sheltered waters, because the Star is a bit delicate for the rough and tumble of coastal racing.

The International Dragon, which is 29 feet overall, was designed in Norway as a 'skerry cruiser' but soon developed into a pure racing machine. It is one of the prettiest small boats, with a classic 'model yacht' profile, and most Dragons are beautifully built and maintained with pride by owners.

More seaworthy than the Star, the Dragon is an ideal coastal racing keelboat even if its rounded bow does tend to bang in a head-sea. This is one of the classes that has gathered strength internationally in recent years.

During the 1970s, the need was seen for a more modern keelboat design for the Olympics than the Dragon, and a set of trials produced the Soling, a much lighter, 26-foot keelboat with a modern fin keel and spade rudder. Thanks to the

pressure of Olympic competition, this became a boat that calls for big, strong men to sail it, and a special style of lying out over the side supported by a body harness was developed. This makes the boat less attractive to the normal weekend sailor, who is unlikely to make the grade in fitness or skill.

However, another design produced at the same time as the Soling, the Etchells 22, has gradually acquired a strong following in the USA, Britain and Australia. A bit bigger and beamier than the Soling, it is also light in weight with a modern underwater profile, and has rules that prevent the extreme style of sitting-out seen on the Soling. As a result, it can be raced effectively by crews of mixed ability while its championships attract some of the world's top yachtsmen.

One of the surprising things about keelboats is the continuing popularity of some of the old designs that have been around since the early years of the twentieth century. To see sixty X-O-Ds racing at Cowes, or fifty Yare and Bure One-Designs racing on the Norfolk Broads, is to realize that the pleasures of sailing are not necessarily dependent on the modernity of the boat involved. Some of these older keelboats seem to have a timeless appeal that, if anything, improves with age.

SPORTSBOATS

Sportsboats have enjoyed a rapid rise in popularity in recent years and look certain to form an important sector of yachting in the future. An initial rush of designs will no doubt settle down as some succeed commercially while others fall by the wayside.

The sportsboat movement has its origins in the frustration felt by many yachtsmen at the high costs and constant uncertainty associated with handicap racing using one of the rating systems such as IMS, and of the poor resale value of boats built to rating rules. Most of today's keenest offshore sailors come from a background of dinghy sailing, where the one-design concept is deeply ingrained and the whole idea of sailing with time allowances is scorned.

The first person to understand the opportunity that this presented was the American designer Rod Johnstone, whose J24 really changed the face of sailing for the better. A light, simple, sporty 24-foot racer with a basic cabin, the J24 made people realize how much more competitive and how much fun racing becomes when all the boats are equal and the outcome depends on the skill of the crew.

This much is familiar territory, but the J24 also appealed to small-boat sailors because it was fast, sporty, planed like a dinghy, and handled nicely because its hull was not distorted to gain advantage under any rating rule.

Large numbers of these boats were built, and J24 racing fleets were established in many parts of the world. However, the J24 is quite a conventional little boat, and the revolution in sailing styles at the beginning of the 1990s saw a number of new and more exciting designs emerge.

Perhaps the most important of these was another American boat the Melges 24, designed by the inventive and very experienced 'Buddy' Melges. This features high-tech composite plastics construction to achieve a high power-to-weight ratio and is fitted with a large asymmetric spinnaker in order to give a supercharged downwind performance. The crew cockpit is big and the cabin minimal—little more than a big waterproof storage locker.

The success of the Melges 24 resulted in a rush of imitators, the majority of which have had little impact on the market. However, the Melges 24, with its exotic construction, is an expensive little boat and in Britain the Hunter 707 showed that many of the advan-tages of the type could be achieved at much lower cost, mainly by using conventional GRP (glass-reinforced plastic) construction and aluminium spars.

This little boat has many attractive features, including an outstandingly clever outboard motor stowage under the cockpit floor. This useful arrangement enables the auxiliary to be set in place and started within a few seconds. This makes ownership more practical, as virtually every racing boat needs to be able to motor in or out of harbour and get home in a calm.

The designer of the 707, David Thomas, has always been very sceptical about the advantages of asymmetric spinnakers, which are only truly effective on a reach and tend to force boats so fitted to sail downwind in a series of zigzags. This can be effective in open water, but in the real world the majority of people sail in places where either the tide or the proximity of dry land are crucial tactical factors that

limit the choice of downwind courses. Thomas therefore gave the 707 a large but symmetrical spinnaker, which is set on an extra-long pole that helps to make it more effective when reaching.

One of the more bizarre developments in sportsboats is the emergence of a special handicap rule in an area where the whole idea was to dispense with handicapping. Nevertheless, so many

slightly different sportsboat designs have emerged that it became logical to devise a means whereby they could race together.

This resulted in the RYA Sportsboat Rule, which in effect is a specialized version of the Channel Handicap. Because of their high power-to-weight ratios and ability to plane, sportsboats tend to rate rather too favourably well under the usual length and

sail-area assessment of performance, and needed this more specialized rating.

Another interesting approach was that of the Royal Cork Yacht Club, which commissioned a new sportsboat for its members' use rather like the day-racing keelboats of old. This boat, the Cork 1720, has proved to be one of the most attractive of the breed and has been enthusiastically adopted by a

number of other clubs in addition to the Royal Cork.

Sportsboats are normally raced by four people, which in itself makes them much easier to manage than an IMS design calling for seven or more crew aboard a 35-footer. They almost all have big cockpits to make handling easier, and small, simple cabins whose main purpose is to store the sails when they are not in use.

In terms of type of racing, sportsboats fit somewhere in between the traditional day-racing keelboats and yachts with proper accommodation.

In other words, they are pretty seaworthy and are suitable for coastal races lasting for a number of hours, but in most cases they are not suitable for overnight racing because they do not carry the essential safety equipment required. Being light in weight, it is a simple matter to hoist them out of the water, and they can be towed by cars with more than about 2 litres engine capacity.

The rise in the popularity of sportsboats can be seen as part of the movement by yachtsmen to get more fun for their money and less trouble. They fit in with the pattern of close, enjoyable racing during daylight hours followed by relaxing evenings ashore.

The fact that they are relatively cheap to own and easy to manage is just as important as their sporty performance afloat. All in all, sportsboats are providing yachtsmen with a very stimulating type of racing, one that is helping to increase the popularity of boat ownership and racing.

THE PROJECTION 762 (above)
An interesting compromise design with a fitted-out interior that makes her suitable for coastal racing, the Projection 762 is one of the speediest of the sportsboats and a potent performer in round-the-buoys racing.

THE MELGES 24 (right)
With its hi-tech composite construction and huge asymmetric spinnaker, the US-designed Melges 24 has a thrilling performance that sets the standard by which the other sportsboats are judged. The success of the Melges 24 has led to a rush of imitators.

THE SIGMA 8 (left)
One of the earliest members of the present generation of sportsboats, the Sigma 8m is relatively narrow and has a conventional cockpit layout. Nevertheless, its high power-to-weight ratio gives a sparkling performance.

BUDGET CRUISERS

There come moments in the lives of most yachtsmen when they long to be able to sail a little farther than their local waters and look forward to the pleasures of live-aboard boats. Cruising is something that has a potent appeal, and although it calls for considerably more skills and knowledge than day-sailing, the learning of those skills is a pleasure in itself.

When people think of cruising, they begin to think of expense, and it is quite true that if you go to a boat show and order the latest 40-footer from a leading builder, then you are looking at large sums of money. But equally, it is perfectly possible to run a small cruiser for no more than a few hundreds of pounds per year, and although you may not have the private cabin and air conditioning of a big boat, you can have a lot of the simple pleasures of cruising.

Two people can cruise in a remarkably small boat, provided their expectations of comfort are not excessive. Tiny cruisers of 20–25 feet can be safe and reliable for coastal cruising and even for short sea crossings. But the fact that adventurers have crossed the oceans in various minute boats should not be allowed to cloud your judgement: 20 feet really is about the bare minimum for a boat that you are going to sleep aboard.

This is because the requirements include a proper cabin with at least two bunks, a simple cooker and some kind of basic toilet arrangement. Without these basics, you are camping afloat rather than cruising. And any boat worthy of being called a cruiser must also be able to carry a decent-sized anchor and chain, a battery and navigation lights, charts and basic navigation instruments, and lifejackets and distress flares, all of which are essential equipment. In addition, it would be foolish to go to sea without a VHF radio of some sort, and not many people would be happy without some kind of engine.

The important thing to realize first is that yachting has a very good secondhand market. Properly built and maintained boats last for many years, and there is always a good selection of small cruisers available for as little as £10,000. Of course, you must be careful when buying and for anyone who does not possess the appropriate technical knowledge, a condition survey is almost always money well spent.

Buying a boat is often easier than finding somewhere to moor it. Marinas are expensive and traditional moorings often hard to find, so the type of mooring that is available is also going to influence the choice of boat. For many people, the only type of mooring available at reasonable cost is one that dries out at low tide, and this means opting for a centreboard or twin-bilge-keel design.

However, centreboard boats can be unhappy on moorings with stony bottoms, which can scar the surface of the hull or get jammed in the centreboard casing, and twin keels can be a problem where the seabed is particularly soft or uneven, because this can result in the boat falling over at low tide.

If you are lucky to live near a deepwater haven, then you may be fortunate enough to find a mooring suitable for a fixed-keel boat. This should always be the preferred option because fixed keels are

simpler, stronger and normally give a better sailing performance than centreboards or twin keels.

An alternative to searching for a mooring is to buy a trailer-sailer, but although the freedom of being able to arrive by car, launch the boat and go can seem attractive, it brings its own problems. There is always the need to moor the boat somewhere—unless you expect to keep on sailing ceaselessly, like the Flying Dutchman—and it is always the case that satisfactory temporary moorings are even more expensive that long-term ones.

THE PARKER 21 (right)

A cruising chute provides that extra little bit of performance downwind, but high performance is not the main attraction of small cruising yachts such as this. Safety, reasonable comfort and low running costs are more important.

THE TRIDENT (left)

Warmly dressed for an afternoon sail on the river. A small cruising boat is ideal for the kind of modest weekend cruises that provide thousands of people with a relaxing escape from the daily grind.

24FT SLOOP (below)

Slipping down the estuary on a quiet evening is the vision of sailing that many people have, and is one that can be achieved without spending a great deal of money. A basic small cruiser can be bought for a few thousand and maintained for a few hundred pounds a year.

Simplicity is the key to successful budget cruising and it will usually be found that the simplest systems work best anyway. In spite of the many alternatives, a simple sloop rig with a reefable mainsail and a roller-reefing jib is usually the best solution.

An inboard diesel engine is a very nice thing to have, but also an expensive one, whereas a 5-bhp outboard motor on a stern bracket is cheap and pretty reliable. And hot and cold running water and a shower sound wonderful until you realize that a 25-footer has difficulty in carrying enough fresh water to make such a system worth having, and a full plumbing system is complex and expensive.

Living aboard a small yacht calls for a lot of organization and self-discipline as you have to eat, sleep, navigate, cook and wash all in the same small space. Tidiness is therefore essential if the interior of the boat is not to turn into a chaotic mess in a short time. In fact, you can often tell cruising people from their obsessive tidiness, for example from the way they carefully clean their shoes before stepping aboard a boat, or their habit of keeping all their food in neatly-labelled boxes. It may seem fussy but it goes with living in very restricted spaces.

The aspect of cruising in a small boat that is hardest to describe is the sheer magic of it: working with the tides and wind in your own tiny vessel and being so close to nature in all its changing moods. Many people think that 'yachting' is for wealthy people only, but when you see the pleasure that people get from small-boat cruising for a very modest outlay, then it is impossible to agree.

FAMILY CRUISERS

The magic size of 30 feet is the one at which most people would agree that a 'budget' or 'pocket' cruiser turns into a 'family' cruiser, and the size range from 30–36 feet encompasses the vast majority of popular production cruising yachts. There are a number of good reasons for this.

From about 32 feet overall, you have a boat that can carry up to six people, even if it is a bit of a squeeze, and a level of equipment that makes a cruise of a reasonable length an attractive proposition rather than an ordeal. A 35-footer can carry an even better range of equipment, and the step up from a 25- to a 35-footer is huge.

Starting on deck, a 35-footer will have more and better sails than the smaller boat. Even if an all-purpose roller genoa is fitted, you can expect to find at least one other headsail and perhaps a spinnaker or cruising chute to enhance downwind performance. Halyards and sheets will be handled by small geared winches, and this is important because it means that no great physical strength is required to set the sails.

The cockpit will be large enough for all the crew to sit in at once, and there will most likely be a folding 'pram hood' over the main hatch to give shelter and prevent water from getting down

below. There will also be enough space on the boat to stow an inflatable liferaft and a dinghy.

The ability to carry an inflatable liferaft is very important feature of any cruising yacht, as a liferaft is one of the most basic safety requirements for a yacht that is going to sail offshore. However well built and equipped a yacht may be, the potential for a disaster such as collision or grounding means that the crew should always have the means of escape available to them. A six-man liferaft is a heavy and bulky item that needs to be stowed in an easily-accessible spot on deck.

Another requirement for a proper cruising yacht is some kind of tender, which in the 30–35-foot size range will almost inevitably be an inflatable dinghy. Smaller yachts that confine themselves to short coastal cruises can tow a dinghy, but for a passage of any length it is essential to be able to carry the tender on deck or, in the case of an inflatable, rolled up in a locker.

THE PARKER 325 (above)
With its lifting keel and rudder, the Parker 325 is a very useful coastal cruising yacht with the special advantage that it can be kept on a mooring that dries out at low tide. The simple rig and diesel auxiliary help to make it a safe and reliable cruising yacht.

THE ISLAND 350 (left)
Fun in the sun—many people get their first experience of cruising on a flotilla holiday, sailing a boat such as this Island 350. Safe, easy to handle and having big cockpits so that everyone can be on deck at the same time, yachts such as this have done a great job in persuading people that cruising is extremely enjoyable and not as tricky as they thought.

Many small cruising yachts offer the option of tiller or wheel steering. People whose background is in dinghy sailing tend to prefer a tiller, which gives a quicker and more direct steering control but the disadvantages include the fact that tiller steering takes up a considerable amount of space in the cockpit. In addition, it is harder to place the steering compass and other sailing instruments in a spot that can be easily seen and not obstructed by other members of the crew. Novice sailors often find that wheel steering is easier to get used to and the wheel plinth provides the ideal place to mount the instruments.

Down below on a 35-footer, you can expect to find an inboard diesel engine. Reliable, economical and safe, a small diesel of, say, 25 bhp will give quite enough power to drive a yacht this size along at its 'hull speed' of around 6 knots. Just as important as the motive power produced are the other types of power generated by the engine—heat and electricity.

The normal arrangement on a family cruising yacht is to fit two storage batteries of around 75 amp/hours each, with a splitter diode to prevent one from discharging into the other. One of these batteries is reserved for starting the engine and the other for 'domestic services' such as lighting and powering the radio and instruments. By running the engine for an hour or two a day, both of the batteries can be kept fully charged.

A cunning device known as a calorifier makes use of the waste heat given off by the engine to heat up water. In effect it is a small water tank, of perhaps 5 gallons capacity, which is warmed by the engine cooling water being passed through a coil. This small tank of hot water is sufficient for a quick shower and ensures that there is hot water for washing up in the galley. However, this system can only be used if there is also a water pressure pump fitted in the system.

In a yacht of 20–25 feet it is barely possible to have a fixed navigation desk but you would certainly expect one on a 35-footer, with a space under the desk for chart storage and a shelf for the inevitable reference books. A bulkhead situated in front of the navigator's desk provides space for the instruments and the radio to be mounted.

Nowadays, what many people are looking for in a cruising yacht is a reasonable degree of privacy so that a mixed or two-family group can operate without too much embarrassment. A 35-footer can accommodate what is rather optimistically known as a 'three-cabin layout', something that is almost impossible to achieve in a 25-footer.

The main feature of this is still the principal compartment or 'saloon' where cooking, eating navigating and general living will take place, and where at least two people will sleep. Behind the engine and below the cockpit, the majority of family cruising yachts manage to find space for a separate 2-berth cabin, and in slightly larger boats this can also include a compact shower/toilet compartment. Forward of the saloon there is normally a further bulkhead and then another reasonably sized two-berth cabin.

The problem with a forward cabin is that being in the fore part of the yacht it is narrow and the bunks are generally of the type that meet at the foot. In addition, the motion is worst in the bow and the space there is also required for uncomfortable items such as wet sails. It is therefore better, if possible, to have four berths in the saloon and regard the fore cabin as sleeping space only when the yacht is at rest.

The need for privacy is more imaginary than real, because when the yacht is on passage at least half the crew will be on deck so the others have the cabin to themselves. Nevertheless, it is obviously very pleasant to be able to shut the door on the rest of the crew before going to sleep in harbour.

LONG-DISTANCE CRUISERS

The dream of many cruising people is a yacht capable of extended cruises over long distances. For many, this remains no more than a dream because large yachts are very expensive, but an increasing number of people take the decision to become 'live-aboards' and swap their houses for boats.

But before selling your house and spending the money on a large cruising yacht, consider that you also need a continuing and not inconsiderable income to run such a boat. Berthing, fuel, insurance, supplies, maintenance, repairs and spares all add up to a considerable annual bill, so it is not really possible to sail off into the wide blue yonder without a healthy sum in the bank back at home.

The key difference between a normal family cruiser and a long-range cruiser is storage space. For a two-week cruise you can live out of a single kitbag, but one lasting for many months calls for an entirely different approach.

For a start, you need to be able to carry much more in the way of food, water and fuel. Rows of cans stowed under the floorboards used to be the standby of ocean cruisers, but nowadays many boats have freezers. Although the type of freezer used on a boat is normally fitted with 'hold-over plates' to keep the temperature down for many hours, the fact remains that freezers use a lot of power. It is normally necessary to run an engine for at least two hours a day to keep a freezer happy.

This brings up the question of power generation. A long-distance cruiser of, say, 45 feet overall will normally carry a diesel of around 50–60 bhp, but running this just to generate electricity is inefficient, so many such yachts carry addition mini-diesels purely for the generation of power. Cruising folk are rightly suspicious about engines and electricity (which tend not to like being soaked in seawater) and many insist on having at least one other source of electricity, such as solar panels or a wind-powered generator. Although these provide a strictly limited amount of power, they are a quiet and cheap method of keeping the batteries charged.

Crossing the ocean can often lead one into areas of complete calm when it becomes a virtual necessity to use the engine. But most family cruisers carry only enough fuel for about 36 hours of continuous motoring, which is not really useful in the middle of the ocean. Tanks holding 250 gallons of diesel would be more appropriate for a mid-sized world cruiser, and this is necessarily pointing towards a vessel with heavy displacement.

Cruising yachts always used to carry at least the same amount of fresh water for drinking, cooking and washing, but modern technology means that most of this can now be made at sea by a reverse-

THE BENETEAU OCEANIS (left)
The capacious hull of the Beneteau Oceanis 40 makes it possible to provide the high level of comfort and equipment needed for long-distance cruising. Notice the safe and secure central cockpit and its folding hood, which is equally useful for keeping off the heat of the burning sun or stinging sea spray.

THE HALLBERG RASSY 45 (below)
With her windscreen and central cockpit, the popular Danish-built Hallberg Rassy 45 seems to possess some of the elements of a motor yacht as well as a sailing yacht. In fact, thanks to modern lightweight diesel engines, cruising yachts such as this generally have almost equal performance under power or sail.

osmosis seawater purifier. However, these things do go wrong occasionally and so it is essential to have an adequate stored water capacity as well.

For coastal cruising, a basic VHF radio is quite sufficient but the ocean-going yacht requires long-range radio communication. Traditionally, this has consisted of high-frequency single-sideband radio with which to contact national radio stations such as Portishead in the UK. However, these sets require a fair amount of experience to use effectively, making it necessary to go on a training course and obtain the appropriate operator's licence.

Nowadays the Inmarsat satellite system provides an easy-to-use alternative. If you are very rich, the Inmarsat A or B systems will give you direct-dial telephone calls anywhere in the world, but for most yachtsmen the Inmarsat C system provides a much more reasonable alternative. This is a text-only system: on board, you type messages into a laptop computer and then despatch them via the satellite to any telephone number capable of receiving them in the form of a fax or e-mail text. Simple and reliable, the Standard C set requires only a small antenna the size of a plate and very little power.

Big and heavy yachts require a big sail area to push them along, but this brings the problem of sail-handling for a crew of moderate strength. In recent years, an enormous amount of effort and ingenuity has gone into developing sails that are easy to handle.

Roller-furling headsails are seen on the majority of cruising yachts, but on the larger sizes in-mast roller furling is another option. In terms of convenience roller-furling mainsails are wonderful—you just wind a winch to make the whole sail disappear inside the mast. In terms of performance, however, they are less impressive because a roller mainsail is always smaller in area and less well-shaped than a normal one.

Alternatives include fully-battened mainsails, which do not flap uncontrollably when they are being set or lowered and can be made to drop down neatly onto the main boom between lazyjacks. The newest idea is for mainsails that roll up inside the boom, but although this is an attractive idea the engineering required is tricky and expensive.

A spinnaker or cruising chute is very desirable on a long run in light weather conditions, but many people quail at the thought of getting one up or down. The solution is a gadget called a spi-squeezer, a tube made of light spinnaker cloth that is pulled down over the spinnaker to muzzle it. Afterwards, it can be safely dropped on deck like a long snake but without any risk of it suddenly filling with wind and taking charge when halfway down.

A reliable autopilot is a virtual necessity on a long-range cruiser because it is a waste of effort to have someone steering all the time. If the person on watch can also adjust the sails, navigate, and make a cup of tea occasionally, then it becomes perfectly sensible to sail with one person in charge and the others resting below. Naturally, all safety precautions must be first class and they should always include wearing a safety harness when alone on deck.

THE OYSTER 70

Particularly popular for long-distance cruising, the Oyster Marine range is often used by live-aboard owners. The Oyster 70 is large enough to be used as a charter yacht with room for up to six guests in addition to the professional crew.

PRODUCTION CRUISER-RACERS

One of the big dilemmas of yacht ownership is whether to go for a one-off or a one-design. If you want to race offshore, you have to have some kind of rating certificate otherwise it will be impossible for the organizing club to give you a result. The trouble is that rating rules are notoriously fickle things.

This is because designers are constantly working on ways to build boats that will be faster for a given rating. Whenever they succeed in scoring a point in this particular game, older boats are outclassed. To cope with this, the rule-makers adjust the rating system to tax the latest breakthrough.

As a result, even if an owner does not change his boat at all, the rating will tend to bounce up and down year after year as the ceaseless skirmishing between designers and rule-makers continues. If a boat owner wants to be at the leading edge of racing, he will have to keep modifying his boat to take account of the latest ideas, and this results in further expense and uncertainty.

One way to escape this vicious circle of change is to opt for a production cruiser-racer that remains the same for a number of years.

This brings some of its own problems because for racing to remain fair between all the members of a given class, controls have to be placed on the way the boats can be equipped and used.

For instance, if one member of the class buys a complete outfit of new sails at the beginning of each year, he will do a lot better than the guy who is making do with a five-year-old outfit. So it will be necessary to have a rule saying how often you can buy new sails and some kind of date-stamp system to ensure that this is obeyed.

That would be an obvious class rule, but there is also a need for more subtle rules to control factors such as weight distribution. For example, how much fuel and water ought to be carried when racing, and how is this to be checked? What is the weight of the standard

anchor and where must it be kept? If one is allowed to stow the anchor and chain under the cabin floorboards there will be a clear gain in weight distribution, but the anchor will not be available quickly in an emergency. How many people can race on the boat? The more people you have on the rail, the quicker you go to windward, but if you limit the crew to a particular number of people, then unscrupulous owners will seek out the heaviest crew, so perhaps it will be necessary to physically weigh the crew.

These and other controls are needed in order to have a successful one-design cruiser-racer such as the Sigma 33. This has been a leading class for many years, mainly because it has a strong class association that has kept things properly under control for the overall benefit of the members. What this means in practice is that the class enjoys large fleets and excellent close racing. The boats remain competitive for many years, command good prices and lose their value very slowly.

The obvious problem is that any design gradually becomes out of date, whereupon sales of new boats start to dry up. Then the original builder begins to lose interest and eventually drops the model from his catalogue. Strangely enough, people do go on sailing production cruiser-racers long after they are out of date, because they still like the boat and it represents an investment. An example might be the Contessa 32 Class, still being keenly raced after 25 years, or the Sigma 33, which is not far behind.

Many yacht builders take a more relaxed attitude. They build and sell a 'stock' boat with a good racing performance but make no specific guarantee to maintain it as a one-design. There is still a big

THE J35
A member of the well known US-designed J-boat range, the J35 has proved to be a very reliable performer over a number of years and can also be equipped for cruising. Unlike other boats in the range, it is completely conventional in terms of its design.

THE IMX 38 (left)

The Danish-built IMX 38 has proved to be an exceptionally successful production boat with the emphasis more on racing than on cruising. A well-balanced design with no extreme features, it is well-treated by most of the rating rules which are in common use.

THE SIGMA 33 (above)

One of the most successful of all cruiser-racers, the Sigma 33 is equally at home cruising with a family crew of four aboard or racing with seven, although the cockpit can become very crowded at times. At events such as Cowes Week, fifty or sixty of these boats can be found competing.

advantage to the owner who will be able to use standard hull measurements in obtaining a rating, thus avoiding the expense and nuisance of full hull measurement. As the years pass, the owners of such a boat may decide to introduce improvements to keep it competitive, or, more likely, sell it on to an owner who will either race at a lower level of competition or use it purely for cruising.

So at club level you will frequently find boats that were 'hot-shots' 15 years ago being raced very successfully in normal weekend events. They may have dropped right out of the rating system and instead be handicapped by some kind of club-based empirical system that rewards failure and punishes success.

One of the better features of the main rating systems in use is that boats are given an allowance for the age of their design. Thus one sometimes finds well-looked-after old boats that are very successful in racing, partly because they are getting a useful age allowance. Indeed there are certain people who seem to be skillful buyers of old boats with good race potential.

Buying a stock cruiser-racer makes sense for all sorts of reasons. For a start, it is liable to be a much better investment than a one-off because popular boats hold their value. The cost of spares and repairs will be low, and good, fair racing will be available at a variety of events. The builder or the class association—if they have any sense—will arrange championships at attractive venues with good racing and social events.

It may sound a bit boring to own just another one of the hundreds of a popular class, but you can be confident that you are not just throwing money into the water when you buy one.

OFFSHORE RACING ONE-DESIGNS

The popularity of racing in standard production boats, which are the 'family cars' of the sea, is not very surprising. But when we get into the area of truly serious, leading-edge racing, things become more tricky because there is so much more pressure that it is hard to make the one-design principle work. Nevertheless, the advantages of close racing without handicap are equally attractive, if not more so, at the highest level.

There have been a number of offshore racing one-designs in the past, and the best have remained popular for a number of years before gradually fading away. In Britain, the OOD 34, designed by Doug Petersen, was taken up enthusiastically by members of the Royal Ocean Racing Club (RORC) in the late 1970s and remained popular and competitive for about ten years. However, it received a bad press after the disastrous 1979 Fastnet Race, when it was claimed that relatively light and beamy boats of this type were capable of rolling right over and remaining upside down.

Ironically, by 1990s standards the OOD 34 was neither particularly light nor particularly beamy, but this scare did lead the RORC to introduce a stability screening test to ensure that all boats that enter for its races have sufficient stability for safety. The yachts were built by an 'approved' builder who was supposed to ensure that all the hulls were as close in weight as possible and that the equipment fitted was substantially the same.

It is very important that a boat like this should have an 'afterlife' so that it does not abruptly lose value when it is no longer being maintained as a one-design class. In this the OOD 34 was also successful in that owners still race their yachts today but under handicap and not at the top level. So the class has faded away gracefully rather than simply fallen off the edge of the world abruptly.

There is a rather different story concerning the Mumm 36, which the RORC promoted from the outset as a boat suitable to race in the Champagne Mumm Admiral's Cup. A design competition was held and the winner, from the Bruce Farr office, was a leading-edge design capable of winning at the highest level under handicap as well as sailing as a one-design. The trouble was that this resulted in features that do not make the boat attractive to the private owner and will tend to militate against the boat having an 'afterlife'.

Being very light in weight, the Mumm 36 needs to carry the maximum permitted crew weight in order to race effectively, and this means that crew selection involves carefully weighing all the candidates and selecting a team with the correct total poundage. The fin keel is extremely narrow and deep and this limits the places where the boats can be kept and raced. The unraked keel with a bulb on the end is also prone to pick up weed. Accommodation is strictly limited and will not readily allow the boat to be adapted as a cruiser-racer.

When the Mumm 36 first appeared, it was quickly taken up by professional skippers and crews, relegating the owner to the position of paymaster. The standard of sailing is so high that not many 'weekenders' can aspire to it. In other words, there is a risk attached to pitching the level of the one-design too high just as there is to pitching it too low.

One sure sign that this is so can be seen in the fact that Mumm 36s very seldom turn out for regular weekend events. For one thing, it is very expensive to put the boat into commission and the owner will not feel like doing this except for a fairly major event.

Another is that in normal mixed racing, they tend to have difficulty beating yachts which have handicap advantages such as cruiser-racer allowances, age allowance and polyester sail allowance. In other words, their status as a 'pure' racer leaves them somewhat exposed in the rough-and-tumble of ordinary racing. They are expected to win and look foolish when they fail to do so.

Interestingly enough, things tend to get a little easier in the larger sizes of one-design. The Corel 45 is of sufficient size that the crew

does not form quite so high a proportion of the displacement, and it also has a higher ratio of ballast to displacement, both factors combining to make the yacht less sensitive to small changes of crew weight. It is also in a size and price range that would make it normal to have at least a proportion of non-professional crew so there are not likely to be many disgruntled amateur owners about.

The costs associated with campaigning a yacht of this kind are pretty formidable, especially as they are usually involved in some kind of 'circus' of racing in different parts of the world. This involves transporting the boat from regatta to regatta, and since schedules often make it impossible to deliver a boat by water, this can involve shipping or overland trucking. Even if a crew consists of a mixture of pro and amateur, when racing they will normally expect the owner to pay for travel and accommodation. Berthing, maintenance, and above all a steady supply of new sails also call for continuous expenditure.

Finally, leading-edge racing boats tend to lose value very quickly. If the designer and the club or group that sponsored the design in the first place have done a good job, then the racing life will last for some years and the residual value will be appreciable. But if they get it wrong, the shiny new racing one-design of today can be found gathering dust at the back of the marina car park after a remarkably short space of time.

THE BASHFORD HOWISON 41 (above)

Although not a strict one-design, the Bashford-Howison 41 is an example of a stock design that has done extremely well under various rating rules in different parts of the world. It is competitive under most conditions—the sure sign of a good design.

THE RODGERS W30 (right)

Why only two people on deck? Because this half-scale version of the Whitbread 60 class is fitted with ballast tanks, which means she can be raced effectively without seven or eight people being needed purely for their weight on the rail. This makes her particularly suitable for short-handed passage racing.

THE CORAL 45 (left)

In 1996, The Corel 45 was the last word in offshore one-designs. Designed by Bruce Farr, she is powerful and fast with the huge, unobstructed cockpit needed for effective round-the-buoys racing. Note the giant steering wheel, which is partly sunk into a trough so it does not obstruct the main boom.

ROUND THE WORLD RACERS

Racing around the world must surely be the greatest challenge that any yachtsman can face. At present there are three types of yacht in use for this type of racing, all 60-footers but all very different.

The 'senior' round the world yacht race is the Whitbread race, which has been held every fourth year since 1973. This has always been a race for fully-crewed yachts and it has always been sailed in stages, with stops for recuperation. Although the stops and the various zigzags between them have changed repeatedly, the Whitbread is basically an eastbound or downwind race.

You can only sail around the world in the southern hemisphere, because the sea north of Canada, Asia and Europe is frozen. Farther south, there is land in the way unless you go through the Suez and Panama canals.

So the normal route around the world from Europe is to sail south down the Atlantic and then 'turn left at the Cape of Good Hope. You then sail south of Australia and New Zealand, cross the Pacific, and turn left again at Cape Horn, the southern tip of South America in order to come back into the Atlantic. In this way, the wind is generally astern as you sail right around the world in the cold and stormy Southern Ocean, which fringes Antarctica.

In the early years, the Whitbread Round the World Race could be entered by any suitable seaworthy yacht and the results were on handicap. This created an 'arms race' with more and more highly-developed 80-foot maxi-yachts being specially designed and built for this one race. As costs began to soar into the stratosphere, the organizers decided to create a special class of smaller yacht, the Whitbread 60, and in 1993 there were two classes, the maxis and the Whitbread 60s. It was immediately apparent that the 60-footers gave much better and closer racing, so from 1997 they were the only class to be used.

The special thing about the Whitbread 60s is that they are built to a 'restricted' rule and race without handicap. They are all similar but not identical so a skipper can choose to have a boat that is, for example, a bit faster in light winds. They are very light, simple sloops that are allowed to carry water ballast in tanks along each side of the hull. By filling up the tanks on their windward sides, the boats get a terrific amount of stability without having the whole crews lined up on the rails, and this gives them dramatic performance in reaching

conditions when they can plane like dinghies. They are also allowed to use either conventional or asymmetric spinnakers, and this also makes for a supercharged downwind performance.

A crew of around 12 is carried, and they have to put up with extremely uncomfortable living conditions for the three weeks or so that the longer legs take as the accommodation is distinctly basic. In fact, racing a Whitbread 60 has been compared to competing in an extra-long dinghy race.

Back in 1969, Chay Blyth amazed the sailing world by sailing nonstop and singlehanded around the world 'the wrong way', that is, westbound and hence upwind. Twenty years later, Blyth conceived the idea of a race over this course, but a race with a big difference. Not only would he built a complete fleet of identical yachts, he would sell the places on them to people with relatively little experience of ocean racing. With professional skippers to supervise them, Chay Blyth's paying volunteers undertook a profound personal challenge by willingly subjecting themselves to this demanding race.

The yachts, used for the British Steel and BT Challenge races, have been a set of identical 67-foot steel cutters which were designed, not for extreme performance like the Whitbread yachts, but to be as strong as possible in order to survive the endless beating to windward in the most arduous conditions.

Like the Whitbread 60s they carry 12–14 people, but there the similarity ends. Heavily built and with sturdy, simple rigs, the Challenge yachts can take it on the chin and often have to. There have been dismastings during the two races and various minor problems, but no really serious accident. If a Whitbread 60 tried to sail the 'wrong way' course it would be much faster but would batter itself to pieces.

The third and most daring type of yacht to be used for racing around the world is the Open 60 used in both the BOC and Vendée Globe races. Both are singlehanded races, the BOC in stages and the Vendée non-stop. The rules for the Open 60 are simple and unrestrictive and have resulted in an unbelievably, light, fast, 'sled' type of yacht, which is only three times longer than its width. Water ballast

and hinged keels that can be canted over to windward are both allowed and huge, fully battened mainsails are normal.

The skipper lives in a kind of 'space-capsule' in the centre of the hull surrounded by batteries of computers and communication equipment. Ashore, teams of 'routeurs' work out the best course for them to follow and transmit daily sets of instructions for the skippers.

Apart from giant singlehanded multihulls, the Open 60 class boats are the most unusual of all the long-distance racers. They are fantastically fast but, as was evident in the 1996–7 Vendée Globe race, they are very dangerous as well. The ultimate stability of the boats is limited, they can remain stable upside down after capsizing, and their twin rudders are vulnerable to damage from floating debris or ice.

Above all, it is a very risky enterprise to go careering downwind at hectic speeds with only one person on board. This is

67-FOOT YACHT (top)
Built to take the worst that the ocean can throw at them, the 67-foot yachts used for the British Steel and BT Global Challenge events are heavily built in steel with reliability rather than speed the most important requirement.

MAXI-YACHT (above)
Maxi-yachts such as the 80-foot 'La Poste' are no longer used at the Whitbread Round the World Race, but they can still compete in handicap racing and remain perhaps the most impressive single-hulled racing machines afloat.

especially true as the farther south the yachts sail, the shorter the distance, so the Vendée yachts steer a risky course along the limits of drifting ice. And with only one person aboard, they cannot keep watch all the time. The people who sail these boats are undoubtedly heroic but also perhaps more than a little crazy in view of the risks.

60FT TRIMARAN
The French are the acknowledged experts in the field of very-high-performance ocean racing multihulls such as this 60-foot trimaran, designed for events such as the Route du Rhum and the Singlehanded Transatlantic Race. Capable of crossing the Atlantic in a week, these are the true ocean greyhounds.

GIANT OCEAN RACERS

Other things being equal, a big boat will always be faster than a small one, and so in any competition series without an upper size limit, the boats tend to keep getting bigger and bigger.

This fact first became apparent in the America's Cup where, under the original rules, the only limit on size was a waterline length of 90 feet. By extending the ends of the yacht beyond the waterline, some remarkably big yachts can result and this process reached its ultimate with the 1903 match when the defender, *Reliance*, was 144 feet overall, drew 20 feet of water, had a rig 175 feet high and carried 64 crew. After that date, new rules were devised to keep things under some kind of control.

The same thing happened with the Observer Singlehanded Transatlantic Race. The originator of the event, Col. 'Blondie' Hasler, thought that having only one person aboard would automatically limit the size of the boat. But he was wrong and each time the race was held the yachts got bigger, until 1976 when the French yachtsman Alain Colas entered the 236-foot schooner *Club Med*.

As it happened, he did not win (because of persistent gear failure) but the writing was clearly on the wall and a top-end limit of 56 feet, later changed to 60 feet, was imposed. (The *Club Med* was later bought by the controversial French businessman Bernard Tapie and renamed *Phocea*, in which guise she set a new record for crossing the Atlantic—a little over 8 days.)

The world of conventional ocean racing has been more sensible and has had a top limit of 80 feet for some years. This limit has to be in terms of maximum rating rather than overall length, since the whole idea of rating is that you can have boats of various shapes and sizes with the same rating, but this has been adjusted over the years so that the limit hovers around the 80-foot mark.

The existence of a limit of this kind presents a temptation to create a class of 'maxi-yachts', and that is exactly what has happened. The Whitbread Round the World Race in particular encouraged the appearance of a continuing class of maxis until it was decided to restrict the race solely to the Whitbread 60 class.

An International Offshore Rule (IOR) or International measurement System (IMS) maxi is a formidable piece of kit that costs millions to build and campaign. A crew of at least 20 is required and several of the personnel must be full-time professionals dedicated to ongoing maintenance. Much of the gear has to be specially made because the levels of strain in the standing and running rigging are way beyond anything experienced in a normal yacht. Masts are 90 feet high and supported by cobalt rod rigging, and a 'wardrobe' of dozens of sails is required in order to achieve maximum performance in all conditions.

In spite of the quite horrific costs involved, there are always a certain number of owners for whom nothing can quite match the buzz of racing at the very top end of the sport. This elite group makes its way around the world in order to race in prestigious events such as the Fastnet Race, Bermuda Race, Sydney-Hobart Race, the Kenwood Cup series in Hawaii, and the Sardinia Cup.

For various technical reasons it is very difficult for a maxi to win a handicap race, and for this reason the maxis are normally competing for 'line honours'—to be the first boat home and never mind the handicap result.

After the Whitbread Race turned its back on maxis, one of the skippers who had been most successful at this level, Pierre Fehlmann of Switzerland, decided to create a new race around the world especially for maxis. The unique feature of this race was that the organizers would design, build and own the yachts, which would then be rented out to the racing

THE MISTRAL 80 CLASS

The 80-foot Grand Mistral class such as 'Merit Cup' was created for a projected round-the-world race in which all the boats were to be identical and rented from the organizers, but financial difficulties have placed the event in doubt.

THE MISTRAL 80 CLASS
Designed by Bruce Farr and like a bigger version of the Whitbread 60, the Mistral 80 class carries water ballast that can be transferred from one side of the boat to the other in order to increase stability. The enormous sloop rig generates, as shown here on the 'Nicorette', a formidable amount of power.

teams. This imaginative idea crystallized as the Grand Mistral 80, a stupendous water-ballasted sloop designed by Bruce Farr along similar lines to the Whitbread 60s but much bigger.

Unfortunately, the race itself ran into financial difficulties and its future is uncertain, but four Mistral 80s were in commission by the end of 1996 and were among the fastest and most impressive offshore racing yachts ever seen. Very light for their size, they are tremendous performers on all points of sailing.

Peculiar sailing conditions create peculiar yachts. The laid-back sailors on the West Coast of the USA prefer to sail always down-wind and to have their boats shipped back to the starting point or carefully sailed back by delivery crews. This is a bit like modern skiing, which is always downhill and depends on ski lifts to get you to the top of the hill again.

The most famous example of this is the Transpac Race from Los Angeles to Honolulu, which can normally be guaranteed to be a 'downwind slide' of over 2,000 miles. For this and similar races, the Californians developed what they called Ultra-Light Displacement Boats or ULDBs, also known as sleds. As their name implies, these boats are light with as little ballast as possible and a huge downwind sail area.

A yacht of this type, named *Merlin* and owned by Bill Lee, startled the sailing world in 1977 by sailing to Hawaii in eight-and-a-half days to create a course record that proved very hard to beat. Although these Pacific sleds are too specialized for European-style offshore racing, their influence has been felt throughout the world as they persuaded owners and designers that it was possible to race offshore in very lightweight yachts.

This in turn influenced the design of yachts such as the Whitbread 60s, which are dramatically lighter than earlier yachts. They also played some part in the concept of the Open 60 yachts, extreme sleds that depend on water ballast or swinging keels to achieve a reasonable level of stability.

SAILING SUPERYACHTS

The really clever thing about large motor yachts is that they do not require many crew, and most of the crew that they do have are hotel staff rather than seamen or engineers. Big sailing yachts, on the other hand, have traditionally needed big crews to handle them. But technical advances have made modern luxury sailing yachts as economical to crew and as easy to handle as motor yachts.

In addition to the fact that the crew have to be paid their wages, they also need somewhere to live, and because the ends of a sailing yacht are much more tapered than those of a motor yacht, the crew quarters occupy about half of all the available space on a typical traditional large sailing yacht. Furthermore, all those masts and sails are very expensive to buy and maintain, and sailing yachts have deep keels so that they cannot enter small harbours or attractive shallow bays. In the past, these factors combined to make luxury sailing yachts much less popular than comparable motor yachts

During the past two decades, however, things have changed dramatically to the extent that each year, nearly as many sailing yachts

over 100 feet (30 metres) in length are built as large motor yachts. The main factors that have permitted this are powered sail-handling machinery and electronic navigation equipment, which make it possible for a small crew to handle a big sailing yacht safely.

The most important feature of powered sail-handling was developed by the Italian yachtbuilder Perini Navi. Signor Perini is an engineer specializing in the design of paper-handling machinery, and it occurred to him that similar technology could be put to use on board his yacht. He therefore designed a captive-reel sheet winch that can pull in sails at the touch of a button. On a captive reel, the rope is wound onto a grooved drum so that it is completely under

control and does not require any human intervention.

Perini placed his powered winches out of sight in lockers, with the ropes running under the decks so that not only is there none of the usual jumble of lines on deck, there are no lines under strain that a guest can be at risk from.

His next step was to link all the winches to a computer control s ystem so that, for instance, when the yacht is tacked, the sheets are automatically eased out on one side as they are pulled in on the other. In addition, the winches can be set to yield at a preset strain so that nothing should get broken in a sudden squall.

The other key development, which had been made some time earlier by Ted Hood and others, was in-mast roller furling of the mainsail. The mainsail luff is fixed to a rotating rod (mandrel) inside the mast, and when this is turned by an electric or hydraulic motor, the sail is rolled up and disappears inside the mast. This enables a big mainsail to be set, reefed or stowed in complete safety by one person

and all he actually needs to do is press some buttons.

In-mast furling is not without its drawbacks, however, as the sail needs to be somewhat flat to roll up easily and it cannot have the usual battens that enable the rear edge of the sail, the leech, to have a curve that makes it bigger and more efficient. A more recent development is in-boom furling, which works on the same basic principle as in-mast furling but calls for some quite tricky engineering to get the sail to roll in evenly and without jamming. However, it does permit a much better-shaped mainsail.

Roller reefing and furling of headsails has been around for some time, and the only additional devel-

THE STEALTH

Very large sailing yachts are being built in increasing numbers. With her black hull and black 'liquid crystal' sails, the Italian-owned Stealth, which is far too large to fit into any accepted racing category, seems a whimsical way of spending several million pounds.

opment needed for the superyachts was to add a motor to the bottom of the stay so that the headsail, too, could be set or furled at the touch of a button.

The problem of excessive draught can be tackled in two ways. Perini Navi and some others favour retractable centreboards, like those used on many dinghies but on a massive scale. However, this takes up space in the hull and requires some expensive engineering. Another solution is to concentrate as much of the ballast as possible in a bulb at the bottom of a short but efficient fin keel. Weight aloft can be saved by fitting a

carbonfibre mast, which will normally turn out to be around 20 percent lighter that the equivalent in aluminium.

Many other less noticeable developments have helped to make it easy to handle these big yachts. Compact, efficient diesel engines give plenty of power without taking up too much space, while feathering propellors cut resistance when sailing. Bow thrusters ease the problem of manoeuvring in tight spaces, while powered windlasses and deck winches take the effort out of anchoring and berthing. Small hydraulic cranes are available to hoist the tender on

board, and equipment such as water-making machines and air conditioning has been miniaturized so that it can be fitted into a crowded engine room.

Big cruising yachts used to be very conservative in design, and frankly dull to sail, but in the past few years some really exciting and fast sailing yachts have been built that also offer exceptionally comfortable living quarters down below. The size of these yacht is steadily increasing: to give an example the Perini Navi sailing yacht *Taouey*, built in 1995, is 58 metres (190 feet) in length and displaces 640 tonnes. She has a sail

SUPERYACHTS

Modern power-operated sail-handling systems, such as those fitted to this 37-metre *Perini Navi,* make it possible for big cruising yachts to be handled by a very small crew—indeed, all sail-handling can be performed by just one person. Meanwhile, the highest standards of luxury are made available for the guests aboard the yacht.

area of 1,364 square metres (14,714 square feet), all of which can be controlled by one person, from the helm position. The total crew numbers just twelve. She is a truly impressive cruising yacht.

TECHNIQUES

Choosing or finding a suitable boat may be difficult enough in itself, but learning to sail from scratch without the benefit of professional instruction can be a nightmare unless the new owner makes adequate preparations and has some idea of what to expect.

Whatever your choice of boat, this section on techniques is a simple guide to some of the more common methods of rigging, handling ashore and afloat and what to do in emergencies.

The actual business of going sailing is relatively simple. The skill levels needed to be reasonably competent are not excessive and you often have sufficient space to make your mistakes without endangering yourself or others.

There is, however, one area which should be avoided (as far as it can be) in the early stages of learning to sail, and that is sailing language and terminology. Complicated technical language can easily confuse the newcomer at a time when he or she is having enough problems learning to sail without the additional burden of learning a new language.

To begin with, try to keep to simple everyday descriptions like 'back' and 'front', 'left' and 'right', 'push' and 'pull'; you can learn the proper nautical terms for the various pieces of string and parts of the boat and its rigging as and when you need to.

Even so, some parts of the boat – such as the boom, mast, mainsail and jib – have names which must be used from the start because they have no everyday alternatives, and you will need to spend some time identifying these and working out how they are used.

Rigging an unfamiliar boat can be difficult. Always try to get the vendor to show you where the bits go, especially if it is an unusual craft. Take photographs or make drawings, and mark assembled items with coloured tape to ensure that you can put them together unaided when the time comes.

Choose your first sailing venue with care and try to get an experienced sailor to 'show you the ropes' and teach you the basics. This will get you through the most difficult phase.

By far the best policy is to invest in a suitable sailing course at a reputable sailing school. Once you have sufficient experience to sail in a variety of wind and sea conditions, the next stage is to learn about those official organizations such as the Coastguard or the rescue services and the requirements they place on you: just as there are rules for driving on the roads, there are 'rules of the road' for seafarers. There is also a comprehensive international system of buoyage for marking obstructions and denoting channels, and a set procedure for sending emergency signals.

Finding your way is dependent upon precise navigation, using either traditional methods of dead reckoning or the very latest satellite navigation aids which can plot your latitude and longitude with great accuracy. However, even if your boat has the very latest and best in electronic navigation systems, you should learn how to navigate without it otherwise a power failure could leave you hopelessly lost.

As a casual sailor, especially of dinghies, you need only learn the basics of boat handling and to keep out of the way of anything really big. But if you are the owner of a cruising boat the book work and learning should be a continuous process, perhaps involving attendance at night schools or special navigation and seamanship seminars.

The topics covered in this section are essentially first steps: the basic information is designed to be developed by the reader and to form a solid foundation for further learning. Don't forget, though, that sailing is intended to be a pleasurable way to spend your time, and if you become sufficiently skilful you will have the courage to use your boat to its maximum, and so get the maximum pleasure from it.

HOW A BOAT SAILS

It is true that there is an incredible amount of aerodynamic and hydrodynamic theory involved in how a boat sails, but many sailors have learned about it by a process of trial and error and a rudimentary understanding of the concepts.

All sailboats are equipped with foils: *aerofoils*, which are above the water, and *hydrofoils*, which are below the water. Those above the water – the sails – are used to create power to drive the boat forward; those below the water – the daggerboard, centreboard or keel, and the rudder – are used to prevent the boat sliding sideways or, in the case of the rudder, to change its direction.

The wings of birds and aircraft and the sails of boats rely on a simple principle to enable them to operate. The top surface of a wing, when viewed from the side, is convex, and therefore longer from front to rear than the flat bottom surface is. As a result, air flowing over the top surface has to speed up to reach the rear of the wings at the same time as air flowing over the bottom surface.

The faster an airstream flows across a surface, the lower the pressure it exerts on that surface. So the air pressure on the top surface of a wing is lower than that on the bottom surface, and this lower pressure creates the *lift* that keeps birds and aircraft aloft.

The sail of a dinghy or yacht acts like a vertical wing, with the leeward side of the sail acting like the curved upper surface of a wing and generating the 'lift' that gives sailboats their driving force. This lift force is augmented by the pressure of the wind on the windward side of the sail.

The sail is angled in the airstream so that the lift it generates drives the boat forward, and for the boat to sail efficiently the sail must be set at the correct *angle of attack* to the wind. As an aid to setting the sail at the correct angle, pairs of tell-tales are attached at regular intervals to both sides of the forward part of it to indicate the airflow over the sail.

Tell-tales can be made from coloured wool sewn through the sails, knotted on either side of the cloth to prevent them slipping through. Red and green are used as contrasting port and starboard indicators, and you can see the tell-tales on the leeward side of the sail because sailcloth is semi-transparent when under tension. About three sets on main and jib will help you set the sails correctly most of the time.

At the optimum angle of attack the sail is creating its maximum lift. At this point the tell-tales on both sides of the sail assume the same slightly upward angle throughout most of the forward edge of the sail.

If the sail is pulled in too much, the leeward tell-tale begins to flutter and rotate. This tells you that the sail

HOW SAILS WORK

On a boat with two sails it is important that they act together as a single aerofoil.
1 Jib sheeted in too far, causing an interrupted or turbulent airflow.
2 Sails trimmed correctly, giving a smooth flow of air over both sails with no turbulence.

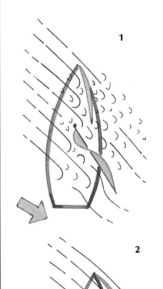
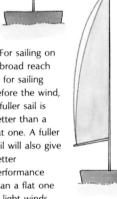

AEROFOIL EFFECT

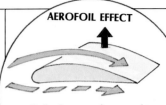

Air flowing over the curved top of an aerofoil has to speed up, creating low pressure, and thus lift, on the upper surface

SAIL SHAPE

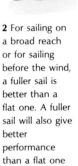

The mainsail should be set to suit the wind and the course sailed. **1** The stronger the wind, the flatter the sail should be. A flat sail is also used when on a close-hauled course.

2 For sailing on a broad reach or for sailing before the wind, a fuller sail is better than a flat one. A fuller sail will also give better performance than a flat one in light winds.

TELL-TALES

These are fine strands of tape or wool which fly free on each side of a sail – red on port, green on starboard.
1 Jib tell-tales parallel: the sail is set correctly.
2 Tell-tales fluttering on leeward side: let out sail or push tiller to leeward.
3 Tell-tales fluttering on windward side: pull in sail or pull tiller to windward.

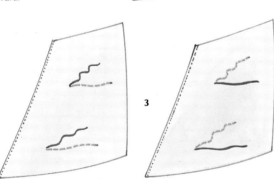

The windward side is normally the one facing the wind, and the leeward side is the one facing away from the wind. With the wind directly behind the boat, however, the side on which the boom is set is designated the lee side.

EFFECTS OF INDIVIDUAL SAILS

WIND

1 Sails set behind the mast tend to turn the bow into the wind.
2 Sails set in front of the mast tend to turn the bow away from the wind.

Each individual sail has a particular effect on the directional stability of the boat.

When balanced together, the turning effects of the sails cancel each other out.

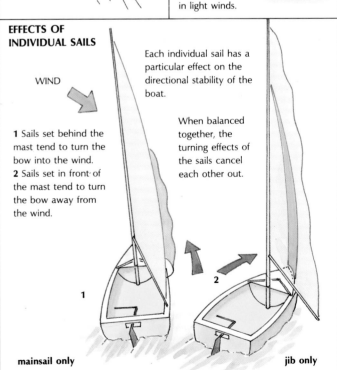

mainsail only   **jib only**

EFFECT OF CENTREBOARD

Wind pressure on the sails pushes the boat sideways as well as forward. The centreboard (or daggerboard) is used to counter this, although as it cannot be stopped completely, sideways motion (called 'leeway') is always present to some extent.

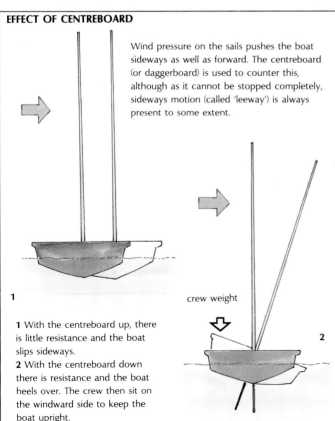

crew weight

1 With the centreboard up, there is little resistance and the boat slips sideways.
2 With the centreboard down there is resistance and the boat heels over. The crew then sit on the windward side to keep the boat upright.

The slot between the jib and the mainsail acts to speed up the flow of air over the mainsail, which improves its performance.

is now at too great an angle of attack and the airflow around the back (leeward) side has broken down into turbulence instead of flowing smoothly.

At this stage, with turbulent airflow over the upper surface of its wings, a bird or aircraft would stall and fall out of the sky. Fortunately, the sailor only loses forward drive, which can be regained by either letting the sail out (toward the fluttering tell-tale) or by pushing the tiller toward the same side as the fluttering tell-tale. When the tell-tales on each side of the sail are flying together, the sail is again creating its maximum drive.

If you let the sail out too much, the windward tell-tale will rotate. This means that the angle of attack is too small and turbulence is occurring on the bottom of the sail. To correct the situation, pull the sail in or pull the tiller toward the same side as the fluttering tell-tale. Again, when the tell-tales on both sides fly together the sail is working correctly.

Single-sailed boats, such as the Optimist and Finn, require sails designed to operate efficiently alone. Boats with two or more sails require each sail to be shaped so as to interact correctly with the others.

For example, the jib of a two-sail boat influences the airflow over the mainsail, and together, especially when the boat is sailing close to the wind, they should act in effect as a single aerofoil. In these circumstances, the front part of the mainsail may not set correctly, and flutter, but this is acceptable because the majority of the sail will be working at maximum efficiency as part of the combined aerofoil.

This efficient working of the mainsail is due to the effect of the slot formed by the gap between the overlapping parts of the jib and the mainsail. This slot constricts the air flowing through it, creating a pressure difference between the air at the windward end of the slot and the air at its leeward end. Because of this pressure difference, the airflow through the slot accelerates.

This means that the airflow over the convex leeward side of the mainsail is faster than it would be if the jib were not there. The air pressure on that side of the sail is correspondingly lower, and so the lift it generates is increased.

So the effect of the slot between two sails is to improve the overall efficiency of the sail behind the slot,

such as a mainsail. This is especially so in sailboats with masthead rigs, where the jib or genoa reaches to the top of the mast and the relatively small mainsail is inefficient by itself.

As well as generating driving forces, individual sails have . a marked effect on the directional stability of the boat. Sails in front of the mast turn the bow away from the wind, and sails behind the mast turn the bow toward the wind. When properly balanced, the sails cancel out these turning movements to produce forward drive.

The combination and interaction of sails, keels, centreboards and rudders determine the sailing characteristics of all boats. When considering the overall efficiency of your own boat, it is important to appreciate that the sails act as a single unit and so they must be tuned together on every point of sailing. The keels and rudder also act as a single unit and must be tuned together, although except in the case of a lifting keel or centreboard only the rudder angle can be changed to tune them.

The keel(s) or centreboard and the rudder(s) act as hydrofoils, which means that the water flow acts on them in the same way as the airflow acts on the sails, creating 'lift' on them if they move through the water at an angle to the forward motion of the boat.

The primary function of keels and centreboards is to reduce the tendency of the boat to move sideways as well as forward when under sail. This sideways motion or *leeway* can never be totally eliminated, but the resistance of the keel or centreboard to being pushed sideways through the water reduces it to a minimum. However, one side effect of this resistance is that it causes the boat to heel over, which is why dinghy sailors often have to use their weight to keep their craft upright.

In the case of fixed keels the most you can do in the way of tuning is to ensure that the finished surface is as smooth as you can get it so that it creates the minimum of drag. Centreboards may not be the perfect hydrofoil section, but they do enable you to adjust the amount of board that is exposed beneath the boat. This is especially important because each point of sailing requires just sufficient centreboard to combat the sideways force generated by the sails.

When sailing as close to the wind as possible you need all the centreboard down, but when sailing downwind you need none at all, or maybe just a little to give some lateral stability.

BASIC SAILING MANOEUVRES

If you can drive a car you may remember how, when you were learning, operating all the controls in the right order was often difficult. As an experienced driver, however, you seldom have to think about what you are doing because your experience has built up what amount to automatic reflex actions.

Sailing a dinghy presents you with similar sequences of operations which, at the outset, will often appear confusing but which soon slot together into reflex actions.

Awareness of the wind direction is the key to successful sailing, and so the first essential is to develop such an awareness. Smoke and flags will give you an indication of wind direction, as will surface waves and wavelets, although these are more subtle. A masthead flag or 'windex' is another useful, and accurate, indicator. However, being able to sense the wind's direction by the feel of it blowing on your face or ears is a useful skill, and one which is essential in competitive sailing.

Getting the boat sailing, and controlling its speed, is the function of the set of the sails. The optimum set of the sails is the one that allows them to work at their maximum efficiency, and so drive the boat at maximum speed.

It follows that to vary the speed from maximum it is necessary to adjust the sails away from their optimum position to give the exact amount of drive you want. This is especially important when manoeuvring to pick up a mooring, to come alongside another boat or to approach a landing place.

Basically, to slow down you let the sails out, and/or turn the boat toward the wind without adjusting the sails. To get the boat moving faster, either pull the sails in to the position that gives you the speed you want, or turn away from the wind.

The principal points of sailing – angles to the wind at which a boat can sail – are *reach, close reach, close-hauled, broad reach* and *run.*

For beginners, the reach (or beam reach) is the key to all manoeuvres, and to the experts it is one of the most exciting points of sail. During the reach, the boat is sailing across the wind, and so the wind is blowing at right angles to the boat and directly onto the skipper's back. (The skipper of the boat is the person holding the tiller and mainsheet, and he or she should *always* sit on the windward side of the boat, facing the sail.) The centreboard should be half down, and the sails pulled in far enough to set them.

As with all vehicles, it is essential to know how to stop your boat. Boats do not have brakes, and only stop completely when they are aground, anchored or moored. In the basic *hove-to* position, though, the boat is almost at a standstill and that is the best that can be achieved once afloat. In this position, the sails are let out so that they no longer convert the wind into a driving force but flap like flags.

To heave-to on a reach, let the sails out to their fullest extent, so that the boom is against the leeward shroud and the jib is almost at right angles to the centreline of the boat. The windex or masthead flag will show the wind at 90° to the centreline, and the boat will virtually stop. When you are learning to sail, one of the useful features of the reach is that it is the point of sailing that offers the greatest safety when the

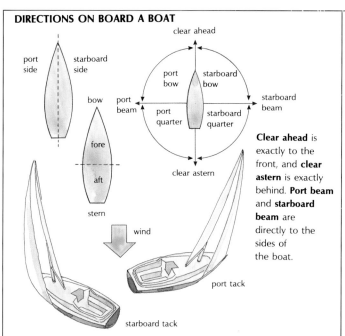

DIRECTIONS ON BOARD A BOAT

port side
starboard side
bow
fore
aft
stern
wind

clear ahead
port bow
starboard bow
port beam
starboard beam
port quarter
starboard quarter
clear astern

Clear ahead is exactly to the front, and **clear astern** is exactly behind. **Port beam** and **starboard beam** are directly to the sides of the boat.

port tack
starboard tack

TACKS With the wind over the starboard side (boom on port side) the boat is on a starboard tack. With the wind over the port side (boom on starboard side) the boat is on a port tack.

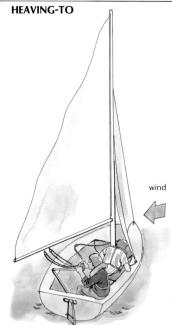

HEAVING-TO

wind

To heave-to, the jib is backed on the windward side and the mainsail eased. The tiller is pushed to leeward to counter the effect of the jib, and the centreboard is set to threequarters down.

In the hove-to position, the boat is almost stationary.

sails are let out.

Experienced sailors also use the reach to heave-to, but with the jib aback (pulled to the windward side) and the tiller pushed away. As the boat *forereaches* – moves forward under its own momentum without any power from the sails – the rudder turns it into the wind while the jib turns it away again. This results in the boat moving in a series of scallops toward and away from the wind.

Another way of stopping or slowing down is to turn the boat toward and into the wind without changing the set of the sails. The boat then slows to the point where it is all but stopped. In an emergency, when things are going wrong or if you have to avoid a collision, turn toward the wind to slow and stop.

To sail on a close reach, begin by sailing on a reach and then push the tiller gently, to turn the boat toward the wind, until the sails just begin to flap. When the boat has turned onto the new course, pull the sails in to set correctly, and move the centreboard from half-down to three-quarters-down to combat sideways drift.

If you turn the boat even farther toward the wind, you will reach a point where the sails – even when they are pulled right in and the centreboard is fully down – will not set and the windward tell-tale will rotate. When this happens, pull the tiller gently until both fully-tensioned sails set correctly. This is the close-hauled point of sailing, which is as close to the wind as the boat will sail.

The boat heels most on this point of sail, and so in stronger winds the crew's weight must be placed as far outboard as possible. To assist in safe sitting-out, toestraps (hiking straps) are fitted at each side of the centreboard casing. These can be adjusted so that the crew can sit right out with his or her backside close to the outer side of the hull. An alternative is to use a trapeze wire.

To sail on a broad reach, start again on the reach and then pull the tiller to turn the boat away from the wind by about 45° and steer a straight course. The sails will appear to be set, but the tell-tales will show that the leeward airflow has broken down. Let the sails out until the tell-tales show that they are set correctly, and raise the centreboard to the quarter-down position.

In strong winds with big seas, the broad reach is the fastest point of sailing, causing the boat to *plane* – to skim over the surface of the water rather than plough through it.

The run is the point of sail when the wind is directly behind the boat. The jib loses most of its drive and should be set on the windward side of the boat (sailing like this, before the wind with the mainsail on one side and the jib on the other, is called *goosewinging*). About six inches of the centreboard should be exposed beneath the boat to give some lateral stability.

Sailing dead downwind can be tricky in strong or gusty winds. If the boat starts to gyrate wildly, the golden rule is to steer it to follow the top of the mast: as the boat rolls to the right, steer right, and as it rolls to the left, steer left.

Remember that any turn *toward* the wind requires the sails to be pulled in and the centreboard to be lowered, and any turn away from the wind requires the sails to be let out and the centreboard raised.

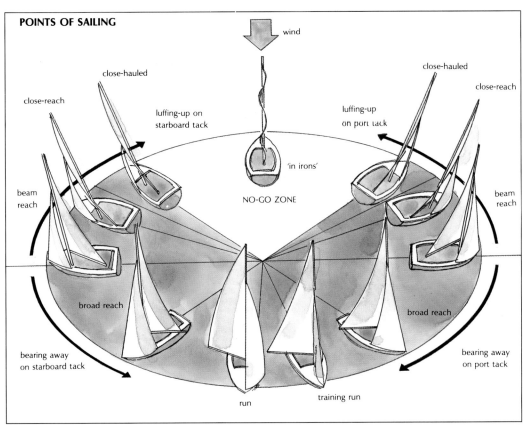

POINTS OF SAILING

wind

close-hauled

close-reach

close-reach

close-hauled

luffing-up on starboard tack

luffing-up on port tack

close-reach

'in irons'

NO-GO ZONE

beam reach

beam reach

broad reach

broad reach

bearing away on starboard tack

bearing away on port tack

run

training run

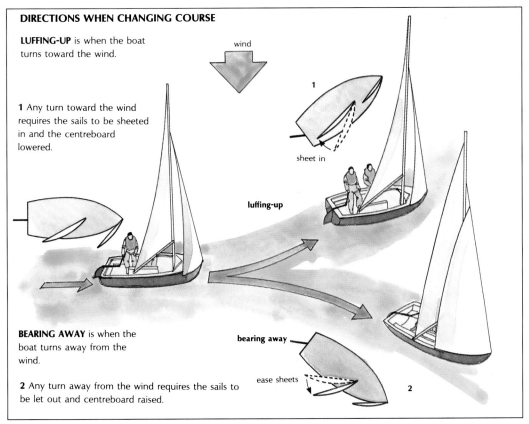

DIRECTIONS WHEN CHANGING COURSE

LUFFING-UP is when the boat turns toward the wind.

1 Any turn toward the wind requires the sails to be sheeted in and the centreboard lowered.

wind

1

sheet in

luffing-up

BEARING AWAY is when the boat turns away from the wind.

2 Any turn away from the wind requires the sails to be let out and centreboard raised.

bearing away

ease sheets

2

CAR TOPPING & TRAILING

One advantage of a small sailing craft is that it is relatively easy to transport on, or behind, a small vehicle. This enables you to keep the craft at home or, if you sail from a club base, to transport it to other sailing venues.

The simplest method is to carry the craft inverted on the vehicle roof, on two bars fitted securely to the existing guttering or into the special roof tracks provided on cars without gutters.

Larger or heavier craft must be trailed on a purpose-built road trailer. To do this, you will need to have your car fitted with a suitable towbar and a connecting socket for the trailer's lighting system. As a general rule, if four reasonably fit

adults cannot lift a boat onto a roof rack, it should be trailed.

Roof racks designed specially to enable you to carry a wide range of summer and winter sports equipment are now widely available. Before you buy any type of roof rack, though, it is essential that you check out the vehicle's handbook to discover the manufacturer's maximum recommended roof loadings. These take into account the aerodynamic loads imposed by bulky objects.

Webbing straps with self-locking, easily-adjusted buckles must be used to secure the load to the vehicle. For added stability, attach a line from the front and back of the load to the respective bumpers (but only

if these offer secure anchoring points for the line).

Loading a dinghy such as a Laser, which has a hull weight of nearly 60 kg (130 pounds), needs careful organization if you have no helpers.

One method is to stand the boat on its transom with its bottom leaning against a wall, and secure it to prevent it falling. Back the vehicle to within about 2 metres (6 feet) of the boat, then gently lower the boat until it makes contact with the rear of the roof rack. Lift the back of the boat and slide it forward onto the rack and beyond its point of balance to its correctly-loaded position. Normally, a boat is correctly loaded when there is an equal amount of overhang beyond the front and rear

roof bars.

If you have a team of helpers, place the boat alongside the vehicle with equal numbers of helpers standing at each side of the boat. To invert it, first lift up one side while pressing down on the other to get it standing vertically on one side. Then push it beyond the vertical with everyone helping to lower the high side to the ground.

With a concerted lift from equal numbers of helpers on each side, get the boat to shoulder height and locate the back of the boat onto the rearmost roof rack bar. Reposition some of the helpers to assist with swinging the front end across onto the rack, and position the craft correctly before securing it.

TYPES OF TRAILER

Right A simple two-wheeled trailer carrying a single dinghy. The boat is lashed to the trailer with ropes at each side as well as at the front.

Below left A four-wheel trailer carrying a small cruiser. The boat is sitting on its keels, and is securely lashed to the trailer at the bow and the stern.

Below right A trailer carrying two dinghies, one inverted above the other. Each of the dinghies seen here has its own launch trailer attached to it, so that it can be launched easily without the road trailer having to go into the water.

Spars, and sometimes sails, may also be carried on roof racks. By far the neatest way is to use a large-diameter, thin-gauge plastic tube which is tailored to accept short spars and rolled-up sails. The tube should be securely attached to the roof bars and have removable end caps, each with a securing lanyard to prevent loss. If you do not use tubes, you must ensure that the spars are securely attached to the racks.

You can lash the boat to the rack with two webbing straps, either one to each roof bar, or criss-crossed over the upturned hull to help stabilize the load. Lash the spars together on the extremities of the bars.

If you prefer to use rope to secure the load, you must use padding (such as sponge rubber or pieces of old carpet) beneath it to protect the hull from abrasion by the rope. The highwayman's or truck driver's hitch is a useful way of tightening down the ropes.

Boats which are too heavy to carry on the roof rack must be trailed behind the vehicle. Again, consult the vehicle's handbook to find the maximum towing weight for it. When calculating towing weights, always add the weight of the boat and all its equipment to the weight of the trailer and then add about 10 percent to allow for extra personal gear.

Each country has specific laws relating to the construction, braking and lighting of trailers, and the display of information on the trailer and the towed vehicle. Check with your local police department or with the supplier of the trailer to ensure that yours conforms to the rules.

The mast of a trailed boat may often be too long to be carried legally on a roof rack, but an adjustable mast support fitted to the front of the trailer will enable the mast to be carried at an angle to clear the roof of the towing vehicle, with the inboard end of the mast located in a specially shaped and padded fitting near the inside of the transom.

Most dinghies require a launching trolley as well as a road trailer, so it's worth investing in one that is designed to load and lock onto the road trailer in one easy movement. This arrangement ensures that the wheel bearings of the road trailers are never immersed (but remember that whether they are immersed or not, they need regular maintenance and lubrication to ensure their reliability).

Protecting a trailed boat is of great importance because road debris, silt-laden rainwater and oil all harm the highly-polished surfaces. Custom top and bottom covers should be used to enclose the boat and its gear completely. If you keep your boat outside, the top cover should be made from a plasticized cloth which keeps rainwater out.

TOPPING AND TRAILING

This sequence of pictures shows a small dinghy being put onto the roof rack of a car, and a trailer carrying a larger boat being hooked to the car's towbar. First, the small dinghy is taken from its launch trolley and placed, inverted, on the roof rack (**1**), and then securely lashed in place with webbing straps (**2** and **3**). Next, the trailer is prepared for towing; here, a board carrying lights, reflectors and the car's registration number is fixed to the stern of the boat (**4**). The rules for marking a trailer in this way vary from one country to another, so check with the relevant authorities if you are planning to take your boat abroad on a trailer. Finally, the small dinghy's launch trolley has been secured on top of it, and the trailer is hooked to the towbar (**5**).

RIGGING A DINGHY

Rigging a dinghy entails fitting the mast, attaching its supporting wires (if fitted) and the boom, and fitting the ropes or wires that haul up the sails and the ropes that control them.

Singlehanded (one-person) boats usually have a single sail, fitted onto an unstayed (unsupported) mast housed in a substantial tube or mast support at the front of the boat. The Optimist, Laser, Sunfish and Topper dinghies are examples boats using this type of mast. In the case of the Laser, the mast is made up of two pieces which slot together like a fishing rod.

Two-person boats, and those which have two or more sails, usually have a mast which is supported (stayed) by three wires. The bottom of the mast (mast foot) is either housed on the deck (deck-stepped) or inside the boat (keel-stepped).

A fixed mast foot has a tenon which fits snugly into a mortice cut into a wooden pad. An adjustable mast foot fits into a track with adjustable pins.

The U-shaped type of adjustable track is drilled at regular intervals to accept the two pins that are inserted to prevent the mast foot slipping forward or back once the position has been chosen. Another type, the inverted T-bar, accepts a grooved mast foot and uses a single pin to locate the mast once it has been positioned.

The mast may be a simple tube (as on the Optimist, Laser, Sunfish and Topper), or a complicated tapered aluminium extrusion with an integral groove to accept the front (luff) of the mainsail.

The foot of the mainsail fits into a groove running along the top of the main boom. The main boom is the horizontal spar, made of aluminium or wood, attached to the aft side of the mast by a fitting called the gooseneck. This may be fixed in a permanent position, or be a sliding fitting that can be adjusted up or down to alter the boom height.

The tack of the mainsail is locked into position by a fitting at the foward end of the boom, and the clew is secured by a line called the clew outhaul. This is lashed to a fitting at the aft end of the boom and used to tension the foot of the sail.

The sail is tensioned overall by a fitting called the kicking strap, kicker or boom vang, which is attached to the underside of the boom, about a quarter of the way from the mast, and to a shackle at the base of the mast. It tensions the sail by pulling down on the boom.

Most tube masts (those of the Optimist and Sunfish are exceptions) fit into a pocket or sleeve at the front of the mainsail, and you should fit the sail to the mast before putting the mast into the hull of the boat. Once the mast is in place, the sail will catch the wind and so the front of the boat should *always* be pointed *into*

the wind while rigging.

Stayed masts are normally supported by three wires, one at each side and one at the front. The two side wires are called shrouds, and the wire to the front (bow) of the boat is the forestay.

The wires are usually attached to a mast fitting called the hounds, which is about threequarters of the way up the mast, by strip shackles or clevis pins. Alternatively, the wires may be swaged into T-bar fittings that slot into holes in the mast wall. Catamaran wires are usually taken to a single large shackle attached to the front edge of the mast.

At their bottom ends, shrouds are attached to the shroud plates by lanyards, adjustable bottle screws or rigging plates. Simple shrouds finish in an eye that is reinforced against wear by a stainless steel thimble.

The forestay, which on modern dinghies is there to keep the mast up when the jib is not rigged, is often kept in place by a simple lanyard lashing. Older boats have bottle screws, especially if the jib is attached to the forestay with metal hanks.

Tensioning the shrouds beyond

Above *Once the mast has been stepped, the supporting forestay and shrouds are tensioned.*
Right *The rudder and tiller should be fitted after the mast and sails have been rigged.*

the normal supporting role causes the mast to bend forward in the middle, while adjusting the forestay determines the amount of rake (forward or backward slope) of the mast. Different wind conditions require different settings of the mast.

In addition to the three supporting wires, the mast will be fitted with wire or rope halyards that are used to raise and lower the sail. These are usually inside the mast and exit at the bottom through pulley blocks contained in a multiple sheave box. This is usually an alloy casting that also incorporates the mast foot.

The jib halyard sheave is at the front of the mast just below the forestay fitting, and the spinnaker halyard sheave is above the forestay. The halyards may be led down to small swivel blocks or fixed rings. The mainsail halyard sheave is often incorporated into the mast head fit-

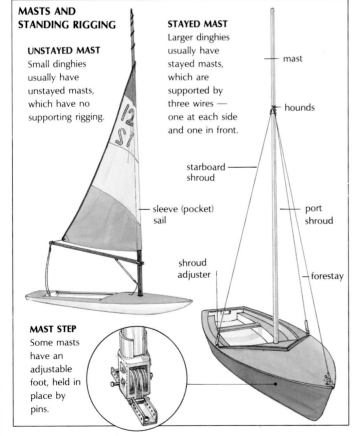

MASTS AND STANDING RIGGING

UNSTAYED MAST
Small dinghies usually have unstayed masts, which have no supporting rigging.

STAYED MAST
Larger dinghies usually have stayed masts, which are supported by three wires — one at each side and one in front.

- mast
- hounds
- starboard shroud
- sleeve (pocket) sail
- port shroud
- shroud adjuster
- forestay

MAST STEP
Some masts have an adjustable foot, held in place by pins.

STEPPING A DECK-STEPPED MAST

STEPPING A KEEL-STEPPED MAST

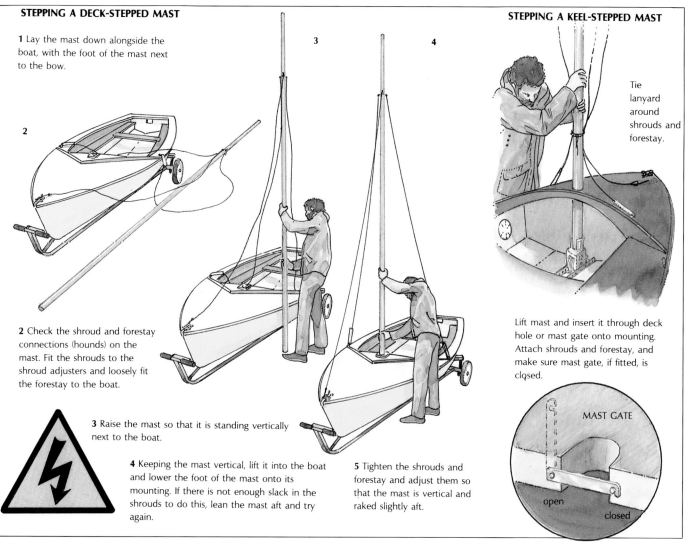

1 Lay the mast down alongside the boat, with the foot of the mast next to the bow.

2 Check the shroud and forestay connections (hounds) on the mast. Fit the shrouds to the shroud adjusters and loosely fit the forestay to the boat.

3 Raise the mast so that it is standing vertically next to the boat.

4 Keeping the mast vertical, lift it into the boat and lower the foot of the mast onto its mounting. If there is not enough slack in the shrouds to do this, lean the mast aft and try again.

5 Tighten the shrouds and forestay and adjust them so that the mast is vertical and raked slightly aft.

Tie lanyard around shrouds and forestay.

Lift mast and insert it through deck hole or mast gate onto mounting. Attach shrouds and forestay, and make sure mast gate, if fitted, is closed.

MAST GATE

open

closed

ting and is at the back of the mast inside the sail track.

Older or very simple rigs may have external halyards that run through pully blocks in the appropriate position for main, jib and spinnaker.

To ensure trouble-free identifi-cation and ease of rigging, always lash or tape halyards to the mast before unstepping it to ensure that they will not get in the way when you next come to step the mast.

To rig a deck-stepped mast, first check that the boat is stable, prefer-ably attached to its trolley or trailer, or on tyres. Lay the mast alongside the boat, with the foot next to the bow. Attach the shrouds to the boat, then fasten the forestay loosely so that when you start to raise the mast it will support it.

Raise the mast to a vertical pos-ition and lift it, against the pull of the forestay, onto its deck mounting. Adjust the shrouds and the forestay so that the mast is raked slightly aft (sloping to the rear).

To ensure that the mast doesn't lean to one side, use the main halyard as a gauge to equal up the shrouds. Apply sufficient tension to the shrouds to produce a 'twang' when you pluck them.

Keel-stepped masts may have to be fed through a hole in the deck, or located in a mast gate. Whichever you have, you need to be inside the boat to place the vertical mast into position. It is advisable to use helpers to steady the mast with the wires, or to pass it to you.

When the mast is in place, lead the halyards to their respective control positions at the front, centre or rear of the boat, and then fit the boom and sails.

Before stepping any mast, it is essential to check that you are well clear of any overhead power lines. Also ensure that you can wheel the boat to the water without the mast touching or even coming close to the power lines.

SAIL RIGGING & REEFING

Sails are extremely sophisticated aerofoils constructed from carefully-shaped panels of closely-woven synthetic sailcloth. Masts and booms are carefully matched to the cut of the sails to give a wide range of sail shapes to suit changing wind and sea conditions, and sails are controlled by ropes which are termed *running rigging* to differentiate them from the *standing rigging* supporting the mast.

To understand the different shapes required of a single sail, we can compare them to the shapes and sections of birds' wings. High speed birds, such as swifts and hawks, have narrow, curved wings which are very thin (flat) in cross-section.

Similarly, a flat sail is needed in strong winds. This is achieved by tightening the boom vang (kicking strap) to tension the sail. This bends the top of the mast toward the stern, and the middle of the mast is bowed forward. The front edge of the sail – the luff – is stretched tight by the halyard and Cunningham tackle, and in section the sail is flat.

In light winds, the sail controls are eased to produce a straight mast and a full-section sail similar to the thick wing of a soaring bird such as an eagle or a buzzard.

Sails come in a variety of shapes and can be triangular or trapezoidal (with four sides). It helps to remember that the tack of a sail faces forward in the boat and the clew is aft. The foot of the sail is always at the bottom.

The foot of the mainsail can be attached to the boom loose-footed, with a lashing at the tack and clew, or it can be laced along its length with rope. More commonly, the clew is fed into a groove in the top of the boom and hauled out to the boom end, the tack being kept in place with a tack pin. The clew is often attached to a rope or wire outhaul to enable the foot to be tensioned.

Halyards are used to haul the sails up the mast or forestay. The simplest rope halyards are tied to the head of the sails either by passing the rope through and tying a double thumb knot, or by the traditional halyard hitch. The usual way, though, is to use a shackle, preferably the type with a captive pin. At their bottom ends, halyards are secured to simple cleats or the wire part is tensioned by a Highfield lever or muscle box.

The jib is either set on its own internal wire stay, or attached to the forestay with plastic or metal clips called hanks. The jib tack attaches to the stem headfitting, which secures the forestay to the bow.

Before hoisting the jib you must attach the jib sheets, either by a shackle (which is dangerous) or by tying a bowline to the clew or, if you wish to use one piece of rope, by tying double overhand knots each side of the clew.

The jib is controlled by ropes led down either side of the mast to fairleads. These can be simple solid bullseyes, or sophisticated ratchet blocks which help to take the strain out of holding the ropes, which are called sheets. Alternatively, the rope can be jammed into a crab's-claw jamming block or a serrated cleat while sailing.

Small jibs normally sheet inside the shrouds, but large genoas sheet outside; spinnaker sheets are rigged outside everything, including the forestay. The spinnaker is usually housed in a bag or pouch adjacent to the mast, and its halyard is led outside the jib and under the jib sheets. When the spinnaker pole is placed on the mast, the windward jib sheet must be on top of the pole.

Numerous devices are used to vary the sheeting position of the spinnaker sheets while sailing. The most common is the Barber hauler, situated just forward of the shrouds and consisting of a ring or pulley.

The various sail controls on a boat are designed to change the shape of the sails to cope with a wide variety of wind conditions. Halyards, for example, control luff tension, and the stronger the wind the greater the tension needed.

Another method of tensioning the luff of a sail is to use a Cunningham tackle, a tensioning line which runs through the Cunningham eyelet, a hole in the sail a little way above the tack. The Cunningham tackle is adjusted so that, when the boat is sailing, the luff has a smooth curve. The luff is too slack if it develops scallops or horizontal creases, and too tight if it has vertical creases.

The boom vang or kicker is attached to the bottom of the boom and runs from there to the foot of the mast, or to the kingpost if the mast is deck-stepped. The vang is usually a multipart purchase with a mechanical advantage ranging from 4:1 to 32:1, and its purpose is to pull the boom forward and down so as to control mast bend, leech shape and sail cross-section.

The mainsheet is usually a 4:1 system used to position the boom at the optimum angle to the wind. It can

This boat is aft-sheeted, the mainsheet being led from the end of the boom to the transom.

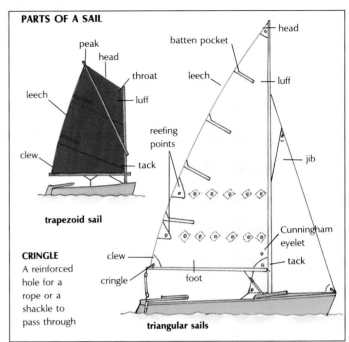

PARTS OF A SAIL

peak · head · throat · luff · leech · clew · tack

trapezoid sail

CRINGLE
A reinforced hole for a rope or a shackle to pass through

head · batten pocket · leech · luff · jib · reefing points · Cunningham eyelet · tack · clew · cringle · foot

triangular sails

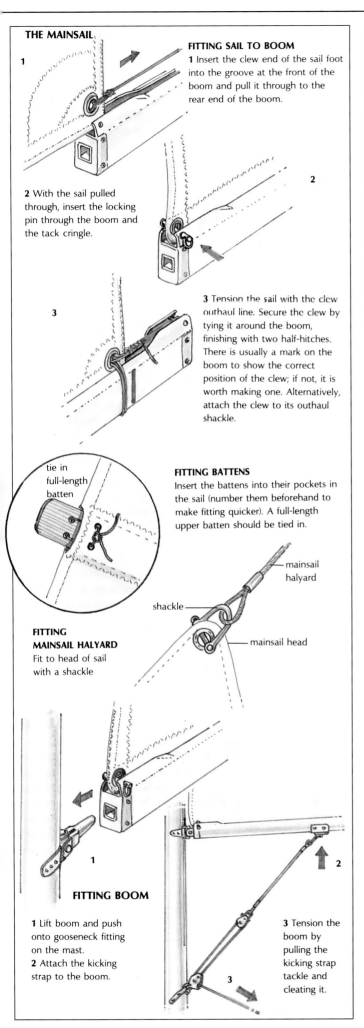

THE MAINSAIL

1

FITTING SAIL TO BOOM

1 Insert the clew end of the sail foot into the groove at the front of the boom and pull it through to the rear end of the boom.

2 With the sail pulled through, insert the locking pin through the boom and the tack cringle.

2

3

3 Tension the sail with the clew outhaul line. Secure the clew by tying it around the boom, finishing with two half-hitches. There is usually a mark on the boom to show the correct position of the clew; if not, it is worth making one. Alternatively, attach the clew to its outhaul shackle.

tie in full-length batten

FITTING BATTENS

Insert the battens into their pockets in the sail (number them beforehand to make fitting quicker). A full-length upper batten should be tied in.

mainsail halyard

shackle

FITTING MAINSAIL HALYARD

Fit to head of sail with a shackle

mainsail head

1

FITTING BOOM

1 Lift boom and push onto gooseneck fitting on the mast.
2 Attach the kicking strap to the boom.

2

3 Tension the boom by pulling the kicking strap tackle and cleating it.

3

THE JIB

3

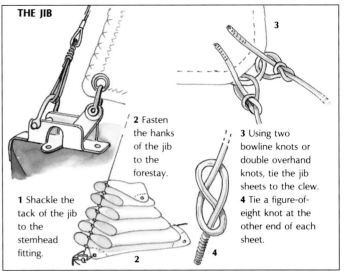

2 Fasten the hanks of the jib to the forestay.

1 Shackle the tack of the jib to the stemhead fitting.

2

3 Using two bowline knots or double overhand knots, tie the jib sheets to the clew.
4 Tie a figure-of-eight knot at the other end of each sheet.

4

SLAB REEFING

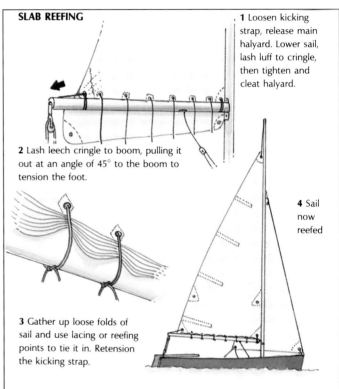

1 Loosen kicking strap, release main halyard. Lower sail, lash luff to cringle, then tighten and cleat halyard.

2 Lash leech cringle to boom, pulling it out at an angle of 45° to the boom to tension the foot.

4 Sail now reefed

3 Gather up loose folds of sail and use lacing or reefing points to tie it in. Retension the kicking strap.

be led to the boom from the transom (aft sheeting) or from the centreboard casing (centre sheeting).

If the wind is too strong to carry full sails, most dinghies can be reefed. Aft sheeting enables you to reef the sail by rolling it around the boom, but the gooseneck fitting at the forward end must have a square shank to prevent the boom rotating when reefed.

To reef a dinghy sail when afloat, heave-to and lower the mainsail, then stow it securely so that it doesn't blow away. With one crew at the tack and one at the clew, first tuck 6 inches of the leech around the boom. Roll the boom, pulling the sail out tight with each roll.

Remove battens as you come to them. Usually, a reef to the first batten is sufficient, but in very strong winds you need small sails so don't hesitate to reef to the second

batten. If you want to use the boom vang, you should make up a webbing reefing strop, or use the sail bag. Roll it in with the last two complete reefs and attach the vang to the strop. Finally, secure the boom to the gooseneck and hoist the sail. The boom should never be lower than parallel to the water after a reef.

Slab reefing will be necessary if you have centre sheeting. In its simplest form, two sets of reef cringles (eyes) at the luff and leech will enable you to lash the sail to the boom in an emergency. Sophisticated systems attach to ram's-horns (hooks) at the gooseneck and have leech lines and jammers to control the leech.

Training dinghies such as the Wayfarer may use smaller mainsails and jibs in strong winds. The jibs require alternate or adjustable fairleads to ensure the correct sheeting angle for the smaller sail.

USING THE CENTREBOARD & RUDDER

Together with the sails, the rudder and centreboard have a major influence on the speed and direction of the boat.

The purpose of the adjustable centreboard or daggerboard (and of the fixed keel of a yacht) is to counteract the boat's tendency to drift sideways as well as move forward when it's under sail.

A centreboard is a small, retractable keel that pivots up into a specially shaped trunking or box on the centreline of a dinghy or cruiser. Some cruisers have an outside stub ballast keel of iron which carries a pivoting plate of iron or steel. Others—lifting keel yachts—have internal ballast plates incorporating a trunking and centreboard.

The advantage of a centreboard over a daggerboard or a fixed keel is that it usually retracts of its own accord if the boat sails into shallow water. It can also be adjusted infinitely from fully down to fully up to match the exact point of sailing you chose.

The sideways drift of a sailboat (called leeway) decreases as the boat sails farther away from the wind. When you're sailing with the wind behind your dinghy there will be no leeway and thus no need for a centreboard, so you should retract it fully.

At the other extreme, when you're sailing close-hauled, the leeway will be at its maximum and so you should adjust the centreboard to its fully-down position. On a close reach, set the centreboard to three-quarters down, on a beam reach to half down, and on a broad reach to a quarter down.

In strong winds, reduce the values by a quarter for beam reach and above but leave a quarter down for the run to provide some lateral stability.

It is well worth laying your boat on its side to observe the positions of the centreboard and to mark the casing with 'down' values—down, threequarters, half, quarter and up. This will help you to set the centreboard quickly to the position you want.

Two areas to watch closely for damage are the gasket through which the centreboard extends—usually a nylon-based membrane—and the edges and bottom of the board.

The daggerboard has the same function as the centreboard, but is slid vertically up and down instead of being pivoted. Its main advantage is that it requires only a small opening in the bottom of the boat, thus eliminating the drag caused by a large centreboard slot.

Its drawbacks are that it jams if the boat sails in too-shallow water and can even damage the hull if the grounding is severe, and you have to take care not raise the board too high when gybing or it will foul the boom, causing an immediate capsize.

Lowering your centreboard or daggerboard will cause the boat to heel, because the board is resisting the sideways drift of the boat. To correct the heeling, you should move your weight farther outboard so as to bring the boat upright again.

Heeling, even if it's only slight, will cause the boat to turn, because the previously symmetrical shape of its waterplane (the area of the hull surface in contact with the water) is transformed into an asymmetrical shape when heeled. The rudder is often used to counteract such a heel-induced turn, as when, for example, a boat is hit by a gust and twists round into the wind.

You may also find that you have to use the rudder a lot to keep the boat on course when the centreboard is down. If you have to keep pulling the tiller towards you, raising the centreboard slightly should cure the problem; if you have to keep pushing the tiller away from you, lower the centreboard a little more.

Rudders come in a wide variety of shapes and sizes. Their principal task is to make large course alterations when tacking or gybing. Their secondary function, of great importance to the skilled sailor, is to act as a trim tab to correct the balance of the boat as it responds to wind and waves.

The simplest is the transom-hung fixed rudder of the Optimist, but

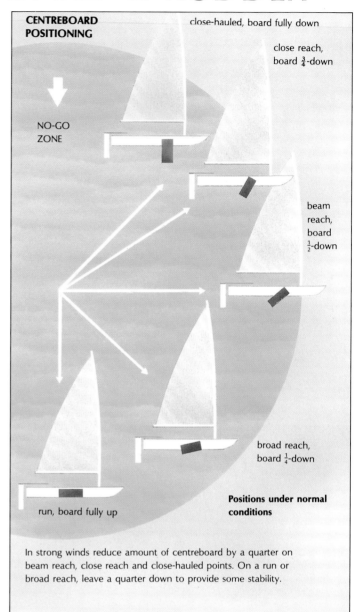

CENTREBOARD POSITIONING

NO-GO ZONE

close-hauled, board fully down

close reach, board ¾-down

beam reach, board ½-down

broad reach, board ¼-down

run, board fully up

Positions under normal conditions

In strong winds reduce amount of centreboard by a quarter on beam reach, close reach and close-hauled points. On a run or broad reach, leave a quarter down to provide some stability.

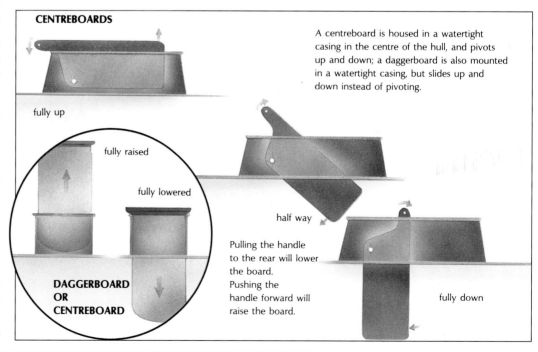

CENTREBOARDS

fully up

fully raised

fully lowered

DAGGERBOARD OR CENTREBOARD

A centreboard is housed in a watertight casing in the centre of the hull, and pivots up and down; a daggerboard is also mounted in a watertight casing, but slides up and down instead of pivoting.

half way

Pulling the handle to the rear will lower the board. Pushing the handle forward will raise the board.

fully down

most dinghies have an articulated lifting rudder which kicks up when striking an obstruction. The transom-bug rudder of the long-keeled ex-Olympic Dragon is protected by the keel itself.

The most vulnerable type is the modern spade rudder which protrudes through the bottom of the boat. To withstand the stresses and strains of sailing it must be strongly constructed of high-grade materials.

The rudder is operated by means of the tiller and works by swinging the stern of the boat around: the stern moves in the same direction as the tiller is moved.

When you move the tiller to the right (to starboard), the rudder moves to the left (to port) and swings the stern to starboard. This turns the bow to port. Similarly, moving the tiller to port causes the bow to turn to starboard.

The reverse happens when you are sailing backwards. Then, the stern moves in the opposite direction to the movement of the tiller, and the bow moves in the same direction as the tiller.

You and your crew should always sit on the windward side of the boat with your backs to the wind. So when you push the tiller away from you, the boat will turn into the wind, and when you pull it towards you, the boat will turn away from the wind. Handle the rudder sensitively, because any violent or excessive rudder movement will have a braking effect on the boat.

Most dinghies are fitted with a tiller extension, attached to the end of the tiller by means of a universal joint so that it can be swivelled both horizontally and vertically. This allows you to move around in the boat and to position your weight correctly while still retaining full control of the tiller.

You should sit with the tiller extension at the side of your body, holding it in your right hand when you're sitting on the port side and in your left hand when you're on the starboard side. Grip the extension as you would a dagger, so that you can move the tiller away from you by pushing the extension and towards you by pulling it.

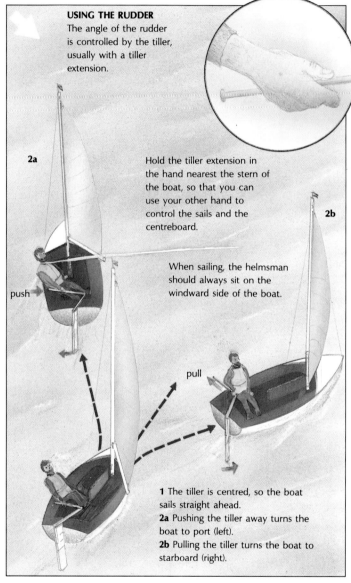

USING THE RUDDER
The angle of the rudder is controlled by the tiller, usually with a tiller extension.

2a

Hold the tiller extension in the hand nearest the stern of the boat, so that you can use your other hand to control the sails and the centreboard.

2b

When sailing, the helmsman should always sit on the windward side of the boat.

push

pull

1 The tiller is centred, so the boat sails straight ahead.
2a Pushing the tiller away turns the boat to port (left).
2b Pulling the tiller turns the boat to starboard (right).

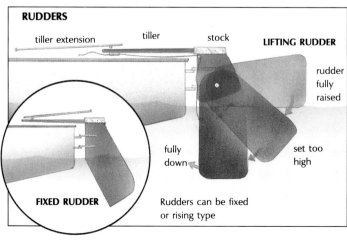

RUDDERS

tiller extension   tiller   stock   **LIFTING RUDDER**

rudder fully raised

fully down

set too high

FIXED RUDDER

Rudders can be fixed or rising type

DAGGER GRIP:
Dinghies fitted with centre mainsheets must be tacked and gybed with the skipper facing forward. The tiller extension is always held across the body at approximately 45 degrees to the vertical and the fore and aft lines. The most natural way to hold the extension is in the 'dagger grip' with the palm toward the body and the thumb extended toward the tip of the extension.

LAUNCH & RECOVERY

If you keep your boat at the water's edge, you have to learn how to launch and recover it in a wide range of wind and water conditions, and sailing on tidal waters adds the complication of tides, which determine the amount of slipway or beach exposed at launching or recovery time.

If you trailer your boat to different sailing venues (or carry it to them on the roof of your car), you face the additional problem of finding a suitable place to launch it and somewhere to leave your vehicle and trailer once you're afloat.

Trailers, by law in many countries, should not be immersed in water because of the inevitable disintegration of the wheel bearings and the seizing of the braking mechanisms.

For that reason, except when dealing with keelboats and very heavy dinghies, a launching trolley is the most commonly-used means of transporting the boat from car to water and back again. Car parking and launching charges are usually paid in advance.

Thorough pre-launch preparation is essential, whether your boat is kept near the water or trailered to the venue. As soon as you arrive at the sailing site you should check on the wind direction, the sea state and, where applicable, the times of high and low water. You should also check out the local weather forecast—listen for it on your car radio, or ask at the harbourmaster's office—and any other safety information applicable to the area.

Your planning should also take account of the fact that once the boat is afloat, someone must hold it while the launching trolley is returned to its allotted parking place. This is no problem if you're sailing two-handed, but if you're going out alone, you will need to arrange for someone to help you with the launch.

Sailing small craft requires considerable personal and boat preparation. Before you change into your sailing clothing, rig the boat to the point where all that is left is to hoist and set the sails, and leave the boat where it will not block the launching area while you change. This may be in the park, or on a wide slipway or beach, close to the water alongside other prepared boats.

Before launching, face the boat into the wind prior to hoisting the sails, and always launch with the bows pointing as near as possible into the wind if the sails are already hoisted.

When you are launching from a weather shore (where the wind is blowing from the land to the water),

Above *Always launch with the bows pointing as near as possible into the wind.* **Below far right** *Unless you lower the mainsail first, you may arrive on a lee shore faster than you expected.*

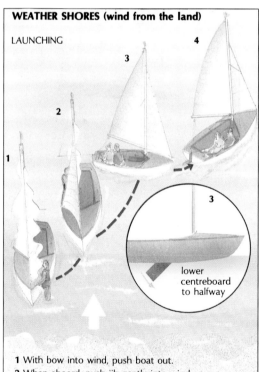

WEATHER SHORES (wind from the land)

LAUNCHING

lower centreboard to halfway

1 With bow into wind, push boat out.
2 When aboard, push jib gently into wind so that the boat drifts backward into deeper water, and push tiller away.
3 Lower centreboard to halfway position, release and sheet in jib.
4 Sheet in mainsail, steer away from the shore, setting sails correctly.

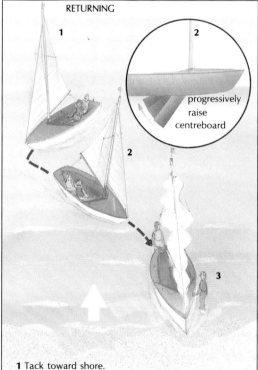

RETURNING

progressively raise centreboard

1 Tack toward shore.
2 Approach on a close reach course, raising the centreboard progressively as the boat sails into shallower water.
3 Point boat into wind, jump out and bring boat ashore.

LEE SHORES (wind from the water)

LAUNCHING

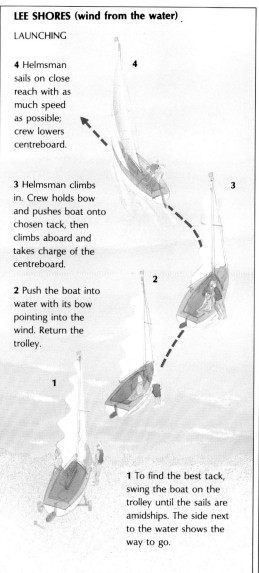

4 Helmsman sails on close reach with as much speed as possible; crew lowers centreboard.

3 Helmsman climbs in. Crew holds bow and pushes boat onto chosen tack, then climbs aboard and takes charge of the centreboard.

2 Push the boat into water with its bow pointing into the wind. Return the trolley.

1 To find the best tack, swing the boat on the trolley until the sails are amidships. The side next to the water shows the way to go.

RECOVERY

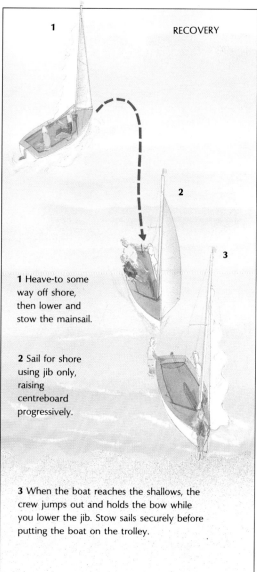

1 Heave-to some way off shore, then lower and stow the mainsail.

2 Sail for shore using jib only, raising centreboard progressively.

3 When the boat reaches the shallows, the crew jumps out and holds the bow while you lower the jib. Stow sails securely before putting the boat on the trolley.

site and jump out as the boat touches the bottom or comes alongside a landing stage.

You can take the boat out of the water with the sails still hoisted, if you wish, but take care to keep the bows pointing into the wind at all times while you do so.

When you are launching from a lee shore (where the wind is blowing from the water to the land), things look markedly different. The wind feels stronger, the waves are larger and break noisily on the shore. Exposed beaches can have waves up to $1\frac{1}{2}$ metres high, which pose a considerable hazard to all but the most experienced sailors.

Assuming the waves are reasonable, and that conditions are suitable for you to go sailing, you must first determine how you are going to get away from the launching area, because the wind and the waves will be pushing you back.

You can row, paddle or sail your boat away from the shore. If you sail, you have to choose the tack which gives you the best angle to the wind. Find this before you enter the water by raising the sails and swinging the trolley until the sails are amidships. Then, the side that is nearer the water indicates the way to go—if the right side is the nearer, sail right; if the left side is the nearer, sail left.

Push the trolley into the water until the boat floats, and have someone (your crew, or a helper) hold the bow while you return the trolley. When you've done that, climb aboard and check the rudder, centreboard and sail controls.

Next, the person holding the bow should pull the boat forward and to the chosen tack and, if he or she is your crew, climb aboard from the windward side and take immediate charge of the centreboard.

Boat speed is the key to getting away from a lee shore. Concentrate on sailing as fast as possible on a close reach, using the mainsail for power. As the depth increases, the crew should lower the centreboard until the boat can be sailed away. Negotiate the waves by pointing into them as they break and bearing away as soon as they have passed.

Returning to a lee shore requires skill and judgement. Very experienced sailors sail in at full speed, round up to 180 degrees in the shallows to face the wind, jump out and back their boat up on to the recovery area.

For the less experienced, though, it will be prudent to heave-to some way off shore, lower and stow the mainsail, and sail in under jib only until the boat reaches the shallows, enabling the crew to jump out and hold the bow while the jib is lowered.

launching is a relatively simple affair. The land affords some shelter and the waves are virtually non-existent. When you trundle the trolley into the water, the boat will float before the water reaches your knees, and it is then a simple matter to pull the trolley out and return it to the park while someone holds the boat to stop it drifting away.

When all is ready, climb aboard and back the jib (that is, push it gently into the wind) so that the boat drifts backward into deeper water. Then release the jib and sheet it on its correct side, lower the centreboard to its halfway position, and sheet in the mainsail to give additional power before bearing away to sail out from the shore.

Returning to a weather shore requires a tacking (zigzag) approach to bring the boat to one side of the launching area. Make the final approach on a close reach and pay particular attention to the centreboard, which should be raised progressively as the boat sails into shallower water.

The final manoeuvre is to point the boat into the wind at the landing

PONTOONS, HOISTS & MOORINGS

Most day sailing dinghies and many keelboats are kept ashore, and so even though many clubs have launching slipways, floating pontoons and finger jetties are increasingly used to ease the congestion at the end of the slipway on race days and at weekends. Many American and European clubs provide electric docking hoists which are operated by boat owners, while heavier boats and keelboats are often kept afloat on a permanent mooring, and the crew either row out in a tender or are ferried out by club launches.

Prior preparation is the key to all successful launching operations, so make sure your boat is fully prepared for sailing before you move it from its land base, floating dock or mooring. Then all you have to do once you are ready to sail off is to hoist whichever sail (or sails) is appropriate to the conditions, just as you would when launching from a beach.

If your boat is berthed on a pontoon, it will usually be chocked upright with padded 'knees' or wedge-shaped trestles. Remove these prior to sliding the boat into the water, and have one person holding the painter as the boat slides gently stern-first off the pontoon.

The wind direction determines your next move. On a weather shore (where the wind is blowing from the shore to the water) your boat's bow should be pointing to the shore. If the wind is strong, rig the jib only so that you can jump in, cast off your painter and, gaining speed, turn the boat onto a broad reach to gain enough sea room to round up and hoist your mainsail.

If the pontoon is parallel to the shore you can rig the sails prior to

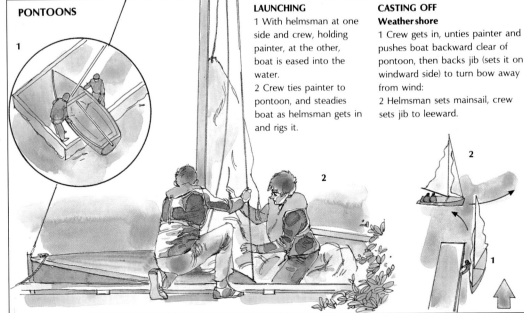

PONTOONS

1

2

LAUNCHING
1 With helmsman at one side and crew, holding painter, at the other, boat is eased into the water.
2 Crew ties painter to pontoon, and steadies boat as helmsman gets in and rigs it.

CASTING OFF
Weather shore
1 Crew gets in, unties painter and pushes boat backward clear of pontoon, then backs jib (sets it on windward side) to turn bow away from wind:
2 Helmsman sets mainsail, crew sets jib to leeward.

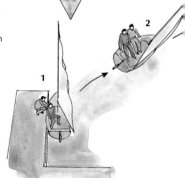

Lee shore
There is only one way for the boat to go.
1 Crew pushes off and jumps in.
2 The sails are set to take the boat on a close-hauled course.

launching. Once afloat, you and your crew both jump in, then you release the painter and the crew backs the jib while you push the tiller to leeward. When the boat is clear of the pontoon, the crew sheets the jib to the correct side and you pull the tiller to windward.

Returning to a pontoon or finger jetty on the windward shore requires a fine judgment, as you need to point the bow up into the wind to come alongside at a slow speed. When a pontoon is at right-angles to the wind, the crew must crawl along the foredeck and fend off as the boat stops head-on to it.

Alternatively, you can lower the sails and paddle alongside.

Launching from a lee shore (where the wind is blowing onshore) always brings additional problems caused by waves and the boat being pressed up against the pontoon, and the first thing to do is to ascertain the most beneficial tack to leave on.

On a finger pontoon you can lay the boat alongside, with sails hoisted and pointing into the wind. As you cast off, push the bow off and sail away on a close-hauled course.

On a shore pontoon it is best to leave the sails stowed ready for

hoisting. The crew pushes the bow off with the paddle and then paddles on the leeward side, while you fend off the back and help by pushing off and forward. Once under way, you apply gentle rudder pressure and the crew paddles against it. Once you have gained enough sea room, the crew hoists the mainsail and the boat is sailed farther offshore until the jib can be hoisted.

On returning to a lee shore pontoon or jetty, reduce sail by rounding up and lowering the main, then under jib alone sail back and round up with just enough room to stop and grab the pontoon.

As with all dinghy manoeuvres, you will need the correct amount of daggerboard or centreboard to enable you to turn correctly or to make headway off a lee shore. Returning to a lee shore you need half to threequarters down to keep the boat under control.

Electric hoists are especially useful on lakes and in areas of high tidal rise and fall. The low, short-armed hoist enables boats to be lifted off trailers and swung out over the dock wall to be lowered quickly into the water. Dinghies and keelboats can be fitted with lifting eyes or permanent strops to enable a team of operators to lift large numbers of boats in a short time.

Ready the boat for sailing before moving to the hoist, and ensure that the lifting strop, straps or wire are in place ready to attach to the hook of the hoist. Then move the boat to the hoist or free the boat from the trailer, and attach the hoist and bow and stern guiding lines. Operate the hoist and swing the boat out, and have someone keep the boat steady while you lower it. When your boat is safely in the water, either retract the hoist or, if another boat has to come out, hand over to the next operator. Once afloat, move away from the hoist area before the next boat comes in on top of you.

Launching and recovering by hoist is one of the simplest ways of handling a boat in and out of the water. Moorings, on the other hand, are about the most complicated and time-consuming option open to boat owners. The boat is kept afloat and so it must be anti-fouled, all the gear has to be transported in and out, and the mooring must be checked regularly for wear and kinking.

When leaving a mooring it is often best to hoist the mainsail, set it correctly, cast off the mooring and hoist the headsail. When returning, lower the headsail to free up the foredeck to enable the crew to handle the mooring.

Left *Prepare your boat for sailing before you cast off from a pontoon.*

Above *Moorings must be checked regularly for wear, and moored boats need antifouling.*

RETURNING

Weather shore
Boat approaches pontoon on a reach, and the sails are let out to slow it. The boat is turned into the wind to bring it alongside, and the crew grabs the pontoon and secures the boat.

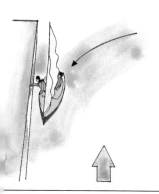

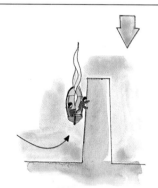

Lee shores
To return to a pontoon at right angles to the shore, sail in on a broad reach close to the shore. Round the boat up head-to-wind as it nears the pontoon, and drift to a stop alongside.

When the pontoon is parallel to the shore, first sail to a point upwind of it. Then turn the boat head-to-wind, lower the mainsail and sail in under jib alone on a broad reach. As the boat nears the pontoon, let the jib flap and drift sideways to come alongside the pontoon.

TACKING

Changing direction into the wind is described as *tacking* or *going about*. The complete manoeuvre involves turning the boat through about 90 degrees from one close-hauled tack to another.

During the manoeuvre, the boat first turns toward the wind, a movement known as *luffing* because, when pointing directly into the wind, the sails are luffing (flapping) over the centreline of the boat. To move from being head to wind to sailing on the new tack, the boat turns away from the wind, and this is called *bearing away*.

Tacking is essentially the same for all boats, but there are differences between dinghy gear and cruiser gear; the procedures described here are for dinghy sailing.

Throughout the tacking procedure, the boom is the key reference point and its position dictates both the progress through the sequence and the actions and positions of yourself and your crew. Before tacking, you both sit opposite the mainsail, balancing the boat to keep it sailing upright.

You initiate the turn by pushing the tiller gently away from you. As the boat turns toward the wind, the sails will lose their driving and heeling forces, so you and your crew must move inboard toward the boom to keep the boat upright. When the boom crosses the centreline you should both be under it and

moving across to the other side, and as the sails fill with wind you both sit opposite them to counterbalance their heeling forces.

This sequence should be followed carefully because the order of events is important; the skipper and crew who find themselves sitting on the same side as the boom after tacking will get very wet.

How you handle the mainsheeting when tacking depends on your boat's mainsheeting arrangements. Most racing dinghies have centre mainsheets, while family or knock-about boats usually have aft mainsheets, and each type requires a different procedure.

With an aft mainsheet, the tail (end) of the mainsheet is led, via blocks, from the transom and over the tiller to the skipper. When tacking, the skipper faces aft when moving from one side of the boat to the other.

For beginners, the best way to practise tacking a two-sail, aft-sheeted boat is to tack from one reach across the wind to another. Tacking is usually a turn of about 90° from one close-hauled course to another, but the reach-to-reach tack, which involves turning through 180°, gives the novice extra time to think and to correct mistakes. It also gives additional time to watch the various changes occur.

To begin with, you and your crew sit opposite to and facing the

mainsail, with both sails set sufficiently to give the boat a reasonable speed. Before turning, you must check that you will not place your boat in the path of oncoming craft or crash into adjacent boats.

Having checked that all is clear, you call out 'Ready about!' Your crew does a similar check, especially under the sails to leeward, and if the way is clear replies 'OK!' or 'Yes!' and prepares to release the jib sheet. Meanwhile, you select a landmark over your rearward shoulder (the one nearest the back of the boat) to use as the new *goal point* toward which you will aim your new tack.

Before tacking, you should have been sailing with the tiller extension in your rearward hand with your thumb uppermost, and the mainsheet over the extension and held in your other hand. As you tack, quickly transfer the mainsheet to your tiller hand and grasp the extension with the other.

After another quick check that it is safe to turn, call 'Tacking!' or 'Lee ho!' and push the extension away slowly to a straight-arm position. As the boat begins to turn into the wind, move toward the centre of the boat with your front foot forward and tiller arm extended.

Your crew should react to the 'Tacking!' command by releasing the jib sheet and grasping the new jib sheet, and balancing the boat while moving toward the centre.

Above *When you're sailing singlehanded, face forward as you move across the boat when the boom swings over.*

You should by now be standing and facing aft. As the boom moves toward and across the centreline, you dip beneath it and turn toward the centre of the boat, pulling and twisting the extension to move the tiller toward the centreline to slow the turn.

As the mainsail fills and sets on the new tack, centralize the tiller and check that the boat is sailing approximately in the direction of your preselected goal point. Your crew should move to balance the boat as it turns onto the new tack, and sheet the jib as the tell-tales dictate.

The tacking procedure for a dinghy with a centre mainsheet is basically the same as that for an aft-sheeted boat, but there are two important differences. This first is that the skipper faces forward during the tack. The second is that, while sailing, he or she holds the tiller extension in the 'dagger' grip, and assumes the 'boxer' position in which both hands are held in front of the chest, like those of a boxer squaring up to his opponent.

Sitting on the side of the boat, hold the extension across your chest in the dagger grip, with your thumb beneath it and toward the upper end. The mainsheet, leading from

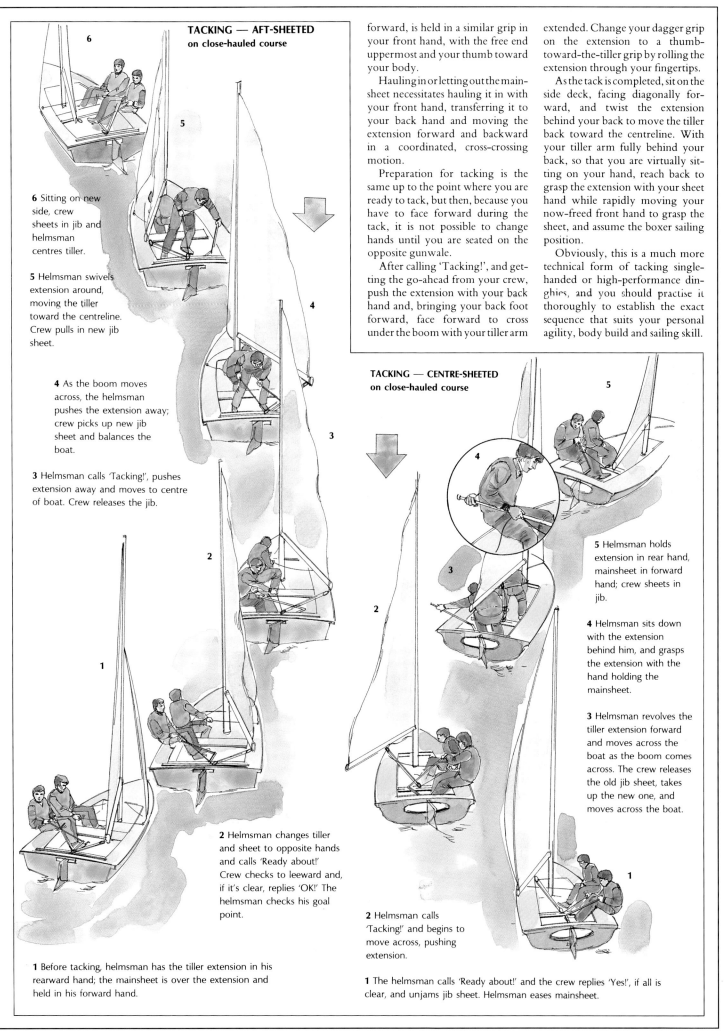

TACKING — AFT-SHEETED
on close-hauled course

6 Sitting on new side, crew sheets in jib and helmsman centres tiller.

5 Helmsman swivels extension around, moving the tiller toward the centreline. Crew pulls in new jib sheet.

4 As the boom moves across, the helmsman pushes the extension away; crew picks up new jib sheet and balances the boat.

3 Helmsman calls 'Tacking!', pushes extension away and moves to centre of boat. Crew releases the jib.

2 Helmsman changes tiller and sheet to opposite hands and calls 'Ready about!' Crew checks to leeward and, if it's clear, replies 'OK!' The helmsman checks his goal point.

1 Before tacking, helmsman has the tiller extension in his rearward hand; the mainsheet is over the extension and held in his forward hand.

forward, is held in a similar grip in your front hand, with the free end uppermost and your thumb toward your body.

Hauling in or letting out the mainsheet necessitates hauling it in with your front hand, transferring it to your back hand and moving the extension forward and backward in a coordinated, cross-crossing motion.

Preparation for tacking is the same up to the point where you are ready to tack, but then, because you have to face forward during the tack, it is not possible to change hands until you are seated on the opposite gunwale.

After calling 'Tacking!', and getting the go-ahead from your crew, push the extension with your back hand and, bringing your back foot forward, face forward to cross under the boom with your tiller arm

extended. Change your dagger grip on the extension to a thumb-toward-the-tiller grip by rolling the extension through your fingertips.

As the tack is completed, sit on the side deck, facing diagonally forward, and twist the extension behind your back to move the tiller back toward the centreline. With your tiller arm fully behind your back, so that you are virtually sitting on your hand, reach back to grasp the extension with your sheet hand while rapidly moving your now-freed front hand to grasp the sheet, and assume the boxer sailing position.

Obviously, this is a much more technical form of tacking single-handed or high-performance dinghies, and you should practise it thoroughly to establish the exact sequence that suits your personal agility, body build and sailing skill.

TACKING — CENTRE-SHEETED
on close-hauled course

5 Helmsman holds extension in rear hand, mainsheet in forward hand; crew sheets in jib.

4 Helmsman sits down with the extension behind him, and grasps the extension with the hand holding the mainsheet.

3 Helmsman revolves the tiller extension forward and moves across the boat as the boom comes across. The crew releases the old jib sheet, takes up the new one, and moves across the boat.

2 Helmsman calls 'Tacking!' and begins to move across, pushing extension.

1 The helmsman calls 'Ready about!' and the crew replies 'Yes!', if all is clear, and unjams jib sheet. Helmsman eases mainsheet.

GYBING

Changing direction *away* from the wind is called *gybing*. The manoeuvre differs from tacking in two ways: skipper and crew have to move the mainsail manually, and the wind fills it for all but a brief period during the manoeuvre.

Gybing calls for a certain amount of boat handling skill, and so, if a novice skipper is forced to gybe, he or she should do it by turning the boat quite quickly and keeping bodies and heads out of the way of the boom as it rattles overhead.

When a boat is running the sails are let out to their farthest extent. To change direction from one gybe to another requires the sail to be moved through about 160° from one side to the other. In light winds the crew can do this, but at all other times the full gybing sequence must be followed.

Until you are an expert, you need all the help you can get when gybing. Fortunately, there is a natural safe course, some 15° off the downwind course, which if held prior to the gybe will prevent an unexpected, accidental gybe.

From a reach, turn the boat away from the wind and adjust the sails and centreboard accordingly. At a point just before the dead run, the jib will collapse and move toward the centreline. Stop the turn at this point and, pushing the tiller away, turn back toward the wind until the jib just sets on the same side as the mainsail.

This point of sailing is the 'training run' used by sailing instructors to encourage students to identify the

As the boom moves across, the helmsman should be in the centre of the boat and facing aft.

correct downwind course from which to start a gybe.

It is essential to keep to this course before you turn, so choose a landmark to bow or stern to help you steer in a straight line while preparing to gybe.

When you're ready to gybe, turn the boat away from the wind by moving the tiller to windward. The wind will cross the stern, and your crew should then help the mainsail across to the other side. Both you and your crew should balance the boat throughout the gybe, especially when the sail crosses the boat and fills with wind.

No two gybes are the same, and the degree of control of the main by the crew increases with experience, particularly with a spinnaker set. Then, control of the boom by the skipper while the crew gybes the spinnaker is the key to successful gybing.

As with tacking, the procedure for gybing an aft-mainsheeted dinghy differs from that used for gybing a centre-mainsheeted boat.

By far the commonest problem with aft mainsheets is that the falls (loops) of the mainsheet catch on the corners of the transom as the boom swings across. If this happens regularly, you will need to incorporate a mainsheet 'flick' into the sequence as the boom moves toward the centre. This flick introduces an S-bend in the sheet which lifts it above the corner. Trial and error will teach you when to flick.

Preparing to gybe involves setting the boat up on a training run with a goal point to aim for. Sailing downwind, you and your crew will normally be sitting inboard to balance the boat, the crew perhaps sit-

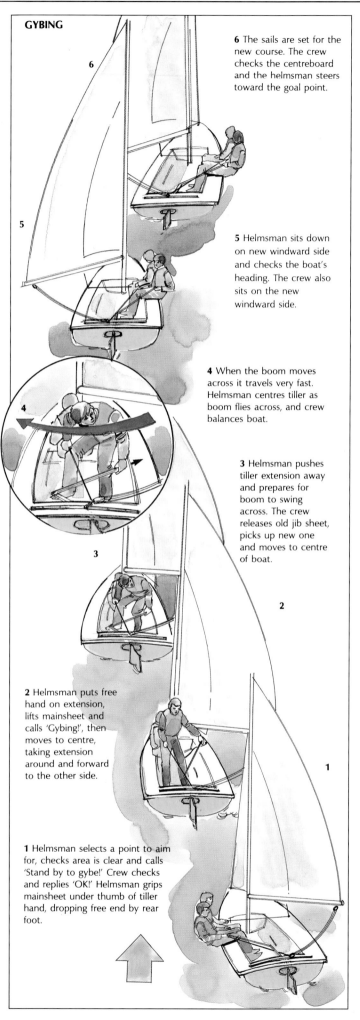

GYBING

6 The sails are set for the new course. The crew checks the centreboard and the helmsman steers toward the goal point.

5 Helmsman sits down on new windward side and checks the boat's heading. The crew also sits on the new windward side.

4 When the boom moves across it travels very fast. Helmsman centres tiller as boom flies across, and crew balances boat.

3 Helmsman pushes tiller extension away and prepares for boom to swing across. The crew releases old jib sheet, picks up new one and moves to centre of boat.

2 Helmsman puts free hand on extension, lifts mainsheet and calls 'Gybing!', then moves to centre, taking extension around and forward to the other side.

1 Helmsman selects a point to aim for, checks area is clear and calls 'Stand by to gybe!' Crew checks and replies 'OK!' Helmsman grips mainsheet under thumb of tiller hand, dropping free end by rear foot.

SLAM GYBE

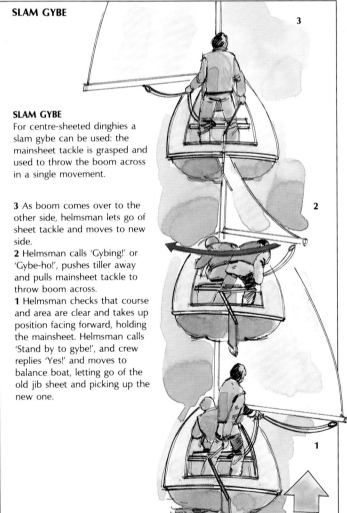

SLAM GYBE
For centre-sheeted dinghies a slam gybe can be used: the mainsheet tackle is grasped and used to throw the boom across in a single movement.

3 As boom comes over to the other side, helmsman lets go of sheet tackle and moves to new side.
2 Helmsman calls 'Gybing!' or 'Gybe-ho!', pushes tiller away and pulls mainsheet tackle to throw boom across.
1 Helmsman checks that course and area are clear and takes up position facing forward, holding the mainsheet. Helmsman calls 'Stand by to gybe!', and crew replies 'Yes!' and moves to balance boat, letting go of the old jib sheet and picking up the new one.

ting on the leeward side. The centreboard will have about 6 inches of its tip protruding through the slot.

When you are ready to gybe, check that you can turn without impeding other boats and call out 'Stand by to gybe!' Your crew should also check that it's safe to turn, and then reply 'OK!' or 'Yes!'

Change hands on the sheet and tiller extension, and move quickly to straddle the centreline with the extension swung 180° up and forward to point to the sail. As you do that, call out 'Gybing!' and push the tiller to windward.

As the boat turns, your crew should move to anticipate boat balance and grab the boom vang to assist the gybe. As the boom swings rapidly across the centreline, centralize the tiller to meet the sudden application of power as the sail fills on the new gybe

In strong winds, the sudden application of power against a centralized tiller will cause the boat to turn slightly away from the wind on the new course. You can correct this by gently easing the tiller to leeward and then centralizing it again.

Successful gybing depends on there being a narrow angle between the original and new courses, because if the boat is turned through a wide angle the sail will not catch any wind on the new course. This will encourage a capsize to windward, one of the commoner sights in a gybing fleet.

When gybing a centre-sheeted dinghy, the change of hands to resume control should be done as rapidly as possible.

It helps to remember that a heeled boat turns away from the angle of heel. This is aggravated by the fact that you may not have a lot of centreboard in the water to start with, and once the centreboard surfaces the boat will slide.

Some skippers advocate pulling in some mainsheet prior to the gybe to reduce the risk of catching the boom end in the water. Any such adjustment must be rapidly followed by the gybe itself.

When you're gybing a centre-mainsheeted dinghy, the most significant difference is that, as with tacking that type of boat, the change of hands occurs *after* the boom has crossed the boat.

Following the preparation and the call of 'Stand by to gybe!', change from the dagger grip to the underhand grip and move to the centre, lifting and rotating the extension toward the sail.

Then call 'Gybing!' and, without pause, push the extension to windward behind your back. As the boat turns, you or your crew should help the mainsail across by pulling on the mainsheet, vang, or boom. As the boom swings across, twist the extension and centralize the tiller while sitting on the side decks facing forward and inward.

TRAPEZING

The trapeze is a device that enables crews, and on some dinghies and catamarans, skippers, to stand on the side of the boat to use their weight to maximum advantage.

There is usually one trapeze on each side of the boat, and each is made up of a number of components. The trapeze wire is attached to the mast above the shrouds or swaged to the shrouds to reduce windage (deflection by the wind). It terminates in a grab handle that is used by the crew as a hand-hold when moving off or onto the boat. An adjustable ring, loop or 'dogbone' is attached to the handle.

This engages in a hook mounted on the front of an adjustable body harness worn by the crew, and is tensioned upward by a thin elasticated 'bungee' cord – the shock cord – which usually runs across the boat to the other trapeze.

Certain dinghies, including the Flying Dutchman, use continuous trapeze wires that enable the crew to remain clipped on while moving across the boat. The ring runs on a block that fits into the hook end of the trapeze wire when the crew is in position.

The trapeze permits crews to place all their weight outside the boat, and while some racing classes impose restrictions on the use of trapezes in competitions, others allow crews not only to use trapezes but also to wear water-filled jackets. These enable them to place even more weight outside the boat so as to give greater righting power.

These 'weight jackets' have pockets that can be filled with water to provide more weight on upwind and reaching legs of a race, but which can be quickly emptied for downwind sailing when the extra weight would be a handicap.

Harnesses are usually padded, and strengthened with webbing. The crew's weight is taken by the hook, which is adjusted to a point between the pubic bone and the belly button. Its exact position is determined by the crew's centre of gravity: if the hook's too high, there is too much weight on the crew's legs; if it's too low, the crew risks hanging upside down.

Most harnesses have high-fitting back supports and a tight-fitting, 'nappy'-type lower body support. Adjustable shoulder straps and front cross-belts ensure a snug fit that keeps the hook as near the body as possible.

If a boat is fitted with a trapeze, it indicates that it is a high-performance dinghy and if the skipper is unused to sailing such a boat he or she will find it difficult to handle in the early stages of ownership. Fortunately, while the skipper is learning to sail the boat the crew can use the trapeze system as a sitting-out aid without having to stand on the outside of the boat.

If you are a newcomer to trapezing, this limited use of the trapeze system will enable you to establish the basic skills of hooking on, sitting out, coming in, unhooking and moving across the boat.

The first thing to practise is hooking on. The shock cord lifts the ring to a point above your trapeze hook when you are sitting on the side of the boat. To engage the hook, grasp the ring with your front hand and clip it onto the trapeze hook. The

Right *On some of the larger, faster dinghies both skipper and crew can trapeze to keep the boat balanced.* **Below** *The crew of a 470 Class dinghy using a trapeze during the 1988 Olympics.*

TRAPEZING — GOING OUT

1 Sitting well out, hook the trapeze onto the harness with your bow (forward) hand. Grab the handle and pull it outboard.

2 Slide out over the side deck, dropping down until your weight is on the wire. Rest your bow foot on the gunwale, next to the shroud.

3 Make sure your bow foot is secure, and push yourself out with your bow leg, keeping your body (as much as possible) at right angles to the boat.

4 Bring your stern (rearward) foot out to rest securely on the gunwale next to your bow foot. Then let go of the handle and straighten your legs.

tension of the shock cord will hold the ring in place.

The correct trapezing position is to have your body parallel to the water when the boat is sailing upright. This means that as you lower your backside over the edge of the boat, you will drop down to a position well outside the boat with your weight totally supported by the trapeze system.

This initial position is the one to use when first starting to trapeze. To get into it, sit on the side with your feet in the toestraps, then reach forward, grab the trapeze ring, and clip it onto the harness hook. (Always clip on from a sitting position, because it is dangerous to clip on while standing.)

Then grab the handle with your front hand and, pushing with your feet or free hand, drop your backside over the gunwale to sit on the outside of the boat, letting go the handle at the same time. Getting back in is a matter of reaching for the handle to pull yourself in again while leaning slightly aft.

In normal sailing trim, the ring of the trapeze will be about 1 to 2 inches above the side deck, but in the initial stages, to help you get back in, it can be raised to 3 to 4 inches above the deck.

To unclip the ring, put your hand inside the trapeze and push down with your palm. **This should be perfected, because in an emergency this method will enable you to release the ring even when your whole body weight is on it.**

To use the trapeze system correctly it is essential to commit your body weight to the wire at the earliest possible moment, as this makes every other movement so much easier. At an advanced level, you will have to handle the jib and spinnaker controls while trapezing.

When you are accustomed to sitting out on the trapeze, you can start going fully outboard on it. From the normal sitting-out position, grab the ring and clip it onto the hook. Then take the trapeze handle in your front hand and, while sitting out and down, swing your body slightly aft so that you can place your front foot against, or near, the shroud.

Now you can put your weight on your front leg and bring your back foot onto the gunwale. If the jib sheet is conveniently placed, you can use it to help you balance while you do this.

Place your feet about shoulder width apart, with your front leg braced to prevent you being thrown forward. From this crouching position, release the handle and adjust your weight, by pushing with your legs, to any point out to the fully-extended position.

COMING IN

5 With your feet at shoulders' width apart, lean back into the fully-extended position. Holding your bow arm behind your head gives more righting power.

6 To get back in, lean toward the stern, bend your knees and grab the handle. Take your weight on your bow leg and bring your stern leg onto the decking.

7 Keeping your body at a right angle, move into the boat, sit on the side decking and unhook the trapeze ring.

DINGHY SPINNAKER HANDLING

Most competitive dinghy classes permit use of a spinnaker, which is set outside all other parts of the rig. Conventionally, it is a symmetrical triangular sail with the head hoisted close to the mast and the clews controlled by sheets leading back to the cockpit. A number of newer dinghy classes have adopted an asymmetric style of sail, which is a cross between a spinnaker and a genoa and is usually set from a projecting bowsprit rather than from a boom.

In the conventional system, the windward clew is supported by a pole that clips to the mast. Its height is controlled by an uphaul/downhaul system and its angle to the wind is controlled by the windward sheet (the guy). The spinnaker pole is usually fitted with spring-piston clips operated by a line joining the ends. In use, the two clips of the pole must always face upward.

Stowage and launching systems can either be of the pouch type in the cockpit or a chute mounted on the bow. There are two techniques for setting the spinnaker from a pouch. It can either be set directly from the leeward side and then pulled around until the windward clew meets the pole end, or it can be set from the windward side, in which case the sail has to be gathered up in a bunch and thrown forward to clear the forestay.

The normal technique involves the skipper standing up in the back of the boat and holding the tiller between the knees. This makes it possible for him or her to use both hands to hoist the spinnaker and then assist in setting the guy.

The sail will go up easily if you are sailing along on a broad reach, but if the course to the next mark is a square reach and there are other boats jockeying for position, life will be more difficult. As soon as

you bear away around the mark, the crew comes inboard from the trapeze (if fitted), releases the halyard and sheets and picks up the pole from its stowage, which may be in the cockpit or under the main boom. Both sheet and guy must be uncleated initially or it will not be possible to get the boom on and/or the sail will fill prematurely.

First the crew clips the boom onto the guy, then attaches the uphaul/downhaul and finally clips the boom onto the mast. As soon as this has been done the skipper hoists away briskly. If it is a leeward set, the sail should now take care of itself; if it is a windward set, this is the moment when the sail is thrown clear. It is vital at this stage for the crew to pull in and cleat the guy, or the spinnaker will belly out to leeward and pull the dinghy over. It is also vital that the guy is running under the reaching hook (the sheet must be free), or the pole

will not stay forward against the clew of the sail.

Finally, the crew pulls in the sheet to fill the sail and, if it is a trapeze boat, he or she must be hooked on and ready to go out immediately as the power comes on. The skipper must now be sitting down again and controlling the boat, sitting to windward if on a power reach and to leeward if on a run so the boat is balanced.

To gybe with a conventional spinnaker, the boat must first bear off sufficiently to let the crew come into the cockpit. The crew flicks the guy out of the reaching hook and then, as the main boom comes overhead, puts the new guy under its reaching hook while also changing over the jib sheets and trapeze harness. The skipper should be free

Below *Good teamwork and close cooperation are essential when using a spinnaker*

to ease the guy to give it sufficient length to get the pole on. After the main boom has gybed, the crew stands up on the new windward side, snaps the pole off the mast, clips it to the new guy, drops the old guy off the free end and clips that end to the mast.

When dropping, the pole comes off first and the sail is gathered last as the skipper stands and uncleats the halyard. If a chute is fitted, the halyard will be continuous and by pulling it 'the other way' the sail is dragged into the chute. With a pouch, the crew gathers in the sail and stuffs it into the stowage.

With an asymmetric, the process begins with extending the bowsprit. As the sail goes up, the guy is brought home to pull the clew out to the end of the sprit, and as soon as the halyard is cleated the sail can be sheeted. Gybing is simple because the sail is treated just like a genoa and turns inside out as it flops across. The only difficulty is to ensure that it does not become entangled with the jib.

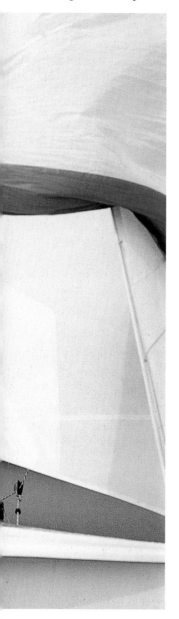

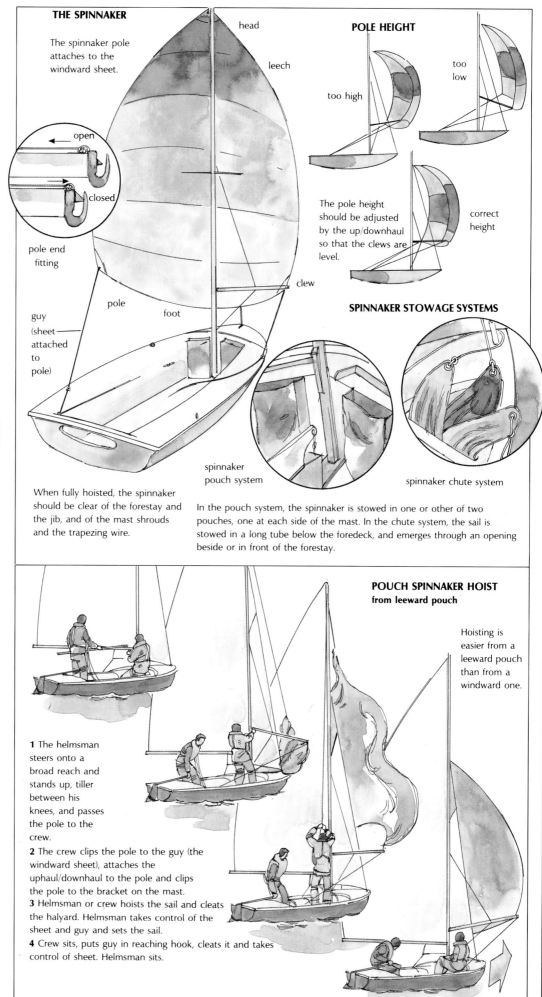

THE SPINNAKER

The spinnaker pole attaches to the windward sheet.

open

closed

pole end fitting

guy (sheet attached to pole)

pole

foot

head

leech

clew

When fully hoisted, the spinnaker should be clear of the forestay and the jib, and of the mast shrouds and the trapezing wire.

POLE HEIGHT

too high

too low

The pole height should be adjusted by the up/downhaul so that the clews are level.

correct height

SPINNAKER STOWAGE SYSTEMS

spinnaker pouch system

spinnaker chute system

In the pouch system, the spinnaker is stowed in one or other of two pouches, one at each side of the mast. In the chute system, the sail is stowed in a long tube below the foredeck, and emerges through an opening beside or in front of the forestay.

POUCH SPINNAKER HOIST
from leeward pouch

Hoisting is easier from a leeward pouch than from a windward one.

1 The helmsman steers onto a broad reach and stands up, tiller between his knees, and passes the pole to the crew.
2 The crew clips the pole to the guy (the windward sheet), attaches the uphaul/downhaul to the pole and clips the pole to the bracket on the mast.
3 Helmsman or crew hoists the sail and cleats the halyard. Helmsman takes control of the sheet and guy and sets the sail.
4 Crew sits, puts guy in reaching hook, cleats it and takes control of sheet. Helmsman sits.

CAPSIZING & MAN OVERBOARD

To be able to follow the correct emergency procedures when your boat capsizes, or someone falls overboard, you need a complete understanding of the boat, its equipment and the way it sails.

In training, both capsize recovery and man-overboard recovery are structured exercises designed to improve boat handling skills. Each is taught as a sequence, and each must be practised and perfected to the point of becoming a reflex action.

Sailing dinghies are actually quite difficult to capsize, especially in a training exercise. The simplest way is to sail close-hauled and tack violently without changing your position. Your weight and the force of the wind on the sails should be enough to cause the boat to lie sail-down on the water.

In real life, dinghies capsize because they are overpowered by a gust before the skipper has time to release the mainsheet, or they roll in while gybing or running in strong winds.

If your boat capsizes when you're sailing single-handed, the first thing to do is to step over the high side as the boat goes over. From a sitting-out position you place your forward leg over the gunwale and sit astride the side. As the sail hits the water, you lower yourself to the centreboard or daggerboard and right the boat by pulling on the gunwale. Then you can climb in and sail on.

The best way to right a two-man dinghy is to use the scoop method, which requires both of you to act

Right *Right a one-man dinghy by standing on the centreboard root and pulling on the gunwale.*

RIGHTING A TWO-MAN BOAT — SCOOP METHOD

1 Both helmsman and crew swim to the stern. The helmsman checks that the rudder is there and fitted properly, and holds it to prevent the boat inverting to the mast-down position. The crew finds the end of the mainsheet.

2 The helmsman takes the mainsheet to use as a lifeline and swims to the centreboard. The crew then swims inside and checks that the centreboard is fully down. The helmsman puts his weight on the centreboard to prevent inverting.

3 The crew finds the top jib sheet and throws it to the helmsman, who tells the crew when he has taken hold of it.

quickly the moment the boat capsizes. You don't need to lower the sails before righting the boat when using this method, but contact and cooperation between you and your crew is essential—so tell your companion exactly what you want to do so that he or she can help you.

The first task is to get your crew to move to the stern, to hold and twist the rudder so as to prevent the boat inverting to the mast-down position.

Then you can swim around the boat to grasp the centreboard or daggerboard protruding through the bottom of it. By pulling down on the board, or lying on top of it, you can prevent the boat inverting. In rough seas, take the mainsheet with you (or have it passed to you by the crew) for use as a safety line.

Once the boat is stable, the crew swims into the boat, finds the jib sheet which is on the high side, and throws it over to you. Having done that, the crew lies face down inside

the flooded boat, head facing forward and knees and arms resting on the lower side of the boat.

Now you can begin to right the boat. Climb onto the board, using the jib sheet as a climbing aid, then stand close to the root of the board (the part nearest the boat) and grasp the rope firmly. It's important to stand near the root of the board, because although you would get more leverage by standing near the tip of it, you would also risk breaking it.

Pull hard on the jib sheet while leaning well back with your knees slightly bent; a jerky motion will help to 'unstick' the sails from the water. As the boat rotates to an upright position the crew will be scooped up inside it.

If you judge the moment correctly, you can climb in as the boat reaches the vertical. If you end up back in the water, your crew can haul you in. When the boat is upright and both of you are safely

aboard, use a bucket to bail or sluice the water out of it.

A completely inverted boat can be brought back to the horizontal by both of you placing your feet on the same gunwale. One of you pulls on the centreboard while the other moves aft to sink the corner of the transom. The boat will slowly rotate to the horizontal, and then it can be righted by the scoop method.

'Man overboard!' is a cry that skippers dread to hear. In a two-person boat, the one remaining crew has to act quickly to bring the boat under control and swing immediately into a well-rehearsed sequence.

The standard dinghy pick-up sequence involves sailing away and returning on a reach, turning on to a broad reach just prior to turning toward the wind to stop alongside the casualty.

In practice, this manoeuvre can cause considerable difficulty to all but the most experienced sailor, so

concentrate on a number of key points.

Keep glancing back at the person in the water. Let the jib sheets go so that the jib flaps out to show where the wind is, and double check that you are sailing at 90 degrees to the wind. Control the boat speed with the main, and ensure that the centreboard is between threequarters down and fully down. Never go more than 50 metres from the casualty.

Tack firmly so that the boat turns through 180 degrees, and adjust your course to be about two boatlengths downwind at a point 45 degrees from the casualty. Round up slowly so that you can stop with the casualty amidships.

Slide forward, still holding the tiller extension and giving it a flick to windward as you make contact with the man overboard. Hold on with both hands until the boat finds its natural drift position and then haul the person back into the boat.

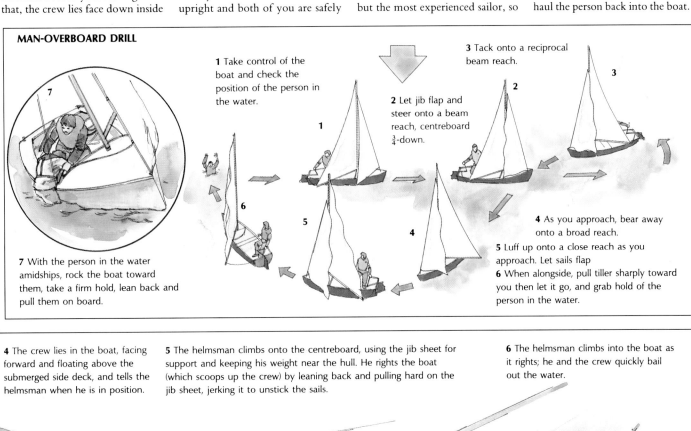

MAN-OVERBOARD DRILL

1 Take control of the boat and check the position of the person in the water.

2 Let jib flap and steer onto a beam reach, centreboard $\frac{3}{4}$-down.

3 Tack onto a reciprocal beam reach.

4 As you approach, bear away onto a broad reach.

5 Luff up onto a close reach as you approach. Let sails flap

6 When alongside, pull tiller sharply toward you then let it go, and grab hold of the person in the water.

7 With the person in the water amidships, rock the boat toward them, take a firm hold, lean back and pull them on board.

4 The crew lies in the boat, facing forward and floating above the submerged side deck, and tells the helmsman when he is in position.

5 The helmsman climbs onto the centreboard, using the jib sheet for support and keeping his weight near the hull. He rights the boat (which scoops up the crew) by leaning back and pulling hard on the jib sheet, jerking it to unstick the sails.

6 The helmsman climbs into the boat as it rights; he and the crew quickly bail out the water.

SAILING SMALL CATAMARANS

Catamarans derive their stability from the span of their slim hulls. On a 2-metre wide craft, the weight of trapezing crew can be 2.5 metres to windward of the immersed leeward hull, exerting a considerable righting movement to counteract the capsizing pull of the sails.

The typical catamaran has a pair of hulls joined by two aluminium beams that are firmly bolted or attached to each hull, and a sheet of sailcloth or a length of close-weave netting forms a 'trampoline' between the two beams and inside edges of the hull. To prevent damage and to simplify production, most hulls have integral keels to eliminate the need for daggerboards or centreboards.

Rudders are sophisticated assemblies designed to lock down while sailing but which spring up if in contact with an obstruction. A tiller bar joins the two rudders, so that both move when the bar is steered.

Hulls are usually made of GRP, but notable exceptions include the Catapult, which is an inflatable, and the French F1 Hurricane which, being made of moulded polyethylene, is a robust knockabout craft ideal for training and family sailing.

Masts and sails have been specially developed to withstand the heavy shock-loadings associated with the high speeds attained by multihulls. Masts are mounted on pivots for easy rotation, and most are fitted with a fixed set of diamond shrouds to ensure a rigid structure.

HULL POSITION

Cats sail fastest on a broad reach or reach; the windward hull should fly just clear of the water, and only an inch or two of the leeward bow should show above the water.

SAILING POSITIONS

In strong winds keep the crew weight well aft. In light airs the crew weight should be near the main beam and both hulls should be equally immersed.

FOOT LOOPS

Most catamarans have foot loops or straps along the outer edge of each hull. These are used when trapezing.

RIGHTING SMALL CATAMARANS

Push down on one end of the hull lying in the water to bring the uppermost hull down and swing the hulls into a vertical position. Then swim around to the mast side and push the boat over into its normal position.

Sails are fully battened at about 1-metre intervals to give an almost rigid, preshaped aerofoil for the wind to act on. Booms, where fitted, are square-sectioned and strong. At the front end a mast 'spanner' determines the amount of overrotation of the mast.

The 8:1 to 16:1 mainsheet is, in effect, the boom vang, and is attached to traveller running on a track attached to the rear beam. The traveller is controlled by a rope so that it can be 'played' in the gusts and adjusted to each point of sailing.

The mainsail luff is kept in position by a masthead lock comprising a protruding clip on the mast and a ring or hook attached to the head of the sail. Once locked in position, the luff can be tensioned by an 8:1 to 16:1 tack downhaul. Jibs are usually small and controlled by a 2:1 jib sheet system.

To assemble a multihull from scratch you need a very good set of instructions or the assistance of someone who has done it before.

When you've assembled and rigged it, put it on a padded, two-wheeled axle to trundle it into the water.

Hoist the mainsail without the mainsheet attached, and tension both jib and mainsail to suit the weather conditions. Once afloat, sail the boat into deeper water before attaching the mainsheet and fixing the rudders in their locked-down position. Baggy sails are bad news to beginners and experienced sailors alike, so always pull the sails in tight and adjust the boom angle with the traveller.

Acceleration and deceleration forces cause crews to be thrown backward and forward, so it's important that trapezing crews lock their feet into toestraps, where fitted, or use the skipper as an anchorage. Some catamarans are fitted with clip-on stern lines which prevent trapezing crews from being thrown forward.

The fastest points of sailing are the reach and broad reach. When sailing these points, keep the crew weight

Top *The crew of a Tornado using a trapeze during the 1988 Olympics.*
Above *At high speeds the windward hull should just clear the water.*

well aft to prevent the leeward bow nosediving and initiating a barrel roll to leeward.

Catamarans are very manoeuverable, as you will find if you gybe to turn during the early stages of learning to sail one. The fully-battened sail allows you to turn downwind, slow down and gybe off onto a broad reach.

Tacking requires more finesse. From a close-hauled position, choose the right time to tack into the waves. Push the tiller bar gently away, gradually tightening up the turn as the boat heads up into the wind. Flick the tiller extension into the water behind the mainsheet and move across the boat, picking the extension up on the other side and being sure to keep the rudders turned to their fullest travel. As soon as the mainsail sets on the new tack, centralize the rudders and sail off on the new tack.

If a jib is fitted, the crew should briefly let it out as the tack commences, then sheet it in again on the same side to back it and help the turn. As soon as the new tack is reached, the jib is released from its backed position and sheeted in on the new tack.

It should be noted that each different design has different handling characteristics when tacking. The position of the crew weight is often critical during the tack and you should start by moving weight after as the boat begins its turn.

Catamarans are noted for their high speed, and the correct attitude for high-speed sailing is to have the windward hull flying just clear of the water. Trim the leeward hull so that only about one or two inches of the bow are showing.

In very strong winds, especially when reaching in waves, there is a very real danger of driving the boat under, so keep the crew weight as far aft as possible. In very light airs, get the crew weight as near the main beam as possible, with both hulls immersed to the same degree.

If you have the misfortune to capsize, you need to act quickly to right the boat because catamarans will invert easily. A small catamaran, such as a Dart, can be righted by bringing the bows or sterns down until the boat is vertical.

To do this, you and your crew swim around to one end of the lower hull, and push down on it to bring the end of the uppermost hull down toward the water. As the end of the uppermost hull drops, grasp it and pull down on it with all your weight, while your crew pushes up midway along the lower hull. This will bring the boat to a vertical position in the water.

Now you both swim to the mast side of the boat, push it over into its normal sailing position and climb aboard immediately, before it sails off on its own.

To right a larger boat, pass a jib sheet over the uppermost hull while your crew steadies the lower one. Grab the jib sheet and stand on the keel of the lower hull, leaning back so that your weight pivots the uppermost hull around the lower one and down to the water.

CRUISER RIGGING

of the waterline length of the boat. Headsails are large and powerful in contrast to the small mainsail, which acts as a secondary aerofoil.

The fractional rig places the mast farther forward in the boat. The mainsail is larger than that of a masthead rig and provides much of the drive. The rig is termed 'fractional' because the headsails emerge seven-eighths or three-quarters of the way from the base of the mast – hence 'seven-eighths rig' or 'three-quarter rig'.

Ketches and schooners have shorter masts and smaller sails in an attempt to make sail handling easier, but recent developments in self-stowing headsails and mainsails make for easy sail handling on other rigs and leave new multi-masted boats in a specialized custom market.

As with dinghies, the standing rigging of stainless steel wire keeps the masts in place. Cruisers are usually rigged with oversize wire to ensure long life and a large safety factor over the designed safe working load.

In older boats the shrouds and forestay will be attached with metal fittings called tangs, but new masts have captive T-bars or ball-and-socket arrangements which are inside the mast section. At the bottom ends of the shrouds and fore-

Left Tensioning the boom vang, which with the mainsheet controls the shape of the mainsail.
Below left Tensioning the backstay.
Below A headsail furling system.

The cruiser market is made up of a small percentage of wooden boats and a large percentage of glassfibre boats, some new but most second-hand and up to about twenty years old.

As with cars and motorcycles, cruising sailboats reflect the development of equipment in the racing sector. The potential buyer is, therefore, faced with a wide variety of rigs and hull shapes reflecting developments over past years.

If you buy a used boat (or if your existing boat is beginning to show its age) you can update the rigging to get better performance, but only to a point beyond which wholesale redesign work will be needed to produce any further improvement. However, there are many ways of improving the performance of an older design without resort to drastic surgery.

The basic rigs of modern cruisers are *masthead*, *fractional*, *ketch* and *schooner*. The masthead rig places the mast just forward of the middle

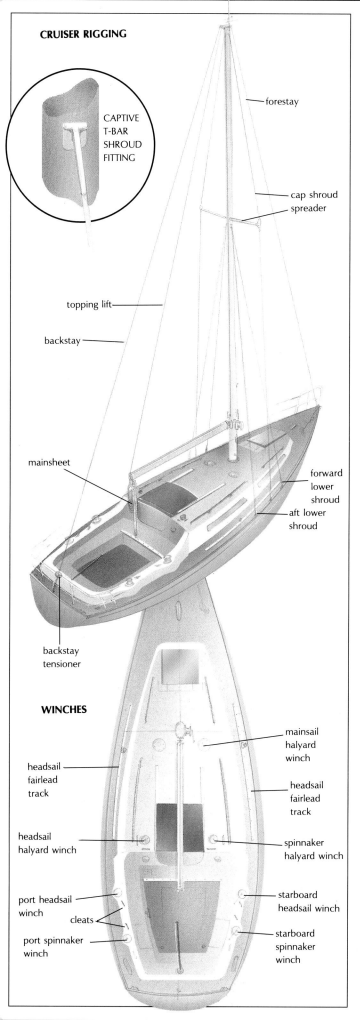

CRUISER RIGGING

CAPTIVE T-BAR SHROUD FITTING

forestay

cap shroud

spreader

topping lift

backstay

mainsheet

forward lower shroud

aft lower shroud

backstay tensioner

WINCHES

mainsail halyard winch

headsail fairlead track

headsail fairlead track

headsail halyard winch

spinnaker halyard winch

port headsail winch

cleats

starboard headsail winch

port spinnaker winch

starboard spinnaker winch

stay, adjustable rigging screws are attached by clevis pins to toggles which act as universal joints to prevent metal fatigue.

In addition to the forestay, there is a backstay leading from the masthead to the stern and usually terminating in a mechanical or hydraulic backstay tensioner to control the forestay tension for upwind and downwind sailing.

All owners of cruising boats should be aware that many boatyards do not 'tune' the rig of cruising boats but usually step the mast and tighten the rigging on a 'that's about right' basis. Any mast which is not tuned will drastically affect the performance of the boat.

Basic tuning is not difficult, though, and even the least mechanically-minded owner can ensure that the mast is upright when viewed from the side and does not lean when viewed from ahead. A mast with more than one set of spreaders must be sighted up the after edge to ensure that no S-bends exist in it.

Most masts are raked aft a little, and you can check the rake by attaching a heavy weight to the main halyard. With the boat in normal trim, measure the distance from the back of the mast to the centre of the weight. Anything from 9 to 18 inches is normal. Raking the mast forward decreases weather helm (the boat's tendency to turn into the wind all the time), and raking it back increases it.

Also check that the mast does not lean to one side. If it does, adjust the rigging screw of each main or cap shroud (the ones that go to the highest point of the mast) until the mast is vertical. Any further adjustment of the screws to increase or decrease shroud tension must be equal on both sides, or else the mast will lean again.

To get the S-bends out of a multi-spreader rig, first ease the backstay and main shrouds. Then ease the intermediate shrouds, which lead to the base of the spreaders. Sighting up the back of the mast, adjust the lower set of spreader shrouds until they are just tight. Then adjust the next set to the same tension. Once the mast is straight all further tensioning must be done in pairs until all shrouds are very tight.

The shrouds should be tensioned enough to keep the mast secure in the boat when it is heeled to 20 degrees. At that angle, the leeward shrouds will just begin to show a little slackness but will not flap.

The principal cruising development in the last decade has been the development of effective, efficient and reliable headsail roller reefing systems. The principle has been around since the early 1900s, but has only recently been developed

for universal use.

A metal or plastic tube, grooved to accept the leading edge of the sail, is placed over the existing headstay, and when this tube is rotated the sail is wound around it and so reefed or furled (reefing is adjusting the amount of sail to suit the wind strength, and furling is rolling the sail up completely when you have finished sailing). At the tube's top end is a captive fitting containing a ball race which ensures that the tube rotates smoothly when the bottom fitting, consisting of another bearing and a rope or wire drum, is rotated by the control rope.

If buying a system from new, get one with two sail grooves to enable you to change sails without having to lower the sail in use before the other is set.

A parallel development is that of in-mast and in-boom mainsail furling systems, which simplify reefing the mainsail without too great a loss in performance. Self-tailing winches for the control lines make the use of sail furling and reefing systems even easier.

If your boat has the traditional hanked-on headsails, you can ease the task of headsail changing by replacing the standard cylindrical sailbag with a flat, zipped bag which accepts a folded headsail. This attaches to the lifelines or the toe rail for hoisting and packing.

It is *essential* for all cruisers to have netting or criss-crossed cord between the toe rail and lifelines from the pulpit to the mast to prevent sails being blown or washed overboard. In addition, permanent sail ties or elastic cords tied to the lower lifelines help control a sail as soon as it is lowered.

Running rigging is reasonably straightforward. Headsails are controlled by sheets which lead from the sail through adjustable fairleads to turning blocks and the winch. The position of the fairlead is critical to the performance of the sail, and this is especially so with roller reefing headsails. As a guide, the sheet should always be pulling equally on the foot and the leech of the sail.

This is achieved when a line drawn at right angles to the luff of the sail passes through the clew and continues along the pull of the sheet. If the sheet is too far back (a common fault), the leech is too loose and will flap. If it is too far forward, the leech is too tight and the sail will be too baggy.

The mainsheet, working in conjunction with the boom vang, controls the position of the sail relative to the wind. Many cruisers have mainsheet travellers which enable the mainsheet to be eased quickly in gusts or when running.

CRUISER SAIL HANDLING

Sail handling is greatly simplified if the sail stowage is properly organized. This involves ensuring that each sail has an easily accessible stowage point, that each sail bag is labelled with the type and number of the sail it contains (for example 'No. 2 Jib') and that the sail has been bagged correctly so that all corners are easily identified as soon as the bag is opened.

Many owners ensure that the tack, clew and head of each sail are tied in with the drawstring of its bag so that no amount of mishandling will dislodge them.

If you sail at night, tactile identification helps you to locate the sail you want. This can take the form of holes punched into a tag, or thick layers of tape around the drawcord or bottom strap of the bag.

Identification of the corners and sides of the sail often eases the job of newly-recruited crews and so speeds packing and hoisting. Many sailmakers stamp the corners and fix a coloured tape to the foot or leech, but if your sails lack these identification aids you can easily mark them yourself.

Roller headsails are often left on the headstay for long periods in the absence of the owner. The sail is then not covered by storm damage insurance, and the sailcloth is vulnerable to the damaging effects of the ultraviolet component of sunlight.

If your furling headsail can be removed easily it should be stowed away and not hoisted until you next sail. The headfoil should be secured with a triangular sailcloth which slots into the foil and which sheets

down to the deck.

To rig a conventional mainsail from scratch, first feed the foot of the sail onto the boom by sliding the clew from front to back. Depending on the design, the foot will either fit into a groove on the top of the boom or run on plastic slugs or metal sliders over a metal track.

At the inboard end, the tack of the sail will be secured by a tack pin or shackle; at the outboard end it will either be lashed to the boom or, more probably, shackled to an adjustable clew outhaul which tensions the foot to match wind strengths.

During hoisting, check that the battens are securely fastened into their pockets. The usual arrangement uses offset batten pockets which ensure that the battens are securely anchored. If they have to be tied in, use a double reef knot.

Before hoisting the sail, first hoist the topping lift by about a foot to ensure that the weight of the boom does not interfere with the hoisting sequence, and then loosen the mainsheet.

Release the main halyard and attach it, usually by captive or snap shackle, to the headboard. What follows depends on whether your mast is fitted with an external metal track which takes metal sliders, an internal track which takes plastic slugs or sliders, or the conventional mast section which takes the bolt rope.

As you hoist the sail, check that the reefing lines are rove (inserted) in the correct order. Each reefing line should be a different colour – for instance green, orange and red – for

increasing degrees of wind strength. Alternatively, if you have fewer reefing lines than reefs you should have thin 'messenger' line of elasticated cord rigged in a continuous loop through the top two leech reefing cringles.

Once the sail is hoisted, tension the halyard until a vertical crease appears in the luff. Then ease the topping lift until the boom tensions the sail, and tension the boom vang to give the leech a firm appearance.

Once you are sailing, you can tell when the sail is set correctly for the wind speed because at that point the vertical luff crease will disappear. If horizontal creases develop in the luff, re-tension the halyard or use the Cunningham tackle to remove the creases.

In strong winds, increase the backstay tension to pull the masthead to the rear. This will make the mast bend forward in the middle and so help to flatten the sail. Downwind, and in light airs, the backstay should be eased to allow the forestay to sag and the masthead to move forward. This will remove any tension on the sail and enable it to fill properly.

Headsails which have to be hanked on to the forestay require crew members to work in the most exposed and dangerous part of the boat. For this reason, even in the quietest conditions they should get into the habit of wearing safety harnesses that clip onto the wire or tape jackstays, rigged lines provided for that purpose.

Headsails should be folded and packed so that when the bag is

opened, the three corners are at the top. On opening the bag, the crew first attach the tack to the tack fitting, which may be a shackle, pin or ram's horn. They then attach the sheets to the clew with as neat a bowline as possible. Preferably with the sail still in the bag the hanks, usually the piston type, are clipped to the forestay starting from the tack and working up to the head.

When the time comes to hoist the headsail, shackle the halyard to the head and pull the sail bag off the sail. Pull the leeward sheet to distribute the sail along the side deck prior to hoisting.

Once again, tension the halyard to create a vertical crease in the luff. When the sail is sheeted correctly with the sheet lead in the correct position, check that there are no creases in the luff. If horizontal creases develop, or the sail is scalloped between piston hanks, release the sheet and tighten the halyard until they disappear.

Changing sails while on the move should be done to suit the safety and working conditions of the foredeck crew, who should work out a plan of action with the skipper. If conditions are bad, the skipper should place the boat on a broad reach to ensure safer working conditions.

Firstly, the new sail should be set up on the windward (weather) rail so that the redundant sheet can be tied on and the sheet lead correctly positioned at its pre-marked point.

The old sail should be lowered and then stowed below through the fore or main hatch, lashed to the rail, or bagged by one crew member

Slugs or sliders ensure that the sail does not escape during hoisting or lowering.

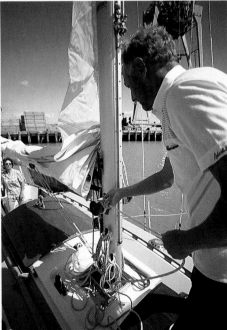

The mainsail can be taken up by hand at first, and winched when it gets too heavy.

The mainsail should be tensioned until a vertical crease appears in the luff.

Above *Spinnakers should be set while a headsail is set on the forestay. Once the spinnaker is set, the headsail can be lowered.*
Below *When not in use, headsails can be stowed along the lifelines.*

while the other hanks on the new sail. Tack the boat so that the new jib can be hoisted and set. The other sheet can then be attached.

Roller reefing headsails give crews a much safer ride, and this is especially important when family crews are sailing quite small boats over long distances. However, every skipper using a reefing headsail system must have a spare headsail which can be set if the system fails or the sail is blown out and cannot be lowered. An old No. 3 jib with a wire luff added is usually sufficient, as it will cover a wide range of windspeeds.

All flying headsails, such as spinnakers, should be set and lowered while a headsail is set on the forestay. This prevents the dreaded 'forestay wrap' – when the flying headsail wraps around the forestay – which can immobilize a boat. The headsail on the forestay is lowered once the flying headsail is set.

Cruising boats also use asymmetrical flying headsails such as cruising chutes and gennekars, often with handling devices designed to offer more control during hoisting and lowering.

The symmetrical spinnaker is a more effective sail because it operates through a greater range of angles to the wind. Its bad reputation stems from early unstable designs and aft sheeting positions which gave rise to wild broaches.

Sheeting systems have been simplified to single sheets, leading aft and running through a floating block controlled by a line running through a toe rail-mounted snatch block in the vicinity of the shrouds. This basic 'Barber hauler' system originated in dinghies, and enables the spinnaker to be pinned down forward of the beam for strong wind conditions, so preventing severe rolling.

Control of the spinnaker during hoisting is easily achieved by 'rubber banding' it: the sail is passed through a bottomless plastic bucket which has rubber bands stretched around it so that they can be slipped off the bucket and around the sail at intervals of 3 feet. The sail is packed in its bag or 'turtle' so that the head is at the front and the clews are on their correct sides.

The spinnaker is hoisted from the rail midway between mast and pulpit or from a pulpit-mounted turtle. To prepare for spinnaker hoisting on a cruiser, steer the boat onto a broad reach, rig the spinnaker bag or turtle, and then rig the spinnaker sheets securely to their appropriate clews.

Place the windward sheet in the spinnaker pole and attach the pole uphaul/downhaul, then hoist the pole so that it is parallel with the deck.

Lightly tension the sheet and guy before loading them onto the winches (preferably self-tailing) and cleating off. Hoist the sail quickly, being certain that it reaches the top by having a clear mark on the halyard.

Sheet the guy so that the sail is pulled to the pole end, and cleat the guy so that the pole is midway between the forestay and shroud. Haul in the sheet so that the rubber bands break and the sail fills. Once the spinnaker is under control, lower the forestay headsail to the deck but have it ready for instant hoisting. The spinnaker is correctly set when the pole is adjusted so that the two clews are level and the windward edge gently 'breathes' by collapsing rhythmically throughout its length.

To lower a spinnaker, first hoist the genoa and steer onto a broad reach. Place a rope over the leeward sheet to ensure that it can be reached to pull it in, and check that the halyard is free to run out without snagging. Ease the pole to the forestay, and release the windward clew from the guy using the tape tail fixed to the snap shackle.

Release the halyard and let it out rapidly. At the same time, pull the sail under the boom from the main cockpit hatch so that it goes into the saloon. Tidy up the sheets and halyard for the next session prior to packing the spinnaker away in rubber bands.

HANDLING UNDER POWER

The majority of cruising boats are fitted with powerful, efficient diesel engines which, if regularly maintained, give good service. More engine problems occur because of lack of regular use than from abuse or heavy use.

User controls have been standardized to a single lever that selects forward (ahead), neutral and reverse (astern) gears and, when used in conjunction with forward and reverse gears, also controls the engine speed. This single lever has made handling under power a much more precise skill than it was in the days of individual gear and throttle levers.

The diesel is designed to be used in a robust manner and manufacturers take account of this when matching drive trains and propellers to specific engines. Cruiser propellers vary considerably in size, shape and format, from the three-bladed, fixed propeller through the streamlined, folding props of racing boats to the variable-pitch propeller of the heavy cruising yacht.

Whatever its size or shape, though, every propeller will produce a sideways turning force which affects the handling characteristics of a yacht. This effect is known as *prop walk* or the *paddle wheel effect*, as the blades bite into the water to produce forward (or reverse) thrust, they also create a sideways thrust.

If a propeller, when viewed from astern, is rotating clockwise, it will tend to swing the stern of the boat to the right. A skipper whose boat is fitted with a right-hand prop (one that turns clockwise when the boat is in forward gear) will know that the shortest turning circle in forward gear is to the left (port), because the back of the boat is kicked to the right by the prop, and this assists the action of the rudder. When going astern, the shortest turning circle will again be to the port side of the boat, because the prop will then be pulling the back to the left.

Knowing the direction of rotation or 'handing' of the prop enables you to use engine revs to advantage. If your boat has a right-hand prop, and you are turning it to port in a confined space, you can use sharp bursts of forward power to kick the stern to the right, interspersed by gentle use of reverse power to stop the boat in preparation for the next forward burst.

You continue this forward/reverse/forward sequence – keeping the tiller or wheel hard over throughout – until the turn is complete. To turn the boat to starboard, use sharp bursts of reverse power interspersed with gentle applica-

tions of forward power to achieve the best results.

If you keep forgetting which way your prop turns, put a little drawing near the controls showing its rotation in ahead (forward) with an arrow below to show the direction of prop walk.

As well as being affected by the rotation of the propeller, the direction of travel of the boat is influenced by the wind acting on the hull. All boats assume a specific *wind rode* angle to the wind, with the bow tending to drift downwind. Except when under sail, the wind acting on the hull and masts will work to push the boat to this angle.

Under power, the high sides and cabins of a cruiser will assist or hamper a turn depending on whether the boat is turning away from or toward the wind, so knowing how your boat drifts is important when you are considering a turn in strong winds. Any turn toward the wind will produce a wider, slower turn, and any turn away from the wind will produce a tighter, faster turn.

Above *An engine can be very useful in very light winds.*
Left *Engine controls have been simplified to single levers.*
Top right *Manoeuvring in crowded areas is better done under power than under sail.*

You can use these effects of the wind to help you manoeuvre, but if you are unsure of how your boat is affected by the wind, before handling it in a confined space practise turning it in open water.

Tidal movement is another variable affecting boat handling and it can also often be used to advantage. Once you have determined the tide's direction, you can face into it and match its speed so as to remain stationary.

Only in exceptional circumstances should you approach a stationary object by moving *with* the tide. This is because you will have to use reverse gear to stop or stay in position alongside the object, and in reverse most boats handle poorly and are notoriously difficult

ENGINE CHECK LIST

Prior to use, check:
fuel quantity
fuel filters
fuel on
crankcase oil level
gearbox oil level
coolant levels
raw water filters
sea cocks open
greasing points greased
electrics on
bilge blowers on
belt tensions

During use: check engine
visually and grease as per
manufacturer's schedules.

After use: use 'Prior to
use' checklist again to
close engine down.

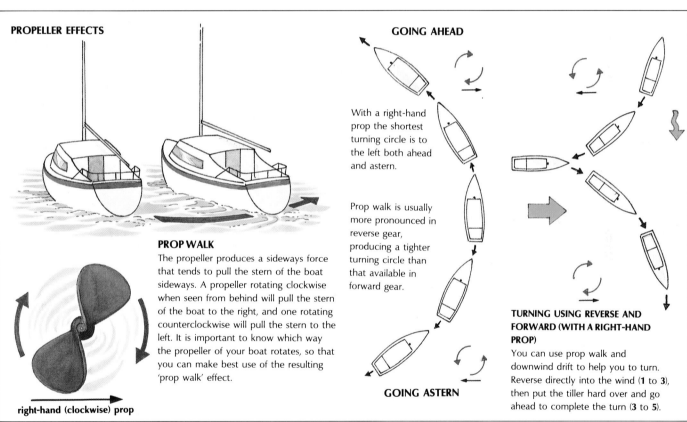

PROPELLER EFFECTS

PROP WALK
The propeller produces a sideways force that tends to pull the stern of the boat sideways. A propeller rotating clockwise when seen from behind will pull the stern of the boat to the right, and one rotating counterclockwise will pull the stern to the left. It is important to know which way the propeller of your boat rotates, so that you can make best use of the resulting 'prop walk' effect.

right-hand (clockwise) prop

GOING AHEAD

With a right-hand prop the shortest turning circle is to the left both ahead and astern.

Prop walk is usually more pronounced in reverse gear, producing a tighter turning circle than that available in forward gear.

GOING ASTERN

TURNING USING REVERSE AND FORWARD (WITH A RIGHT-HAND PROP)
You can use prop walk and downwind drift to help you to turn. Reverse directly into the wind (**1** to **3**), then put the tiller hard over and go ahead to complete the turn (**3** to **5**).

to steer accurately. Additionally, many engine/prop combinations do not produce sufficient power in reverse gear to combat a strong tide.

Your boat's speed should always be regulated to the minimum needed to complete the task in hand efficiently, but beware of being over-cautious and moving too slowly, because then you might not be able to counteract the effects of the wind or tide.

Picking up or releasing a mooring should be done carefully so that the crew member never has to take any weight on the mooring strop. Similarly, when coming alongside, the whole boat should cover the last few feet moving sideways so that crew members can jump out and fix their mooring lines with the minimum of fuss and without having to fight the weight of the moving boat.

The momentum of a boat is enormous. It may weigh 3 to 4 tons or more, and even when moving at half a knot it can cause considerable damage if it hits a solid object. Large, well-secured fenders, set low for coming alongside pontoons or high for walls, should be generously arranged on the side which is expected to make contact. One or two large fenders, in the hands of experienced crew members, should be kept in reserve for unexpected problems.

Gaining confidence in handling under power requires a period of concentrated practice, preferably under the guidance of a competent instructor or experienced boat handler. Without tuition, the average weekend sailor will probably continue to repeat mistakes rather than gain experience.

Whenever a boat is under power, it is the guy at the controls who determines what will happen, and proper management of the boat and its crew is vital for successful docking, mooring or anchoring. All ropes, warps and fenders must be prepared well in advance, and the crew must know their individual tasks, for instance to jump ashore with both warps and secure the one which will prevent the boat drifting away with the tide or wind.

Similarly the operational maintenance of the engine is the skipper's responsibility. Unlike an automobile engine, the marine diesel needs to be given a series of checks before, during and after use, to minimize the chances of something going wrong when the boat is away from shore.

LEAVING & BERTHING

The advent of marinas, with their finger berth pontoons placed at right angles to the main catwalks, has resulted in the need for some very close-quarter boat handling under power when leaving or entering them. In such situations, a proper understanding of the use of warps to assist in turning in confined spaces goes a long way toward preventing the wind or the tide taking control.

Every member of the crew must understand what is going to happen and what is expected of them. Leaving your permanent berth with a crew of non-sailing friends is the severest test of your ability to handle your boat in a confined space: either you know you can do it yourself with the minimum of help or you will have to brief your crew thoroughly.

The first thing they should learn is to look at you when they are speaking, so that you will hear clearly what disaster is about to happen. The second thing is that situations change quickly and they must always be listening for new instructions – you shouldn't have to shout at them to attract their attention before giving them instructions.

The majority of marina berths enable two boats to occupy each section. This gives a little manoeuvring space and enables you to use your neighbour to assist if the wind or the tide are pressing you onto your finger berth.

When leaving a berth, you should use warps to windward or uptide to

check drift or assist your turn. You may have to send a crew member, with a warp, to a boat on the adjacent set of pontoons so that you can haul your boat astern, particularly if the wind is blowing strongly from astern. Aim to collect the crew member at a more accessible point on the marina, such as at the fuel berth.

The general plan is to reverse out of your berth, turn on to your desired exit course, change into forward gear and leave the marina.

Assume that you are moored with bow, stern and breast ropes, and bow and aft springs (a bow spring is a mooring rope led forward from the stern, an aft spring is one led aft from the bow). With the engine running and the boat prepared for sea, two of your crew members go ashore.

They first set up a warp which leads from the stern to the bollard/-cleat/ring on the end of the pontoon, and back to the stern. This is referred to as *singling-up* a warp, and it

enables the warp to be retrieved by a crew member on board as soon as it has done its job. The on-shore crew then release the bow, stern and breast ropes, steadying the boat with their hands, and prepare to release the springs.

You should now be ready to leave as soon as the springs are cast off by the on-shore crew. After releasing the springs, they push the boat away from the pontoon and guide it astern as you engage astern. As they jump on, they push the boat away some more.

The stern warp is kept under control by a crew member under instructions from you. To use it to turn the boat, the crew takes a turn around the cleat and hauls it tight, easing out a bit at a time as the pull gets too great. The bow will be flicked out as the stern is held by the warp. During the turn, make sure that you always have sufficient space to manoeuvre in at both bow and stern.

As soon as the boat is facing in the new direction, you engage forward gear and the crew hauls in the rope as the strain decreases and the boat moves forward.

To kick the stern out prior to leaving the berth, a singled warp is attached from the bow to the end of the pontoon. You first push the tiller away from the pontoon and then, with short gentle bursts in forward gear, kick the stern out against the pull of the singled warp prior to cen-

Right Properly positioned fenders are essential, especially when boats are rafted up alongside others.

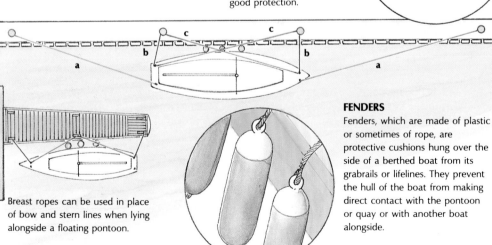

WARPS
All ropes used for mooring are known as warps, but when they are rigged in position they are given particular names:
(a) are bow and stern lines
(b) fore and aft breast ropes
(c) fore and aft springs.

PROTECTING WARPS
Warps are particularly prone to chafe where they go through fairleads or over the edges of quays. Threading a length of plastic tube on them gives good protection.

Breast ropes can be used in place of bow and stern lines when lying alongside a floating pontoon.

FENDERS
Fenders, which are made of plastic or sometimes of rope, are protective cushions hung over the side of a berthed boat from its grabrails or lifelines. They prevent the hull of the boat from making direct contact with the pontoon or quay or with another boat alongside.

Left A typical yacht marina, with finger berth pontoons placed at right angles to the main catwalks.

tering the tiller, engaging reverse and backing out prior to the turn. Then the warp is pulled aboard. Always use favourable winds or tide to assist your turns.

Returning to a marina berth has one advantage over leaving it, in that even a first-time crew now know a bit more about sailing and where everything goes.

As you approach, double-check that you are entering the section of the marina that contains your berth and that no-one else is in your space. Have all warps and fenders strategically placed, and brief the crew on what they have to do, especially those with 'wandering fenders' for unexpected contact with other users. Remember that it is often easier to go alongside your neighbour than the smaller finger pontoon, so have a few fenders ready on that side.

Your approach should 'test out' the wind and tide effects so that your final turn into the berth will take account of both. Place the boat well into your space so that a crew

member can jump ashore with the springs. Go astern to stop, being careful not to kick the stern out. Once the springs are secured, the breast ropes are attached followed by the usual berthing ropes. Often, owners have specially-protected permanent marina warps which are left attached to the pontoon. On return, these ropes are picked up and placed on their correct cleats or mooring posts.

When berthing at quaysides or long pontoons, you either have to raft up to previous arrivals or occupy a narrow space between them. First do a dummy run to assess wind and tide effects, usually by aiming straight at the quay or pontoon, then go around, prepare long bow and stern warps and plenty of fenders, and go alongside the chosen vessel or into the chosen space. Unless you are very experienced, never try mooring alongside with a strong following wind or tide unless you are certain that you can get a stern warp secured quickly.

Rafting alongside or mooring to a tidal quay requires a minimum of 50 metres of bow and stern warp to reach the shore and allow for rise and fall of tide.

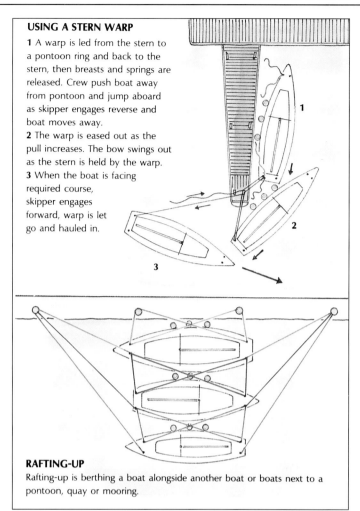

USING A STERN WARP
1 A warp is led from the stern to a pontoon ring and back to the stern, then breasts and springs are released. Crew push boat away from pontoon and jump aboard as skipper engages reverse and boat moves away.
2 The warp is eased out as the pull increases. The bow swings out as the stern is held by the warp.
3 When the boat is facing required course, skipper engages forward, warp is let go and hauled in.

RAFTING-UP
Rafting-up is berthing a boat alongside another boat or boats next to a pontoon, quay or mooring.

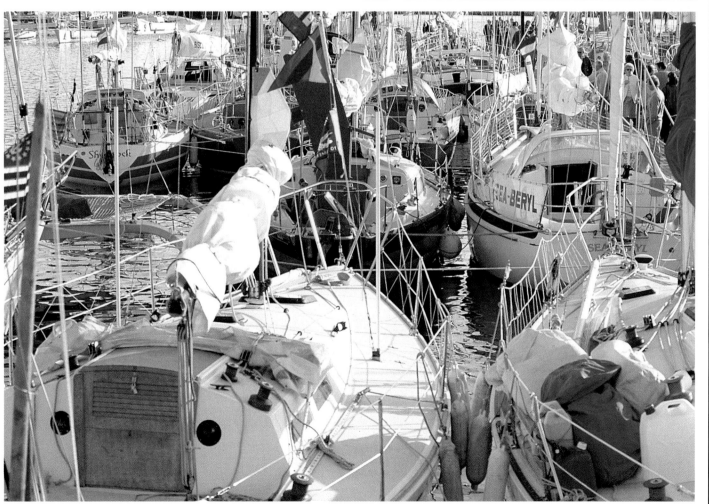

MOORING & ANCHORING

A mooring is a permanent anchorage where you keep your boat when it's not in use. It may be tidal, in which case the boat dries out twice a day, or deepwater, where the boat is afloat at all states of the tide. Anchoring is a temporary method of mooring your boat for reasons of safety or for convenience and comfort, such as for an overnight stop.

Mooring and anchoring involve the use of heavy gear, and you should handle this carefully to avoid permanent injury, especially to your back. The anchors and anchor chains on most cruising boats of up to 10 metres can be handled safely without winches, but on boats above 10 metres the weight of the anchors and chains makes the use of manual or electric anchor winches essential.

The working parts of a mooring are a large, spherical buoy that supports the weight of the heavy mooring chain, and a smaller buoy attached to the chain, wire or rope mooring strop that attaches the boat to the mooring.

When you moor your boat, lead the strop through the bow roller to a substantial cleat, bollard or sampson post, and cleat the lighter rope of the pick-up buoy over the strop to prevent it jumping off. Insert the bow roller pin to prevent the strop jumping out.

Before you leave a mooring, prepare your boat for the voyage. Choose the sails to suit the weather conditions, and run the engine to warm it up, even if you plan to leave under sail.

Ready the mooring by removing the pin from the bow fitting, uncleating the buoy line from the strop, and placing the buoy through the front of the pulpit and up over the guardrail so that it is free when the mooring is released.

In a tideway, check that the boat is wind rode and that hoisting the mainsail will not cause the boat to sail about wildly. Ready the headsail but keep it rolled, bagged and stowed on the rail.

Drop the mooring by uncleating the strop and then walking the boat forward by pulling on the mooring. Steer the boat away in an arc, sheeting in the main, and hoist the headsail when clear of obstructions. To back off under sail, push the boom into the wind.

To pick up the mooring under sail, first decide whether other moored boats are facing into the wind or tide, and then sail in – under mainsail, headsail or no sails – to position your boat to match those already moored. The secret of successful mooring is practice, plus a slow unhurried approach with a planned exit in case of emergencies. Have your engine running as a back-up.

Your boat should be equipped with two anchors which can be relied on to hold it securely in gale-force conditions. The main or 'bower' anchor should be the heavier of the two and should be matched to at least 50 metres of chain. Your second or 'kedge' anchor should have 6 metres of heavy chain and at least 100 metres of plaited or braided nylon anchor warp, preferably stored on a drum.

Chain must be carried for one anchor because it resists abrasion and its weight, combined with its catenary, acts as a spring in violent gale-force conditions. Stowing chain is a problem on modern boats, but a large plastic bin or box securely bolted inside a locker may be a good solution.

The end of the chain (the *bitter end*) must be secured to a strong eyebolt with a rope lashing which can be cut in an emergency. Anchors must be securely stowed in their lockers to prevent structural damage in rough conditions.

When choosing an anchorage, check your tidal curves to ascertain the minimum depth at low tide. Make due allowances for boats already moored, especially if some are on rope and others on chain, because they will have vastly different swinging circles.

If anchoring with chain, flake about twice the depth onto the side decks, then lower the anchor to just above the surface and motor into the choosen position. Come to a stop facing into the wind and, as the bow blows off, lower the anchor to the seabed. Reverse away, letting out a

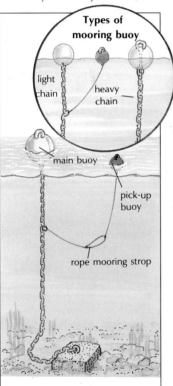

Types of mooring buoy

light chain
heavy chain

main buoy

pick-up buoy

rope mooring strop

MOORINGS

Moorings have three basic elements: a floating buoy, a chain and a sinker. They may simply have a ring on top to tie the boat to, or have a rope strop which can be secured to the boat. Some have a smaller pick-up buoy, attached to a ring on the chain to which the boat is tied.

TIDAL WATER

A moored boat will face either into the wind or into the tide, whichever is the stronger. A boat facing into the wind is said to be 'wind rode', and a boat facing into the tide is said to be 'tide rode'. When the effects of wind and tide are equal but opposite, a moored boat will line itself up at right angles to both, and is said to be 'across the wind'.

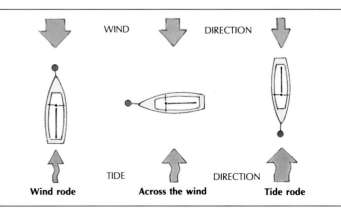

WIND   DIRECTION

TIDE   DIRECTION

Wind rode   Across the wind   Tide rode

length of chain about three times the high-tide depth of the water.

Check that the anchor has bitten and, when the boat has settled down, take anchor bearings to enable you to check for drift. Hoist a black ball in your forward rigging by day and replace it with an anchor light at night.

The kedge is used as a 'lunch hook' for short stays or as a second anchor when bad weather is expected from another direction. The classic example is during the passage of a cold front. In the Northern Hemisphere, when a cold front passes through, the wind veers from southwest through west to northwest, so the kedge should be motored, or laid by dinghy, in a northwesterly direction.

In the Southern Hemisphere, the wind backs from southeast through east to northeast during the passage of a cold front, so the kedge should be positioned to the northeast of the boat.

To retrieve two anchors, first pick up the kedge and then the main anchor.

ANCHORING

To find the minimum length (scope) of chain needed at an anchorage, multiply the depth at high water by three, and add extra length to allow for the distance from the windlass to the water. The weight of a chain causes it to hang down in a curve, known as a 'catenary'. Because rope isn't heavy enough to hang in a deep catenary, an anchor rope needs a longer scope (of at least five times the depth of water).

Once a boat is anchored, a black signal ball must be hoisted in the fore rigging, and at night this must be replaced by an anchor light.

The weight of an anchor alone is not enough to hold a boat: the anchor has to bite.

BITE
An anchor has bitten when it has dug into the bottom.

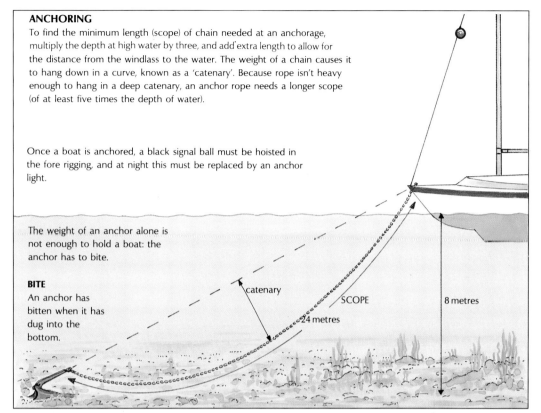

catenary · SCOPE · 8 metres · 24 metres

Above left *A typical mooring. The mooring strop runs from the bow of the boat to the underwater chain securing the mooring buoy.*

Above *Boats moored at buoys in a sheltered estuary. The boats are tide rode, facing into the incoming tide.*

BASIC CRUISER MANOEUVRES

The basic manoeuvres of tacking and gybing are essentially the same for cruisers as for dinghies, but the sail-handling gear is different and the manoeuvres take longer because a cruiser reacts more slowly than a dinghy.

Another difference is that winches have to be used to sheet in the headsail, because it is much larger than that of a dinghy. If your boat has self-tailing winches they can be operated by a single crew member, but if it has ordinary winches and you have sufficient crew, detail one to turn the winch and another to do the tailing. Tailing involves looping the sheet or halyard around the winch, and pulling on the end of it while the winch is being turned.

The procedures described here can be carried out by a skipper and one crew member, but if you have more than one crew you can divide the tasks among them, if you wish. For example, you could have one crew releasing the old headsail sheet and another handling the new one, or perhaps two handling the new one, with one of them tailing the winch and the other winding it if it isn't a self-tailer.

Before you begin to tack, your boat should be sailing fast and not too close to the wind, and you and your crew should double check that it is safe to tack and that you won't be obstructing other vessels when you do.

When you are ready to tack, call 'Ready about!' to inform the crew, who then uncleats the headsail sheet but does not ease it. Then call 'Lee-ho!' and push the tiller to leeward (or turn the wheel) to bring the bows round into the wind while the crew releases the headsail sheet.

As the sails move across to the other side of the boat, the crew should move across to take up the slack in the new headsail sheet and you should also change sides, keeping the tiller hard over. The crew now winches in the new headsail sheet to set it while you steer the boat onto its new course.

Gybing a cruiser is much simpler than gybing a small dinghy, because the larger boat is inherently more stable. Even so, you must maintain full control of the boat throughout the manoeuvre because the sails remain full and so they cross to the other side of the boat with some force. You must also, of course, check that it is safe for you to turn before you begin to manoeuvre.

With the boat on a broad reach, tell the crew you are about to gybe by calling 'Stand by to gybe!' The crew should ready the new headsail

sheet and take up the slack in it, and prepare to release the old one. Steer onto a dead run, and haul in the mainsheet to bring the end of the boom over the quarter (midway between the stern and the beam) so that it doesn't simply swing right across the boat.

Now call 'Gybe-ho!' and cross to the other side of the boat, changing hands on the tiller as you do. Let the boat turn until the sails begin to swing across to the other side, then stop the turn by centring the tiller and use the mainsheet to control the swing of the boom as it transfers to the other side.

The crew can now release the old headsail sheet and ease or winch in the new sheet to set the sail on the new side, while you steer the boat onto its new course and set the mainsail correctly.

The downwind performance of a cruiser can be improved by

Above At night, deck lights greatly assist foredeck work; otherwise, the simple mountaineer's head light can prove of great benefit to a crew member struggling in the dark.
Top Before you make any manoeuvre, check that it is safe to do so.

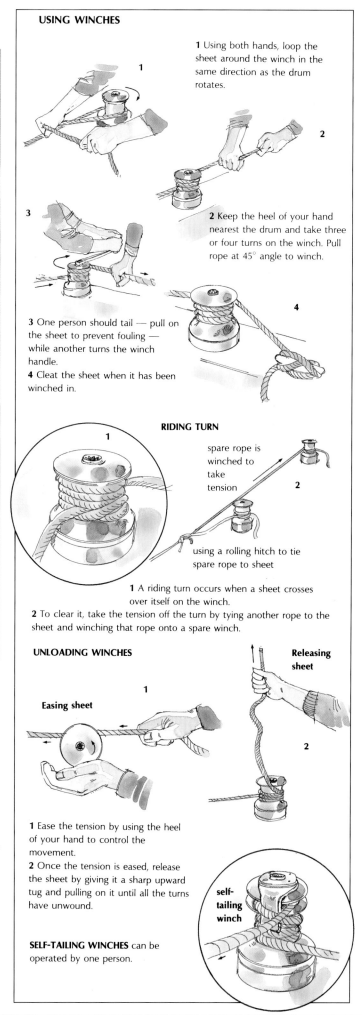

USING WINCHES

1 Using both hands, loop the sheet around the winch in the same direction as the drum rotates.

2 Keep the heel of your hand nearest the drum and take three or four turns on the winch. Pull rope at 45° angle to winch.

3 One person should tail — pull on the sheet to prevent fouling — while another turns the winch handle.

4 Cleat the sheet when it has been winched in.

RIDING TURN

spare rope is winched to take tension

using a rolling hitch to tie spare rope to sheet

1 A riding turn occurs when a sheet crosses over itself on the winch.

2 To clear it, take the tension off the turn by tying another rope to the sheet and winching that rope onto a spare winch.

UNLOADING WINCHES

Releasing sheet

Easing sheet

1 Ease the tension by using the heel of your hand to control the movement.

2 Once the tension is eased, release the sheet by giving it a sharp upward tug and pulling on it until all the turns have unwound.

SELF-TAILING WINCHES can be operated by one person.

self-tailing winch

using a cruising chute, a poled-out headsail or a spinnaker. Cruising chutes or poled-out headsails are usually preferable for family cruisers because they are much easier to handle than spinnakers.

You can gybe a cruising chute as you would a jib or genoa, if it has two sheets, but if it has only one then you will have to lower it before you gybe and reset it after. With a poled-out headsail, you remove the pole before the gybe and fit it on the new side after it.

To gybe the spinnaker, work on the principle of flying the sail without a pole so that it does not collapse. Ideally, only the mainsail should be swung across the boat to gybe, rather than the boat turned through a large arc.

Begin from a run, and with the pole set aft ease the uphaul/downhaul to enable the foredeck crew to move the pole. Prior to the gybe, the foredeck crew should place the leeward genoa sheet over his or her shoulder to ensure that it ends up on top of the pole.

As the pole is eased forward the crew releases it from the guy, unclips the pole from the mast, clips the new guy to the pole and places the pole on the mast fitting.

This sequence is called *end-for-ending*. It's a complicated task, and the skipper and the crew handling the sheets and pole controls must give the foredeck crew plenty of time and space to complete it. Once the pole is secure, the sail is sheeted to the new course.

Racing crews use a *dip pole gybe* in which the pole remains attached to the mast. As the pole is eased forward and dipped to the deck, the foredeck crew releases the old guy and inserts the new one, then the pole is hoisted again. The mainsail is gybed during the manoeuvre.

CRUISER SAILING

Most sailboat skippers rely upon pilotage – the identification of landmarks and seamarks – while in familiar waters. This basic, easy-to-recall form of navigation frees them up to concentrate on their sailing and boathandling skills.

Except for the very few who use their boats for extended periods, the majority of owners are bound by schedules, even when taking a two- or three-week cruise. All too often, skippers opt for using the engine, not realizing that the boat will sail almost as fast if sailed properly. The term 'cruising boat' should not imply that it cannot sail well, given the right skipper.

Attention to the set of the sails on their spars, correct luff and foot tensions for the given wind conditions, and a basic concept of target speeds rather than closeness to the wind, go a long way to producing an efficient sailboat.

All displacement boats have a theoretical maximum hullspeed, which is related to the immersed waterline length. Designers incorporate hull features into their boats which increase waterline length when the boat is heeled, so as to increase the length of the wave created by the hull as it displaces the water.

Because the speed of a wave is governed by its length (the crest-to-crest distance), the length of the wave created by the hull dictates the speed of the yacht.

The formula for wave speed is 1.34 times the square root of the wavelength in feet. Therefore, the hullspeed of a 30-foot yacht with a static waterline of 25 feet will be 1.34 times the square root of $25 = 1.34 \times 5 = 6.7$ knots.

When the boat is heeled to about 20 degrees, the increased waterline length might give 7 knots as a maximum, and so the first fact which must be accepted is that no matter how much sail you put up, that boat will seldom exceed 7 knots.

Fit an inclinometer to show when you reach 20 degrees of heel; not only is this a reasonably comfortable working angle below, it also tells you that you have the correct amount of sail for the given windspeed. Obviously, in light airs the boat will be heeled less, but in such conditions the more upright the boat is the better, because you then need to reduce the wetted surface to reduce hydrodynamic drag on the hull.

To maintain maximum boat speed on all points of sailing you will need to either consult or construct a *speed polar* diagram for the principal points of sail – close-hauled, fetch (sailing close-hauled without tacking), close reach, beam reach, broad reach and run – for a given number of wind strengths, for example 6 knots, 10 kts, 16 kts, 21 kts, 27 kts and 33 kts. Sail combinations for each windspeed are shown on the left side of the diagram and are especially useful as a reminder of which sails are needed and how they should be reefed. It may take a season to complete the construction of a speed polar diagram for your boat, but it's a seaman-like exercise which will improve your sailing speed.

Another factor which seriously affects the speed of cruising boats is the sea state produced by the wind or the tide, or a combination of the two. Waves in coastal waters are usually short and steep and, remembering the formula used to find hull speed, a wave with a length of 4 feet will move at 2.68 knots. If you are sailing a 25-foot cruiser close-hauled you will be sailing against at least five of these oncoming waves at any one time.

To overcome the resistance of short, steep waves, change course to a fetch or a close reach to both increase the sail power and decrease the impact of the waves by meeting fewer crests at a greater angle.

The concept of having to reef the sails in strengthening winds is one readily accepted by racing crews, who appreciate that too much sail heels the boat excessively, slows it down, makes it difficult to steer, and is unnecessary.

Using 20 degrees of heel as a guide, start reefing if the boat repeatedly heels beyond 25 degrees and/or if the gusts turn the boat into the wind despite the application of opposite rudder.

With masthead rigs the headsails are the first to be changed or reefed. Fractional rigs start with a reduction in the area of the mainsail, while ketches douse their mizzens first.

The strategy for reefing any sailboat is four-fold: to maintain

Racing crews make good use of the extra hull speed that heeling can give them.

MAXIMUM HULL SPEED

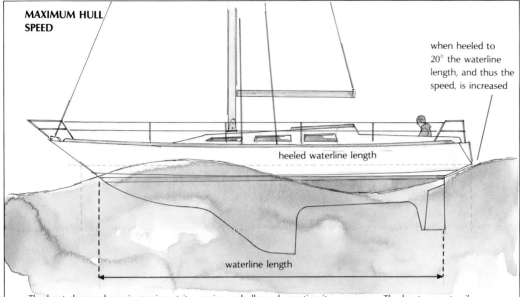

when heeled to 20° the waterline length, and thus the speed, is increased

heeled waterline length

waterline length

The boat shown above is moving at its maximum hullspeed, creating its own wave. The boat cannot sail faster than the speed of this wave, and the wave's speed is governed by its length (crest-to-crest distance). In its turn, the wave's length depends on the waterline length of the boat's hull, and so this distance dictates the speed of the boat.

The formula for calculating the wave speed, and thus the maximum speed of the boat (in knots), is 1.34 times the square root of the boat's waterline length in feet. So for a 30-foot boat with a static waterline length of 25 feet, the maximum speed is 1.34 × the square root of 25 = 1.34 × 5 = 6.7 knots.

Heeling the boat to about 20° might increase the waterline length enough to give a maximum speed of 7 knots.

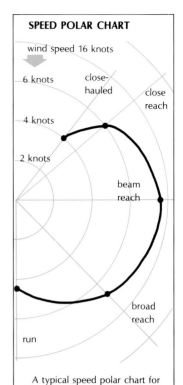

SPEED POLAR CHART

wind speed 16 knots

6 knots — close-hauled — close reach

4 knots

2 knots

beam reach

run — broad reach

A typical speed polar chart for a wind speed of 16 knots. The sail combinations are not shown on this example.

maximum hullspeed; to maintain an angle of heel; to retain the balance between headsails and mainsails so that the boat is not difficult to steer; and to keep the boat as comfortable and dry as possible below, given that circumstances may dictate a specific course of action.

In a progressively rising wind the degree of preparedness and organization of the boat begins to show through. For example, well-engineered furling and reefing systems continue to produce a headsail which is flat enough to drive the boat, and slab reefing systems pull down effective and secure reefs in the main without exposing the crew to unnecessary risks.

Fabric cockpit dodgers and main hatch pram hoods are substantial enough to prevent the ingress of water below. The cockpit is kept free of water by substantial cockpit drains which work even when the boat is well heeled, and bilge pumps operated from below and above deck have the capacity to clear large amounts of water. Down below, the stowage of all heavy items – batteries, anchors, chains, cans and so on – is such that nothing can be thrown out of its locker or stowage lashings even if the boat is knocked down flat.

All these considerations apply to every sailboat which cruises on exposed coastal or large inland

waters. Sudden squalls, often associated with thunderstorms or cold fronts, can produce wind and sea conditions bordering on storm force, often at very short notice.

The short-term answer to the sudden onset of very severe weather is to lower and lash all sails to 'lie a-hull' with the boat fully battened down – especially the main hatch

boards. Experienced skippers may want to keep a storm jib set and to sail off on a broad reach to keep the boat under control and to ride the waves as they rapidly increase in size. The main problem in such conditions is regulating boatspeed to a safe maximum due to the power of breaking crests and the steepness of the waves.

Heeling increases the waterline length of a boat and thus its maximum possible speed.

Heavy-weather strategy is a subject in its own right, and you should refer to some of the standard works on the subject just in case you ever get caught out in life-threatening conditions.

CRUISER EMERGENCY DRILLS

At sea, any potentially life-threatening situation must be treated as an emergency. Successful remedial action will downgrade it to an event, but unsuccessful action will result in the need for help.

The shock of the sudden onset of an emergency can be a mind-numbing experience. To deal with the emergency in a methodical, seamanlike manner, all crew members (and especially the skipper) must know where the emergency equipment is stowed and how to use it. A detailed stowage plan of all emergency equipment should be displayed in the saloon or pasted to the underside of a cockpit locker, and your responses to possible emergencies should have been thought out beforehand.

The VHF radio features prominently in emergency drills, because there are three internationally accepted states of emergency. 'Pan' and 'Securité' are advisory emergency calls, telling the outside world that you have a problem but not actually requesting help, while the third – 'Mayday' – is a call for immediate outside assistance.

It is far better to alert rescue agencies to a *possible* Mayday situation as the emergency develops, rather than to make a frantic Mayday call when the situation gets out

of control, and when you may be unable to give the essential information on who, where and what is involved. The emergencies you are most likely to encounter are man overboard, being holed or running aground, fire, and medical emergencies.

A man-overboard emergency can occur on any point of sail, or even at anchor, but it's always a real emergency and you must do everything and use everything – including daytime orange smoke, nighttime white flares or strobe (flashing) lights – to locate and rescue the person in the water.

The first essential is to mark the position of the man, woman or child overboard with a dan buoy with attached lifering, or orange smoke or strobe light, and assign a crew member to point at the man overboard.

The second is to stay as close as possible to that position while you get the boat under control to situate yourself for the pickup. The third is to make contact with the victim prior to rigging equipment to lift him or her from the water.

The reach-to-reach under sail man-overboard drill, which originated in the United States in the 1960s, assumes that the boat is not carrying spinnakers or boomed-out

headsails when the person falls overboard.

You first steer onto a beam reach for about ten boat-lengths, and then tack round onto a close reach to bring you back to the person in the water. Slow down by letting the headsail fly, and then heave-to to windward of the victim by letting the mainsail fly as well.

The worst-case situation is when you are sailing downwind with a spinnaker set. You then have either to ditch the spinnaker by letting the sheets and halyard run through their blocks, or to release the halyard for a 'float drop' and lash the spinnaker to the rail. Whichever option you choose, the person in the water will have a long wait before being picked up and so will need all the markers you can throw.

In all recovery situations you should lower and lash the headsail and pull all ropes inboard before using the engine to position the boat correctly for the pickup. You should try to make contact with the victim at the first attempt, preferably by throwing a rescue line with a buoy or weighted floating loop.

Thereafter the man overboard can be winched to the boat and hoisted aboard using the mainsheet or two halyards around two different winches. During the rescue,

Recovering a man overboard. The crew had to drop the spinnaker before turning the boat.

delegate a spare crew to issue a Securité call on Channel 16.

If at any time visual contact is lost for more than a minute, issue a Mayday call for outside assistance. It can always be cancelled if you locate the man overboard.

Floating debris such as drums or huge containers is an increasing passive hazard, while submarines and other vessels pose an active threat. A hole six inches across will sink a keelboat very quickly, giving the crew almost no time to issue a Mayday call, gather essential gear, don lifejackets and launch the liferaft.

If a boat suddenly starts letting in water, and it rises above the saloon floor, the first thought is to find the source. Unfortunately, most yachts' batteries are placed low down, and so while someone is looking for the site of the damage a Securité call must be made, alerting the coastguard to a possible emergency, *before* the batteries become immersed.

Your emergency equipment should include tapered softwood plugs with which to plug failed seacocks. Any hole in a GRP hull, however, will be a split or jagged fracture, and while it may be possible to plug it with bunk cushions, clothing or sails, the water usually rises so quickly that the crew will be working in deep water after a few minutes.

If the flow cannot be stemmed, and the pumps fail to prevent the level rising, it must be accepted that unless the boat can be beached, then sooner rather than later it will sink. A Mayday call giving *who*, *where* and *what* together with a description of the action taken will ensure that rescue services or local ships will come to your aid.

When you launch the liferaft or dinghy, try to keep everyone dry. Take the ship's flare pack and documents and any easily accessible high-energy food such as chocolate. As soon as the boat shows signs of instability, climb into the liferaft and cut the painter so that the raft is clear of the boat when it sinks.

If you are close inshore, let off smoke and a pattern of flares as soon as you abandon. If offshore, give rescue services time to reach you and space out the flares – red and white – at sensible intervals, saving the smoke for the final rescue.

If you go aground and are holed, the boat will not necessarily be lost. If the tide is ebbing, you may be able to make a temporary repair with a GRP repair kit, plywood screwed over the hole with self-tappers, or even plastic sheet and duct tape. Most damage occurs when the boat settles onto rocks as the tide recedes, so use fenders, bunk cushions, even bagged sails to protect the hull from damage. However, think carefully before inflating either the dinghy or liferaft to use as hull protection because you may need one or both of them if the situation develops into an emergency.

Use a Securité call to advise the coastguard of your problem, but **do not accept offers of professional assistance to tow you off unless you really need them and have agreed to insurance terms or on a specified fee**. Maritime laws concerning salvage, which is what this is, are quite clear as to how much of the yacht's value the salvage vessel can claim.

Just about every part of a yacht is combustible and gives off lethal fumes when it burns, and diesel fuel, bottled gas, engines and electrical systems can all trigger off a fire. Effective extinguishers and fire blankets must be easily accessible, preferably sited away from probable sources of fire. Always try to fight the fire in its confined space, without having to open the space up. As soon as you think that you are not winning, make a Mayday call before it becomes impossible to stay below. Once you decide to abandon, get out and away as quickly as you can, turning off gas or fuel cocks only if safe to do so.

Because of the risk of explosions, try to get at least 100 metres away. Anyone who is burned should have cold seawater poured over their burns to cool the flesh and prevent further injury.

A serious physical injury accompanied by broken bones or bleeding may need outside assistance. Once the casualty has been made comfortable a Pan Medico call should be made. This will result in on-the-spot treatment by the crew or evacuation of the casualty by rescue services. A well-stocked First Aid kit can be augmented by tea towels, sleeping bag liners, heavy-duty paper rolls and sailcloth.

Helicopter evacuation by static line transfer requires the yacht to be motored into the wind. The helicopter takes station on the port side and lowers a line to the cockpit which must be hand-held, *never* cleated. The helicopter crewman uses the line as a guide to transfer from helicopter to cockpit, and casualties are winched up from the cockpit.

Alternatively, the casualty, accompanied by a crew member, can be drifted astern in the dinghy on a long line. The helicopter crewman transfers down and lifts off the casualty.

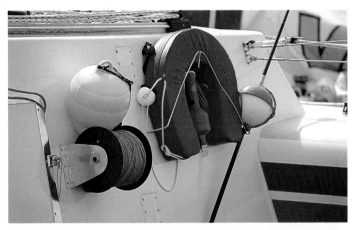

STOWING EMERGENCY EQUIPMENT
All the different items of emergency equipment on a cruiser should be stored securely but should be immediately accessible when they are needed. Lifebuoys and dan buoys, for example, should be kept on properly-designed brackets in the cockpit.

LAUNCHING A LIFERAFT
To launch the liferaft, secure the static line or painter to the boat, then pick up the valise or canister containing the raft and throw it overboard on the leeward side. Pull on the static line to activate the raft's inflation system, maintaining your pull on the line until the raft begins to inflate. When the raft has inflated fully, one person should climb on board and the others should pass down any gear, food, water or other items needed on board. Then the others can climb aboard, and the last one on should cut or untie the painter to free the raft from the boat.

DISTRESS SIGNALS

S O S
Morse code emergency signal, may be sent by radio or by flashing a light

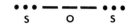

FLAGS
N flag over C flag: 'I am in distress. Help'

W flag: 'I require medical help'

V flag: 'I require assistance'

FLARES AND ROCKETS
Collision avoidance
All vessels sailing at night should carry at least four handheld white flares to use to attract the attention of larger craft when there is any danger of a collision

Inshore signals
When within 3 miles (5 km) of land or of potential rescuers, use handheld flares to attract attention and, when help is on its way, to pinpoint your position. Use handheld red flares in high winds, in poor visibility, and at night, and handheld orange smoke in clear daylight with light winds.

Coastal signals
When between 3 and 7 miles (5 and 11 km) from land, or when cloud is low, attract attention by firing rockets which discharge red stars. When help gets within sight, use handheld red flares or orange smoke to pinpoint your position.

Offshore signals
When more than 7 miles (11 km) from land, attract attention by using rockets which deploy parachute-suspended red flares. Pinpoint your position, when rescuers get within sight, by using red handheld flares (in poor visibility, darkness or high winds) or buoyant orange smoke (in clear daylight with light winds).

MAYDAY CALL (on radio)
1 Mayday (spoken 3 times) **2** This is [ship's name] spoken 3 times **3** Mayday **4** Ship's name **5** Position **6** Nature of emergency and assistance required **7** Any other relevant information

TENDERS & INFLATABLES

'Tenders' is the collective word for a wide variety of small craft used to service the needs of yachts. Originally, yacht tenders were of heavy clinker construction and were hoisted aboard in davits.

Today, two types are available. The first is the rigid GRP tender, which is usually used in conjunction with a swinging mooring. It is large enough to carry the crew and their equipment and strong enough to withstand robust use and storage ashore.

The second type is the inflatable dinghy, designed to be easily stowed on board when deflated. In use, it often gives its occupants a wet ride and is prone to windage (being swept off course by the wind). Nevertheless, it has found universal acceptance as being the best compromise for the many tasks it is called upon to perform.

When buying an inflatable, check that you can sit on a seat or inflated buoyancy compartment while you are rowing. If there's no seat, you will have to sit on the wet floor in an impossible rowing position. A plastic or plywood floor is an essential fitment on an inflatable. Not only does it give a more stable platform to work from, it also increases the craft's performance both when rowed and under engine.

Rowing both forms of tenders requires practice. The rigid tender is often heavy, and clumsy to manoeuvre, but it tracks well and carries large loads. The rowing action is long and measured. The inflatable needs a quick, dipping rowing action where the aim is to keep the oars in the water as much as possible to prevent the wind taking over. Captive oars can complicate the rowing action, however, especially in choppy seas.

A modern lightweight outboard engine is a must for all-weather operations, and a small 2-hp engine with self-contained tank will push most heavily-loaded inflatables against everything except a strong spring ebb.

The outboard attaches to a bracket on the transom of the inflatable, and a safety lanyard is permanently attached to the engine and clipped to the tender while in use. When not in use, the outboard is usually stowed on its own mounting board which is fixed to the back of the yacht's pushpit, and the safety lanyard is always clipped to the pushpit.

When transferring the outboard from its stowage to the dinghy it should always be clipped to something. While being handed down

Top Using a small outboard motor to drive an inflatable is easier and safer than rowing.
Above Inflatables can be towed, but only in calm conditions.

1 When getting into a tender, step carefully into the middle.

2 Release the painter, taking care not to lose your balance.

from the yacht, it is clipped to the crew member's wrist. As soon as it is in the tender it is clipped to the transom and then attached to its mounting.

Because of their light weight and considerable windage, inflatables do not tow well except in calm conditions. The principal danger to a towed inflatable is of being flipped upside down and creating so much drag that the painter breaks or, worse, pulls out its anchorage patches.

If your foredeck is large enough you can pull the inflatable aboard, invert it and lash it down. If it isn't, you have to deflate it and roll it up so that it can either be stowed on deck or placed into its bag and stowed in a locker.

Once ashore, it may be placed vertically in special shore stowage racks resembling toast racks, or placed on car roof bars and taken home, where it can be hoisted into the garage roof space using permanently-mounted hoisting strops.

When using the tender, each occupant should wear a life preserver. Statistics show that more people drown through accidents with tenders than through falling from cruising yachts.

In many cases, problems occur at night when crews return from an evening ashore. Skippers must accept that night work from an inflatable is both difficult and dangerous. The load should be kept within the maximum capacity and the driver should be skilled and capable of finding the mother ship.

The tender should be equipped with a torch, a pump, spare fuel, a toolkit and flares, and all items should be secured with line or placed in special sailcloth 'dinghy bags' fixed to the tender.

As well as its primary use for ferrying the crew to and from the yacht, the tender is a workboat which should be capable of carrying out the various traditional sea-

manship tasks, such as laying out an anchor.

Laying out a second anchor at an angle to the first is a task which calls for thought. Inflatables do not tow well because they skid across the surface when turned. They work best in reverse with the towed object attached to the bow painter. The engine, now at the front, can be aimed at your objective and everything else follows. If the anchor and chain are heavy, they should be placed in a box to prevent damaging the inflatable's fabric, and slung beneath the tender with a quick-release hitch.

If you have to use the tender to move your cruiser it is best to lash it firmly alongside using springs and bow and stern lines. The spring leading aft from the bow of the tender tows the boat forward, the stern spring tows it backward. The yacht is steered normally so that, in effect, the tender is being used as an auxiliary engine.

Cleaning the yacht's hull from the tender, especially the waterline, is often complicated because the tender tends to drift away. Place two large fenders along the sides of the dinghy and stern so that they leave a working space. You can then lash the dinghy tightly to the yacht to keep it in position.

Caring for and repairing tenders is usually on a 'permanent' first-aid basis. GRP dinghies can be fixed with the standard automobile repair packs and inflatables usually have a repair pack containing wooden plugs for emergencies and fabric patches for repairs.

Fortunately, the development of really tough laminated fabrics makes the inflatable a long-lived proposition requiring a visit to a servicing agent about once every three years. Sand, especially at the junction of floorboards and fabric, can be a threat to the fabric, though, and so regular washing and twice-a-season inspections are called for.

3 Carefully push the tender clear of the boat.

4 Fit the oars or start the engine and move off.

PILOTAGE

Pilotage is essentially navigating by using the landmarks and seamarks which are shown on charts. It relies upon the accurate identification of charted objects such as buoyage systems, lighthouses and prominent landmarks. Charts are contour maps of the seabed, drawn to show features and depths at the lowest low water (*lowest astronomical tide* or LAT) normally experienced in the area shown.

An experienced navigator will have the skills to interpret the depths shown on charts, but the newcomer would be wise to start out by sailing only in the areas which show sufficient charted depth, for example 2 metres, until the skills to fix the boat's position by using a handbearing compass have been mastered.

Fixing your approximate position by means of a handbearing compass, which is a special handheld compass incorporating a prism, is an essential skill which can be practised ashore in any open space.

To obtain an accurate magnetic bearing *from* your position *to* an identified charted feature, such as a lighthouse or a headland, you sight over the compass so that you can see both the feature and the bearing (0 to 360 degrees) in the prism. (The recently-developed electronic compasses record the bearing automatically if you press a button when pointing the compass at the feature.)

An accurate bearing gives you a line of position running from your position through the charted feature. You mark that line on your chart, and you then know that your boat's position is somewhere on that line.

To find out where on that line you are, you need to take a second bearing – preferably at right angles to the line – and transfer that second line of position to the chart. The point on the chart where the two lines cross shows the position of your boat, and you should mark it on the chart as a *fix*, a dot within a circle. If the two features you took bearings of are close together, you should take a third bearing to improve the accuracy of your fix.

The difference between true (or charted) north and magnetic north is shown on the chart's compass rose as *variation* to the east or west of true north. The reason for the difference is that the earth's magnetic poles do not coincide with the geographic poles, and the earth's magnetic field is constantly changing at different rates in different parts of the world.

Each chart and each compass rose printed on it carries the variation which existed when the chart was drawn, and the annual increase or decrease in variation. At the start of each season, amend the variation on each compass rose to take account of the increase or decrease in variation since the chart was drawn, or since you last marked the variation on it. Each rose on the chart will show a true and a magnetic rose, printed concentrically.

Also printed on the chart are vertical lines representing longitude and horizontal lines representing latitude. Each is measured in degrees. There are 180 degrees of latitude, 90 degrees north and 90 degrees south of the equator, and there are 360 degrees of longitude, 180 degrees east and 180 degrees west of the *Greenwich Meridian*. Each degree is divided up into 60 minutes (') and each minute into 60 seconds ("). So a point on the earth's surface described as being 53°.21'.24" N, 12°.42'.02" W would be at latitude 53.21.24 north (of the equator) and longitude 12.42.02 west (of Greenwich).

The reintroduction of latitude and longitude, in place of local chart references, has been brought about by the availability of electronic navigation equipment such as Loran and Decca systems, and it is important to understand it and to be able to chart it correctly.

If you are determined to go through the conversion of all bearings to true north you will have to learn, and remember, the conversion sequences. Various mnemonics such as C-A-D-E-T will help you to get it correct. C-A-D-E-T is used to complete the conversion of a Compass bearing to a True bearing. However, the basis of the mnemonic – *C*ompass *A*dd *D*eviation *E*ast for *T*rue is only half the story. The full conversion sequence is *C*ompass course, *A*dd *D*eviation *E*ast (or subtract deviation west) to give magnetic course, add *E*ast variation (or subtract west) to give *T*rue course.

Using C-A-D-E-T to convert a true course to a magnetic one you change the 'add deviation east' to 'subtract deviation east'. You can probably understand why most weekend navigators prefer to work in magnetic only.

Charts are produced by national agencies, and each country has developed its own style of presentation and symbols for land and sea

---

TAKING A FIX — Using a handheld compass

The most usual type of fix is taken by finding the bearings of two charted objects about 90° apart. These bearings are plotted on the chart, and the point at which they intersect is the position or fix of the boat. The closer the boat is to the objects, the better the fix. Taking the bearings of three objects, preferably about 60° apart, will give an even more precise fix.

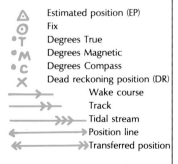

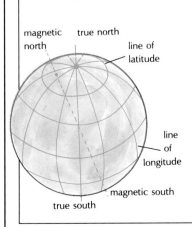

NAVIGATIONAL TERMS
MAGNETIC VARIATION

This is the angle between the True (geographical) North Pole and the Magnetic North Pole as shown by magnetic compasses. This angle varies over the earth's surface, and changes from year to year.

magnetic north — true north — line of latitude — line of longitude — magnetic south — true south

---

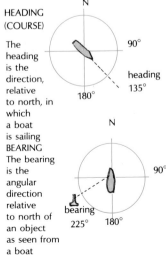

DIRECTION
Direction is measured clockwise from North

HEADING (COURSE)

The heading is the direction, relative to north, in which a boat is sailing

N — 90° — heading 135° — 180°

BEARING
The bearing is the angular direction relative to north of an object as seen from a boat

N — 90° — bearing — 225° — 180°

MEASUREMENTS
Knot The knot is the unit of speed used by boats and aircraft, and is equal to 1 nautical mile per hour.

Nautical mile The international nautical mile is a distance of 1.852 km (1.15 miles or 6067.12 feet). The international nautical mile has replaced previous units such as the British standard nautical mile of 6080 feet.

Metre The metre is a primary unit of measurement in the metric system, and is equivalent to 3.28084 feet (39.3701 inches).

Fathom The fathom, used for centuries to measure water depth, is being replaced by the metre. 1 fathom equals 6 feet.

SYMBOLS FOR USE ON CHARTS

Below are the symbols commonly used when plotting a course on charts. Using symbols is quicker than writing words and takes up less space on a chart

△ Estimated position (EP)
⊙ Fix
°T Degrees True
°M Degrees Magnetic
°C Degrees Compass
× Dead reckoning position (DR)
→ Wake course
⇉ Track
⇛ Tidal stream
⇐ Position line
⇚ Transferred position

Symbols should be marked on chart in plain or coloured pencil.

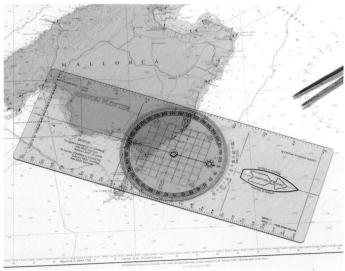

Top Using a parallel rule and dividers to plot a course on a chart.
Above A Breton Plotter, a very useful charting instrument devised by Captain Yvonnick Gueret. It has a rotatable plastic circle marked in compass degrees to allow easy conversion from magnetic to true bearings or vice versa.

features. It is necessary to obtain the relevant publication listing all the symbols on the charts you intend to use.

If you can already read a land map, it doesn't take too long to learn the most-used charted symbols. Start with those nearest the land, such as sandbanks which dry, and rocks which are awash or dry, then move on to shoreline types followed by charted depths and buoyage systems.

Charted features, especially those underwater (such as sandbanks) may change after the chart has been drawn. 'Notices to Mariners' are published at regular intervals to enable you, or a chart agent, to update your charts.

Charts are designed to be drawn on with a medium-grade pencil, and you can use a good-quality eraser to clean them after use. You should stow them in their numbered se-quence, either folded flat in the chart table or stowed vertically in a spe-cially-made easy-stowage rack.

When entering details on your chart, keep to a standard set of sym-bols. Use the 24-hour clock to show times, and mark your DR (dead reckoning) position with an 'X'. Show a fix as a circle with a dot in the centre, and an estimated position as dot inside a triangle. When con-structing navigation *vectors* indi-cate their functions with arrowheads: one arrowhead on the course to steer, two on the track you wish to sail along, and three on the tidal stream. If you are using mag-netic values as your norm, you must identify other values in your chart-work. Show degrees true as °T, and degrees compass as °C.

Accurate chartwork requires using whichever method best suits your capabilities, especially when under stress in adverse conditions.

PASSAGE MAKING

As soon as you leave the confines of an estuary and emerge into the open sea, pilotage becomes less useful and you must adopt a more demanding method of keeping track of or calculating your position.

On the open sea, your reliance upon your main steering compass requires you to know its *deviation values*, which are compass errors caused by factors external to the compass. All compasses are influenced by large masses of ferrous metal or electric fields built into the boat's structure, such as the keel, the engine, and the electrical system.

Deviation is found by checking (swinging) the vessel through 360 degrees by reference to shore marks, or by cross-checking the main compass readings with a handbearing compass, and built-in correcting magnets are adjusted to damp down large errors. (A professional compass adjuster should be employed when fitting new compasses.)

Deviation values are taken at 45-degree intervals and entered on a deviation card as 'east' and 'west' values. Display the card in the navigation space and enter the values in your Decca, satnav or Loran system. For most purposes, because it is not possible to steer within 5 degrees of a given course, errors of 2 to 3 degrees can be ignored on short passages.

Plotting your intended course requires proper passage planning before you set out. With the appropriate corrected charts you consult the almanac, tidal stream atlas and local sailing instructions to determine when you can sail and where you can sail; 'when' is determined by the tides, which govern depths and the speed and direction of the stream, and 'where' is determined by the wind.

When planning, you aim to take advantage of the wind and tide, and to negotiate tidal gates at slack water just before the stream turns in your direction, or to pass through the gates with the stream if sea state permits.

Your passage plan as drawn on the chart will be a series of vector calculations based on one-hourly units of tide. You can choose between letting the tide take you where it wishes while maintaining a steady course, or keeping to a predetermined track by allowing for the tide each hour. A coastwise plan would show as a series of waypoints.

The wind direction, and to a certain extent its speed, will determine whether you can follow those tracks. If you can't, you may have to tack to your waypoints. Calculating how long it will take to tack to an objective embodies the basic

chartwork which must be understood before you venture offshore.

The vector triangle of calculation incorporates the leeway or drift of the boat caused by the wind, the tidal stream direction and speed, and the speed and direction of the vessel. The result of the calculation will be a course to steer when you are passage planning, or a dead reckoning (DR) position once you are out of sight of land and relying solely on published information and your instruments. Only the depth

sounder will give you an observation, and you shouldn't forget its importance.

When you add an electronic or visual bearing to your DR it becomes an estimated position (EP), the change of name denoting that there is a greater degree of accuracy. Only a fix on identified charted features can be taken as an accurate position.

To construct your vector you draw a track, a line joining your point of depature to a waypoint destination. You then consult a tidal

If you plan your course before you sail, you will have less to do when under way.

stream atlas, a tidal diamond or an almanac to determine the tide's speed and direction (which is always given in degrees true) for a given time. Using the true compass rose, mark in the tidal vector at the point of departure so that the arrows point in the direction of the stream. The vector's length is equal to one hour's worth of flow, so if, for example, the tide's speed is 5 knots, the length

COMPASS DEVIATION

A compass needle points north because it is attracted by the earth's magnetic field. However, it will also be attracted by large metal objects on board, such as the engine. These objects will make the compass needle point a little to either east or west of magnetic north, to a direction known as compass north.

SWINGING THE COMPASS

When you instal a compass, find its deviation by 'swinging' it. On a calm day, with all gear in place, sail to a point where you can observe a transit between two charted objects. From your chart, find the transit's bearing and sail slowly past it on eight different headings. Each time you pass the transit, note your heading and the transit's bearing as shown by the compass. The difference between the actual transit bearing and the observed bearing on each heading will be the compass's deviation on that heading.

DEVIATION CARD

Use the information obtained from swinging your compass to draw up a deviation card. Mark each deviation on the card at the point where the vertical line representing its value crosses the line representing the heading on which the measurement was made. When you have marked all the values, draw a curve to connect them. Then you can use this curve to find the deviation on any heading.

360°

315°   45°

270°   90° compass deviation

225°   135°

180°   Chart bearing 135°

boat compass bearing 141°

Boat Heading °COMPASS	WEST					EAST				Boat Heading °MAGNETIC
	8°	6°	4°	2°	0°	2°	4°	6°	8°	
000°c										003°M
045°c										043°M
090°c										084°M
135°c										128°M
180°c										176°M
225°c										226°M
270°c										274°M
315°c										321°M
360°c										003°M

of the vector should represent 5 nautical miles.

The final construction is to draw in one hour's worth of estimated boatspeed from the end of the tidal vector and mark where it cuts the track. You now have the course to steer to move along your charted track. Before you measure its angle you can draw in your leeway angle to windward of the course to steer. Measure this angle to get a course to steer which will cancel out leeway and tidal drift. If you then add or subtract steering compass deviation, you will get a compass course to steer.

Once on your passage you are not theorizing. You have to take account of boatspeed, wind direction and tide for your DR position, and an estimate of the course steered by your helmsman.

If the wind direction makes it impossible to sail along your neat passage plan track, then the track becomes your rhumb line (the direct line to your destination) and you will zigzag along it.

You should update your chartwork hourly, and if you can also make one hour-tacks the updating will be simpler. However, half-hour

tacks are often needed to work inshore of a foul tide, in which case you should note in the log the time of the tack, the average course steered during the preceding half hour and a note on leeway in degrees, especially when in short steep seas.

Your DR calculation will show a line, representing the course steered, starting at your last fix, EP or DR and ending at a point which coincides with your logged distance run in the preceding period. From this point the tidal vector (degrees T) is drawn in the direction of flow to a length with coincides with the time since your last DR. This time will usually be an hour, but if it isn't, beware of adding an hour's worth of tide. The end of the tidal vector is your DR position and you should mark it with an 'X'. If you wish to allow for leeway, apply it to windward of your course steered before you draw in the tidal vector.

Measuring from your previous fix, EP or DR to the new DR position will give your *speed over the ground* (SOG) and *course made good* (CMG). Of course, if you have Decca, satnav or Loran, you can get this information by simply pressing the appropriate button.

The key to successful manual navigation, on short passages out of sight of land, is to know that your steering compass is accurate to 3 degrees on all points of sailing at 20 degrees angle of heel; not to place steel cans or other large magnetizable or magnetic objects near the compass; have a reliable log to measure speed and distance; know how to find accurate tidal information related to local high water and springs and neaps; and to have vector triangles drawn into the front of your log book to show how to plot a course to steer and how to calculate a DR position.

Electronic navigation aids using ground- or space-based transmitters are rapidly replacing all other forms of aids such as radio direction finding and radio lighthouses. When using Decca, satnav or Loran systems it is essential to keep a traditional navigation system 'ticking over' in your ship's log. You should also plot an hourly electronic fix and compare it with a rough DR calculation. If there is a large discrepancy, suspect the electronic aid and immediately re-work your position from the ship's log data.

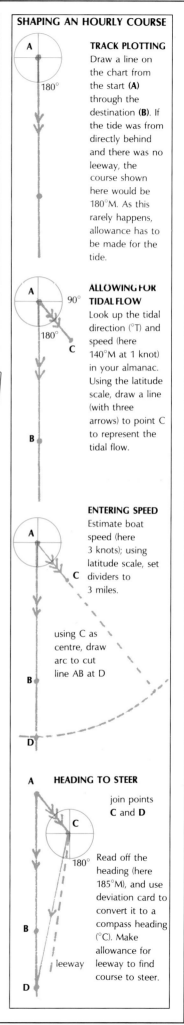

SHAPING AN HOURLY COURSE

TRACK PLOTTING
Draw a line on the chart from the start (A) through the destination (B). If the tide was from directly behind and there was no leeway, the course shown here would be 180°M. As this rarely happens, allowance has to be made for the tide.

ALLOWING FOR TIDAL FLOW
Look up the tidal direction (°T) and speed (here 140°M at 1 knot) in your almanac. Using the latitude scale, draw a line (with three arrows) to point C to represent the tidal flow.

ENTERING SPEED
Estimate boat speed (here 3 knots); using latitude scale, set dividers to 3 miles.

using C as centre, draw arc to cut line AB at D

HEADING TO STEER
join points C and D

Read off the heading (here 185°M), and use deviation card to convert it to a compass heading (°C). Make allowance for leeway to find course to steer.

leeway

MARITIME BUOYAGE

If you intend to sail along coasts and in estuaries you will need to understand buoyage, the system of buoys and other markers used to identify features such as channels or obstructions. Two buoyage systems – Lateral A and Lateral B – were adopted in 1976 by IALA, the International Association of Lighthouse Authorities, for implementation worldwide by 1990. System A is used in the British Isles, Europe, Australia, New Zealand, Africa and most of Asia, including India. System B is operated in North, Central and South America, Japan, South Korea and the Philippines.

The need to mark the sides of shallow, winding channels was appreciated early on in the history of sailing. Originally, the markers were sticks, tree branches or floating barrels, but they became more sophisticated as larger vessels needed to gain access to inland ports.

A uniform colour coding of red for port (left) and green for starboard (right) markers was adopted, but the Europeans marked their channels from seaward while the Americans marked theirs from landward. Nonetheless, these *lateral systems* work well and confusion only arises when you sail from waters using one system into waters using the other, or into waters where neither system has yet been implemented.

The 'direction' of buoyage is determined by the direction in which the flood tide flows. Where two tides meet, such as in a narrow strip of water separating an island from the mainland, a change of buoyage direction is made at a specific point, which is marked on charts of that water.

The Lateral A system has red flat-topped cairns to port on entering, and green conical marks to starboard. With Lateral B, there are green flat-topped marks to port on entering and red conical marks are to starboard. In both systems, the marks may or may not have lights mounted on them.

The lateral systems are used in conjunction with the universally-adopted *Cardinal System* of buoys. This system marks the positions of hazards in relation to the four cardinal points of the compass (north, south, east and west), and the buoys are identified by shaped-top marks and colour coding. In principle, minor estuarial channels are marked with the lateral system and the approaches and major obstructions are marked with the cardinal system.

The identifying marks of cardinal buoys tell you their position in relation to the hazard they are marking, so a north cardinal will be placed to the north of the hazard, an east cardinal to the east of it, and so on.

The top marks of cardinal buoys consist of two black cones, mounted one above the other on the top of the structure and arranged as follows: both cones pointing up = north cardinal; both pointing down = south cardinal; one pointing up and the other down with their bases together = east cardinal; one pointing up and the other pointing down with their points together = west cardinal. If you get confused between east and west cardinals, think of the west as being waisted.

The colours used are black and yellow. North is a black pillar on a yellow buoy, and south is a yellow pillar on a black buoy. East is a black and yellow pillar on a black buoy, west a yellow and black pillar on a yellow buoy.

The colours are often quite confusing, especially when weed or bird fouling occurs, so always start with the colour of the buoy to identify north or west (yellow) and south or east (black), and then positively identify the top mark, making sure that no resting birds are confusing the issue.

Three additional types of mark in the IALA systems are the isolated danger mark, the safe water mark and the special mark. An isolated danger is one, such as a rock, that has navigable water all around it, and the marker for this has horizontal black and red bands and has two black spheres on top.

The safe water mark is a spherical buoy, or a pillar or spar, with vertical red and white stripes and with a red ball on top, and is used to mark landfalls and as a mid-channel marker.

Any special marks to zone off recreational areas, for instance for water skiers, are yellow and may have an X-shaped top mark. They may be any shape, as long as they cannot be confused with a navigational mark.

At night, shapes and colours are of no use to the mariner and so an equally organized system of top lights is used to identify lateral and cardinal systems.

When entering a channel from seaward at night you should have a prepared list of all lights which may be visible during the approach. Your chart of the channel will tell you the characteristics of the lights you will see, and you will find detailed descriptions of the lights used on buoys in any good nautical almanac.

INTERNATIONAL BUOYAGE

Used in conjunction with lateral buoyage, regions A and B.

CARDINAL SYSTEM

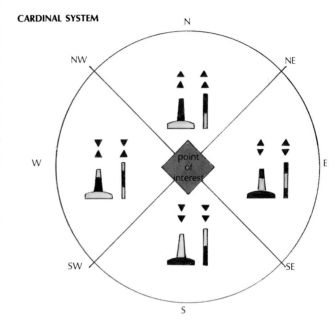

Cardinal buoys warn of hazards, and their identifying marks tell you their position in relation to the hazard they are marking. A north cardinal, for example, is placed to the north of the hazard.

SAFE WATER MARKS

A safe water mark (placed, for instance, in the middle of a channel) indicates that there is navigable water all around it.

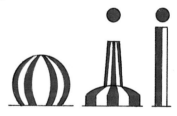

ISOLATED DANGER MARKS

These mark a danger spot that has navigable water all around it.

SPECIAL MARKS

Special marks are not intended primarily to assist navigation but are used to indicate features or areas that may be referred to in nautical almanacs or local sailing directions. A special mark may be any shape, provided that it cannot be mistaken for a navigational mark.

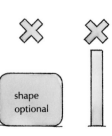

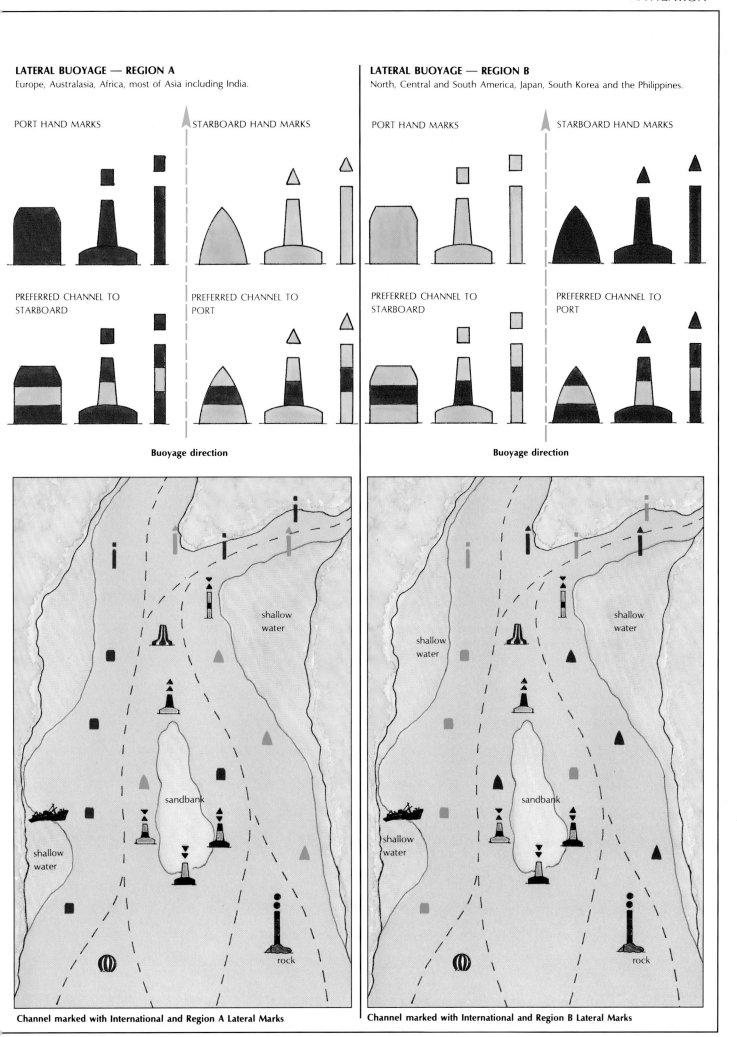

LATERAL BUOYAGE — REGION A
Europe, Australasia, Africa, most of Asia including India.

PORT HAND MARKS

STARBOARD HAND MARKS

PREFERRED CHANNEL TO STARBOARD

PREFERRED CHANNEL TO PORT

Buoyage direction

Channel marked with International and Region A Lateral Marks

LATERAL BUOYAGE — REGION B
North, Central and South America, Japan, South Korea and the Philippines.

PORT HAND MARKS

STARBOARD HAND MARKS

PREFERRED CHANNEL TO STARBOARD

PREFERRED CHANNEL TO PORT

Buoyage direction

Channel marked with International and Region B Lateral Marks

shallow water

shallow water

sandbank

shallow water

rock

ROPES & KNOTS

Being able to tie secure, reliable knots is an essential skill for all sailors, and it's important to use knots that are suitable for their intended purposes, such as attaching halyards or sheets to a sail.

The introduction of Kevlar and prestretched polyester ropes has enabled owners of all but the hottest racing machines to revert to using ropes for halyards. Racing boats continue to use the wire halyard/rope tail because it is the least affected by stretch.

Kevlar-based polyester braids offer the next least stretch, but Kevlar does not take kindly to repeated kinking in the same spot, as for example over a halyard sheave. It is used primarily in dinghies, keelboats and cruiser racers of up to 15 metres.

Traditionally-laid, 3-strand, super-stretched polyester is popular with cruiser racer owners who prefer to dispense with wire. Its sheave abrasion characteristics are good and it can be spliced easily. Sixteen plait multibraid over a 3-strand core is the ideal combination for spinnaker and genoa halyards. Although you can splice it yourself, it is often better to get a rigging specialist to splice multiplait, especially if it is joined to Kevlar or wire tails.

To prevent a halyard running back up the mast, use the double thumb knot, which is easy to tie and easily untied again after years of use. For attaching halyards directly to the head of a sail, and possibly a sheet to a headsail if the bulk of a bowline is not acceptable, the figure-of-eight overhand hitch is a very useful knot to use.

One of the prime requirements of ropes used as sheets is a high resistance to the abrasion caused by running through blocks and around winches and being dragged around shrouds. In use, sheets develop a slightly 'furry' finish which helps them to resist abrasion and improves their grip on winches and rope jamming devices.

Because sheets have to be handled by crew members, it is essential that they are of sufficient diameter to give a comfortable grip when under severe load. For this reason, many dinghy sailors use a thin Kevlar sheet to run through the blocks and splice on a 10- to 12-mm diameter braided tail leading back to the helmsman or crew.

Cruising boats usually cover more ocean than racers and are at sea for longer periods. This adds up to considerably more wear on all ropes and gear, and for these boats' sheets 16-plait matt finish polyester over a 3-strand core gives the required

strength and longevity. Dayboats and dinghies can often use 8-plait polyester and lightweight multifilament polypropylene for all running lines.

Sheets are attached to sails by a bowline, which is the one general purpose knot that all sailors need to be able to tie in any situation. The sheet bend is the traditional method of attaching a sheet to a strop spliced to the clew, and is also used for joining ropes of different diameters. Note that the two short ends of rope must be on the same side of the finished 'bend'. It can be doubled for extra security or slipped if an easy getaway is required.

The rolling hitch is an essential emergency hitch when a sheet fouls and jams on a winch when an inexperienced tailer pulls down instead of up at an angle of 45 degrees. To free a sheet jammed under load, attach a spare rope or sheet to it with a rolling hitch. Then take the tail of that rope or sheet to a spare winch and winch it in until the load on the jammed rope is eased and you can free off the riding turn.

The rolling hitch works on the principle of tightening its grip as the pull increases, so remember to construct the early parts in the same direction as the intended final pull.

To cleat a rope, lead it to the back of the cleat, and secure it with a round turn and at least one figure-of-eight around both horns of the cleat. Small cleats require a half-hitch to finish.

Ropes suitable for mooring and anchoring have good stretch characteristics derived both from their fibres (nylon) and from their loose construction. The introduction of nylon to replace chain has made short-stay anchoring a far less cumbersome prospect, but chain is still preferable for serious cruising and for anchoring in heavy weather. Warps used to moor alongside need to be chafe-resistant.

There is a wealth of knots, bends and hitches with which to attach your vessel and its tender to rings, bollards, poles and other ropes, but if your mind goes blank you can revert to the bowline to create a loop in the shore end. Once your vessel is safely attached, you can think about the alternative knots at your leisure. These include the round turn and two half-hitches, which is quick and simple.

To tie a rope to an anchor ring, use a fisherman's bend with two half-hitches to finish; it may need seizing (trying back) for extra security. The figure-of-eight overhand hitch is useful for anchoring or attaching dinghies to the shore.

PARTS OF A KNOT

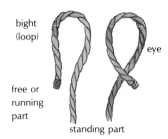

bight (loop)

free or running part

standing part

eye

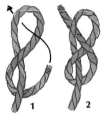

Stop knot — figure-of-eight knot

simple stop knot to prevent rope slipping through blocks or fairleads

1   2

Half-hitch — simplest form of knot, basis for many others

Slipped half-hitch — quick release knot, used where speed of untying is needed

Reef knot — originally used to tie reefing lines. Can be used to join equal thicknesses of rope but will spill if one end is pulled sharply. Good flat knot

1   2   3

Round turn and two half-hitches — for tying rope to standing objects

 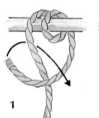  

1   2   3   4

make two round turns around object   make half-hitch   make second hitch   pull tight

Belaying a cleat

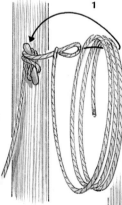

1 take turn around cleat, then over horn

1

2

2 wind around horn in a figure-of-eight

3 several figure-eights can be wound on. Finish with another turn around cleat or tie a slipped hitch

Securing spare rope

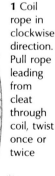

1

1 Coil rope in clockwise direction. Pull rope leading from cleat through coil, twist once or twice

2 hang the loop on top of the horn of the cleat

2

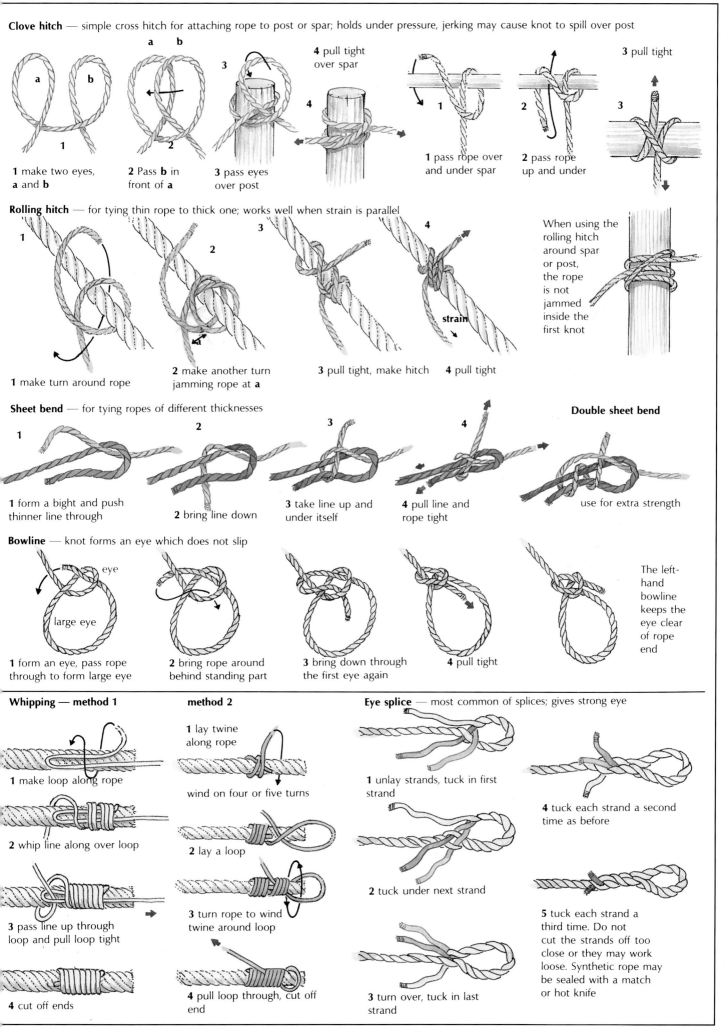

Clove hitch — simple cross hitch for attaching rope to post or spar; holds under pressure, jerking may cause knot to spill over post

a b

a b

3

4 pull tight over spar

4

3 pull tight

1 make two eyes, **a** and **b**

2 Pass **b** in front of **a**

3 pass eyes over post

1 pass rope over and under spar

2 pass rope up and under

3

Rolling hitch — for tying thin rope to thick one; works well when strain is parallel

1

2

3

4

When using the rolling hitch around spar or post, the rope is not jammed inside the first knot

strain

1 make turn around rope

2 make another turn jamming rope at **a**

3 pull tight, make hitch

4 pull tight

Sheet bend — for tying ropes of different thicknesses

1

2

3

4

Double sheet bend

1 form a bight and push thinner line through

2 bring line down

3 take line up and under itself

4 pull line and rope tight

use for extra strength

Bowline — knot forms an eye which does not slip

eye

large eye

The left-hand bowline keeps the eye clear of rope end

1 form an eye, pass rope through to form large eye

2 bring rope around behind standing part

3 bring down through the first eye again

4 pull tight

Whipping — method 1

method 2

Eye splice — most common of splices; gives strong eye

1 lay twine along rope

1 make loop along rope

wind on four or five turns

1 unlay strands, tuck in first strand

4 tuck each strand a second time as before

2 whip line along over loop

2 lay a loop

3 pass line up through loop and pull loop tight

3 turn rope to wind twine around loop

2 tuck under next strand

5 tuck each strand a third time. Do not cut the strands off too close or they may work loose. Synthetic rope may be sealed with a match or hot knife

4 cut off ends

4 pull loop through, cut off end

3 turn over, tuck in last strand

COMPETITIVE SAILING

If you analyze it in terms of skill levels, sailing is a relatively simple physical exercise. If, however, you analyze the *sport* of sailing, you will find that it is one of the most complex of sports to master because of the huge range of skills and activities involved in it.

The majority of dinghy and open keelboat sailors spend at least part of their sailing careers in the competitive side of the sport. This requires them to develop more advanced close-quarter boat handling skills than are needed for leisure sailing, plus an ability to understand and interpret the often-complicated racing rules while involved in tactical and strategic sailing. These skills spill over into the big-boat racing arena, where the degree of sophistication of the craft is matched by the racing pedigree of the crews and the sophistication of the electronic navigation equipment.

Sailboat racing can be as exciting and demanding as any other sport which relies upon complicated racing machines. At world championship and Olympic levels, you need not only the fitness and strength of an athlete but also the mental power of a chess player, so that you can interpret wind, waves and strategies to produce a winning combination.

Fortunately, however, racing is conducted at many levels, not just at international or Olympic level. These range from casual weekday evening races through regular club series to cut-throat one-design class meets and championships, and so there is ample opportunity for any competent sailor to enjoy competitive sailing at a level that suits his or her abilities.

As with all other sports, coaching, physical fitness and practice are all essential to success at higher levels of competition. The casual racer will often gain immense benefit by asking an experienced, successful skipper or crew aboard so that they can sort out the systems and tune the rig. The serious aspiring competitor will need to participate in a structured, land-based physical training schedule in addition to on-the-water sail, boatspeed and technique evaluation sessions either with another boat or with a coach in attendance.

The basis of all sailboat racing is a universal set of rules administered by national sailing authorities on behalf of the International Yacht Racing Union (IYRU). These rules, based on the International Rules for the Prevention of Collisions at Sea (IRPCS), have been developed over a century of racing and are extremely complex. Fortunately, you don't have to learn them all at once. They progress from a few simple, basic rules which everyone *must* know and are easy to learn, through rules which everyone *should* know to rules which you have to look up in a book because they are so obscure.

Rules for the conduct of racing require a proper course to be set, a period of preparation before the start, and a recognized starting signal to be given when all the boats are in position behind the starting line. The race finishes when boats which have correctly sailed the course without infringing any of the rules cross the designated finishing line in the correct direction. Because the rules are usually enforced by the competitors, in most races any infringements are resolved as the race continues. If this is not possible, the aggrieved boat signals a protest, which is then resolved by a jury or protest committee after the race has finished.

The great majority of dinghy owners participate in handicap racing against boats of different designs, and in one-design racing against boats of the same design. Handicap racing thrives in small dinghy clubs and among cruiser racer owners who wish to race against each other in inshore and offshore events. One-design or 'boat-for-boat' racing gives the closest racing and places a premium on boat-handling skills. It also enables the owner to trail to other venues as part of the class points and ranking system.

Boat-for-boat competitions are typified by the various match racing-series held throughout the world. These may involve two boats being matched against each other, as in the America's Cup, or be aggregate competitions such as the Congressional Cup, where a group of selected skippers and crews race against each other in a round-robin series to determine the finalists, or the outright winners.

Yacht racing did not become a media sport until the involvement of certain politicians and pop stars, and the publicity caused by the 1979 Fastnet storm, brought it to the attention of the general public. Since then, in countries such as the United States, France, Australia and New Zealand, racing yachtsmen and women have been elevated to the status of national heroes because of their ability to win prestigious events. In the wake of this public awareness has come an increasing commercial interest from companies wishing to use the not-inconsiderable expanses of hulls and sails as billboards in exchange for sponsorship money.

In many ways, the commercialization of the sport has been a good thing because it has enabled sailors to choose between being amateur or professional, and allowed organizers to run sponsored events with a clear conscience. Sponsorship has already secured the future of many exciting competitions, and has encouraged the design and construction of new breeds of monohulled and multihulled racers that otherwise would never have seen the light of day.

INDIVIDUAL DINGHY RACING

The encouraging aspect of competitive dinghy sailing is that success often comes to those who apply themselves wholeheartedly to the sport. For example, many skilled and enthusiastic young sailors have been selected by top sailing coaches for specialist squad training and have gone on to win Olympic medals.

Less spectacular, but nonetheless rapid, progress can be made by newcomers to racing who take the trouble to practise and to understand the rules. Very little advanced coaching will be available at club level, and you will need to learn by observation, experience and by reading the many excellent books available covering all aspects of competition.

As an example, suppose you have bought a two-man, 14-foot dinghy of international status, suitable for both racing and family use, and you want to take up racing. During the first year of ownership, you and your crew will be primarily engaged in learning to sail the boat in a wide variety of wind conditions at your club.

Racing will usually be a fairly haphazard affair to start with because of your lack of sailing skill. You should concentrate on successfully negotiating the race course and learning the fairly complicated

Jaap Zeelhuis (Holland) fights off Roger Schultz (Germany) in the 1988 Laser Worlds.

procedures of starting and the basic racing rules. Most of your activity will be confined to the club waters, with the occasional excursion to the coast or other sailing venue to gain experience in towing, launching, and navigating in unfamiliar waters.

At the end of the first year, you and your crew will have become able to handle the boat with confidence in medium winds. You will both have a reasonable understanding of what racing entails and an idea of whether your boat has the potential to be tuned to a competitive level.

The second year usually determines whether you will be 'average' club racers or have the potential to become very good racing sailors. Much depends on your degree of organization and whether you are working to a proper 'game plan'.

Before the second season starts, draw up a rough itinerary to show the pattern of competition, which may well include an excursion to the Class Association's 'Nationals' to gain experience in big-fleet sailing and to meet up with other enthusiastic owners.

Spend the early part of the season perfecting starts and sailing good windward courses. Later in the season it should be possible to engage in boat-for-boat tactical racing and to develop an overall strategy for each race dependent upon the prevailing weather conditions. Aver-

age finishing positions somewhere above the bottom third of the fleet will indicate good progress.

If a handicap series is available, sail it to improve your ability to overtake or to block an overtaking boat. Your results will often serve to encourage rather than discourage you. Sail in local regattas at other clubs, prior to attending the National Championships if they are being held in a reasonably sheltered area. The experience of attending a National for the first time is worth all the frustrations of big-fleet racing when your sailing and racing skills may not match your ambitions. Finish the season with a short series and only sail the 'frostbite' (winter series) if it provides relaxation.

During the third year you can expect to see a few first places coming your way in some of the less competitive series. Boathandling and racing skills, especially in the area of boat-to-boat tactics, will develop quite quickly as confidence builds and you are prepared to contest starts, initiate tacking duels and fight off challenges at rounding marks. The racing rules will begin to make sense to you by then, and you should begin to use the rules to advantage and to protest about those who infringe them.

If you have decided to develop your racing skills further, you will now have to make a decision about the competitiveness of your boat. By attending a series of class open

meetings at different venues you can assess its overall performance. It may be that new foils and/or sails will suffice, or that the boat needs a complete overhaul during the winter.

The Nationals will be less of an unknown quantity and you should seek a finishing position somewhere near the middle of the fleet, given reasonably good sailing conditions. Near the end of the year your club rating should be within the top third of your class, with a number of top placings in some of the races.

At the start of the fourth year, you will appreciate that application and attention to detail are the keys to success, and if you have a new boat it will have to be race-tuned. The best way to tune your boat is to find another good skipper and crew to tune up with, so that each of you can benefit from a set of on-water tune-up exercises.

Much will depend on the strength of the class in your area or country; if the Nationals are attended by upwards of a hundred boats, the class is healthy. Sailing at the club will be confined to known popular and closely-contested events and a spring or autumn series which will provide the opportunity to win a trophy. Otherwise, open meetings and championships will form the basis of your summer programme, culminating in a serious attempt to put together a good set of results at the Nationals.

Probably the most popular small catamaran in the world, the Hobie 16 gives a fast and thrilling ride.

TEAM DINGHY RACING

Team racing in dinghies is perhaps one of the most tactically demanding forms of sailing, as sailors are able to make great use of the rules to prevent their team from losing. For example, certain moves intended to slow the opposition down are permitted by the rules, and slowing the opposition down is very much a feature of team racing. Only rarely are the tactical skills inherent in this used in other forms of racing, such as championship racing.

Typically, team racing will be between two teams of three boats per team, all of the boats being from the same class, but two-boat and four-boat team racing are common variants.

Scoring in team racing is under the place points system, with 3/4 point for the first place (except in two-boat team racing) and the number of points for each other place being numerically equivalent to the boat's position in the finishing order, for example 2 points for second place, 3 points for third, and so on. The team with the lowest aggregate points score will be the winners.

It is essential that, in a tight team race, close attention is paid to the team's overall score, so that winning combinations of finishing places can be sought. Tactical considerations must be aimed at getting the team into a winning position.

For instance, one boat a long way out in the lead will not always ensure a win for its team, and 2-3-4 is one of the classic winning team race patterns as the leading boat is isolated from the rest of its team and is ineffective in the tactical battle for the remaining places.

The highest points total with which it is possible to win in three-boat team racing is 10 points compiled from placings of 2, 3 and 5, not immediately obvious as a winning total. As has already been suggested, two boat team racing is scored slightly differently in that the scoring system is modified so that the team with the last boat over the line loses.

While team racing takes place throughout the world, in many ways the United Kingdom and the United States are the leading centres of the sport because of their flourishing university and college racing circuits. The British Universities Sailing Association (BUSA) runs a team racing league and hosts an annual championship, and there is a similar league and championship for poly-

technic colleges.

In the United States, university and college racing is organized by the Intercollegiate Yacht Racing Association (IYRA), whose annual events include the IYRA Team-Racing Championship and the National Women's Intercollegiate Championship. The United States Yacht Racing Union (USYRU) also organizes team races, including the US team-racing championship (the Hinman Cup).

The British National Team Racing Championship, sponsored by the Royal Yachting Association (RYA), seems to have fallen a little by the wayside and has been replaced by the World Team Racing Championship (the Wilson Trophy) which is hosted by West Kirby SC. This is sailed in Firefly dinghies supplied by the club and sponsored by local companies, and each team is given boats and sails of a particular colour so that the spectators can eas-

ily see how the race is developing.

The boats used for team racing range from the 12-foot Firefly dinghy up to 36-foot yachts which are used for the British-American Cup team racing series, and include dinghies such as the International 14 and the 505 which are raced using trapezes and spinnaker. The use of trapezes and spinnakers adds to the excitement, but it does rather detract from the tactical aspect of team racing as boatspeed may

Any type of dinghy can be used in team racing. Here, six Lasers vie for a winning combination.

become a more significant factor in deciding the race winners.

In general, team racing is best suited to two-man racing dinghies raced without trapeze or spinnaker, and on the college circuit in the UK the most popular classes are the Lark and Laser II. Both boats are very simple to sail and accelerate and decelerate quickly, which is a key feature for good team racing.

Good acceleration and deceleration are important in team racing because of the techniques employed to slow down the opposition. There are a number of such techniques, which involve a skipper slowing an opposing boat so that his or her team-mates can overtake it, and most are used on the upwind legs.

One of the main techniques is to cover a boat so as to get between it and the wind, thus placing it in a wind shadow. This needs careful positioning of the boat, and a very close cover is most effective.

The leebow tack is another very effective way to slow a boat down. By sailing to leeward of a rival, and staying just ahead of its wind shadow, a boat can get close enough for its sails to bend the wind onto the leeward side of its rival's sails.

Away from the beat, the most common site for team-racing place changes is at marks, where intelligent placing such as stopping in the two-boat-length circle to force an opponent's boat wide can have its role.

On a reach, the most common tactic to allow place changing is to luff so as to force an opposing boat way above the rhumb line (the direct line to the next mark). Alternatively, if an opposing boat tries to go to leeward it can be blanketed by the wind shadow of a windward boat, and the windward boat can exacerbate the slowing effect by overtrimming its mainsail.

The tactics and techniques of team racing are many and various, and a free-thinking approach is needed so that tactics can be matched to the prevailing conditions. Usually, a team will race two races in matched flights of boats, swapping boats between races. In this way, the effect of any differences in boatspeed between the flights of boats can be offset, and this is important if a fair race is to result.

BOAT CLUB RACING

Organized racing within boat clubs is the foundation on which all the higher levels of sailing competition are based, and clubs come in all shapes and sizes. The Royal Yacht Squadron at Cowes was originally constituted as an arm of the British Navy, and its members still fly the Royal Navy Ensign. The New York Yacht Club, famous for its long custody of the America's Cup, created a chain of clubs along the Eastern Seaboard so that its members could benefit from the services of the club when they visited popular ports such as Newport, Rhode Island. In contrast to these large, prestigious clubs, hundreds of clubs throughout Europe and the Americas sail on small lakes and reservoirs, some as small as a few acres in size.

A common theme running through these clubs is the quasi-naval hierarchy of club officials, which includes such ranks as Admirals, Commodores, Flag Officers, Sailing Masters, Officers of the Day, Gunners, Cadets and Bosuns. Many clubs, especially those 'senior clubs' with large memberships and a tradition of social activities, also have their own club dress uniforms and codes of conduct.

If you wish to join a club, membership is usually by election by the club committee. What type of club you join will depend largely on the area in which you live or sail, and the type of sailboating in which you wish to participate.

The majority of newcomers to dinghy sailing will join a local club so that they can participate in local activities midweek as well as at weekends. Cruiser racer owners living some distance from the sea will have to join a coast-based club, or a Class Association which organizes races through a club or group of clubs.

Another factor which influences the type of racing you will become involved in is the availability of one-design or handicap racing. In the United States, one-design racing is the order of the day and there is comparatively little dinghy handicap racing. In the UK, the majority of dinghy clubs organize racing for both one-designs and handicap fleets. The cruiser racer scene was originally based on handicap fleets, but the popularity of one-design fleet racing increased during the last decade as owners became dissatisfied with local and international handicapping systems.

Perhaps the best option is to join a club which offers one-design and handicap racing to all boat owners. One-designs race on equal terms, and first home is always the winner as long as all the racing rules have been complied with.

There are many different handicapping systems. The Royal Yachting Association's 'Portsmouth Yardstick' system allocates a particular number to each of 114 different classes of dinghy and keelboat. The number is based on annual reports, supplied by clubs, suggesting changes based on their handicap race results. The objective is to enable the slowest boats to compete on equal terms with faster boats by allowing them additional time on

Right *The International Canoe class provides exciting racing worldwide in a craft which is sailed from a sliding seat and is very difficult to control.*
Below *A typical mixed bag of dinghies competing in a club handicap race.*

the course. The amount of extra time is calculated from a set of tables which relate to the boat's number and the time taken to sail the race course.

Cruiser racer handicap systems, such as the Channel Handicap System, operate to a secret formula. Owners must supply accurate details and measurements of their boats to the measurement office. They then receive a CHS number or rating which is applied to all races run to the CHS system. It goes without saying that the historical path of yacht racing is littered with discarded handicap and rating systems, abandoned as owners became disgruntled with them and demanded new ones.

Your choice of boat for racing will depend on the designs adopted by the club you want to join – it's no use buying a Dragon if the club doesn't allow keelboats. Conversely, if you already have a boat, or you have decided on the type of boat you want to race, you will have to find a club that races that type.

Once you have joined a club and bought your boat you will be pitched into racing at the deep end. Most racing sailors learned that way, so you should seek all the advice you can get beforehand from fellow club members, especially about the basics of the immensely complex International Yacht Racing Rules. Ideally, you should attend a series of courses in racing procedures and the racing rules during the early part of your racing career.

The pattern of club racing has become standardized around the world into seasonal series. For instance, in northern latitudes 'frostbite' or winter sailing takes place from November to March or April or until the waters freeze over and sailing is impossible.

A spring series encourages sailors onto the water in sufficient time to compete in the summer series, which lasts until the main holiday season of late July and August when many crews will take their boats away to national or regional championships and to local regattas staged at nearby clubs. An autumn series gives those who missed out on the earlier series the opportunity to win something before the frostbite season comes around again.

Prizes usually centre on a principal cup or plate donated by an ex-club member or passed down from earlier competitions, and prizewinning can extend down to 10th place in a well-attended series. Most clubs have so many individual class and handicap trophies for the numerous series and individual championships that the annual prize-giving can last for up to two hours as the silverware is distributed.

The majority of clubs encourage family membership, and many incorporate junior fleets and have extensive summer programs. In the United States, the larger clubs are prominent social centres and stage summer-long junior programs staffed by professionals. In the UK, junior programs tend to be ongoing with the emphasis on spring and fall training courses, leaving the summer free for racing.

The wide choice of venue – inland lake or reservoir, river, estuary or open sea location – combined with the great number of clubs, means that most sailors can find a club that suits them.

Above *Racing in Optimist dinghies provides children with an excellent introduction to competitive racing.*
Right *The Salcombe Yawl, originating in Salcombe, Devon, is one of the many flourishing local one-design classes.*

PERFORMANCE CRUISER RACING

The performance cruiser offers the comfort of a cruising yacht plus enough speed and manoeuvrability to ensure that its owner need not feel outclassed in local racing. Cruiser racing, whether handicap racing where all yachts are different, or class racing between identical yachts, is organized through clubs at weekends and, usually, one or two evenings a week.

Racing is relaxed and informal with little of the cut-and-thrust of offshore racing. Courses are shorter – perhaps over a maximum of 20 miles – and the racing is an ideal way for an owner to compare the performance of his yacht with that of others of a similar size.

Racing at this level is a good way to hone skills that will, inevitably, come in useful during cruising. For example, it offers a chance to use the spinnaker and to indulge in a little close-quarters tacking. Apart from that, most modern cruisers owe much of their design to their racing cousins, and this type of racing gives their owners the opportunity to put their speed and manoeuvrability to good use.

Cruiser racing takes place at all levels and owners find their own level quickly, most being content to leave the offshore racing to those who enjoy the discomfort, and occasional thrills, of long passages out of sight of land. The average owner of a modern cruising yacht usually prefers to combine a day's sailing with a little not-too-strenu-

ous racing, improving his or her skills and sharpening up the crew.

Some classes enjoy close racing. Fleets build up, owners get together and soon the top yachts are beginning to consider entering class championships. Here the line between offshore racing and cruiser racing starts to blur. If an owner decides to take racing seriously there is no reason why he should not enter some of the longer, offshore races, especially if his family or regular crew have caught the bug sufficiently to make up the numbers.

Unless the class is one-design, the owner will then need to have the boat measured according to whichever rule is in force where he wants to race. This could be the International Offshore Rule (IOR), the International Measurement System (IMS), the Channel Handicap System (CHS) or one of a number of others, all designed to equalize the performances of widely differing yachts and their rigs.

With such a rating the yacht can now be entered in major regattas like Cowes or Burnham Week, where the owner will meet owners of similar, or identical, yachts and through enjoyable racing compare performance and different gear and thus improve both his yacht and his racing.

Many areas have associations that organize racing among clubs. For instance, on the East Coast of England there is the East Anglia Offshore Racing Association, in Ireland

Above *Stripped-out racing boats like these can be converted into performance cruisers when their racing days are over.*

Left *One-design cruiser racers, such as these Ranger class yachts, are often used for international match racing.*

the Irish Sea Offshore Racing Association, and in Poole the Poole Yacht Racing Association. There are many equivalents elsewhere in Britian and throughout America.

Performance cruiser racers make up the vast bulk of yachts both in England and America. The successful compromise between the two roles which the yacht is designed to

play depends on many factors, most important of which is the need for good accommodation without the boat becoming too much like a caravan. The owners of small cruiser racers usually have to put up with limited headroom but when designing yachts of over 30 feet, naval architects have perfected clever ways to keep the profile sleek without cutting down on comfort.

Modern out-and-out racing yachts are, by and large, useless for cruising. In the effort to keep weight to a minimum all superfluous interior furniture is left out, leaving an almost-bare hull that is only tolerated by dedicated crews in their quest for victory. The performance cruiser, on the other hand, provides comfortable accommodation and will have a sparkling windward performance – vital in racing – without the complexities of a racing rig that requires maximum concentration and tuning to get the best out of the sails.

Performance cruisers are, in effect, de-tuned racing boats with easily-handled rigs. They are the marine equivalent of sporty family cars, built and styled to appeal to those who like comfort but dislike being overtaken. Their construction is sturdier than that of their racing counterparts, and they are nowhere near as exotic.

For, perhaps, half the price of a dedicated racer, the cruiser racer offers far more than half the performance and twice the comfort. Not dissimilar in profile, with deep keels and adequate rig, its life expectancy and usefulness far outstrips that of a racing yacht.

That high performance is not wasted when it comes to cruising because, in many respects, speed is of greater importance in a cruising yacht than in a racer. Racing depends on closely-matched yachts, whose crews are expected to get the best out of whatever they sail, whether it be a high-performance yacht or a sailing barge. The skipper of the barge may be sailing slowly, but as long as he is sailing the boat as fast and efficiently as it can go, he will beat the other barges and win the race. The race can take all day; winning is the important thing, not speed.

The cruising skipper, on the other hand, may have a hungry, tired family aboard, longing to reach the nearest port. It is essential that he gets there before the tide turns, and for that he needs a yacht that is not only comfortable, but swift. The cruising skipper races every time he goes sailing. A little cruiser-racing practice will allow him to polish the skills needed to bring his yacht safely home to port before the pubs close or the family lose their tempers completely.

OFFSHORE RACING

The origins of offshore racing can be traced back to 1866, when a group of wealthy New York yachtsmen were arguing over who had the fastest yacht. To settle the matter, they decided to race across the Atlantic for a wager of $30,000. Three yachts took part ,and the winner was newspaper owner James Gordon Bennett's *Henrietta*, which arrived at Cowes on Christmas Day.

Most people considered this to have been an act of complete madness, and forty years were to pass before another transatlantic race was proposed—by Kaiser Wilhelm of Germany in order to get American yachts to come to Kiel Week. This time there were eleven entries and the winner was the magnificent 3-masted 187-foot schooner *Atlantic*, whose record of just over 12 days stood until 1988.

More important in the long run than such 'spectaculars' were the relatively short race up the east coast of the USA from New York to Marblehead, Massachusetts, organized by the journalist Thomas Fleming Day, and the race that he subsequently organized to Bermuda. These were for normal cruising yachts and formed the basis of what we now recognize as offshore racing.

With this example before them, British yachtsmen organized the first Fastnet Race in 1925 and afterwards formed the club that later became the Royal Ocean Racing Club (RORC), which to this day is perhaps the most authoritative voice on the subject. The same year there were 49 starters in the Bermuda Race while in 1939, 37 yachts raced from San Francisco to Honolulu.

Immediately following the Second World War, the naval officer John Illingworth began to introduce a completely new style of racing. In this, the yachts taking part were real racing machines instead of slightly modified cruising yachts, and the people taking part took a much more dedicated approach. The design firm he set up, Illingworth and Primrose, dominated the field for some fifteen years, and he was responsible for originating the Sydney to Hobart Race while serving in the Royal Navy in Australia. His book *Offshore* become something of a bible for the sport.

By 1957, Illingworth, together with Sir Miles Wyatt and Peter Green, had conceived the idea of the Admiral's Cup (now the Champagne Mumm Admiral's Cup, or CMAC). Like the Kaiser's Cup, this was originally a way of attracting American boats across the Atlantic and consisted of a points series for teams of three boats, which competed in a variety of races during Cowes Week culminating in the Fastnet Race. Other nations soon joined it and the Admiral's Cup became effectively the world championship of offshore racing.

Nowadays the CMAC attracts mainly professionals, so the RORC has taken the step of organizing a parallel event, held on alternate years and called the Commodore's Cup, in which there is a strict limit on the number of professionals taking part.

A persistent problem afflicting offshore racing is that different handicap rules are used in different parts of the world, and this makes it difficult to have fair competition between yachts from various nations. To get over this problem, the major yachting nations got together in the 1970s to create the International Offshore Rule (IOR). Although technically complex, this rating rule was responsible for an explosive growth in the sport with literally thousands of yachts being built all over the world and rated by the same method.

The French yachtsman Jean Peytel conceived the brilliant idea of running races in which all the yachts had to have the same rating so that they could compete without handicap. This became, rather confusingly, known as the One Ton Cup, not because the boats weighed one ton or anything like it but because that was the name of an old trophy that Peytel presented for the new event.

In time, this idea spawned many imitations at various rating levels until there were 'ton cups' ranging from mini-ton to two-ton. Sadly this initiative has gradually faded, although the idea of racing without handicap at a fixed rating is still used for various events.

Unfortunately, the IOR gradually buckled under the strain of so many brilliant designers constantly trying to outwit it, and it came to

Above *The Champagne Mumm Admiral's Cup, with its mixture of short regatta courses and longer races, is considered the world championship of offshore racing.*

be seen as the cause of offshore racing yachts becoming too expensive and specialized. By the early 1990s, the IOR was fading fast but the system that was supposed to replace it, the International Measurement System (IMS), proved to be no better or possibly worse and has not achieved universal support.

As a result, offshore racing has split three ways. Some nations and clubs persevere grimly with the unpopular IMS, while others use the Channel Handicap System (CHS), which works well but is regarded as less serious because it uses a secret formula that the RORC rating office can tinker with whenever one type of boat seems to be getting an unfair advantage. The third approach is toward one-design yachts that race without handicap, and there are many such classes emerging.

At the top end, offshore racing is strictly for experts with many professional crew taking part, but the wide part of the pyramid is formed by thousands of weekend enthusiasts for whom no racing presents quite the same level of challenge as offshore racing.

Above *Long-distance racing across the oceans of the world calls for special skills and a great deal of stamina on the part of crews. It also makes great demands on the yachts competing.*
Left *Competition in an offshore one-design class such as the Mumm 36 can be incredibly close and competitive. Every scrap of crew weight is needed on the rail to increase stability.*

MULTIHULL RACING

Despite the fact that multihull craft have been sailed successfully in the Pacific and Indian oceans for many centuries, and were carefully described by European explorers, the developed nations were extraordinarily slow to accept the advantages of boats that achieved their stability from their shape rather than their weight.

During the eighteenth and nineteenth centuries there were just a few isolated experiments in multihull design, the most successful of which, in 1876, was the celebrated American designer Nathaniel Herreshoff's 32-foot catamaran *John Gilpin*. This proved to be a fast and able boat and

incorporated many ingenious features that have since become standard, such as toed-in tillers linked by a crossbar to allow for the fact that in a turn, the outside hull turns less sharply that the inside one—like the front wheels of a car. Unfortunately, after a few outings, Herreshoff was asked to stop racing his catamaran because it was beating much larger yachts and was obviously 'unfair'.

This heralded a problem that has dogged multihulls ever since: it is practically impossible to devise a workable system under which multihulls and conventional yachts can race together without argument and recriminations on all sides.

Today, therefore, multihulls either race only against each other or compete with conventional yachts in long-distance races, which they tend to dominate.

The first of the offshore racing multihulls appeared in Europe and the United States in the 1960s, and different styles immediately developed. The American multis, such as *Aikane*, designed by Rudy Choy, were basically Hawaiian beach boats with deep, rockered hulls. Although fast downwind and relatively easy to build, they were fairly poor performers to windward because they slid off to leeward and tended to 'hobby-horse' in short waves.

In England, the Prout brothers built a quite different catamaran for the former test pilot Don Robertson. *Snowgoose* had round-bottomed hulls with little rockers and centreboards for lateral resistance. She was a much more efficient sailer but because she was rather low, her bridge deck tended to bang on waves.

The next important development came in 1968, when two new 40-footers were built for that year's Round Britain Race. One was the very light and shapely Macalpine-Downie catamaran *Mirrorcat*, which was occasionally devastatingly fast but often broke things, while Derek Kelsall built the ugly but strong and effective trimaran *Toria*. The latter won the race and began a long line of successful offshore racing trimarans.

There are two big advantages to this layout: it is much easier to step the mast in the central hull of a trimaran than on the bridge deck of a cat, and the outriggers are slightly raised so that only one is in the water at any one moment. This reduces the boat's wetted surface drag and transforms the windward hull into useful ballast.

In the years that followed, bigger and faster trimarans were built to compete in major events such as the Observer Singlehanded Transatlantic Race (OSTAR). They soon came to dominate such

Left *The French trimaran 'CDK/Media de la Mer' powers to windward in a Formula 40 Grand Prix event.*
Below *The Olympic gold medallist Randy Smyth reaches downwind in his catamaran 'The Smyth Team'.*

events, although it was by no means a walkover and many important big catamarans continued to be built, such as the 80-foot *Jet Services* which set a number of ocean records including being the first to sail nonstop around the world in less than eighty days.

The great French offshore skipper Eric Tabarly commissioned the hideous but very efficient trimaran *Manureva* in which he set several new passage records, including the west-east Atlantic crossing in 1980, before selling the boat to Alain Colas, who used it to sail nonstop around the world. In England, John Shuttleworth and later Nigel Irens produced some remarkably effective trimarans. The latter designed and built the 60-foot trimaran *Apricot* for Tony Bullimore and with him won the 1985 Round Britain Race by a commanding margin, and then went on to humble some much larger French cats and tris in the Round Europe Race.

Big, ocean-going multihulls have always been more popular in France than anywhere else because they suit their 'cult-of-personality' spectacular races such as the Route du Rhum and others. The success of *Apricot* led to Nigel Irens becoming one of the favourite designers in France, and this resulted in his being chosen to design and build the 80-foot catamaran *TAG* in Canada.

Unfortunately, the 80-foot unlimited multihull class was then in the process of disappearing due to runaway costs, but after languishing in various Brittany ports for a while, *TAG* was bought by the New Zealand Apple and Pear Marketing Board and became *ENZA* (Eat New Zealand Apples).

She was then refitted and lengthened in order to attempt the record for sailing nonstop around the world. At the first attempt, in 1993, she hit an obstruction and was disabled. She was refitted again and in 1994, with Peter Blake and

Robin Knox-Johnston in charge of a crew of seven, sailed around the world in the incredibly short time of 74 days.

This performance gives some indication of the huge power and speed potential of a big multihull as, in the early stage of the run, she averaged over 20 knots for nearly two weeks. At the same time, it was certainly no pleasure trip as at that speed the spray comes over the boat with the force of a firehose. The ride is violent and jerky, making it exceptionally difficult to get any rest, and the rig and gear has to be checked constantly to make sure that nothing is about to break under the heavy strains.

These big boats are the trailblazers of multihull design, but a regular offshore circuit for multihulls of moderate size has developed, albeit very slowly. Micro-multihulls, up to 25 feet in length, race on coastal courses and are incredibly fast for their size but quite tippy.

OLYMPIC RACING

First seen at the Games in 1900 but not an official Olympic sport until 1908, Olympic sailing is for many the ultimate in sporting endeavour. Since the Olympics come around only once every four years, a chance to compete in them is a rare prize to be seized by anyone of sufficient ability to qualify.

Eight different types of sailing boat now take part in the Olympics but two of them are used for both men's and women's competitions giving a total of ten 'disciplines', as the Olympic authorities term them. Of these ten disciplines, three are uniquely for men, three for women and four are open.

There are now three different singlehanded dinghies in the Olympic fleet: the Europe dinghy is for women, the Finn for men and the Laser for either, although in reality there are at present no women competing at the top level in the Laser Class.

The Europe is a 'frozen Moth', with a design dating back to the 1960s, and being quite light and small with a modest sail area, it is suitable for women of normal physique. A great mistake was made by this class when, prior to the 1996 games, it failed to take steps to ban the use of carbonfibre masts. This abruptly increased the cost of the boats without conferring any general advantage.

The Finn is very different, being a big, heavy dinghy that calls for big, heavy men to sail it. It is very hard work to race and this, of course makes it a demanding competition, a bit like rolling rocks up a mountain. The Finn is also a very highly developed boat from which virtually all technical problems have been ironed out.

It is also one of the classes that is supplied to sailors by the organizers, and this helps to make the competition even. But it does not make it cheap, because as soon as the builder of the boats for the next Olympics is announced, all sailors hoping to qualify need to obtain one in order to practice with it.

When the new 49-er dinghy was proposed for the 2000 Olympics, everyone supposed that the Finn would be dropped to make way for it, but instead it was the Star keelboat that got the chop. However, since nearly every committee of the International Sailing Federation includes people who race Stars, its eventual return can be confidently predicted.

As the most popular one-design in the world, the Laser clearly deserves its place in the Olympic fleet and there is no doubt that its inclusion has raised the standard of singlehanded sailing dramatically. Although fairly tall and very fit people are favoured, this effect is not too marked and people of various physiques can win. This is another of the boats that are supplied by the organizers so that in theory all are equal.

The 470, a run-of-the-mill 1970s trapeze dinghy with nothing particularly special about it, is used as the two-person dinghy for both men and women. Back in the 1980s there were some successful mixed 470 crews, but this is no longer permitted. Because these boats are sailed all over the world, competition is fierce and tiny differences in sails and tuning can make all the difference between success and failure.

The 470 is not supplied by the organizers, and this means that a large part of the preparation for the Olympic regatta consists of developing and perfecting sails. Its very ordinariness makes the 470 a good Olympic boat as crews have to work very hard over several years to produce equipment and techniques that are slightly better than anyone else's.

The only multihull in the Olympics is and always has been the Tornado, a B-Class catamaran sailed by two people. Being quite big, expensive and technical it is not the most popular of Olympic boats, but most people agree that there should be at least one multihull in the competition. Attempts to change to a cheaper and more popular boat, such as the Dart or Hobie 16, tend to set off severe political and commercial warfare so it has been found safer to stick with the Tornado.

The Soling three-man keelboat is used for both fleet and match racing. Normal races are used to select the top twelve teams, which go into a match-racing regatta to decide the medals. Though not the very latest technology, the Soling is another very highly developed boat from which big surprises have been ironed out.

It calls for a fairly heavy and fit crew, who use a unique style of sitting out in which they slip right overboard and sit on the outside of the hull, supported by a body harness. Getting back in is the hard part. Some of the very best keelboat sailors and match-racers in the world are attracted to this class, which is exceptionally difficult to win in—a high level of training and dedication is needed.

The most recent recruit to the Olympic family is the 49-er dinghy. This very fast, two-person dinghy with twin trapezes and standing-out frames calls for a very athletic type of sailor. In theory, at least, this is an open class and it will be most interesting to see if any woman skipper or crew makes it to the highest level.

Sailboards have been an established part of the Olympics since 1984 and there are divisions for both men and women. But because there are no weight divisions, the winners always tend to be tall and thin since people with that physique have the greatest leverage. Sailboards race up to four times per day over short courses.

The influence of the Olympics extends far beyond the actual games, because the great majority of big regattas are run along Olympic lines, using the same rules, courses and points systems. In Europe, for example, most nations have at least one big Olympic classes regatta per year, and these are linked together to produce the Eurolymp series.

It is possible to criticize the Olympics for soaking up so much money and talent, but it does give what can be a very diverse sport some focus. Junior training programmes, national squad training, technical development and coaching are all focused on the goal of Olympic medals and without this the whole small-boat racing side of the sport would be pretty chaotic.

Left *The Soling three-man keelboat is unique in being used first for a normal fleet regatta followed by a match-racing tournament for the top group. Although it is not a very new design, years of development have produced a boat that offers fast, competitive racing. The unique style of sailing, requires crews to be reasonably heavy and fit.*

Top *The Tornado is the only catamaran which has been used in Olympic competition, but it was designed in the 1970s and is now considered to be a little old-fashioned.*

Above *Since all the boats and equipment are supplied by the organizer, the singlehanded Laser provides the purest form of Olympic competition.*

SINGLEHANDED RACING

The earliest known singlehanded ocean crossing took place in 1786, when Josiah Shackford sailed a 15-ton gaff sloop east to west across the Atlantic from Bordeaux, France to Dutch Guiana (now Surinam). The first west to east singlehanded Atlantic crossing did not come until 1876, when Alfred Johnson, a Grand Banks fisherman, made the journey in a 20-foot dory called *Centennial*. The problems he encountered, of damage, gales and fatigue, are well known to all those who have attempted to sail the oceans of the world alone.

The motivations behind these voyages are many. Some have done it for spiritual enlightenment, others to prove themselves in competition, or out of philanthropy, and even as a result of mutiny. In 1877, Richard McMullen set off from Greenhithe, Kent for Cherbourg with two crew. A week after their arrival, the crew became so truculent that McMullen sacked them and returned alone.

Ten years earlier Rob Roy MacGregor, a Cambridge graduate with a taste for adventure of all kinds and a gift for self-publicity, had made many voyages in his small canoe. In 1867, he decided to sail alone from London via Boulogne to Paris to deliver a cargo of Protestant tracts to what he considered the 'godless' French Roman Catholics. His accounts of his adventures captured a wide readership at the time.

Captain Cleveland, of Massachusetts, claimed to have crossed the Indian and Pacific Oceans in a 15-foot boat in 1800, but the first substantiated claim to a singlehanded Pacific crossing was that of Bernard Gilboy from Buffalo, New York. He achieved this incredible voyage in 1882-3 in his 18-foot boat *Pacific*.

However, the true father of singlehanded sailing was undoubtedly Captain Joshua Slocum. In 1895, at the age of 51, he said off from Newport, Rhode Island in his 36 ft 9 in gaff yawl *Spray* to become the first to circumnavigate the world alone. The 46,000-mile journey, which took him via the Magellan Strait, took three years.

Slocum, a professional seaman but a non-swimmer, was lost during a subsequent voyage, but after him came a string of pioneering sailors including Harry Pigeon, whose four-year round-the-world voyage ended in Los Angeles in 1925, and Fred Rebel and Edward Miles, who both made solo crossings of the Pacific from west to east in 1932.

Most of the early pioneers were American, but by the 1950s the list of singlehanded sailors had become more cosmopolitan with Australians, Norwegians, Argentinians, French and Germans joining in. These included Alain Bombard, of France, who crossed the Atlantic in an inflatable, living off fish caught along the way.

The great era of competitive singlehanded sailing dawned in the 1960s, a decade that saw the first singlehanded one-stop circumnavigation by Francis Chichester, who had already won the first Observer Singlehanded Transatlantic Race (OSTAR). The interest shown in these voyages by the media helped to encourage and finance more attempts, while improvements in radio technology and satellite communications made it possible for voyagers to keep the public in touch with their efforts.

Chichester was followed by Alec Rose in his old cruising yacht *Lively Lady*, but the real breakthrough came in 1968, when the *Sunday Times* proposed a nonstop round-the-world race for singlehanders. There was only one finisher: Robin Knox-Johnston in his little homebuilt sloop *Suhaili*. Like Slocum, Knox-Johnston was a professional seaman, but his stubborn refusal to give up and ability to overcome all kinds of practical problems were the key to this remarkable feat.

There not seem much that could be done to better this tremendous voyage except do it again more quickly, but Chay Blyth had other ideas when he set off in 1969 to sail around the world nonstop 'the wrong way', heading west against the prevailing winds.

This voyage was not exactly a race, of course, but it subsequently inspired Blyth to set up his 'Challenge' fleet of identical 67-foot steel yachts, which have since been used for two races over the same course, the British Steel Race and BT Global Challenge.

Two of the people who sailed in the British Steel Race have subsequently made the same trip singlehanded, both racing against the clock. Mike Golding managed to complete the trip nonstop and now holds the record for a west-east circumnavigation. Samantha Brewster was the first woman to perform this remarkable feat, although an enforced stop in Brazil to repair damage prevented her epic journey from qualifying as a nonstop voyage.

Real singlehanded ocean racing began properly with the Observer

Right *Looking a bit like enormous model yachts, the Unlimited 60-footers are used for major singlehanded ocean races such as the Vendée Globe and the BOC Challenge.*

Singlehanded Transatlantic Race which was conceived by the former marine commando 'Blondie' Hasler and won in the first instance by Francis Chichester in *Gypsy Moth III*. This event takes place every four years and has spawned many imitators, such as the Route du Rhum.

There are two singlehanded round-the-world races, both of which take place in monohull yachts with a maximum size of 60 feet. The BOC Race is in stages while the Vendée Globe is the only nonstop, singlehanded, round-the-world race.

Competing craft grew bigger and bigger until the appearance of the enormous *Club Med* forced the Royal Western Yacht Club to limited the maximum size to 60 feet. Any kind of seaworthy yacht can enter these events, but in recent years multihulls have dominated the results.

It has to be said, of course, that singlehanded racing is highly dangerous, and it is also technically illegal because the lone sailor cannot keep a constant lookout as required by the International Regulations for the Prevention of Collisions at Sea. A number of lives have been lost in events of this kind, and one only needs to look at the drama that surrounded the 1996-7 Vendée Globe event to see that racing of this kind is controversial to say the least.

The list of singlehanded sailors who have died at sea, although not necessarily while sailing alone, includes Alain Colas, who sailed his trimaran to a new circumnavigation record of 168 days in 1974; Loic Caradec, lost in the Atlantic in 1987; Daniel Gilard from his catamaran *Jet Services*; and Jacques de Roux. Most of the great solo sailors, including Eric Tabarly, winner of the 1964 and 1976 ODTARs, Chay Blyth and Philippe Jeantot have survived capsize and disaster.

Despite modern position-plotting and efficient rescue services, solo sailors are as vulnerable as ever to the power of the sea. However, like Formula I motor-racing or climbing Mount Everest, there are always people who want to take on the ultimate challenge. As far as sailing is concerned, singlehanded ocean racing is definitely that.

Above *'Jester', the boat with which Blondie Hasler started it all. She was abandoned to the Atlantic in the 1988 race.*

TRANSATLANTIC RACING

The history of ocean racing is inextricably bound up with the history of racing across the Atlantic. The very first ocean race, in 1866, was from New York to Cowes, and ever since, the Atlantic has been the forcing ground for the design of ocean-going racing boats.

The reasons for this are not hard to understand. It is generally only in relatively wealthy countries that yachting can develop on a large scale, because it involves spending a lot of money on something that is done purely for the satisfaction of the people involved.

From the mid-nineteenth century onward, the two wealthiest parts of the world were Western Europe and the USA. These two great centres of wealth and yachting are separated by 3,000 miles of some of the most unpredictable ocean in the world. For yachtsmen in either Europe or America, the Atlantic was bound to represent the big challenge.

The very first ocean race, which resulted from a wager and was won by James Gordon Bennett in his schooner *Henrietta*, was regarded at the time as an act of complete foolhardiness by a group of people with more money than sense and did, in fact, result in the loss of six people who were swept overboard

from *Fleetwing*. As a result of this disaster, it was many years before the racing of yachts across the Atlantic Ocean became accepted as a sensible thing to do.

It is difficult to imagine the climate of opinion of those days, but there were many respectable authorities who strongly condemned the whole idea of racing long distance as unseamanlike and dangerous. Fortunately, American yachtsmen took a more enlightened view, and during the 1920s and 1930s, transatlantic races became regular affairs.

The impetus for these was the desire of American owners to send their yachts over to Europe for one or more of the major regattas such as Cowes Week or Kiel Week, following which they could cruise down the European coastline to the Mediterranean, and eventually return to the United States in the autumn via the West Indies.

It still took some time for something recognizable as an ocean racing yacht to emerge. One of the most important steps along the way came in 1931, when the brothers Rod and Olin Stephens produced the 52-foot yawl *Dorade*, which easily won that year's transatlantic race. She was a slim, easily driven and, by modern standards, heavy

Above *British sailor Tony Bullimore drives the trimaran 'Apricot' over the start of a two-handed race.*
Left *'Chic Boba II', seen here at the start of the 1972 singlehanded transatlantic race, was typical of the early monohulls.*

yacht that was like a more robust version of contemporary 8-metre and 12-metre inshore racing yachts. The great success of this yacht led the brothers to set up what in time became the most successful yacht design partnership of all time: Sparkman & Stephens of New York.

One of the partnership's very first commissions was for another 'go-anywhere' yacht, the 54-foot *Stormy Weather*, which in 1935 won that year's transatlantic and went on to win the Fastnet Race the same year. Happily, this fine old yacht

survives and has been restored to her original condition. She returned to Cowes in 1995 and raced in the Fastnet Race, sixty years after first winning it. By modern standards she looks terribly heavy and underpowered, but she represented the leading edge of design in 1935.

In the years following the Second World War, transatlantic racing soon came to be regarded as fairly unremarkable, especially in the west-east direction which is generally downwind. However, things changed dramatically in 1957, when H G Hasler proposed a singlehanded race from Plymouth to Newport, Rhode Island.

He himself thought that this would help to develop small, seaworthy, easily handled yachts, but in fact it led to a kind of arms race of bigger and bigger yachts. When

the Royal Western Yacht Club was eventually forced to place an upper limit on size, it became inevitable that the race would always be won by multihulls, and faster and faster catamarans and trimarans have appeared for this race, which is held every four years.

These are some of the fastest seagoing yachts in existence, and on a number of occasions, multihulls have first taken part in the Singlehanded Transatlantic Race and then returned to Europe, having a crack at the record for crossing the Atlantic on the way.

Atlantic's record has been broken on numerous occasions since 1988, but in 1994, Laurent Bourgnon, sailing the 60-foot trimaran *Primagaz*, sailed from the Ambrose Light Tower (outside New York Harbour) to The Lizard, at the entrance to the English

Channel, in the quite astonishing time of 7 days, 2 hours, 34 minutes. Not the least amazing thing about this was that Bourgnon did it singlehanded.

A quite different type of race, which seems to reflect a much older and less frenetic spirit of seafaring, is the annual Atlantic Rally for Cruisers (ARC), which takes yachts across the Atlantic via Las Palmas and the West Indies. The original idea of this was simply for a group of cruising yachts to sail across in company for fun and safety, arriving in the sunny Caribbean in time for the Christmas holidays. In recent years, however it has grown into a large event in which competition forms an important element, but the yachts taking part are not racers but a wide variety of typical modern cruisers, with amateur crews of families and friends.

THE WHITBREAD RACE

The Whitbread Round the World Race, held every four years, was the first fully-crewed circumnavigation event to be established in the yachting calendar. Since it was first held, in 1973, it has grown in stature until it is now acknowledged to be the second most important yachting event in the world, after the America's Cup.

The race was the idea of the publisher Anthony Churchill and the publicity agent Guy Pearse. Having worked hard but failed to get it off the ground themselves, they generously handed over all their files to the Royal Naval Sailing Association (RNSA), which caught the ball and ran with it for the next 20 years.

The key event that allowed the RNSA to go ahead was obtaining the sponsorship of the brewers Whitbread, who not only were the most reliable of all sponsors but gradually took more responsibility, finally buying the rights to the race and appointing their own operating staff.

The very first race was won by *Sayula*, a more-or-less standard Swan 65 ketch owned by the Mexican refrigerator millionaire Ramon Carlin and skippered by 'Butch' Dalrymple-Smith. It is

interesting to note that the Swan 65, designed by Sparkman and Stephens, was a yacht in a direct line of descent from *Dorade*, in which the Stephens brothers won the 1931 transatlantic race.

Fourteen yachts finished the first Whitbread Race, in 1973/4, and much of what befell them on their 27,000-mile voyage has become the stuff of legend. For a start, three people lost their lives, amply justifying the pre-race doubts of various pessimists. The winning yacht survived a complete 360-degree loop, which caused so much damage down below that the crew spent weeks repairing her. Eric Tabarly's *Pen Duick* lost her mast, Les Williams' *Burton Cutter* split her aluminium hull, and nearly all the others had tales of breakage or near-disaster. It was abundantly clear from the beginning that racing around the world was no easy undertaking.

Four years later there were fifteen finishers in the second Whitbread Race, and a massive ten days were knocked off the record because this time there were some real racing yachts as well as up-rated ocean cruisers. The fastest time was set by the foam-sandwich ketch *Great Britain II* that had been

built for Chay Blyth four years previously. Skippered by the late Rob James, she not only beat the time set by Blyth and his crew of paratroopers but did it with a crew of 'guests' paying £4,000 each for the privilege.

The handicap winner was Cornelis van Rietschoten's *Flyer*, a yacht specially designed and built for the event and meticulously prepared over a period of many months. It was van Rietschoten, for instance, who commissioned Keith Musto's company to produce a set of foul-weather clothing that would be dramatically superior in performance than anything that had been available up to that time. Musto designed the 'three-layer' system that has been the basis of deep-sea racing clothing ever since.

Flyer's win was significant in another way in that she was locked in competition right around the globe with the sloop-rigged Swan 65 *King's Legend*, and they were only two hours apart at the finish. The idea that a boat-for-boat race could go on for day after day and week after week like this had not occurred to anyone previously.

The man whose name will for ever be associated with the Whitbread race is that of Sir Peter

Top *Due to a change of rules, the spectacular 80-foot maxi-yachts such as "Merit" were not seen in the Whitbread Race after the 1993 event.*

Above *The Whitbread Trophy symbolizes the essential elements of the race. The winners of this maritime marathon are a very select and highly regarded band.*

Right *The Whitbread 60 became the only size of yacht used from 1997 onward, resulting in exceptionally tight and competitive racing.*

Blake, whose persistence in the face of adversity could hardly be bettered. In the very first race he was sailing on *Burton Cutter*, which had to pull out with a split hull. Four year's later he was a watch-leader on *Heath's Condor*, which had one of the very first carbonfibre masts (which unfortunately broke).

The third race saw him as skipper of the 68-foot Bruce Farr-designed *Ceramco New Zealand*. Clearly a potential race-winner, she was dismasted on the first leg. In 1985, he was back again with *Lion New Zealand*, a yacht that proved to be not a cat but a dog with very little chance of winning.

Pierre Fehlmann was first home in *UBS Switzerland* while Lionel Pean's *L'Esprit d'Equipe* won on handicap. Finally, in 1989, Blake got the right boat, the got right crew and made the right preparations for an outright win in the maxi-ketch *Steinlager II*.

This was also the year that Tracy Edwards skippered the first all-girl crew in *Maiden Great Britain*, something that attracted almost more attention than all the other yachts put together. There was also a reminder that this race can place an intolerable strain on the people involved when the skipper of the first Russian yacht ever to take part committed suicide after the end of the first leg.

That was the year in which the maxi-ketches dominated the event, but it was also the one in which it was clear that the writing was on the wall for such excessively expensive yachts.

From 1993 onward, the Whitbread 60 was the boat to sail and the maxis were fading fast. New heroes emerged, such as Britain's Lawrie Smith who took over the command of the European Whitbread 60 *Intrum Justitia* after the first leg and immediately leapt into top gear to win the second.

The New Zealand skipper Chris Dixon had probably the most dedicated campaign and was set to win overall in *Tokio* until her mast fell down in the penultimate leg. This led the organizers to redesign the points system on a 'per leg' basis so that in future one failure will not prejudice a boat's chances completely.

The very strong line-up for the 1997 race—all Whitbread 60s—showed that the race was still going from strength to strength, especially as modern communications have made it possible to keep in touch with the yachts and monitor their progress virtually hour by hour.

THE ADMIRAL'S CUP

The Admiral's Cup, a biennial event held in the Solent off Cowes and in other nearby waters, is the most important series for offshore yachts held in Britain and perhaps the world. It has benefited greatly from supporting sponsorship, first from Dunhill and subsequently from the French champagne house C H Mumm.

Organized by the Royal Ocean Racing Club (RORC), the original idea of the Admiral's Cup was to attract American yachts to Cowes Week by offering them a series of races for a team trophy. From its inception in 1957, the event quickly grew in size and stature until it became the *de facto* world championship of offshore racing. At its peak in the late 1970s, 19 nations sent three-boat teams, although numbers subsequently dwindled due to world recession and the confusion caused by a change in the rating rule.

The format of the Admiral's is for a mixture of short and long races, culminating in the 605-mile Fastnet Race. In the early years, the Admiral's Cup yachts raced in two of the best-known Cowes Week races, the New York Yacht Club Cup and the Britannia Cup. But it soon became obvious that this involved the risk of competitors being accidentally balked by other yachts that were not involved in the Cup, and so the decision was made to run special short races just for the Admiral's Cup fleet. However, they do still join in the melee of the Channel and Fastnet races.

A team wishing to challenge for the Admiral's Cup has to send a fleet of three yachts, each of a specified size and type. The definition of the three different yachts has been changed repeatedly, reflecting the rating rules in force at the time, but the basic idea is to have one large, one middle-sized and one small yacht in each fleet. In recent years, there has been a move to have no-handicap level racing within the individual classes, but this has not always been possible because of the difficulty of finding enough yachts with the same rating from different parts of the world. However, use of the one-design Mumm 36 as the small boat points the way ahead.

The programme of races has also been changed several times. It now begins with two short races in the Solent, held two days before the start of Cowes Week. This is followed by the Channel Race, designed to last for about thirty hours. Next, the whole fleet decamps to Christchurch Bay, between the Solent and Bournemouth, where a series of short races are run over two days. There is then a rest day before a short offshore race designed to last eight hours. Finally, on the second Saturday of Cowes Week, in company with many others, the fleet begins the Fastnet Race. This starts at Cowes, goes around the Fastnet lighthouse near Baltimore in Ireland, and finishes at Plymouth.

Above *Each competing nation puts forward a three-yacht team, with the result that the Champagne Mumm Admiral's Cup is really three regattas rolled into one.*

Right *The racing is incredibly close, especially in the inshore events.*

Below *The Admiral's Cup remains the premier trophy for the sport of offshore racing.*

The points are loaded to give more weight to the longer races, especially the Fastnet Race, so that in spite of grumbling by some crews who don't much like having to spend three or four days on board a smallish yacht such as a Mumm 36, which has very basic accommodation, this is still an off-shore championship.

In the early years of the event, Britain, the United States and Australia dominated the results, but more recently Germany, France, New Zealand and Italy have also been successful. The dogged persistence of some countries can only be admired. Holland, for instance, had by 1995 competed in 17 out of a possible 20 Admiral's Cup series without ever winning. Australian and New Zealand teams are clearly disadvantaged by having to travel from the opposite side of the world, especially if they decide to bring all three yachts with them. Partly as a reaction to this, Australian yachtsmen set up the Southern Cross Series, which is a mirror-image Admiral's Cup held in December. Italy holds a similar series, the Sardinia Cup, in alternate summers to the Admiral's Cup.

The year 1971 was a highly significant one in two ways. Firstly, the Dunhill company came up with a serious level of sponsorship that enabled the RORC to raise the status of the event very significantly. For instance, it became one of the first sailing events to have a proper press office, with press boats to take journalists to watch the racing. As a result, by 1995, a total of 429 journalists were accredited and TV bulletins were broadcast in 25 countries. The majority of yachts are now sponsored and are allowed to carry advertising slogans on their hulls and sails. In later years, when Champagne Mumm became the title sponsor, the level of publicity increased still further.

The second significant feature of 1971 was that the British Prime Minister of the day, Edward Heath, was captain of the home team and sailed in every race aboard his yacht *Morning Cloud*. The fact that someone this much in the public eye could actually take part in a major yachting competition attracted enormous attention, and Heath's participation undoubtedly helped to raise the public status of the sport in general.

The 1970s were the boom time for yachting in every form, and the Admiral's Cup had 19 teams competing on three consecutive occasions, but the 1980s were rocky and the 1990s pretty disastrous, with entries falling right back to eight teams. World economics was certainly the most important reason but the fading of the International Offshore Rule (IOR) and the shaky introduction of the International Measurement System (IMS) undoubtedly had a lot to do with it as well, because yachtsmen in different parts of the world were not all singing from the same hymn-sheet. Italian yachtsmen, for instance, were keen to continue with IOR while Americans insisted on changing over to IMS.

Another difficulty facing the Champagne Mumm Admiral's Cup is that the competitive level is so high that most of the participants are professional and this raises costs all round. Whether the event will continue in its present form remains to be seen, but if not, one can still say that it was the leading yachting event of its time and set many trends.

THE SYDNEY TO HOBART RACE

The instigator of the Sydney to Hobart Race – now one of the world's classic offshore races – was a visiting sailor on attachment to the Royal Australian Navy at the end of the Second World War. The sailor was John Illingworth, who, with his Laurent Giles-designed *Maid of Malham,* had already done much to promote the racing of well-found craft back in his native England.

Illingworth, hearing that Sydney's newly-formed Cruising Yacht Club was organizing a cruise to Hobart, Tasmania, signed up for it and persuaded the other eight participants to make a race of it. During the race a gale blew up (as has happened in many subsequent Sydney to Hobart races) and Illingworth, in his recently-acquired, double-ended 34-foot cutter *Rani* pressed on through the gale while the others sought shelter. He crossed the finishing line, well up the Derwent river, some seventeen hours ahead of his nearest rival.

Since Illingworth's win in the 1945/46 race, the Sydney to Hobart has been held every year, starting on Boxing Day and, for some of the later finishers, continuing into the New Year. In 1967, after winning the Admiral's Cup, the Cruising Yacht Club of Australia introduced its own international team series, the Southern Cross, comprising three inshore races plus the Sydney to Hobart.

One thing which sets the Sydney to Hobart apart from all other long-distance races is the intensive media coverage coupled to a genuine and knowledgeable public interest throughout Australia. A contributory factor to the continuing interest in the race has been the mandatory position updates that all competitors have to supply every eight hours. These positions are broadcast as overall line-honour and corrected positions, so that the public knows what is going on and the competitors know what is expected of them. Australians are among the best sailors in the world, and the public

Left *At the first turning mark off Sydney Harbour, 'Police Car' holds on to her spinnaker while 'Highland Fling' drops hers.*

Above *The fleet gathers for the start of the Sydney to Hobart Race.*

interest generated by the Sydney to Hobart races fuelled the near hysteria when Alan Bond won the America's Cup in 1983.

In common with those of other long-distance races, the Sydney to Hobart course can be divided into a number of sections, each with their own characteristics. The race begins at a starting line inside Sydney Harbour during the Christmas holidays when, in Australia, it's midsummer and even if there were no Sydney to Hobart Race the harbour would be alive with pleasure craft.

Surrounding the harbour, and especially on the headlands around the entrance, tens of thousands of spectators line every vantage point to watch the spectacle and see the fleet away on its 500-mile (800-km) trek south to Hobart. The start is always well policed, and the thousands of spectator craft usually keep well out of the way of the competitors as they make their way out of the harbour to the turning mark off the heads, before beginning the long haul down the New South Wales coastline.

Having completed the first phase of the race, the competitors' next objective is to make best possible speed along the coast, with the prospect of picking up a southerly set (tidal current) of some 2 knots which is generated by the seasonal northwesterlies. Those going in search of the drift may have to go fifty to sixty miles (80 to 100 km) east of the rhumb line (direct course) to benefit from it.

Once clear of the New South Wales coastline, the fleet then has to face up to the gales and storms that frequently occur in the Bass Strait, which separates Tasmania from the mainland, and to the strong southeasterlies that may be encountered on the approaches to the Tasmanian coastline.

The entrance to the Derwent river is the aptly-named Storm Bay, which is often reached after a hard beat up the Tasmanian shore. The last phase of the race, inside the Derwent, is usually conducted in light, flukey conditions which can see an apparent win fade away to a lowly place as a new breeze carries the back markers up the river.

After John Illingworth's win in the first race, he donated a trophy – the Illingworth Cup – to be awarded to the first boat to cross the finishing line. The boat that wins the line honours is often accorded more hospitality than the boat that wins on corrected time, and is the boat that the spectators come to see.

One notable exception to this occurred in 1969, when the boat that took the line honours was overshadowed by the winner on corrected time, a boat called *Morning Cloud* which was skippered by the then British Prime Minister, Edward Heath.

It is not often that a serving prime minister or head of state wins a major sporting event, and the attention of the world's media placed Australian sailing and the Sydney to Hobart Race squarely on the sporting map.

Morning Cloud was designed by the legendary Olin Stephens and was an almost-standard Sparkman & Stephens 34 production yacht. Heath was the first Englishman since Illingworth to win the Sydney to Hobart, and his account of the race in his sailing autobiography *A Course of my Life* gives an insight into the nature and characteristics of the race as seen through the eyes of a first-time entrant and eventual winner.

THE AMERICA'S CUP

The America's Cup is believed to be the oldest international sporting trophy of any kind—dating back to 1851—and is certainly the most famous of all yachting events. It began when the Royal Yacht Squadron (RYS) planned a series of races off Cowes, Isle of Wight, to celebrate the Great Exhibition of 1851, and the Commodore, Lord Wilton, wrote to the Commodore of the New York Yacht Club (NYYC), John Cox Stephens, inviting him to enter.

Stephens, a keen sportsman, was inspired by this invitation to form a syndicate of prominent New York businessmen who between them commissioned a racing version of a New York pilot schooner. This was not their idea of a flat-out racing yacht but rather of one that was capable of first sailing across the Atlantic safely and then giving a good account of herself in racing after arrival.

Designed by George Steers and built by William H Brown, she was a two-masted schooner in the Baltimore Clipper tradition with a deep wine-glass shape and sharply-raked masts. The sails, which were a key feature of *America*, as she was named, were made from machine-woven American cotton, which was much superior to the heavy flax canvas sailcloth still being used in Britain at the time.

America crossed the Atlantic and duly appeared at Cowes ready to take on all-comers, but ran into an embarrassing delay. Firstly, Stephens thought he could challenge the English yachts for an enormous wager of 10,000 Guineas (£10,500), but was told that this kind of thing was 'not done'. Then,

when he tried to enter for the Queen's Cup race, he was told this was not possible because *America* was owned by a group rather than an individual.

Eventually, it was agreed that *America* could enter for a race round the Isle of Wight on 22 August for a specially-made 100 Guineas Cup. Though the details of the race are still somewhat unclear, it is certain that *America* beat the whole of the English fleet by a large margin and took the cup.

Shortly afterwards *America* was sold, but Stephens and his friends returned to New York where, after a few years, it was decided to draw up a Deed of Gift donating the 100 Guineas Cup to the New York Yacht Club for perpetual competition by 'Any organized yacht club of any foreign country.' Nothing happened for a while because of the American Civil War, but in 1870, James Ashbury's schooner *Cambria* was sailed over from England to make the first of 23 unsuccessful challenges spread over the next 132 years.

Some of these challenges, particularly those involving the Earl of Dunraven, were rather ill-tempered and argumentative, but then a series of challenges by the more diplomatic Sir Thomas Lipton brought things back to a more sporting level. Britain came nearest to winning in 1934, when the aviation millionaire Tom Sopwith challenged with the Nicholson-designed J-Class cutter *Endeavour*, which was clearly superior to the defender *Rainbow*. But, sailing with an amateur crew, Sopwith fluffed his tactics and missed his chance.

After the Second World War, it was agreed to revive the competition using the 12-metre class, which was considerably smaller and cheaper than the J-Class monsters seen in the inter-war period or the even larger monsters used at the turn of the century. But although Britain made two challenges, they were both feeble efforts that were repulsed with embarrassing ease and it was not until Australia, France and Sweden brought some new blood into the game that the competition came back to life.

It was agreed that in future, multiple challenges would be accepted with a preliminary knock-out series to find the eventual challenger, who would sail a 'match' against a single defending boat. This gave the challengers a much better chance because they were fully race-tuned by the time they entered the final.

In 1983, the seventh Australian challenge was finally successful when *Australia II*, owned by Alan Bond and skippered by John Bertrand, beat the rather lacklustre *Freedom*, sailed by Dennis Conner. *Australia II* had a controversial 'secret weapon' in the shape of a winged keel, an innovation that helped to give her better stability and acceleration. This momentous victory by Australia was one of the great days in that nation's enviable sporting history, made all the more poignant in retrospect by Alan Bond's subsequent imprisonment for fraud.

Conner was not a man to take defeat lying down and, after a preparatory programme of relentless efficiency, he won back the cup in a wonderfully spectacular heavy-

The America's Cup was made by the Garrards, the Crown Jewellers, and contains 134 ounces of fine silver. It was originally named the 100 Guineas Cup, because that was what it had cost.

weather series sailed off Perth, Western Australia, in 1987. Australian attitudes to this can be summed up by the poster that read 'Well done Dennis you bastard' — the word 'bastard' is often used as a term of endearment in Australia. His success meant that the famous cup was now back in the USA, but in San Diego where the yacht club proved even more truculent that the NYYC.

The next serious challenger for the America's Cup was the New Zealander Michael Fay, who attempted to take the Americans by surprise with a monstrous 90-foot waterline sloop that met the terms of the original Deed of Gift.

After much legal wrangling this farcical challenge went ahead, and the massive New Zealand yacht was trounced by a catamaran that had been hastily designed and built by Conner's team. This at least forced all the parties to get together to eatablish a new set of rules and to agree on a new type of boat to be used in future, the International America's Cup Class, big, exciting lightweight sloops of around 75 feet.

In the second challenge held in these new boats, in 1995, the Australian boat sank and the New Zealand team, which was led by Sir Peter Blake, completely overwhelmed the weak defence put up by Dennis Conner and carried off the cup for the first time. With Australia and New Zealand now dominant in the sport, it could well turn out that the 100 Guineas Cup will remain in the Southern Hemisphere for some time to come.

Above 'Stars and Stripes' and 'Team New Zealand' do battle off San Diego, California.
Left The win by 'Team New Zealand' in 1995 took the trohpy from the USA for only the second time in the race's long history.

RULES OF THE ROAD

When you go afloat, even in a small inflatable, you immediately become a 'Master' of a vessel subject to the International Regulations for the Prevention of Collisions at Sea (IRPCS). You can buy copies of these regulations, which are also reprinted in almanacs, and you should take the trouble to learn the most important of them because every Master is liable for their proper application, especially in relation to other water users.

Sailors talk about the 'rules of the road' which are, in effect, the rules they are most familiar with and which apply to their everyday use of the highways of the sea, usually when in confined channels where they have to apply the rules when they meet other vessels.

Other responsibilities include keeping a proper lookout at all times, proceeding at a safe speed, and taking into account the state of the sea and strength of the wind when close to navigational hazards.

The owner of a sailing vessel fitted with a motor has to be aware of the different rules which apply when sailing and when motoring, while for racing yachtsmen there are additional rules which are based on the IRPCS.

The main purpose of the rules is to prevent vessels crashing into each other, given that at most times ships are free to move in any direction they choose. Large ships don't, in practice, move in just any direction, because they follow well-charted sea routes, but smaller sailing vessels have greater freedom and do crisscross these routes.

The risk of collision exists when two boats are in sight of each other. If another boat appears to be on a converging course to your own, take a series of compass bearings on it. If the angle remains constant, you are on a collision course and should prepare to take avoiding action.

As an alternative to taking compass bearings, you can use a part of your boat, such as a stanchion, as a reference point. If the other vessel stays in line with it, you are on a collision course; if it moves forward of the stanchion it will pass ahead of you, if it falls back you will pass ahead of it.

Because the rules are quite specific there are duties that each vessel much observe. The rules describe situations in which two vessels are approaching each other, and designate one as the *give-way* vessel, which must take avoiding action, and the other as the *stand-on* vessel, which has the right of way. To avoid a collision, the give-way vessel must take positive action in plenty of time and the course alteration or change in speed must be obvious to the other vessel. The master of each vessel is entitled to expect the other to act according to the rules, but must be prepared to take action himself if necessary.

When in narrow navigable channels, it may not be possible to make large changes of course without going aground. Yachts should keep to the periphery of channels when commercial vessels, which are constrained by their draft, are in the channels.

The main 'rule of the road' is that traffic keeps to the right (starboard) while navigating channels. Another rule, especially applicable in a channel with blind bends, is that the appropriate sound signals should be made prior to carrying out specific manoeuvres.

Sound signals are short blasts of I second duration and prolonged blasts of from 4 seconds to 6 seconds. A vessel approaching a blind bend should sound one prolonged blast. If another vessel approaches the bend from the opposite direction it should sound a prolonged blast in reply.

When in sight of each other, vessels (mostly those in excess of 12 metres) sound one short blast to indicate an alteration to starboard, and two short blasts to indicate an

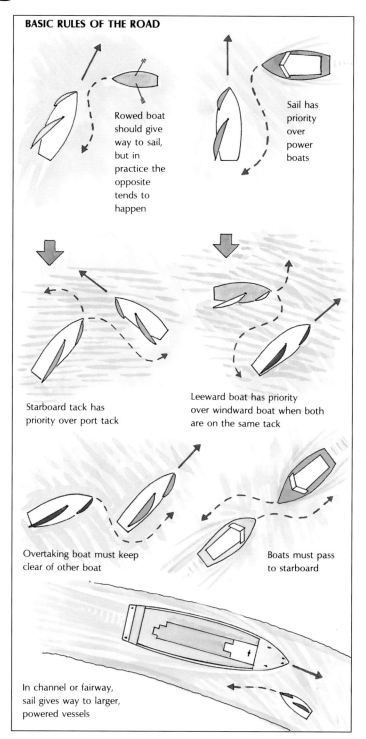

BASIC RULES OF THE ROAD

Rowed boat should give way to sail, but in practice the opposite tends to happen

Sail has priority over power boats

Starboard tack has priority over port tack

Leeward boat has priority over windward boat when both are on the same tack

Overtaking boat must keep clear of other boat

Boats must pass to starboard

In channel or fairway, sail gives way to larger, powered vessels

SAIL SYMBOLS

Boats can be identified by the symbols and numbers on their sails. The simplest identification is a symbol or logo to identify the class of boat, plus a number. The class owners' association, along with the manufacturer, issues numbers to new boats. Most classes and all international racing classes now use the three-letter national code. These have recently been changed, for instance, the symbol for the United Kingdom was changed from K to GBR.

class symbol
registration number
country prefix

ARG	Argentina	HKG	Hong Kong
AUS	Australia	IND	India
AUT	Austria	IRL	Ireland
BEL	Belgium	ISR	Israel
BRA	Brazil	ITA	Italy
CAN	Canada	JPN	Japan
CHN	China	MEX	Mexico
DEN	Denmark	NED	Netherlands
ESP	Spain	NOR	Norway
EST	Estonia	NZL	New Zealand
FIN	Finland	POR	Portugal
FRA	France	RUS	Russia
GBR	United Kingdom	SUI	Switzerland
GER	Germany	SWE	Sweden
GRE	Greece	USA	USA

alteration to port; three short blasts tell other craft that the sounding vessel's engines are going astern. Five short and rapid blasts can mean anything very rude you can think of; this signal shows that the sounding vessel has no idea what you are doing and wants you to get your act together to avoid a collision.

In a narrow channel, if a vessel coming up behind you gives two prolonged blasts followed by a short one, it means 'I intend to overtake on your starboard side.' Two of each means 'I intend to overtake on your port side.' To learn these signals, think of the first two prolonged

blasts as meaning 'Wake up!' in each case; then you only have to remember that one short following blast means 'starboard', and two mean 'port'.

The signal is acknowledged by four blasts – one prolonged, one short, one prolonged and one short – meaning 'I agree and will keep my course.'

In restricted visibility there are numerous signals which must be understood. The principal rules governing a motor sailing vessel are: when sailing, one prolonged and two short blasts at not more than two-minute intervals; when motoring, one prolonged blast at not more than two-minute intervals. If you are at anchor in an area where a risk of collision exists, ring a bell or strike a gong (even a saucepan, if you've nothing else available) for five seconds once a minute.

In clear visibility the rules are

designed to get vessels to take positive early action. For the yachtsman there are three categories of vessel to watch out for. The first category is fishing vessels, which are a 'law unto themselves' because they move in all directions. The rules acknowledge this and advise everyone to keep clear of vessels identified, by the appropriate lights or shapes, as fishing vessels.

The second category is commercial shipping, and these vessels should be treated with great caution. In theory they should give way to sailing vessels, but in practice they are on autopilot in open waters and restricted in narrow channels, so you should plan accordingly to make your intentions clear. Don't insist on your right of way over commerical shipping; it's as unwise as arguing with trucks on the highway.

The third category is other sailing

vessels, which will expect you to know and obey the sailing rules.

When two powered vessels meet, the following rules apply. When they are approaching each other head-on, each should alter course to starboard, so that they pass each other port-to-port. When crossing each other's path, the vessel which has the other vessel on her starboard side should keep out of the way, preferably without crossing ahead of the other vessel. The rule can be remembered by 'If I am on the right, I am in the right.' Lastly, an overtaking vessel, which will usually be approaching from about 22 degrees either side of dead astern, must keep well clear of the overtaken vessel.

The rules relating to sailing vessels form the basis of the racing rules. When two boats are on different tacks, the vessel on a port tack (with the wind blowing over its port

The rules of racing are based on the IRPCS rules for sailboats.

side) must keep out of the way of one on a starboard tack (with the wind over its starboard side).

When two boats are on the same tack, the windward boat (the one closest to wind) must keep out of the way of the vessel to leeward. Any vessel on a port tack and unsure of what tack another vessel is on must keep out of its way. In the racing rules, the windward side is determined as being the opposite side to that on which the mainsail is carried.

Overtaking rules are the same as for powered vessels and are designed to keep the overtaking vessel away from the vessel being overtaken.

Generally, a commonsense approach to the rules will stand you in good stead as long as you do what is expected of you, either as a stand-on vessel or a give-way vessel.

LIGHTS, FLAGS & SIGNALS

The standard patterns of lights for both vessels and buoyage systems ensure their identification at night, and while most signalling is now confined to the VHF radio, shapes, flags and Morse still have a role to play in communications.

When entering a channel from seaward at night you should have a prepared list of all buoyage or other fixed lights which may be visible during the approach and when within the channel. These should include distant lighthouses which, even though not directly visible, can be identified by their *loom* as the light sweeps the night sky below the horizon.

Your list should also include inland features such as radio and television transmitter masts, which are very good navigational features because of their height and distinctive aircraft warning lights.

The correct details of each light visible in or from the channel will be contained in the *Admiralty List of Lights*, which is often reproduced in nautical almanacs, and this list, rather than your chart (which will also give details of the lights), should form the basis for your own list. As you identify each light, mark it on the chart with a tick, and as you sail past it and leave it abeam, change the tick to a cross.

The description or characteristic of a particular light, as given in a published list or on a chart, tells you its colour and period and, for some types, its elevation and range.

The lights that are to be carried by different types of vessels is a complex subject, but one that is usually well-covered by most almanacs. In essence, most vessels must show a red light to port and a green light to starboard, plus one or more white or other coloured lights depending on the vessel's size, type and use.

Yachts under power display port, starboard and stern lights low down, with a single white 'steaming' light higher up. When under sail a yacht may show the three lowers or, more commonly, a masthead tricolour (which uses less electricity). Very small sailboats may simply show a single all-round white to avoid collisions.

Signalling by flags and lights has largely been superseded by spoken messages over VHF radio. Nevertheless, the international code of flag signals and the Morse code are still in daily use, and should be learned because they may be used by larger vessels or shore stations to send a message to you.

You should also learn the international phonetic alphabet, in which each letter of the alphabet is assigned a word, such as 'Alpha' for 'A' and 'Delta' for 'D'. By using this phonetic alphabet, names and other words can be spelled out over the radio without confusion between, say, 'F' and 'S', or between 'B', 'P' and 'D'.

FLAGS, PHONETIC AND MORSE ALPHABETS

SINGLE-LETTER MEANINGS

The single-letter signals are the most important of all the code signals, and you should try to learn them by heart so that you can act upon them immediately. They may be made by any method of signalling, but if they are made by sound they must be made in accordance with the relevant rules (34 and 35) contained in the International Regulations for the Prevention of Collisons at Sea (IRPCS).

THE THREE SUBSTITUTES

Flags used to repeat other flags

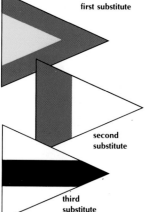

first substitute

second substitute

third substitute

A ALPHA · —

I have a diver down; keep clear and pass at low speed

B BRAVO — · · ·

I am loading, unloading or carrying dangerous goods

C CHARLIE — · — ·

Yes; confirmation of preceding signal

D DELTA — · ·

Keep clear, I am manoeuvring with difficulty

J JULIET · — — —

I am on fire and have dangerous cargo on board; keep clear

K KILO — · —

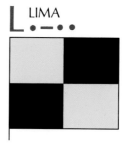

I wish to communicate with you

L LIMA · — · ·

You should stop your vessel immediately

M MIKE — —

My vessel is stopped and making no way through the water

S SIERRA · · ·

I am going astern under power

T TANGO —

Keep clear, I am engaged in pair trawling

U UNIFORM · · —

You are running into danger

V VICTOR · · · —

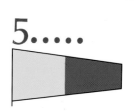

I require assistance

1 · — — — —

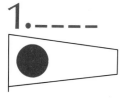

2 · · — — —

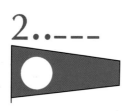

3 · · · — —

4 · · · · —

5 · · · · ·

LIGHTS

A. Masthead (steering light) white with unbroken arc of 225°

B. Side lights green starboard red port unbroken arc of 112.5°

C. All-round light unbroken arc of 360°

D. Stern light white unbroken arc of 135° placed as near stern as possible

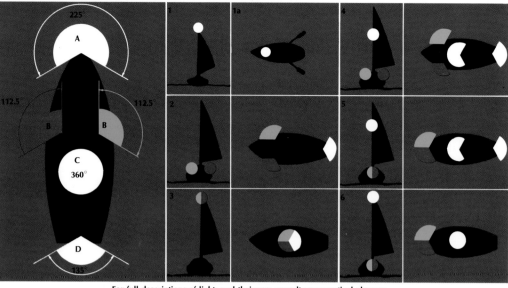

Boats under 7 m
1, 1a All-round white light

Boats 7 to 20 m
Under sail
2 Side and stern lights or **3** combined tricolour light on masthead

Under power
4 Side, stern and steaming lights or **5** combined side lights, stern and steaming light

Under 12 m
Side lights and all-round masthead light

For full descriptions of lights and their use, consult your nautical almanac.

E ECHO .

I am altering course to starboard

F FOXTROT ..—.
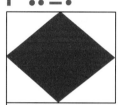
I am disabled, communicate with me

G GOLF ——.

I require a pilot or (on a fishing vessel) I am hauling in nets

H HOTEL ....
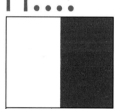
I have a pilot on board

I INDIA ..
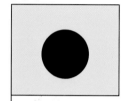
I am altering course to port

N NOVEMBER —.

No; the preceding signal should be read in the negative

O OSCAR ———

Man overboard

P PAPA .——.

I am about to put to sea

Q QUEBEC ————

My vessel is healthy and I request clearance to come ashore

R ROMEO .—.

Single letter code R has no allocated meaning; see the IRPCS

W WHISKY .——

require medical assistance

X X-RAY —..—
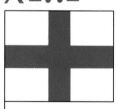
Stop carrying out your intentions and watch for my signals

Y YANKEE —.——

I am dragging my anchor

Z ZULU ——..

I require a tug or (on a fishing vessel) I am shooting nets

ANSWERING PENNANT AND CODE FLAG
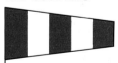
The code flag is flown to show that the International Code is being used, and to acknowledge a message.

6 —....
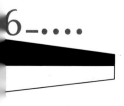

7 ——...

8 ———..
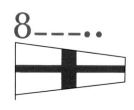

9 ————.

0 —————
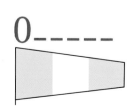

SAILING TERMS

A

Aback A sail is said to be aback when its clew is to windward and the wind is pressing it against the mast, for instance when the boat is hove-to, or as a result of a sudden change in the wind.

Abaft Toward the stern.

Abeam At right angles to the centreline of a boat.

About To go about is to change tack.

Adrift Free-floating, without power or control.

Aft At, toward, near or behind the stern.

Afterpart The part of a boat aft of the beam.

A-hull A boat is lying a-hull when hove-to with all sails furled (see also **Lie**).

Aloft Overhead.

Amidships Midway between the stem and the stern of a boat.

Anabatic wind A wind created by air blowing up a slope. It is the result of the air at the bottom of the slope being warmer than the air at the top, and rising by convection (see also **Katabatic wind**).

Anchor light An all-round white light displayed at night (usually on the forestay) by an anchored vessel. Also called a riding light.

Antifouling A protective compound (usually a paint) applied to a hull to inhibit the growth of marine life, such as barnacles, on it.

Apparent wind The perceived wind flowing over a moving boat. It is the resultant of the speed and direction of the true wind and the speed and direction of the boat (see also **True wind**).

Aspect ratio The ratio of the length of the foot of a sail to the length of its luff. A tall, narrow sail has a high aspect ratio, and a low, broad sail has a low aspect ratio.

Astern Behind a boat. To go astern means to reverse.

Athwart from side to side across the centreline of a boat.

Avast 'Stop!' (see also **Belay**).

Aweigh An anchor is said to be aweigh when it has come free of the ground.

B

Back To push a sail out so that the wind fills it from the other side.

Backstay A stay leading aft from the masthead.

Ballast Weight (usually metal) placed in the bottom of a boat or fitted to the keel to increase stability.

Bar An offshore ridge of sand, mud or shingle, parallel to the shore and across the mouth of a river or bay or the approach to a harbour.

Barber hauler A line or tackle attached to a sheet, at a point between the clew and the fairlead, which is used to adjust the angle of sheeting.

Battens Thin strips of wood or plastic inserted into pockets in a sail to preserve its shape.

Beam The maximum width of a boat.

Bear away To change course away from the wind.

Bear down To approach from upwind.

Bearing The direction of an object expressed in compass notation.

Beating To sail to windward by repeated tacking.

Becket A small loop or eye in the end of a rope or on a block.

Belay To secure a rope to a cleat or a belaying pin; an instruction meaning 'Stop!' (see also **Avast**).

Bend One of various types of knot; to knot two ropes together; to attach a sail to a spar.

Bermudan rig A rig with a triangular mainsail. Also known as a Marconi rig.

Bight Any part of a rope between its ends; a curve or loop in a rope; a wide indentation in a coastline, or the water bounded by that indentation.

Bilge The part of a vessel's hull where the side curves in to form the bottom; the part of a vessel between the lowermost floorboards and the bottom, where water often collects.

Bitter end The end of a line or chain, especially the end secured in the chain locker or to the bitts.

Bitts A pair of small posts on the deck of a vessel for securing mooring lines.

Block A casing containing one or more freely-rotating pulley wheels (sheaves).

Bollard A sturdy wood or metal post, fixed to a quay or wharf, to which mooring lines are attached.

Bolt rope A strong rope sewn around the edge of a sail to reinforce it.

Boom A spar used to extend the foot of a fore-and-aft sail, such as a mainsail, and to control its position relative to the wind.

Boom preventer A line or tackle that prevents unwanted movement of a boom, such as an accidental gybe.

Boom vang A line or tackle that prevents the boom from riding up when the mainsail is set. Also called a kicking strap.

Bosun's chair A canvas bucket seat on which a person can be hoisted up a mast.

Bow The forward end or part of a vessel.

Bower A main anchor carried at the bow of a vessel.

Bowsprit On some boats, a heavy spar projecting ahead from the bow, enabling headsails to be set farther forward.

Breast line (breast rope) A rope, used for tying up to a jetty, which is led from forward or aft at right angles to the side of the vessel.

Bring up To stop or come to anchor.

Broach to To swerve sharply and dangerously in a following sea, slewing broadside-on to the waves.

Bulkhead An upright, wall-like partition within a boat.

Bulwarks A solid, fencelike parapet along the outer sides of a deck.

Burgee A small, triangular or swallow-tailed flag, flown from the mast of a yacht to indicate the owner's membership of a particular yacht club, or to act as an indicator of the apparent wind direction.

By the head Having greater draught forward than aft (see also **By the stern**).

By the lee Sailing on a run with the wind over the same side as the mainsail (over the lee side). This can result in an accidental gybe.

By the stern Having greater draught aft than forward (see also **By the head**).

C

Cable An anchor chain or rope; one tenth of a nautical mile.

Camber The curve of a set sail; the slight upward curve from the side to the centre of a deck.

Capstan A vertical drum for hauling in or letting out the anchor chain.

Careen To heel a vessel onto one side so as to be able to work on her bottom.

Carvel-built Having a wooden hull whose planks are made flush at the seams (see also **Clinker-built**).

Cast off To release the lines securing a boat to a dock or mooring.

Caulking Waterproof material packed into the seams between planks to make the structure watertight.

Centreboard A pivoting wooden board let down through the bottom of a sailboat to provide lateral stability and reduce leeway (see also **Daggerboard, Keel, Leeboards, Leeway**).

Centreline The fore-and-aft line through the centre of a boat.

Chain plates The metal fittings at the sides of a boat to which the shrouds are attached.

Chart datum The water level — usually the level of the lowest astronomical tide — from which all depths shown on a chart are measured.

Chine A sharp angle between the side and the bottom of a boat.

Chord An imaginary straight line, parallel to the foot, joining the leading edge (luff) and trailing edge (leech) of a sail.

Claw ring A C-shaped fitting, slipped over the boom when the sail has been roller-reefed, which allows the kicking strap (vang) to be re-attached.

Cleat A two-armed metal or wooden fitting to which ropes can be secured.

Clew The lower aft corner of a fore-and-aft sail, where the leech meets the foot.

Clinker-built Having a wooden hull whose planks overlap at the seams (see also **Carvel-built**).

Close-hauled Sailing as close to the wind as possible.

Cockpit The well at the stern of a sailboat, where the helmsman stands or puts his feet.

Coffee grinder A large, pedestal-mounted winch with two handles on a horizontal spindle.

Committee boat In racing, the boat carrying the race officials.

Companionway A stairway or ladder leading from the deck to the cabin or saloon.

Cringle An eye or loop set in the bolt rope of a sail.

Cross-trees Struts on each side of a mast to increase the spread and holding power of the main shrouds. Also called spreaders.

Cunningham hole An eye in the luff of a sail, just above the tack, to which a tackle (Cunningham tackle) is attached to adjust the luff tension.

Cutter A single-masted boat rigged with a staysail and jib. It may be Bermudan-rigged or gaff-rigged.

D

Daggerboard A sliding wooden board let down through the bottom of a sailboat to provide lateral stability and reduce leeway (see also **Centreboard, Keel, Leeboards, Leeway**).

Day mark An indicator, usually a white-painted shape, which marks a shore feature by day.

Dead reckoning Navigating by using the measured speed, elapsed time and course steered from a known position to calculate the boat's present position (see also **Fix, Observed position**).

Deck The structure completely or partially covering the interior of a boat.

Deckhead The underside of a deck; the roof of a boat's cabin or saloon.

Displacement The weight of the water displaced by a floating boat; the displacement is equal to the actual weight of the boat.

Dodger A canvas strip fitted between the guardrail and the gunwale of a yacht to protect the crew from spray.

Dolphin A pile, post or buoy for mooring a vessel in a harbour.

Double-ender A boat which has a hull that is pointed at bow and stern.

Downhaul A rope or tackle used to haul down a sail (such as a spinnaker or to tension the luff of a sail by pulling down the tack (see also **Uphaul**).

Draught The depth of water occupied by a vessel, meaured as the vertical distance from the waterline to the lowest point of the hull or keel.

Drogue An object, such as a canvas sea anchor, towed behind a boat to reduce its speed.

Drying features Features, such as sand banks, which are covered at high water but exposed as the tide drops.

E

Ease To let out a line, sheet or anchor chain gradually.

Ebb tide The flowing back of the tide from high to low water (see also **Flood tide**).

Ensign A flag flown by a vessel to indicate its nationality.

F

Fairlead A channel, ring, eye, loop or bolt for guiding a rope in the required direction.

Fairway The main shipping channel in restricted waters.

Fall The part of the rope, leading from a tackle, that is hauled on.

Fathom A unit of measurement of water depth, equal to 6 feet (1.8 metres).

Fetch To sail close-hauled without tacking.

Fin keel A single, centrally-placed and ballasted keel (see also **Keel**).

Fix A vessel's position, as obtained by taking accurate bearings (see also **Dead reckoning, Observed position**).

Flood tide A rising or flow tide (see also **Ebb tide**).

Flukes The pointed parts of an anchor that dig into the ground.

Following sea A sea travelling in the same direction as the boat (see also **Head sea**).

Foot The bottom edge of a sail.

Fore At, toward or near the bow.

Fore-and-aft Along or parallel to the centreline.

Foresail A triangular sail, such as a jib, set ahead of the main mast (see also **Headsail**).

Forestay A stay leading from the masthead to the bow.

Forward Toward the bow.

Freeboard The distance between the deck and the waterline.

Furl To roll a sail and fasten it to its boom when it is not in use (see also **Reef**).

G

Gaff The spar that supports the head of a gaffsail.

Gaff-rigged Having one or more gaffsails.

Gaffsail A four-sided, fore-and-aft sail.

Galley The kitchen of a yacht.

Gaskets The small cords used to tie up a furled sail. Also called ties or furling lines.

Genoa A large foresail that extends aft beyond the mainmast.

Gimbals A pair of pivoted, concentric rings used to hold a compass or stove horizontal, regardless of the motion of the boat.

Gnomonic projection A type of map or chart projection with straight longitude lines and curved latitude lines (see also **Mercator projection**).

Go about To turn a boat head-to-wind to change tack.

Gooseneck A pivoted fitting that secures a boom to a mast.

Goosewing To sail downwind with the mainsail set on one side and the foresail on the other.

GRP Glass-reinforced plastic, made by impregnating glassfibre matting with resins such as polyesters.

Gunter rig A rig in which gaff is used as an extension of the main mast.

Gunwale (or **gunnel**) The top edge of the side of the hull.

Guy A rope or wire used to steady a spar.

Gybe To move a fore-and-aft sail from one side of the boat to the other when changing course on a run.

H

Halyards Ropes or wires used to hoist sails.

Hanks Clips or rings that attach sails to stays.

Harden up To sail closer to the wind.

Hawse pipes Bow pipes through which the anchor cables pass.

Hawser A heavy rope used for towing, mooring or warping.

Heading The compass direction in which a boat is pointing.

Headsail A sail, such as a spinnaker, set forward of the main mast (see also **Foresail**).

Head sea A sea travelling in the opposite direction to that of the boat (see also **Following sea**).

Heads The toilets on a boat.

Head-to-wind With the bow pointing into the wind.

Heave-to To stop a boat, for instance by backing the foresail or by letting the sails flap on a beam reach.

Heaving line A light rope thrown ashore when berthing and used to haul a heavier mooring line ashore.

Heel To lean over or list; the bottom of a mast; the aft end of a keel.

Helm The tiller or wheel.

Helmsman The person steering a boat.

Hitch To tie a rope to a spar or stay; a knot that can be undone by pulling against the direction of the strain that holds it tight.

Holding ground Ground that an anchor can dig into.

Hounds The part of the mast to which the shrouds and stays are attached.

I

Inboard Situated within the hull; toward the centreline.

Inshore Close to the shore; toward the shore from the water.

Irons A boat is said to be 'in irons' when it is pointing directly into the wind and unable to move forward.

Isobars Lines on a weather map joining points of equal barometric pressure.

IYRU The International Yacht Racing Union, which is the controlling body for international yacht racing.

J

Jamming cleat A cleat into which a rope may be jammed to secure it.

Jib A triangular sail attached to the forestay.

Jury rig A temporary replacement for damaged rigging.

K

Katabatic wind A wind created by air flowing down a slope. It usually occurs at night, when the air at the top of a slope cools quicker, and so becomes heavier, than the air at the bottom (see also **Anabatic wind**).

Kedge A small anchor used in conjunction with the main anchor; to move a boat by deploying the kedge and pulling on it.

Keel The underwater extension of the hull of a sailing boat that provides lateral stability and reduces leeway. It is usually fixed, but on some boats can be raised and lowered (see also **Centreboard, Daggerboard, Leeboards, Leeway**).

Ketch A two-masted boat, rigged fore-and-aft. The forward mast is the main mast, the aft mast is called the mizzen.

Kicking strap A line or tackle that prevents the boom from riding up when the mainsail is set. Also called a boom vang.

Knot A speed of one nautical mile per hour (see also **Nautical mile**).

L

Land breeze A breeze blowing from the land. It occurs mainly at night and in the early morning, when the land is cooler than the sea because it has lost more heat after sunset (see also **Sea breeze**).

Landfall To sight or arrive at land.

Lanyard A short length of rope or cord for attaching one thing to another.

Lash To tie something in place by binding it tightly with light rope.

Latitude The angular distance of a position in degrees north or south of the equator (see also **Longitude**).

Launch To slide or lower a vessel into the water; a small motor-driven tender.

Lay up To take a boat out of use, for example during the winter.

Lee The area downwind (to leeward) of a boat or other object (see also **Weather**).

Leeboards Boards fixed vertically to the sides of a boat's hull to provide lateral stability and reduce leeway (see also **Centreboard, Daggerboard, Keel, Leeway**).

Leech The rear edge of a fore-and-aft sail.

Lee side The downwind (leeward) side of a boat or other object (see also **Weather side**).

Lee tide A tide running with the wind (see also **Weather tide**).

Leeward (Loo'ard) Toward the lee side; the direction to which the wind is blowing (see also **Windward**).

Leeway The sideways drift of a vessel, to leeward, caused by the wind; the distance between the course steered and the course actually run.

Let fly To let go a sheet so as to spill the wind from the sail it controls.

Lie To keep a boat stationary; to keep a boat as steady as possible during a gale, for instance by lying a-hull (see also **A-hull**).

Lifeline A safety line for the crew to hang onto, fitted fore-and-aft or around the deck.

Lift A rope or wire supporting a spar (see also **Topping lift**).

Line squall A usually violent squall accompanying the cold front of a depression. Its low black cloud forms a distinct line or arch.

Log An instrument used to measure a boat's speed through the water; a book (logbook) in which the details of a boat's voyages are recorded.

Longitude The angular distance of a position in degrees east or west of the Greenwich Meridian (0°) (see also **Latitude, Meridian**).

Loom The reflection on the clouds of the light from a lighthouse or lightship, when the light itself is still below the horizon.

Loose To let go of a rope; to unfurl or set a sail.

Loose-footed A loose-footed sail is one whose foot is not laced to a boom.

Low water Low tide.

Lubber line The line marked on a compass to indicate the fore-and-aft axis of the vessel.

Luff The forward edge of a sail; to bring a boat closer to the wind.

Luff up To turn a boat directly into the wind.

Lug (lugsail) A four-sided, fore-and-aft sail.

Lugger A boat rigged with a lugsail.

M

Make fast To secure a rope.

Marconi A rig with a triangular mainsail. Also known as a Bermudan rig.

Mark A fixed onshore or offshore feature used as a guide when navigating.

Marlin(e) spike A pointed metal or wooden spike used for separating the strands of a rope to splice it.

Mast A vertical pole or set of poles for supporting a sail or sails.

Mast gate The fixture that secures the mast of a dinghy where it passes through the foredeck.

Masthead The top section of a mast.

Masthead sloop A sloop on which the forestay (which carries the foresail) extends from the bow to the masthead.

Mast step A fixture into which the foot of the mast is fitted, either on the deck (for a deck-stepped mast) or on top of the keel (for a keel-stepped mast).

Mercator projection A type of map or chart projection with straight longitude and latitude lines crossing at right angles (see also **Gnomonic projection**)

Meridian An imaginary circle drawn around the earth and passing through both poles. All lines of longitude are meridians (see also **Longitude**).

Millibar A unit of barometric pressure, used on weather maps. 1000 millibars (1 bar) is equal to 29.53 inches of mercury. From the earth's surface, atmospheric pressure decreases by about one millibar for every 28 feet (8.5 metres) of increase in altitude.

Miss stays When tacking, a boat is said to miss stays when it fails to go about and so remains on its original tack.

Mizzen The aftermost mast of a two-masted vessel; on a vessel with three or more masts, the third mast from the bow; the sail set on a mizzen mast.

Moulded hull A hull made of GRP or built up by bonding layers of marine ply.

N

Narrows A narrow channel.

Nautical almanac A book, published annually, containing navigational, tidal, astronomical and other data of use to sailors and navigators.

Nautical mile A unit of length, used in navigation, equal to 1852 metres or 6076.103 feet (see also **Knot**).

Navigation lights The identifying lights that vessels must show at night.

Neap tides The tides that occur at around the first and last quarters of the moon, and have a relatively small range (see also **Spring tides**).

No-go zone The area, about 45° to either side of the wind, into which a sailboat cannot sail without tacking.

O

Observed position A vessel's position as obtained by direct observation of charted features (see also **Dead reckoning, Fix**).

Offshore Away from the shore.

Offwind Any point of sailing away from the wind.

One-design A boat built and equipped to conform to strict rules, so that it is identical to all the other boats in its particular class.

Onshore On or toward the land.

On the quarter Something is said to be on the quarter when its bearing is 45° abaft of the beam of the boat (see also **Quarter**).

Outhaul A rope used to tighten the foot of a sail by hauling the clew along the boom.

Overfall A turbulent stretch of water resulting from currents flowing over an underwater ridge.

P

Painter A line attached to the bow of a small boat for tying it up.

Pay out To ease a line or chain.

Pennant A tapering or triangular flag.

Pilot Someone authorized to navigate vessels in and out of a port, or through a channel; a book of sailing directions.

Pitch The downward motion of a boat's bows as it plunges into the trough of a wave (see also **Yaw**).

Pitchpole To tumble stern-over-bow when upended by a wave.

Plane A boat is said to plane when it lifts onto its bow wave and skims over the water rather than moving through it.

Plot To mark a chart with bearings, directions and courses.

Points of sailing The main angles to the wind on which a boat may sail.

Pontoon A floating platform or walkway to which boats may be secured; a float supporting such a platform.

Port The left-hand side of a boat as seen when facing the bow.

Port tack A boat is said to be on a port tack when the wind is blowing over its port side (see also **Starboard tack**).

Position line A line on a chart along which a vessel's position lies.

Preventer A line, tackle or stay that prevents unwanted movement of a mast or boom (see also **Boom preventer**).

Prop walk The tendency of a propellor to pull the stern of a vessel to one side.

Prow The fore part of a vessel, including the bows.

Pulpit A guard rail set around the bow or stern of a boat. That at the stern is also called the pushpit.

Purchase A tackle or lever mechanism used for raising, moving or tightening things (see also **Tackle**).

Pushpit A guard rail set around the stern of a boat (see also **Pulpit**).

Q

Quarter The part of a boat between the beam and the stern (see also **On the quarter**).

Quarter berth A bunk under the side of the cockpit.

Quartering With the wind or waves on the quarter of the boat.

R

Race A rapid current, especially through a narrow channel.

Rake The rearward slope of a mast.

Range The difference in water level between low and high tide.

Rating A way of classifying boats of different types and sizes so that they can race on a handicap basis.

Ratlines small lines fixed between adjacent shrouds to form steps.

Reach To sail with the wind blowing approximately abeam; the stretch of water between two bends in a river.

Reefing Folding or rolling a sail to reduce its area.

Reef points Short pieces of rope used to tie up the reefed part of a sail.

Ride To lie at anchor; to ride out a storm when at sea is to wait for it to pass (see also **A-hull, Lie**).

Riding light An all-round white light displayed at night (usually on the forestay) by an anchored vessel. Also called an anchor light.

Rig The arrangement of masts, spars and sails carried by a vessel.

Rigging The ropes and wires on a boat that keep the mast or masts in place and work the sails (see also **Running rigging, Standing rigging**).

Roach The curved part of a fore-and-aft sail, bounded by the leech, that projects behind an imaginary straight line from the clew to the head.

Rudder A movable underwater vane at the stern of a vessel, used for steering.

Rudderpost The aftermost timber of a boat.

Run To sail with the wind aft or nearly aft.

Running rigging The sheets and halyards that raise, lower and control the sails (see also **Standing rigging**).

S

Safety harness A harness attached to a line secured to the boat, and worn by crew in bad weather.

Sam(p)son post A vertical wooden or metal post to which warps or cables may be secured.

Schooner A vessel with two or more masts (the aftermost of which is the main mast) and all lower sails rigged fore-and-aft.

Scupper An opening let into the bulwarks of a vessel to allow deck water to drain away; to sink one's own vessel deliberately.

Sea anchor A drogue deployed as a floating anchor to help a vessel ride out a gale or storm.

Sea breeze A breeze blowing from the sea. It occurs mainly during the day, when the land is warmer than the sea (see also **Land breeze**).

Seacock A valve in the hull of a vessel, below the waterline, for admitting seawater or pumping out bilge water.

Shackle A U-shaped link, closed by a bolt or pin.

Shackle key A metal tool for unscrewing shackle pins.

Shake To loosen or cast off.

Shank The main shaft of an anchor.

Sheave A pulley wheel (see also **Block**).

Sheer The deck line of a vessel, as seen from the side.

Sheet The rope attached to the clew of a sail, with which the sail may be trimmed or tensioned.

Shock cord A strong, elasticated rope.

Shrouds Wires fixed at each side of a mast to support it (see also **Standing rigging, Stays**).

Side lights The red (port) and green (starboard) lights that a vessel must show at night.

Slack tide The short period at high or low tide when there is no tidal flow. Also called slack water.

Slip To release or let go, for instance to slip anchor.

Sloop A single-masted boat, Bermudan-rigged or gaff-rigged, with a single headsail.

Snatch block A block into which a rope can be inserted quickly from the side instead of being threaded through.

Sound To measure the depth of the water; a relatively narrow stretch of water linking two larger areas; an inlet or deep bay.

Spars A general term for the various pole-like pieces of gear on a boat, including masts, booms and gaffs.

Spinnaker A large, light, three-cornered headsail.

Spit A thin strip of sand or shingle projecting from the shore.

Splicing Joining two ropes by intertwining their strands.

Spreaders Struts on each side of a mast to increase the spread and holding power of the main shrouds. Also called cross-trees.

Spring A mooring line led forward from the stern or aft from the bow.

Spring tides The tides that occur at or near full and new moon, and are the lowest low tides and the highest high tides (see also **Neap tides**).

Sprit A spar extending from the mast to the peak of a four-cornered sail.

Square-rigger A ship rigged with four-sided sails hung on yards athwart (across) the ship.

Stanchions The upright posts that support the guardrails and lifelines.

Standing rigging The shrouds and stays that support the mast or masts (see also **Running rigging**).

Stand on To maintain course.

Starboard The right-hand side of a boat as seen when facing the bow.

Starboard tack A boat is said to be on a starboard tack when the wind is blowing over its starboard side (see also **Port tack**).

Stays Wires fixed fore and aft of a mast to support it (see also **Shrouds, Standing rigging**).

Staysail An auxiliary sail, usually triangular, attached to a forestay.

Steerageway A boat is said to have steerageway when it is moving fast enough to allow it to be steered.

Stem The main timber or structure at the bow of a boat; the foremost end of a boat, as in the phrase 'from stem to stern' (see also **Stern post**).

Step The fixture into which the heel of a mast is fitted.

Stern The after (rear) part of a vessel.

Stern post The main timber or structure at the stern of a boat (see also **Stem**).

Stiff A vessel is said to be stiff if it is relatively resistant to heeling or rolling, and returns quickly to the vertical (see also **Tender**).

Stock The part of a rudder to which the tiller is fitted.

T

Tack The forward lower corner of a fore-and-aft sail; to turn the bows of a boat through the wind; to sail a zigzag upwind course by repeated tacking; to sail with the wind blowing from forward of the beam (see also **Port tack, Starboard tack**).

Tackle A rope and block purchase system (see also **Block, Purchase**).

Take up To tighten.

Tangs The metal fittings that secure the shrouds and stays to the mast.

Tell-tales Small lengths of wool sewn to each side of a sail to indicate the airflow over it.

Tender A small boat towed or carried by a larger vessel and used to ferry people and stores between the larger vessel and the shore; a boat is said to be tender if it is easily heeled over by the wind (see also **Stiff**).

Thwart A seat running across a dinghy or other small boat.

Tide The regular rise and fall of sea level caused by the gravitational pull of the sun and the moon; the horizontal flow of water resulting from these changes in sea level.

Tide rode A moored or anchored boat is said to be tide rode when it has swung round so that its bows are facing into the incoming or outgoing tide (see also **Wind rode**).

Tiller A wooden or metal handle attached to the top of a rudder and used to control it.

Toe straps Loops into which dinghy crews can put their feet to keep them secure when sitting out.

Topping lift A rope or tackle that supports the end of a boom.

Track The intended course of a vessel.

Transit Two objects are said to be in transit when, from the point of view of an observer, they are directly in line with each other.

Transom The stern surface of a vessel.

Trapeze A support used by the crew (and sometimes the helmsman) of a racing dinghy to place his or her weight outside the boat.

Traveller A sliding fixture, travelling on a track, to which a sheet is attached so that its angle can be altered.

Trim The fore-and-aft inclination of a boat; to change or adust the set of a sail.

True wind The actual speed and direction of the wind, rather than the apparent wind as perceived on a moving boat (see also **Apparent wind**).

Trysail A loose-footed, triangular sail used in place of the mainsail in heavy weather.

U

Under way On the move.

Uphaul A rope or tackle used to haul up a sail (such as a spinnaker) (see also **Downhaul**).

V

Vang A rope used to support a gaff or sprit (see also **Boom vang**).

W

Wake course The course actually travelled by a vessel.

Warp A rope used to secure or move a vessel; to move a vessel by hauling it with ropes.

Weather The area upwind (to windward) of a boat or other object (see also **Lee**).

Weather side The upwind (windward) side of a boat or other object (see also **Lee side**).

Weather tide A tide running against the wind (see also **Lee tide**).

Weigh anchor To lift the anchor off the bottom.

Whipping Binding the end of a rope to stop it fraying.

Whisker pole A pole used as a boom for the jib when sailing goosewinged (see also **Goosewinged**).

Winch A hand-operated or powered machine for hauling in sheets or halyards.

Wind rode A moored or anchored boat is said to be wind rode when it has swung round so that its bows are facing into the wind (see also **Tide rode**).

Windward Upwind; toward the weather side; the direction from which the wind is blowing (see also **Leeward**).

Y

Yard A spar suspended from a mast to spread a sail.

Yaw The sideways motion of a boat's bows as it plunges through waves (see also **Pitch**).

Yawl A two-masted vessel, rigged fore-and-aft, with a large main mast and a small mizzen (rear) mast stepped just aft of the rudderpost.

SAILING ORGANIZATIONS

British Marine Industries
Federation (BMIF),
Boating Industry House,
Meadlake Place,
Thorpe Lea Road,
Egham,
Surrey TW20 8HE
01784-473377

British Sub-Aqua Club,
Telford's Quay,
Ellesmere Port,
South Wirral,
Cheshire L65 4FY
0151-357-1250

British Telecom Marine Radio
Services,
43 Bartholemew Close,
London EC1A 7HP
0171-583-9416

British Waterways Board,
Willow Grange,
Watford,
Herts WD1 3QA
01923-226422

Cruising Association,
CA House,
1 Northey Street,
Limehouse Basin,
London E14 8BT
0171-537-2828

Coastguard Headquarters,
Spring Place,
105 Commercial Road,
Southampton SO1 0ZD
01703-329486

HM Customs and Excise,
OAS,
5th Floor East,
New King's Beam House,
22 Upper Ground,
London SE1 9PJ
0171-865-4742

Hydrographic Office,
Ministry of Defence,
Taunton,
Somerset TA1 2DN
01823-337900

International Sailing
Federation (ISAF),
27 Broadwall,
Waterloo,
London SE1 9PL
0171-928-6611

Jubilee Sailing Trust,
Jubilee Yard,
Merlin Quay,
Hazel Road,
Woolston,
Southampton SO19 7GB
01703-449108

Lloyd's Register of Shipping,
Yacht and Small Craft
Services,
71 Fenchurch Street,
London EC3M 4BS
0171-709-9166

Maritime Trust,
2 Greenwich Church Street,
London SE10 9BG
0181-858-2698

Meteorological Office,
London Road,
Bracknell,
Berks RG12 2SZ
01344-420242

Radiocommunication Agency,
Ship Radio Licensing Unit,
South Quay Three,
189 Marsh Wall,
Docklands,
London E14 9SX
0171-211-0119

Royal Institute of Navigation,
Royal Geographical Society,
1 Kensington Gore,
London SW7 2AT
0171-589-5021

Royal National Lifeboat
Institution (RNLI),
West Quay Road,
Poole,
Dorset BH15 1HZ
01202-663000

Royal Naval Sailing
Association,
17 Pembroke Road,
Portsmouth,
Hants PO1 2NT
01705-823524

Royal Ocean Racing Club,
20 St James' Place,
London SW1A 7LF
0171-493-2248

Royal Yachting Association,
RYA House,
Romsey Road,
Eastleigh,
Hants SO5 9YA
01703-629962

Small Ships Register,
DVLA,
Swansea SA99 1BX
01792-783-355

Solent Cruising and Racing
Association,
18 Bath Road,
Cowes,
Isle of Wight PO31 7QN
01983-295744

Sports Council,
16 Upper Woburn Place,
London WC1H 0QP
0171-388-1277

Trinity House,
Tower Hill,
London EC3N 4DH
0171-480-6601

UK Offshore Boating
Association,
1 Carbis Close,
Port Solent,
Portsmouth PO6 4TW
01705-219949

Whitbread Round the World
Race,
Whitbread Centre,
Tollbar Way,
Hedge End,
Southampton SO30 2ZB
01489-799000

INDEX

Page numbers in bold type (eg **134–5**) indicate main entries, and those in italics (eg *74*) indicate photographs or diagrams.

CREDITS

AUTHORS:
Bob Bond
Jonathan Clark
Brian Grant
Adrian Morgan
David Pelly

EDITORIAL:
US Consultant Editor
Madelyn larsen
UK Consultant Editors
Bob Bond, David Pelly
Editor Ian Wood
Art Director Steve Leaning
Computer consutant Ray Leaning

ARTISTS:
Rod Sutterby, Tony Garrett, Ian
Heard, SB Design

PHOTOGRAPHY:
Studio photography
Theo Bergström
*Additional equipment
photography* Mike Millman
Boats section photographs supplied by
PPL

Location photography Mike Millman,
Bill Jenner, John Darling, Theo
Bergström
Additional photography
Jonathan Eastland of Ajax News
and Features Service; Colin Jarman
of Eyeline Photos; Roger Lean-
Vercoe of Yachting Photographics;

ACKNOWLEDGEMENTS
*Our special thanks to the following for
supplying materials and providing
assistance:*

Simon of
Captain O M Watts Ltd
45 Albemarle Street
Piccadilly
London W1X 4B

The Secretary and Members of
Grafham Water Sailing Club
Perry
Huntingdon
England

All the manufacturers especially
Brookes & Gatehouse
Cetrek,

Ian Proctor Metal,
International Paint,
McMurdo Ltd.,
Navico Ltd,
North Sails (UK) Ltd.,
Raytheon,
Retreat Boatyard,
Volvo Penta UK Ltd

DETAILED CREDITS

Page 6: *photo* Lean-Vercoe
8: *photo* Jarman
10–11: *illustration* Garrett
12: *photos* Eastland (top), North
Sails/Michael Richelson (bottom
left), Jenner (bottom right)
13: *illustrations* Garrett
14: *photo* Lean-Vercoe
15: *photos* Bergström (top left),
Proctor Masts (bottom left),
Darling (top right), Millman
(middle and bottom right)
16–17: *photo* Bergström, *supplier*
Captain O M Watts Ltd
18–19: *photo* Bergström, *supplier*
Captain O M Watts Ltd
20–21: *photo* Bergström, *supplier*
Captain O M Watts Ltd, *inset photo*
Millman, *illustration* SB Design
22: Courtauls/DML, *inset photo*
Rick Tomlinson
23: *photos* Millman
24: *photo* Bergstom
25: *photos* Millman, (bottom right)
Brookes & Gatehouse
26: *photos* (top) Millman,
(bottom) Yanja Visser/PPL
27: *photos* (top right) Raytheon,
(centre left) ICS/PPL (others)
Millman
28: *photo* Navico Ltd
29: *photos* (top left) Millman, (top
centre) Darlin, (top right) Brookes
& Gatehouse, (centre) Navico
Ltd., (bottom) Cetrek
30–31: *photos* Millman
32–33: *photos* Millman
34: *photos* Millman
35: *photos* (top) Volvo Penta,
(centre) Millman

37-37: *photos* Bergstrom, (insert)
McMurdo Ltd.
38-39 *photos* Bergstrom
40: *photo* Lean-Vercoe
42–43: *photos* Millman,
illustrations Sutterby
44: *photo* Bergström, *illustration* SB
Design
45: *illustration* Garrett
46: *photo* Eastland, *illustration* Heard
48–49: *photo* Millman
50–51: *photo* Eastland

52: *photo* Jenner
54: *photos* Jenner
55: *photos* Millman (top),
Lean-Vercoe (bottom)
56: *photos* Millman (top), Jenner
(bottom)
57: *photo* Darling, *illustration*
Garrett

58–97: *all photos supplied by* PPL

98: *photos* Lean-Vercoe
100–101: *photo* Darling,
illustrations Sutterby
102–103: *photo* Eastland,
illustrations Heard
104–105: *photos* Bergström
106: *photo* Bergström
106–107: *illustrations* Sutterby
107: *photo* Millman
108–109: *photo* Millman,
illustrations Sutterby
110–111: *photo* Jarman,
illustrations Garrett
112: *photo* Bergström,
illustrations Garrett
113: *photo* Darling
114: *photo* Lean-Vercoe,
illustrations Heard

115: *photo* Bergström
116–117: *photo* Jarman
illustrations Heard
118: *photo* Millman
118–119: *illustrations* Heard
119: *photo* Bergström
120: *photo* Eastland
120–121: *illustrations* Heard
121: *photo* Lean-Vercoe
122–123: *photo* Jarman,
illustrations Heard
124–125: *photo* Pickthall Picture
Library, *illustrations* Heard
126–127: *photos* Lean-Vercoe (top),
Bergström (bottom),
illustrations Sutterby
128: *photos* Darling (top, bottom
left), Millman (bottom right)
129: *illustration* Garrett
130: *photos* Darling
131: *photos* Lean-Vercoe (top),
Pickthall Picture Library (bottom)
132: *photos* Millman (top), Darling
(bottom)
133: *photos* Darling, *illustration*
Sutterby
134–135: *photos* Millman,
illustrations Sutterby
136–137: *photos* Millman,
illustrations Sutterby
138–139: *photos* Lean-Vercoe,
illustrations Heard
140: *photo* Eastland
141: *photo* Pickthall Picture
Library, *illustrations* Heard (left), SB
Design (right)
142: *photo* Jarman
143: *photos* Millman,
illustrations SB Design
144: *photos* Eastland (top) Millman
(bottom)
145: *photos* Darling

146: *illustrations* SB Design
147: *photos* Navico Ltd (top),
Bergström (bottom)
148–149; *photo* Darling,
illustrations SB Design
150–151: *illustrations* Sutterby
152–153: *illustrations* Sutterby

154: *photo* Jarmen
156 *photo* Jarmen
157 *photo* Bentley/PPL
158-159 *photos* Jarmen
160-161 *photos* (top centre) Lean-
Vercoe, (bottom left) Jenner, (bottom centre) Lean-Vercoe, (bottom
right) Millman
162-163 *photos* (top) Lean-Vercoe,
(bottom) Eastland
164 *photo* Nasn/PPL
165 *photos* (top) Fisher/PPL,
(bottom) Novak/PPL
166 *photo* Eastland
167 *photo* Jarmen
168 *photo* Bentley/PPL
169 *photos* Bentley/PPL
170 *photo* Lean-Vercoe
171 *photo* Pickthall/PPL
172-173 photos (top) Eastland,
(bottom) Lean-Vercoe
174 *photo* Guerrini/PPL
175 *photo* Pepper/PPL
176 *photo* Pepper/PPL
177 *photo* Lawson-Johnston/PPL
178 179 *photos* Jarman
180 *photo* Nash/PPL
181 *photo* Borsari/PPL

182: *illustrations* Sutterby (top),
SB Design (bottom)
183: *photo* Lean-Vercoe
184–185: *illustrations* Sutterby,
SB Design (185 top)